Property without Rights

Major land reform programs have reallocated property in more than one-third of the world's countries in the last century and impacted over one billion people. But only rarely have these programs granted beneficiaries complete property rights. Why is this the case, and what are the consequences? This book draws on wide-ranging original data and charts new conceptual terrain to reveal the political origins of the property rights gap. It shows that land reform programs are most often implemented by authoritarian governments that deliberately withhold property rights from beneficiaries. In so doing, governments generate coercive leverage over rural populations and exert social control. This is politically advantageous to ruling governments but it has negative development consequences: it slows economic growth, productivity, and urbanization and it exacerbates inequality. The book also examines the conditions under which subsequent governments close property rights gaps, usually as a result of democratization or foreign pressure.

Michael Albertus is Associate Professor of Political Science at the University of Chicago. He is the author of the award-winning book *Autocracy and Redistribution* (Cambridge, 2015) and *Authoritarianism and the Elite Origins of Democracy* (Cambridge, 2018). Albertus also writes regularly for popular outlets such as the *New York Times*, *Washington Post*, and *Foreign Policy*.

CAMBRIDGE STUDIES IN COMPARATIVE POLITICS

GENERAL EDITORS

KATHLEEN THELEN *Massachusetts Institute of Technology*

ASSOCIATE EDITORS

CATHERINE BOONE *London School of Economics*
THAD DUNNING *University of California, Berkeley*
ANNA GRZYMALA-BUSSE *Stanford University*
TORBEN IVERSEN *Harvard University*
STATHIS KALYVAS *Yale University*
MARGARET LEVI *Stanford University*
MELANIE MANION *Duke University*
HELEN MILNER *Princeton University*
FRANCES ROSENBLUTH *Yale University*
SUSAN STOKES *Yale University*
TARIQ THACHIL *Vanderbilt University*
ERIK WIBBELS *Duke University*

SERIES FOUNDER

PETER LANGE *Duke University*

OTHER BOOKS IN THE SERIES

Christopher Adolph, *Bankers, Bureaucrats, and Central Bank Politics: The Myth of Neutrality*

Michael Albertus, *Autocracy and Redistribution: The Politics of Land Reform*

Michael Albertus, *Property without Rights: Origins and Consequences of the Property Rights Gap*

Santiago Anria, *When Movements Become Parties: The Bolivian MAS in Comparative Perspective*

Ben W. Ansell, *From the Ballot to the Blackboard: The Redistributive Political Economy of Education*

Ben W. Ansell and Johannes Lindvall, *Inward Conquest: The Political Origins of Modern Public Services*

Ben W. Ansell and David J. Samuels, *Inequality and Democratization: An Elite-Competition Approach*

Adam Michael Auerbach, *Demanding Development: The Politics of Public Goods Provision in India's Urban Slums*

Ana Arjona, *Rebelocracy: Social Order in the Colombian Civil War*

Leonardo R. Arriola, *Multi-ethnic Coalitions in Africa: Business Financing of Opposition Election Campaigns*

David Austen-Smith, Jeffry A. Frieden, Miriam A. Golden, Karl Ove Moene, and Adam Przeworski, eds., *Selected Works of Michael Wallerstein: The Political Economy of Inequality, Unions, and Social Democracy*

S. Erdem Aytaç and Susan C. Stokes, *Why Bother? Rethinking Participation in Elections and Protests*

Andy Baker, *The Market and the Masses in Latin America: Policy Reform and Consumption in Liberalizing Economies*

Continued after the index

Property without Rights

Origins and Consequences of the Property Rights Gap

MICHAEL ALBERTUS
University of Chicago

CAMBRIDGE
UNIVERSITY PRESS

CAMBRIDGE
UNIVERSITY PRESS

University Printing House, Cambridge CB2 8BS, United Kingdom

One Liberty Plaza, 20th Floor, New York, NY 10006, USA

477 Williamstown Road, Port Melbourne, VIC 3207, Australia

314–321, 3rd Floor, Plot 3, Splendor Forum, Jasola District Centre,
New Delhi – 110025, India

79 Anson Road, #06–04/06, Singapore 079906

Cambridge University Press is part of the University of Cambridge.

It furthers the University's mission by disseminating knowledge in the pursuit of
education, learning, and research at the highest international levels of excellence.

www.cambridge.org
Information on this title: www.cambridge.org/9781108835237
DOI: 10.1017/9781108891950

First published 2021

Printed in the United Kingdom by TJ Books Limited, Padstow Cornwall

A catalogue record for this publication is available from the British Library.

Library of Congress Cataloging-in-Publication Data
Names: Albertus, Michael, 1983– author.
Title: Property without rights : origins and consequences of the property rights gap / Michael
Albertus.
Description: Cambridge, United Kingdom ; New York, NY : Cambridge University Press,
2020. | Series: Cambridge studies in comparative politics | Includes bibliographical references
and index.
Identifiers: LCCN 2020028711 (print) | LCCN 2020028712 (ebook) | ISBN 9781108835237
(hardback) | ISBN 9781108891950 (ebook)
Subjects: LCSH: Land reform – Latin America. | Right of property – Latin America.
Classification: LCC HD1333.L29 A54 2020 (print) | LCC HD1333.L29 (ebook) | DDC
333.3/18–dc23
LC record available at https://lccn.loc.gov/2020028711
LC ebook record available at https://lccn.loc.gov/2020028712.

ISBN 978-1-108-83523-7 Hardback
ISBN 978-1-108-79983-6 Paperback

Contents

Figures

Tables

Acknowledgments

The taproot of this book is buried in the fieldwork I conducted when writing my first book on land reform. In the many conversations I had with land reform beneficiaries, land reform losers, bureaucrats, officials, and academics across Latin America, a strange and puzzling contradiction emerged. Time and again someone would declare that a land redistribution program that had broken up large landholdings and redistributed that land to peasants was necessary for the country. Land reform was judged as critical to make a clean break with the colonial era, modernize, end feudal landlord–peasant relationships, and advance social and economic equality. But later in the conversation that same person would declare the land reform a disaster.

At first I thought that perhaps I was talking to the wrong people. After all, land reform – like any major government-driven program that redistributes assets within society – is fundamentally controversial. It would not be particularly surprising for a landowner whose property was stripped from them by the government to declare land reform a misadventure, even if they had to publicly declare it necessary so as not to appear reactionary. But many peasants who had received land similarly decried the deficits of land reform. These were not just the rural children of land recipients who may have resented the upward mobility of their urban counterparts; original recipients themselves often had the same opinion. Nor could it be chalked up to contemporary political propaganda or a radical reinterpretation of the past. To many land beneficiaries, their experience with land reform was in equal parts loved and hated.

This narrative of land reform sat uneasily at the back of my head for several years until I began to teach a course on long-term economic and political development in Latin America. I returned to a fascinating debate that economists had engaged in a decade prior: Why were the richest parts of Latin America prior to colonization now incorporated into some of its least developed countries? Some authors attributed this reversal of fortune to the political institutions the conquistadors created in the colonies; others pointed to geographic features of the colonies that determined settlement patterns of land appropriation and forced labor. Regardless, the result throughout most of the region was the creation of vastly unequal landholding that persisted at least until the early or mid-twentieth century. Those few large landowners at the top of the pyramid underinvested in public goods such as schools, opposed taxes, sought to restrict the franchise, and systematically won policies favorable to protecting their interests. Economies were sluggish and the predominantly rural populations of the region remained poor and marginalized.

Logically, then, it struck me that redistributive land reform that leveled the distribution of landholdings should rid countries of key obstacles that were holding back development. I knew from writing my first book the enormity of many land redistribution programs around the world. In Latin America alone, the redistribution of privately held land since the 1920s covered roughly 40 percent of all cultivable land in the region. This was a seismic shift. And yet development did not follow. To the contrary, building on data I had collected in my first book I found that development had generally stagnated following land reform. There was a missing piece to the puzzle.

It was then that I began reconsidering other aspects of land reform as it was typically conducted and the conversations that I had with those who had a front-row seat to land reform. Many land reform beneficiaries relayed to me stories of government abuse and inadequate support. Others told me that they had been forced to work the land in modes and methods they never desired. Former large landowners told me stories of government incompetence and ways in which a real opportunity for change was squandered. Bureaucrats decried the corruption of the past but vowed that the ship had been righted. Academics and policymakers pointed to the downsides of political expediency or outdated ideologies.

Very quickly a core insight emerged. Land reform beneficiaries often received their land with a web of restrictions and in most cases could not use their land or transfer it as they pleased. Their property rights were ill-defined or entirely absent, and as a result they relied on fickle, unresponsive, or manipulative government agencies to have their daily needs met. The root of the book began to grow.

My first acknowledgments are therefore due to these individuals I interacted with during and beyond my fieldwork. Land reform beneficiaries shared their stories in their fields, homes, and town squares. Former large landowners reflected on their travails with me in their homes, in offices, and at social events. Dedicated bureaucrats and officials in a wide range of land reform agencies schooled me in processes of land reform; the implementation of reform programs from administrative, legal, and practical angles; and how agencies interacted with beneficiaries. They also played another crucial role in this project: facilitating my collection of data on both land reform and on property rights over land. I thank officials and bureaucrats at the Instituto Nacional de Reforma Agraria (INRA) in Bolivia, the Instituto Nacional de

Colonização e Reforma Agrária (INCRA) in Brazil, the Servicio Agrícola y Ganadero (SAG) in Chile, the Instituto Colombiano de Desarrollo Rural (INCODER) in Colombia, the Instituto Nacional de Desarrollo Agrario (INDA) in Ecuador, the Registro Agrario Nacional (RAN) in Mexico, the Comisión de Formalización de la Propiedad Informal (COFOPRI) in Peru, the Ministério da Agricultura, Florestas e Desenvolvimento Rural (MAFDR) in Portugal, the Instituto Nacional de Colonización (INC) in Uruguay, and the Instituto Nacional de Tierras (INTi) in Venezuela for invaluable assistance. These agencies were fundamental to my data collection along with numerous national statistics agencies, archives, and libraries. Finally, local experts and academics aided my understanding of the broader context of land reform and property rights in many cases and provided critical accounts that shed light on government motivations.

Only later did the ideas from my initial insights begin to flower as I kept returning to a common theme: the lack of property rights that land beneficiaries had despite receiving land, and the political utility that this generated for incumbent governments. Many colleagues and mentors provided me with invaluable feedback that aided the development of this idea. I benefited greatly from early discussions with Alberto Diaz-Cayeros and Beatriz Magaloni regarding Mexico's experience with land reform. Steve Haber was a fount of knowledge on the many ways governments could structure property rights for political gain. I profited greatly from ongoing conversations with Dan Slater about authoritarianism and the coercive side of distributive government programs, as well as discussions about why democratic governments would sometimes relinquish leverage over their populations. I also benefited in the early stages of the project from interactions with and the work of several titans of Peruvian politics, especially Cynthia McClintock and Enrique Mayer, who encouraged the project and helped to convince me that Peru was indeed fertile terrain for further study. As the project began to develop, I also had the great fortune of former dissertation advisors who graciously and periodically served as a sounding board. I cannot thank David Laitin, Jim Fearon, Steve Haber, and Jonathan Rodden enough for the training that they gave me during graduate school as well as their consistent dedication to scholarship and their relentless – and constructive – critical thinking.

The Center for International Social Science Research at the University of Chicago, with Jenny Trinitapoli at the helm, supported an invaluable daylong workshop for the book manuscript. Alberto Diaz-Cayeros, Cynthia McClintock, Leo Arriola, and Dan Slater all carefully read the full manuscript and provided trenchant and productive feedback. Alberto offered rich insights into the Mexican case and ways in which I could better organize and present my empirical evidence. Cynthia deeply engaged with the Peru case based on a wealth of knowledge built over decades and encouraged me to link it more closely with the other chapters while doing justice to the specificities of Peru's unique history of land reform. Leo encouraged me to focus my empirical analyses and provided brilliant suggestions for classifying common paths of property rights gaps. Dan pushed me farther on regime coercion and intentionality in withholding property rights versus alternative arguments, and provided a characteristically insightful comparative perspective. All offered ideas on framing the project and engaging with other scholarship. And that is just the tip of the iceberg.

I ended the day swimming in pages of notes and inspired by a wealth of new ideas and points to consider. It took a full nine months to edit the manuscript accordingly, and it improved immeasurably. Their engagement with the work reflects a deep dedication to scholarship as well as a rich generosity of spirit. I thank them profusely. Colleagues and graduate students at Chicago also participated wholeheartedly in the workshop, for which I am appreciative. In particular, Sue Stokes, Ben Lessing, Yanilda González, Paul Staniland, Noah Schouela, Maura Cremin, and Mark Deming provided carefully considered comments that enriched the discussion and in turn the manuscript.

Two anonymous manuscript reviewers at Cambridge University Press engaged with the manuscript and provided thoughtful and constructive reviews that led me to reconsider several important points, clarify others, problematize assumptions, and delve back into related literatures. The manuscript consequently improved considerably. I thank Robert Dreesen at Cambridge University Press for soliciting such excellent and timely reviews. Robert was responsive and encouraging at every stage of the process. And when he passed the project off to Sara Doskow for a final round of review and other steps prior to production, Sara took the torch with enthusiasm and professionalism. Yet again I gained immensely from the careful comments of an anonymous manuscript reviewer. Kathy Thelen then deftly and quickly steered the finished manuscript through review at the Cambridge Studies in Comparative Politics series.

In addition to the especially large impact that these individuals had on the final book manuscript, numerous others have helped to shape my thinking on the project. Of particular note are a growing group of scholars studying the politics of land, including Catherine Boone, Francisco Garfías, Scott Gehlbach, Evgeny Finkel, Alexandra Hartman, Allison Hartnett, Mai Hassan, Lauren Honig, Ethan Kapstein, Kathleen Klaus, Shivaji Mukherjee, David Samuels, Emily Sellars, and Henry Thomson. Various portions of the project and the ideas linked to it similarly benefited from the comments of Jenna Bednar, Pablo Beramendi, Larry Diamond, Mark Dincecco, Mary Gallagher, Miriam Golden, Guy Grossman, Anna Grzymala-Busse, Steve Haber, Allen Hicken, Pauline Jones, Didi Kuo, David Laitin, Margaret Levi, Steve Levitsky, Beatriz Magaloni, Rob Mickey, Brian Min, Noah Nathan, Jennifer Pan, Allison Post, James Robinson, Rachel Riedl, Jonathan Rodden, Ken Scheve, Deborah Yashar, Joe Wong, and Daniel Ziblatt. I also thank seminar and workshop participants at the University of Michigan, Georgetown University, and Stanford University for critical and productive comments.

The University of Chicago Center in Beijing provided me funding to cohost, with my colleague Dali Yang, a formative conference in Beijing on land and development in 2015. That forum gave me the opportunity to learn an immense amount about China's history of land reform, property rights, and development, and also stimulated my thinking about the link between property rights and development comparatively through conversations with Alain de Janvry, Meg Rithmire, and numerous others.

My colleagues at the University of Chicago also provided an incredibly rich and stimulating intellectual environment for the development of this project. The department, and the university as a whole, is indefatigably devoted to the pursuit of ideas. The incisiveness of discussion around conceptualization and theory is unrivaled. The energy around scholarship is infectious. This book is much better for it. John McCormick, Monika Nalepa, Jim Robinson, Sue Stokes, Lisa Wedeen, and Dali Yang have shaped my thinking about political regimes in fundamental ways. Yanilda González, Ben Lessing, and Paul Staniland have influenced my understandings of coercion and state repression. And Dain Borges, Brodie Fischer, Emilio Kourí, Mauricio Tenorio, and numerous other visitors during my interim tenure as the Director for the Center for Latin American Studies have broadened my horizons on the many ways and many issues to study in Latin America.

Institutional support and generous funding facilitated and propelled the research that forms the bedrock for this book. Well before I had even conceived of the idea for this book, but as I was already laying the groundwork for it through data collection, I was supported through a series of fellowships toward the end of my graduate study at Stanford University, including a predoctoral fellowship at the Institute of Economic Policy Research and a postdoctoral fellowship at the Center on Democracy, Development, and the Rule of Law. A sabbatical fellowship at Stanford's Hoover Institution in 2015–2016 provided me the time to write an initial paper version of what would ultimately become this book. The Center for International Social Science Research at the University of Chicago then provided several years of funding to conduct additional fieldwork in several different countries, most importantly Peru, Portugal, and Mexico. That funding also aided in hiring research assistance for the project and in facilitating an enormous amount of data gathering and data construction on Peru. Finally, a sabbatical fellowship at Stanford's Center for Advanced Study in the Behavioral Sciences in 2019–2020 provided the final landing strip for the project. I was able to finish drafting revisions to the full manuscript and further revisions to a final review in no small part due to the long, quiet mornings and afternoons perched atop the hill with a view over the live oaks of the Dish and the hum of Silicon Valley, punctuated by lively and generative conversations with the other fellows.

The project also benefited from valuable research assistance by Josh Corona, Joey DeMarco, Mark Deming, Claudia Fernandez, Johnny Guy, and Eddie Yang. All of them compiled case study materials on land reform, property rights reforms, and development for countries in Latin America, southern Europe, and East Asia. These materials were crucial in gaining insights into how and when governments extend property rights to land reform beneficiaries and formulating initial theoretical foundations for the project. The cases also provided critical glimpses into popular demands for property rights. And they propelled me to make a stronger case that my main argument applies more broadly beyond Latin America to nearly every region of the world. Most of these assistants also aided at some point in chasing down bits and pieces of data, historical details, or bibliographical sources.

The chapters on Peru would not have been possible without the fruitful collaboration of Peruvian scholars. Ricardo Fort in particular shared my decade-long fascination with Peru's agrarian reform and helped to build a formidable team of research assistants based in Lima to painstakingly and systematically gather data on all land expropriations in the country between 1969 and 1985. He also generously shared his data on subsequent land titling by the Special Land Titling and Cadaster Project (PETT) and Agency for Formalization of Informal Property (COFOPRI). And together with Mauricio Espinoza, over the course of several years we constructed, digitized, and compiled reams of district-level data on Peru from a plethora of sources on land characteristics, demographics, social and economic factors, state presence, and much more. These data alone will bring historical data coverage and availability in Peru much closer toward that of Brazil, Colombia, and Mexico. I hope that this opens the door to a new generation of research on Peru. In addition to this collaboration, Ricardo graciously provided space for me to work and present my research at the Grupo de Análisis para el Desarrollo in Lima and introduced me to numerous Peruvian historians, economists, political scientists, and policy practitioners. Separately, my understanding of Peru's history and the treatment of it in this book has been informed by a wide array of interviews, archival work, trips into the hinterlands, and conversations and correspondence with Peru scholars.

Related pieces of a small selection of mainly descriptive materials in Chapters 6 and 7 were published in my articles "Explaining Patterns of Redistribution under Autocracy: The Case of Peru's Revolution from Above," *Latin American Research Review* 50(2); "Does Equalizing Assets Spur Development? Evidence from Large-Scale Land Reform in Peru," *Quarterly Journal of Political Science* 15(2); and "Land Reform and Civil Conflict: Theory and Evidence from Peru," *American Journal of Political Science* 64(2); and in my book *Autocracy and Redistribution: The Politics of Land Reform* (Cambridge University Press, 2015). There are also small portions of my discussion of the Mexico case in Chapter 2 drawn from my article "Authoritarian Survival and Poverty Traps: Land Reform in Mexico," *World Development* 77(2). Separately, related versions of a limited number of selections in Chapters 2 and 3 are drawn from my book *Autocracy and Redistribution: The Politics of Land Reform* (Cambridge University Press, 2015) and my co-authored book *Coercive*

Distribution (Cambridge University Press, 2018). I thank the publishers of these pieces for their permissions.

The great debt of gratitude I owe to all of the intellectual support and inspiration I received in the formulation and writing of this book is only rivaled by that which I owe to my closest family and friends. Without the everyday joy and adventure with them that ran in parallel to this project, the task would have been far more daunting and monotonous. My family continues to grow while remaining incredibly tight-knit. Whether hiking with my siblings, reading to my nieces and nephews, or picking fruit in Michigan's orchards with my parents, their presence is consistently refreshing and rejuvenating.

I am also especially appreciative of the constant enthusiasm of my wife, Ally, who has seen far more of forgotten or ignored swathes of the countryside across continents than she surely would have if she had not met me. A spirit forged in the backwoods of Vermont, she shares my deep appreciation of the rugged, the rustic, and the hardscrabble. Her companionship in trekking for days at 15,000 feet in the Peruvian Andes, searching out community leaders in small villages in Mexico, and traversing the ruins of abandoned estates among wheat fields and cork groves in southern Portugal is in equal parts steadfast and encouraging.

And as I set to copyediting this book, we had just begun our greatest journey yet: welcoming our daughter Sierra into the world. She has already profoundly deepened our lives and stolen our hearts. May we live up to the calling to leave her and the others of her generation a more just, equitable, and wild world.

I

Introduction

José swung the gate open, hopped back into the bed of the truck, and tapped the window to the cab gently with the butt of his rifle. Iván cut the headlights and put the truck in gear. We inched forward along the bumpy road that carved through the broad Southern Venezuelan plains, the dust rising in a thick cloud just behind us. In a low voice, I asked José: "Wouldn't it be easier to find capybara with the headlights on?" "I'll tell you tomorrow," he whispered in reply. "You'll see, on a night like tonight, the moonlight reflects off their eyes."[1]

Before long, Iván brought the truck to a halt and José, William, and I hopped out. José and William stalked slowly into a set of reeds and began whistling intermittently. Iván and I hung back near the truck. The pale light of the moon illuminated the water just beyond the reeds. Iván told me that he was recently freed by the feared Revolutionary Armed Forces of Colombia guerrilla group, which had held him hostage for two months across the border in Colombia until his family scraped together ransom money. Suddenly a shot rang out. Something splashed repeatedly in the water. A few minutes later, José and William approached the truck. José dragged a large capybara behind him over the hard, parched dirt and rocks. He had shot it in the head. "See?" he said to me with a victorious grin.

The next morning, I found out why we were hunting capybara under the light of the moon. José's relationship with his neighbor, who happened to have the better capybara hunting grounds given the size of his property, was fraught and no one knew what might happen if there was a confrontation. After all, José's small plot of adjacent land used to belong to his neighbor. Under Venezuela's new land reform, José had successfully applied for a *carta agraria*, a usufruct certificate that allows applicants to legally occupy the private property of individuals that might run afoul of landholding size and productivity criteria under Venezuela's 2005 land reform law until compliance and ownership are verified. If they cannot be verified in a timely fashion, the occupant receives the land. José was the second occupant to cleave off a chunk of his neighbor's land, and for all anyone knew, he was unlikely to be the last.

---

[1] This event occurred in February 2009. I have changed the names of these individuals to preserve their anonymity.

1

Both existing property owners and recipients of *cartas agrarias* have been trapped by Venezuela's Kafkaesque land reform law that has enshrouded the countryside in a suffocating fog of murky property rights. The law is a near replica of a 2001 law that Venezuela's Supreme Court struck down, only to be resuscitated after President Hugo Chávez upended the court and packed it with his allies in his quest to eliminate opposition. Under the 2005 iteration, *latifundios* – defined as properties larger than the regional average and whose yield is less than 80 percent of that suitable to its extent – are subject to expropriation and redistribution. Productive private lands that are not exceptionally large are protected, at least in theory. Practice is another story. The agency in charge of land reform, the National Institute of Lands (INTi), does not know what average property sizes are by region because they lack complete cadastral data on the actual distribution of property.

Property owners are required to register their property with INTi to rectify its lack of information. To receive a definitive title, however, owners must provide documents that prove a consistent chain of title from 1848 (when the Law of Public Lands was passed) until the present, even if their family has not occupied that land since 1848. Very few owners have such documentation.[2] The result was the generation of a pool of land that the government can – and in many cases does – expropriate and redistribute.

What about the land reform beneficiaries like José? Individual land claims like his spread like wildfire in Venezuela given that any Venezuelan citizen can challenge the ownership of a given property. There are several routes to receiving land through the law. The most common are *cartas agrarias* and declarations of permanence. Successful land claimants that obtain *cartas agrarias* receive provisional rights to their plot from INTi subject to submitting a production plan that INTi must sign off on. INTi is supposed to conduct a follow-up review after two years to verify that the land claimant has put the production plan into action; otherwise, the land can revert to state ownership. However, in many cases INTi does not follow up on the production plan, leaving the property rights of possessors of *cartas agrarias* in legal limbo. It was no surprise that José was holding off on building a house on his new property until he was more certain that it would remain his.

In a similar fashion, a declaration of permanence allows an applicant to remain on and continue occupying a plot of land over which they hold no title such that they cannot be removed except through a separate proceeding that must pass through INTi. Again, these individuals often become de facto land occupants that lack property rights.

---

[2] Informal land transfers in Venezuela have been common historically and most land titles dating from the 1800s that do exist are vague: many historical property delimitations relied on impermanent features of the landscape such as trees. Subsequent titles referred to and built on these originally imprecise titles. Even if an owner can prove an unbroken chain of legal title to land, the productivity criteria in the land law are also vague and politicized.

Alongside individual land claims, the government has opened a second front against private landowners by itself targeting private landowners for expropriation. It then typically converts these lands into state-run farms and hires local rural laborers to work on them while vesting property rights with the state rather than workers. Workers on state-run farms are monitored, screened for their support of the government, and mobilized to turn out during elections.

Millions of hectares of formerly private land in Venezuela have transferred hands through these various channels under the 2005 law. Consequently, a large portion of the rural sector now has property with highly incomplete property rights or no property rights at all. Pervasive property rights insecurity has wreaked havoc on agricultural production, which twinned with exchange rate and import controls has caused devastating food shortages and widespread hunger as the economy as a whole crumbled in the late 2010s. But property rights insecurity has also given the Venezuelan government a much tighter grip on the countryside and its precarious inhabitants than on cities. Although rural areas lack the investment and policy attention targeted at cities, they more reliably turn out to politically support the government. This is in part driven by people like José who hope to retain their new access to land but worry that they may lose it if they are flagged as disloyal.

The rampant weak property rights associated with land redistribution in Venezuela is hardly exceptional among land reform programs that have occurred over the last century. Take the example of Mexico. In the wake of the Mexican Revolution that drew to a close in 1920, the hegemonic ruling party (the Institutional Revolutionary Party, or PRI) methodically expropriated more than 50 million hectares of private land – more than a quarter of all of Mexico's land area – over the course of more than 70 years and redistributed that land to peasants. Land was granted communally as *ejidos* to whole villages. Peasants acquired the right to use and work the land individually or collectively but faced a host of restrictions to property rights. Neither villages nor individual peasants could sell the land or use it as collateral to access commercial loans. Peasants could not rent plots and were not permitted to leave their plots idle for more than two consecutive years.

Similarly in Peru, an anticommunist military regime that ruled from 1968 to 1980 expropriated and redistributed half of all of Peru's private agricultural land. Land reform beneficiaries, however, were not granted property rights over their land. Rather, large private estates were mostly converted into cooperatives of former workers. The regime withheld land titles from cooperative members, maintained co-ownership of cooperatives until the mortgage on the land was paid, and prohibited land sales, leasing, and the use of assets as collateral for loans. Centralized control dissipated when the military regime retreated to the barracks in 1980 and cooperatives informally dissolved, splitting land up among their members. Consequently, an enormous swathe of Peru's rural population drifted into informal individualized ownership. Today the Peruvian state is still working to extend property rights to former land reform beneficiaries.

These dynamics are not unique to Latin America. The Soviet Union redistributed private land to peasants at a massive scale without ever granting them property rights. The same transpired in much of Eastern Europe during the Cold War and China after its Civil War. Zimbabwe's Robert Mugabe seized land owned by white farmers in Zimbabwe and redistributed it to black Zimbabweans in the 1990s and 2000s while withholding property rights from land recipients. Military regimes in Egypt and Portugal of various political stripes similarly redistributed large tracts of private land while imposing onerous restrictions on the property rights of peasant beneficiaries.

Why do governments that redistribute property on a massive scale so frequently fail to grant property rights to land beneficiaries? This is particularly puzzling given that some governments do extend property rights to land beneficiaries, and that a lack of property rights often stunts and distorts investment, markets, and long-term decision-making. Indeed, in many of the examples given previously, the redistribution of property without rights was ultimately followed by economic stagnation or decline, even where governments stoked their economies in the short term through subsidies and investment.

Rather than refashioning the rural sector toward smallholding farmers or communities with secure property rights, governments typically steamroll large landowners through expropriation but leave land reform beneficiaries adrift with highly imperfect property rights and even insecure land access, paving the way for eventual stagnation and underdevelopment. In short, the history of land redistribution is largely a history of reallocating property without rights. This book attempts to make sense of this puzzling regularity.

1.1 CONCEPTUALIZING THE PROPERTY RIGHTS GAP

When free markets prevail over the allocation of resources in society, governments shape and regulate market rules that guide allocation but do not directly reallocate resources. This scenario, however, is historically uncommon. The history of land redistribution – a highly interventionist public policy – is indicative. One-third of the world's countries implemented redistributive land reform programs in the last century (Albertus 2015). Land reform has impacted at least 1.5 billion people since 1945 and hundreds of millions of hectares of land.

Land redistribution entails the expropriation or purchase of private land from large landowners and the distribution of that land to laborers and the land-poor. Government is at the core of this process.

Governments are also central to providing property rights. A property right is an enforceable authority to undertake particular actions in a specific domain (Commons 1968). The specific domain of interest in this book is land. Property rights over land vary in several important dimensions: whether rights are privately or publicly held, whether rights are formal and defensible, whether rights are alienable, and whether rights are collective or individual in nature.[3] Land that lacks any formalization (typically a title), is indefensible, or is inalienable indicates an absence of property rights.[4] By contrast, land that has a formal, registered title to an owner that faces few consequential restrictions on alienability reflects complete property rights.[5]

The core phenomenon that this book examines is the juridical gap between the government-led redistribution of private land and the allocation of property rights over that same land. When a government redistributes land but does not grant land beneficiaries property rights over that land, I term this gap a "property rights gap."

Property rights gaps can be measured on an annual or cumulative basis. If a government redistributes land over the span of years but does not grant property rights over that land, a property rights gap can accumulate in the countryside.

Property rights gaps can also be negative, effectively forming a "property rights surplus." In this case, a government grants property rights over land that was previously redistributed without property rights but does not simultaneously redistribute new land without property rights (or, in some cases, grants property rights over more land than is concurrently redistributed).

To reiterate, this book focuses on property rights gaps and surpluses *in the land reform sector*. Governments may erode or bolster property rights over land that was not distributed by the government to begin with. While these actions can sometimes be driven by similar theoretical considerations as those considered here, that is not always the case. Broader property rights regimes can also be driven by factors such as economic inequality (Engerman and Sokoloff 2002), class-based political competition (Ansell and Samuels 2014), ethnically based political competition or affirmation (Boone 2018; Klaus 2020), enforcement capacity (Soifer 2013), strategies of colonial rule and their postcolonial aftermath (Boone 2014), social status within customary

---

[3] Although I focus on these as major dimensions of property rights that are critical for empirically assessing this book's theory, property rights over land vary in other ways as well, such as how long rights endure (Barzel 1997), the degree to which they generate externalities by encouraging certain forms of resource use (Libecap 1993), and whether enforcement is centralized or decentralized (Ostrom, Schroeder, and Wynne 1993a). See Chapter 2 for further discussion.

[4] An important literature demonstrates that in certain circumstances, longstanding and uncontested informal ownership or customary tenure can provide as much or greater property security as formalized ownership (e.g., Brasselle, Gaspart, and Platteau 2002). However, as Chapters 2 and 3 detail, while these conditions may prevail in some countries, particularly in parts of sub-Saharan Africa and Oceania (Boone 2014), they are empirically rare in the Latin American cases that are the principal empirical focus of this book.

[5] Chapter 2 unpacks these definitions in detail along with the scenario of partial property rights – property rights that reflect incomplete or imperfect formal ownership, consequential restrictions on alienability, or serious limits to defensibility.

institutions (Honig 2017), and population growth and demographic change (Boserup 1965; Barbier 2010).

Governments can of course create property rights gaps over property other than land as well. Indeed, the creation of markets and the management of property rights in those markets is a generic concern in all developing countries. For instance, a government could distribute houses to beneficiaries but not grant property rights over those houses. This occurs on a massive scale with public housing in Singapore (Trocki 2006). Or as another example, the government could allow some private actors to run companies or engage in financial transactions without giving them property rights to protect their assets or transactions from encroachment by other private actors or the state. This characterizes many of China's private business enterprises (Bai et al. 2006; Hou 2019; Wang 2015).[6]

Figure 1.1 graphically depicts a stylized property rights gap in the land reform sector for illustrative purposes. The building blocks for the property rights gap are displayed in Figure 1.1a. Suppose that a new government takes power in period 1. This government engages in land redistribution over several periods. But it does not provide property rights to the beneficiaries of land reform.

A new government comes to power in period 5. This government faces pressure to provide property rights to the beneficiaries of land redistribution from the previous government. At the same time, remaining large landowners organize to block further land redistribution. The extension of property rights over formerly redistributed land, for instance through a formal land titling program, begins slowly under the new government but outpaces further land redistribution, which slows to a trickle. The extension of property rights under the new government then picks up pace in period 6 while land redistribution ends. The extension of property rights continues through period 8. In this period, property rights are extended over the last remaining lands that had been redistributed but that lacked property rights. There is no new redistribution in period 9 and no remaining redistributed land to grant property rights over.

Figures 1.1b and 1.1c demonstrate how the patterns of land redistribution and the provision of property rights over land in Figure 1.1a generate two related but distinct property rights gap measures: a yearly property rights gap measure and a cumulative property rights gap measure. While the chief focus of this book is to understand broad trajectories of property rights gaps, and therefore the evolution of cumulative property rights gaps, the change in these cumulative gaps is of

---

[6] Of course, those with a relative lack of property rights can seek ways to protect themselves. Hou (2019) demonstrates how business entrepreneurs in China seek local legislative positions to gain selective and individualized property rights. Wang (2015) shows how foreign-invested enterprises in China that control valuable assets but lack political connections can demand more effective formal law enforcement than state-owned or domestic private enterprises.

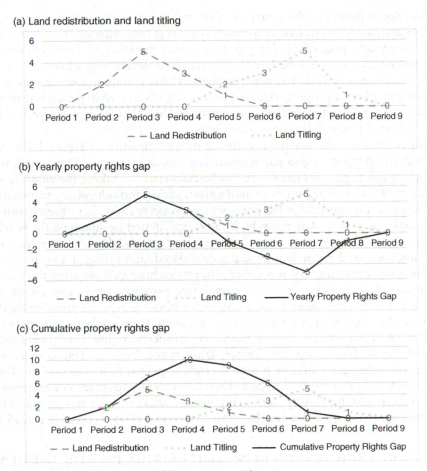

FIGURE 1.1 A stylized picture of the property rights gap
(a) Land redistribution and land titling
(b) Yearly property rights gap
(c) Cumulative property rights gap
Note: The y-axis in each subfigure indicates the amount of land affected in millions of hectares.

necessity comprised of changes in yearly property rights gaps. It is therefore useful to illustrate how each is constructed and how they relate to each other.

The yearly property rights gap displayed in Figure 1.1b is calculated by taking the annual amount of land redistribution and subtracting from it the annual amount of that land over which property rights are granted. In other words, the yearly property rights gap measure is a "flow" variable. In periods 1–4, land redistribution proceeds without granting land beneficiaries property rights over their land. This generates a yearly property rights gap over redistributed land that equals the amount of land redistributed on an annual basis. But in period 5, the yearly property rights gap turns negative: property rights are extended over twice as much land as is redistributed. From periods 6–7, the yearly property rights gap grows more negative as the extension of property rights over formerly redistributed land accelerates while new land redistribution is stalled. The yearly property rights gap diminishes in period 8 as the extension of property rights slows and returns to zero in period 9 as there is no new land redistribution and no more land that had been previously redistributed that still lacks property rights.

In contrast to the yearly property rights gap measure in Figure 1.1b, the cumulative property rights gap measure is a "stock" variable. The cumulative property rights gap in Figure 1.1c can be calculated by taking the cumulative amount of land redistribution up until a given period and subtracting from it the cumulative amount of that land over which property rights have been granted up until that period. Alternatively, it can be calculated by summing the yearly property rights gap over time. It therefore captures the net difference in accumulated land redistribution and accumulated land titling at a given point in time. By definition, the cumulative property rights gap is nonnegative.

Figure 1.1c indicates that the cumulative property rights gap grows in periods 1–4 as land redistribution proceeds without extending property rights and yearly property rights gaps therefore accumulate. It reaches a maximum in period 4, after which the extension of property rights over previously redistributed land outpaces further land redistribution. The cumulative property rights gap therefore begins to erode in period 5. It continues eroding in periods 6–8. By period 8, property rights are extended over the last remaining lands that had previously been redistributed without property rights. The cumulative property rights gap therefore returns to 0 where it began in period 1.

1.2 THE RADICAL SHIFT IN PROPERTY RIGHTS IN LATIN AMERICA OVER THE LAST CENTURY

This book builds a general theory of property rights gaps like that depicted in Figure 1.1. But the main, though not exclusive, empirical focus of this book is property rights gaps in Latin America. Most countries in Latin America entered the twentieth century with the bulk of their rural land area guided by private property rights regimes. Extreme social and economic inequality prevailed, rooted in the skewed distribution and use of land.

The colonial period along with events and policies in the nineteenth century had generated these circumstances. Colonial-era land settlement along with land grants, land sales, and forced labor practices set in motion the appropriation of indigenous lands by the Spanish and Portuguese crowns, powerful private individuals, and the Catholic Church. Military officers who fought in the independence wars at the start of the nineteenth century also won large land grants in parts of Latin America. Many states in the region then confiscated church-owned lands between the mid-nineteenth and early twentieth centuries and sold them to private individuals. Frontier areas shrank as development and population growth drove the privatization of public lands. In some countries, such as Mexico, Peru, and Bolivia, private property at the outset of the twentieth century existed alongside communal property structures within indigenous communities that were pushed to the margins of their economies. But communal lands were shrinking, exacerbated by the late nineteenth century commodity boom.

To be sure, private property rights in the region were often poorly documented and enforced by powerful landholders rather than impartial courts. Furthermore, in most Latin American countries, private smallholders had relatively weak protections of their property rights and in some cases merely had de facto possession of state-owned land or private land. Nonetheless, private property rights largely ruled the day and eventually became fairly stable.

Take the example of Mexico. *Haciendas* dominated much of the rural sector at the start of the twentieth century. These holdings evolved from Spanish colonial land grants to notables (*mercedes*) as well as grants of jurisdictions (*encomiendas* and *repartimientos*) to individuals that included both villages and peasants. Grantees were allowed to levy taxes and demand labor of the villagers that lived within their land grant. Peasant residents on haciendas typically were given an individual plot in exchange for labor on the hacienda (often six days a week) and a predefined share of the harvest (Thiesenhusen 1995, 31). The wives and daughters of male peasants often performed household tasks for the landowner.

The policies of Mexico's Porfiriato period (1876–1910) supported the export economy and accelerated land concentration. The south saw an increase in forced labor and subjugation of indigenous groups alongside traditional peasant communities. Haciendas in the central region, oriented toward agricultural production for export, encroached on communal lands and turned free indigenous villages into rural laborers (Sanderson 1984, 16).[7] This trend was intensified by the 1857 Ley Lerdo that confiscated land from the Catholic Church and sold it to individuals.

By 1910, roughly half of the total rural population, comprising 82 percent of all inhabited communities, were debt peons who worked as resident laborers on haciendas and smaller ranchos under a variety of different arrangements (Sanderson 1984, 18). The haciendas held most of the fertile and irrigated land in the country, leaving residents of free agricultural villages with fragmented and insufficient lands at the agricultural periphery, often on mountainsides and unirrigated flat areas (Sanderson 1984, 19). Less than 11,000 hacienda owners controlled 57 percent of the national territory. One landowner's holdings were as large as all of Costa Rica. Remaining communal

---

[7] In northern Mexico, however, scarce labor led to wage increases.

lands were being rapidly absorbed into haciendas. At the same time, about 15 million peasants were landless (Thiesenhusen 1995, 30).

Major land reform programs in Latin America beginning in the twentieth century rocked private property rights regimes like an earthquake. The redistribution of privately held land in particular, which impacted approximately 40 percent of *all cultivable land* in Latin America, generated an enormous spike in informal ownership. A property rights twilight zone emerged: the private, excludable ownership structure of large landowners ebbed as new forms of provisional and informal ownership arose. Newly important land tenure relationships, and especially cooperative and communal ownership, took root on a massive scale. Where individual ownership continued to prevail, albeit among a new set of land reform beneficiaries, the new owners often never received formal land titles, received provisional titles that were never converted into unconditional, full titles, or received land titles that were never linked to a property register or land cadaster. In other cases, land ownership was formally vested in the state, which granted individuals or groups usufruct over land or shares to collective profits.

These enormous "property rights gaps" often endured for years or decades. Only later did many of the same countries that upended property rights seek to reintroduce them at a large scale. The shift back toward more secure property rights almost invariably occurred after the governments that eroded property rights had left the scene. Relatively young democratic regimes that replaced them often led the way, especially in the last several decades. But in several cases, such as Chile, Mexico, and Peru, authoritarian regimes took the first major steps in restoring property rights to rural areas.

In some countries, like Chile, the most recent shift back toward property rights security came after many original land reform recipients had sold their land or migrated to urban areas. In others, like Bolivia or Peru, informal rural transfers during the property rights twilight zone along with state weakness generated trouble in extending property rights to former land reform beneficiaries. In still other countries, like Mexico, the government strengthened property rights, but there was never a shift to more individual forms of ownership.

1.3   THREE CANONICAL PATHS OF PROPERTY RIGHTS GAPS

This book's main focus is on explaining why and when governments generate, maintain, and close property rights gaps. Over time these actions create different property rights gap trajectories within countries. It turns out that there are a small number of clear patterns that repeat themselves across countries. These broad patterns have important consequences for a host of development outcomes that later chapters examine.

The shift in many Latin American countries over the last century from relatively stable private property rights over land to a property rights twilight zone and finally back toward property rights security is only one of three main paths that countries tend to follow with respect to property rights gaps. Figure 1.2 displays three canonical paths of property rights gaps over time. The figure displays cumulative property rights gaps like that depicted in Figure 1.1c.

If a country traces Path A, it never generates a property rights gap in the countryside. This could be for one of two reasons. First, a country simply may never redistribute land to begin with, foreclosing the ability to open a property rights gap. While this is relatively common outside of Latin America, every country in Latin America in the last century has engaged in at least some land redistribution. A country may also approximate this scenario by going many years without any land redistribution, followed by a brief and nearly negligible period of redistribution in which land beneficiaries are granted property rights, which is in turn followed by a return to inactivity on land redistribution. One example would be Argentina. Land redistribution was off the table until the mid-1940s, at which point the government expropriated a handful of private properties and distributed them to beneficiaries with property rights. Governments since the early 1950s have not redistributed private land and therefore it was impossible for rural dwellers to receive land without property rights.

Alternatively, a country could follow Path A by redistributing land over a longer period of time and concurrently granting property rights over that land throughout that period. Historically, this has occurred only rarely. One example is Colombia. Over the last century, Colombia's government has engaged in limited purchases of private land for redistribution, twinned with some seizures of land (typically those involved in drug production or trafficking). When the government distributes these lands from the state land bank, beneficiaries receive title and property rights over their land.

A more common path in Latin America is Path B. A country that traces Path B at first redistributes property to land beneficiaries but withholds property rights over that land. A property rights gap opens in the countryside as that process continues. The lives of beneficiaries come to be deeply marked by holding land but lacking property rights over it. This is particularly the case if the property rights gap endures for years or decades. A property rights gap as shown in Path B of Figure 1.2 can be large and longstanding. In countries such as Bolivia, Mexico, and Peru, governments forged property rights gaps exceeding half of all cultivable land in the rural sector. Indeed, in Mexico and Peru, governments went on to distribute marginal lands as well, generating property rights gaps that swallowed up both productive and mediocre farmland.

Countries that follow Path B, however, eventually close the property rights gap. This occurs when a government grants land beneficiaries property rights over the land that they had initially received without property rights. Typically, this is a different government than the government that had initially distributed property without rights. Often it happens after a country transitions from dictatorship to democracy, but not always.

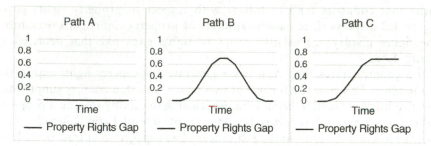

FIGURE 1.2 Three canonical paths of property rights gaps
Note: The y-axis in each graph indicates the proportion of a country's land under a property rights gap.

Finally, a country can trace Path C. Like Path B, this path begins as a government redistributes property but withholds property rights from land beneficiaries. This generates a property rights gap. But unlike Path B, this property rights gap is not closed. It is instead maintained for a long time period. One example is Cuba. The ruling Communist Party redistributed or nationalized nearly all of Cuba's privately owned property in the first five years after Fidel Castro seized power through the Cuban Revolution. But peasants that received land were never granted property rights over that land. The Dominican Republic and Paraguay have also followed Path C, redistributing property without rights from the 1930s through the 1970s but never appreciably extending property rights to land beneficiaries.

Of course, countries that have traced Path C could eventually extend property rights to former land reform beneficiaries. This would ultimately yield a Path B pattern by closing a property rights gap. But there are many countries that have long been on Path C. Outside of Latin America, countries such as China and Zimbabwe have also followed this path.

I.4   MEASURING THE PROPERTY RIGHTS GAP

How can we measure trends in the security of property rights over property such that we can discern whether a country follows Path A, Path B, or Path C as indicated in Figure 1.2? This is a novel and difficult task. Measuring a property rights gap is complicated because rural dwellers hold a wide panoply of rights over property. This makes for diverse definitions and concerns tied to property rights.

One major contribution of this book entails the construction of an analytical framework that differentiates among a set of common, observable, and consequential distinctions in property rights that are theoretically relevant and the subsequent classification of property rights gaps according to these distinctions.

I focus on three key aspects of property rights: land formalization, defensibility, and alienability. Land formalization entails delineating property delimitations, granting legal recognition of property rights and uses, and registering or recording this information. Defensibility entails the ability to defend property rights by calling on and retrieving clear property rights information and by appealing to the state for rights enforcement. Alienability entails the right (which need not be exercised) to sell or lease exclusion, management, or withdrawal rights associated with a property.

Property that lacks any formalization, is indefensible, or is inalienable reflects an absence of property rights. On the other end of the spectrum, land that has a formal, registered title with few consequential restrictions on alienability reflects complete property rights. To be sure, rights over property can, and often do, reside in a middle ground between these two extremes. I therefore classify property rights characterized by incomplete or imperfect formal ownership, consequential restrictions on alienability, or serious limits to defensibility as partial property rights. Chapter 2 explores these property rights definitions in detail.

The property rights definitions I employ do not require property to be held individually for rights to be complete. There is a rich history of communal property holding, particularly among indigenous groups. Collective groups can hold a full bundle of property rights just as private individuals do – although the organization of those rights differs. But if land is held collectively or communally, the group as a whole must at least have the *option to decide* whether or not its members can alienate their land for property rights to be complete.

Using these definitions, I conducted extensive fieldwork and archival work to collect original data on both the redistribution of landed property and the property rights held by the beneficiaries of land redistribution for all Latin American countries between 1920 and 2010. There was very little to no land redistribution within Latin American countries of the type I examine here prior to 1920.[8] Data on land redistribution and property rights over land are housed by land reform agencies, ministries of agriculture, or archives of the state throughout the region and have not been otherwise widely disseminated. Of course, data are not always classified in accordance with the theoretical distinctions that guide this project. This required gathering supporting information on the nature of compensation for land seizures, laws and practices regarding the rights and duties of property ownership, the coverage and use of property registers, and other supplementary material. Chapter 2 discusses these issues at length.

---

[8] There was a small amount of land redistribution in Mexico just before 1920 during the final years of the Mexican revolution. Chapter 2 also discusses the distinct phenomenon of nationalizing or selling off lands owned by the Catholic Church in many Latin American countries between the mid-nineteenth and early twentieth centuries.

I gathered data on land redistribution and property rights over that land separately from one another since property rights over land can and do change over time. The result of this fieldwork is the most comprehensive and systematic dataset ever gathered on rural property rights. Furthermore, the data are comparable across countries and over time.

What emerges is a first, fascinating glimpse into rural land ownership and property rights in Latin America – or any region, for that matter – over a significant time period. I use the separate measures of land redistribution and property rights to construct "full" and "partial" property rights gap measures. I construct these measures annually as well as cumulatively over time in order to examine how property rights gaps expand, close, or persist in a stable fashion.

The coding scheme that I employ to measure the property rights gap is not tailor-made to Latin America. It can also be applied to other regions with land tenure structures and landholding patterns that differ from those in Latin America. Many countries around the globe have generated property rights gaps. Some countries, such as Portugal, generated large property gaps only to close them quickly, following Path B in Figure 1.2, whereas other countries, such as China, generated property rights gaps and then maintained them for decades at a time, following Path C.

Most of the governments within Latin America that implemented large-scale land redistribution simultaneously underprovided property rights to land reform beneficiaries, embarking either on Path B or Path C. Bolivia, Brazil, Chile, Cuba, the Dominican Republic, El Salvador, Guatemala, Mexico, Nicaragua, Panama, Paraguay, Peru, and Venezuela all generated large and positive yearly property rights gaps. These yearly property rights gaps sometimes stacked up so large that they came to dominate the rural sector. Governments in Bolivia, Chile, Cuba, Mexico, Nicaragua, and Peru distributed more than half of all cultivable land to land reform beneficiaries that then languished without property rights. Sometimes this transformation happened quickly, as in Cuba and Nicaragua; in other cases it occurred more slowly and methodically, as in Mexico.

In many of the cases where governments generated large property rights gaps, subsequent governments extended property rights to former land reform beneficiaries without further redistributing land, following Path B. This resulted in negative yearly property rights gaps that chipped away at longstanding cumulative property rights gaps in the countryside. The cumulative property rights gap closed relatively quickly in some cases. In El Salvador, for instance, much of it had been eliminated about 20 years after it was generated. But in other cases, such as Bolivia and Mexico, large cumulative property rights gaps took between 30 and 70 years to close. And in still other cases, such as Cuba, the Dominican Republic, and Paraguay, large cumulative property rights gaps were never closed and continue to prevail over enormous swathes of the countryside. These countries have followed Path C in Figure 1.2.

Figure 1.3 displays a series of graphs of land redistribution and property rights over redistributed land in a canonical Path B case: Mexico. These graphs follow the same order as the stylized picture of the property rights gap in Figure 1.1. Figure 1.3a shows the amount of land in Mexico that the government redistributed over time from large landowners to new peasant communities. It also shows how much redistributed land was granted property rights through the Certification of Ejido Rights and Titling of Urban Plots (PROCEDE) program, a large-scale land titling program that started in 1993. Figure 1.3b displays the yearly property rights gap. This is calculated by subtracting the amount of land titled from the amount of land redistributed. Figure 1.3c displays the cumulative property rights gap, calculated by summing the yearly property rights gap over time. Figure 1.3c indicates that Mexico clearly follows Path B from Figure 1.2.

1.5 FRAMING THE PUZZLE: PROPERTY RIGHTS, DEVELOPMENT, AND LAND REFORM

The fact that so many countries trace Paths B or C instead of Path A constitutes a major puzzle from the perspective of much of the study of property rights. Why do many governments redistribute property without extending property rights to land beneficiaries? And why do other governments grant secure property rights to beneficiaries, whether contemporaneously with land redistribution or long after it has occurred?

This puzzle is made more perplexing from several of the dominant perspectives on land reform and property rights that struggle to make sense of both the variation in property rights provision across governments as well as the propensity of most governments to withhold property rights from land beneficiaries.

Consider the perspective that granting property rights to land beneficiaries can enable them and those around them to flourish by generating economic returns used to pay for land reform or to invest in human capital or infrastructure. It is conventional wisdom that, in general, secure property rights can underpin long-term economic development by encouraging accumulation, production, and economic dynamism (Acemoglu et al. 2001; North 1990). People can confidently make productive investments when property rights are secure because they will not worry that their property or investments might be arbitrarily seized. And the transparent and enforceable nature of ownership and interests enable people to leverage their property as collateral to gain access to financing in order to improve their assets or invest in human capital such as education. Secure property rights also underpin liquid markets for property, which can put property into the hands of those that would use it most efficiently (Demsetz 1967).

Secure property rights over land as an asset are anticipated to have similar positive consequences. A large literature demonstrates that well-established and secure property rights are critical for the functioning of rural land markets, for

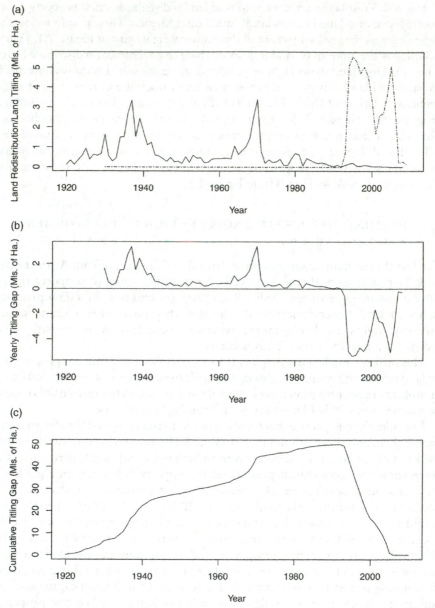

FIGURE 1.3 The property rights gap in Mexico, 1920–2010
(a) Land redistribution and land titling
(b) Yearly property rights gap
(c) Cumulative property rights gap
Note: The y-axis in each subfigure indicates the amount of land affected in millions of
hectares. In Figure 1.3a, land redistribution is indicated with a solid line and land titling
with a dashed line.

generating incentives to invest in agricultural production and infrastructure, and for the rise of access to private credit (e.g., Deininger et al. 2004; De Soto 2000; Rajan and Zingales 2003). Secure land access also supports the accumulation of human and physical capital (Besley and Burgess 2000; Galiani and Schargrodsky 2010; Galor et al. 2009). It is therefore widely accepted that property rights – albeit not always formal or individual – strongly support the efficient exploitation of land (Demsetz 1967; Feder and Feeny 1991).[9]

Incomplete and insecure property rights over land, by extension, can inhibit accumulation and production as they depress the value of land and make it difficult to sell, lease, partition, or leverage as collateral to gain access to loans. Incomplete or insecure land rights can encourage an emphasis on planting short-term crops (Do and Iyer 2008) and a reticence to fallow land for fear of counterclaims or appropriation (Goldstein and Udry 2008). Both of these dynamics can reduce long-term land productivity and deplete soils. Widespread property informality can scare off foreign investors and capital (Songwe and Deininger 2009).[10] It can force domestic investors to pursue creative strategies to protect their investments (Post 2014).[11] And it can generate contestation over ill-defined and poorly documented property delimitations (Boone 2014; Deininger 2003; Klaus 2020). This last consideration encourages individuals to remain on their property to protect it against counterclaimants rather than migrate seasonally to work and complicates the ability to sell land.

Despite the anticipated positive consequences of secure property rights, insecure and incomplete rural property rights are endemic throughout most of the developing world. Furthermore, major land reform programs that overhauled the allocation of property in over a third of the world's countries since the dawn of the twentieth century only rarely granted beneficiaries complete property rights. Land reform programs instead tended to grant beneficiaries land in usufruct with state ownership, land with restrictions on partitioning, alienability, and mortgaging, or land with provisional titles or no titles at all. As de Janvry et al. (2014, 216) put it in terms of conventional

---

[9] The importance of land formalization and individual ownership in securing property rights is an area of much more active debate than the importance of property rights themselves. See, e.g., Brasselle, Gaspart, and Platteau (2002); Ellickson (1993); Goldstein and Udry (2008). Chapter 2 takes up these issues in detail.

[10] Customary forms of land access and common property rights, however, can also be exploited by foreign actors in order to acquire land at a large scale that they would otherwise be prohibited from acquiring (Wolford et al. 2013).

[11] Post (2014) demonstrates in an analysis of the privatization of urban water and sanitation systems in Argentina that alternatives such as firm organizational structure can help substitute for weak formal property rights to make credible commitments for investment. Cross-sector diversification enables domestic investors to gain valuable informal contractual supports that underpin investment.

wisdom in economics, land reform is "vastly ill-used as a policy instrument in spite of its well-recognized potential to generate efficiency and welfare gains."

The puzzle of the underprovision of property rights is further complicated by the fact that land reform represents a relatively rare opportunity to supercharge development. A large body of scholarship suggests that the concentration of land in the hands of a few large landowners is key to understanding the historical roots of inequality, poverty, and underdevelopment in the contemporary world (Ansell and Samuels 2014; Moore 1966; Rueschemeyer et al. 1992). Where landholding was concentrated, as in Latin America, Southern Europe, and East and South Asia, smallholders, tenants, and wage laborers could not – or were not permitted to – accumulate enough land or capital to save, invest, and send their children to school where they could be trained to work in more dynamic economic sectors (Cinnirella and Hornung 2016; Galor et al. 2009). Land concentration can undermine dynamic rural labor markets (Rueschemeyer et al. 1992; Ziblatt 2008) and even the establishment of representative government (Acemoglu and Robinson 2006; Moore 1966).[12] And Engerman and Sokoloff (2002) show that high historical inequality in parts of the Americas during the colonial period lowered subsequent investments in public goods, generating worse development outcomes in the long run.

For these reasons, scholars point to landholding inequality as a root cause of the "Great Divergence" between rich and poor countries over the last few centuries (Galor et al. 2009). By eliminating large landowners and equalizing land access, land redistribution should unlock economic dynamism and development (Baten and Juif 2014; Galor et al. 2009; Lipton 2009). This relationship should be particularly straightforward given that land reform avoids the typical equity-efficiency trade-off (Besley and Burgess 2000). In other words, greater equity in the distribution of landholding does not sacrifice productivity in the way that equity-enhancing reforms sometimes do in other markets. This is in part due to the generally inverse farm size–productivity relationship: land reform can contribute to rural well-being given that, all things equal, small farms are often more productive than large farms (Deininger 2003).

Consequently, many scholars and policymakers beginning around the late 1940s advocated land redistribution as a way to tackle poverty and inequality in the developing world and encourage development (Ladejinsky 1977; Prosterman and Riedinger 1987).[13] Redistributive land reform held the potential to vastly and directly improve peasant livelihoods, facilitate human capital formation, and pave the way for new public goods and services.

---

[12] For a dissenting view that instead emphasizes the importance of rural labor market conditions, see Mares (2015).

[13] See, e.g., Kapstein (2017) for a discussion.

Although studies of the development consequences of land reform are few and far between, several such studies provide supportive evidence linking land reform to rural well-being. At the macro level, scholars have long pointed to post–World War II land reforms in South Korea and Taiwan as generating both equality and high economic growth as rural families could better afford to send their children to school, ultimately yielding urbanization and industrialization (Galor et al. 2009; Haggard and Kaufman 1995). Besley and Burgess (2000) similarly tie land reform – and specifically tenancy reform – to lower rates of rural poverty in Indian states. At the more micro level, Keswell and Carter (2014) link land allocations in contemporary South Africa to higher consumption and household living standards in the medium term.

This book demonstrates that these cases are the exception rather than the rule. Most countries that have conducted land reform over the last century have squandered its development potential. To a large degree, this is tied to the typical withholding of property rights from beneficiaries.

1.6 EXISTING EXPLANATIONS FOR THE UNDERPROVISION OF PROPERTY RIGHTS

Why have so many countries failed to grant the beneficiaries of land redistribution programs property rights over the land that they receive? Few existing accounts examine the creation of property rights gaps per se through policies of redistributing property but withholding rights. Nonetheless, there are several prominent explanations for the more general dearth of secure property rights in some countries that could be extended in an effort to shed light on the property rights gap. These include myopia, ideology, and insufficient state capacity.

The myopia explanation comes in several stripes. It could be, for instance, that governments were unaware that underproviding property rights would drive negative economic and social consequences, or that they could more productively shape property rights. Relatedly, governments may have identified the importance of property rights but took ineffective steps to provide them – for instance by creating decentralized property registers that were not linked to a land cadaster. A final myopia explanation lies with the need of governments to wrestle with multiple and often conflicting goals simultaneously. For instance, the drive to feed cities, maintain agricultural economies of scale, and avoid land reconcentration provided powerful motivations for some policymakers to pursue land collectivization and to withhold property rights from land reform beneficiaries.

A second explanation for the lack of property rights is ideology. Skeptics of free market capitalism have long pointed to market volatility, an imbalance in power relations in the countryside, and logics of extraction and social domination as powerful forces that tend toward land concentration, peasant dispossession, and labor repression. Many leftist governments, and especially socialist ones during the heyday of the Cold War, sought to avoid these outcomes by organizing land reform beneficiaries collectively and prohibiting land alienation.

A third explanation for prevalent insecure and incomplete property rights is that many states lack the capacity to provide complete property rights. Providing and maintaining property rights can be costly and complex, requiring significant administrative and infrastructural power that some states lack.

Chapter 3 details each of these existing explanations in much more depth and roots them in broader historical context. I find support for each of these explanations to varying degrees in this book. But none is sufficient to fully explain the timing, extent, and characteristics of property rights gaps. There are too many anomalous cases, too much conflicting evidence, and often too loose a match with the realities of the countryside for these explanations to be entirely satisfactory, whether individually or in concert.

1.7 REEXAMINING THE POLITICAL ORIGINS OF THE PROPERTY RIGHTS GAP

Existing explanations shed light on but do not entirely resolve the puzzle of festering incomplete rural property rights or patterns in the upending of rights through land redistribution without granting property rights to land reform beneficiaries. Why, then, do some governments generate large property rights gaps over rural land whereas others do not? Why do some governments close these gaps when they encounter them whereas others allow them to persist or even exacerbate them? And what effects do property rights gaps have on critical development outcomes such as economic growth and well-being, urbanization, educational outcomes, inequality, rural political voice, and links between parties and voters? This book provides a novel set of answers to these important questions rooted in the political nature of land ownership, property rights, and development.

The Generation and Maintenance of Property Rights Gaps

The generation of a new property rights gap requires two elements: the redistribution of property and the withholding of rights over that property from new beneficiaries. Land redistribution itself is a monumental political project. It requires deliberate executive action, legislative support, a judiciary that sustains the legality of property transfers, and a bureaucratic and military apparatus that can physically seize or purchase land from large landowners and transfer it to rural workers.

Political regimes are therefore fundamental to the implementation of redistributive land reform. Land redistribution often dies at the doorstep of democracy as heterogeneous interests across a plurality of institutions make deliberate action and consensus building on land redistribution close to impossible. Large landowners can win legislative seats, challenge land redistribution in independent courts, and lobby politicians in an effort to stymie or entirely block land redistribution.[14]

Authoritarian regimes, by contrast, have much greater capacity to steamroll opposition to policies that they pursue. But not all authoritarian regimes seek to redistribute land. For every Castro or Cárdenas, there is a Castelo Branco. For every Velasco there is a Videla, and for every Mao or Mugabe there is a Mussolini. Authoritarian regimes that rule with political coalitions that exclude large landowners will brook no appeals to protect them. To the contrary, they will often view out-group elites as rivals to be crushed. After all, powerful landowners have resources that can be used to attempt to displace the incumbent regime. They can also make ruling difficult because they stand at the apex of rural social and economic relations and therefore mediate between the state and its broad swathe of rural subjects.

Crushing rival landed elites through land redistribution leaves authoritarian regimes with a valuable resource – land – and a choice: how should land and the property rights over it be allocated? Reallocating enormous tracts of land to regime insiders poses the serious risk of empowering a new set of rivals. It also forecloses the opportunity of gaining popular support from society. Few authoritarian regimes pursue this route.

On the other hand, widely distributing land grants to rural dwellers along with complete property rights gives beneficiaries a considerable degree of autonomy and independence from the state. While this can stoke economic dynamism, it too carries risks given that authoritarian regimes seek economic cooperation and reliable political support from their populations in the form of extractive revenue and pro-regime mobilization. Granting property with rights to land reform beneficiaries can be self-undermining because it can enhance their power to oppose the incumbent regime.

There is a third, particularly tempting route under these circumstances: redistribute land to rural workers without attendant property rights over that land. The strategy of widely distributing property without rights activates a set of additional political mechanisms that provide an opportunity to enmesh land

---

[14] Of course, some "popular democracies" are characterized by few institutional constraints (e.g., Albertus and Menaldo 2018). These regimes are more capable of implementing land redistribution than institutionally constrained democracies, as illustrated by land reforms under Salvador Allende in Chile and Jacobo Arbenz in Guatemala. However, these are exceptional cases within Latin America. The history of democracy in the region has largely been characterized by strong institutional constraints (Albertus 2015). Furthermore, democracies across the range of institutional constraints can channel popular demands more effectively than dictatorships, as will be discussed later in the chapter. In light of the distribution of constrained versus unconstrained democracies in Latin America during this period and the theoretical considerations this book raises, I do not split democracies into subgroups.

reform beneficiaries in relations of dependence on the state. This paves the way to creating a politically pliable and dispersed support base.

The key to recognizing these mechanisms lies in understanding the everyday obstacles that rural dwellers face when they hold property without secure property rights as well as the ways that states can fix the market failures that they themselves create. Rural dwellers deprived of property rights face difficulties in using land as collateral to obtain loans and credits from banks for critical production inputs and capital improvements. The result is underinvestment in land and agricultural production. A lack of property rights also makes it hard to sell, lease, partition, or mortgage property. This stunts rural land markets and depresses land value. Weak or absent property rights also makes it difficult to defend land against counterclaimants or those who seek to encroach upon or enclose it. This renders landholders wary of migrating to obtain seasonal employment or schooling, lest they come home to find someone else living on their land.

A precarious rural sector balancing between poverty and prosperity presents a ruling authoritarian regime the opportunity to create tools that require rural dwellers to interact with the government on an iterated basis and enable them to scrape by if they remain in the government's good graces. Examples include state banks that monopolize rural credit and loans, agencies that monopolize the provision of fertilizers and subsidies, and agencies that manage land access. These tools can be used to manage threats such as rural rebellions and blockades of crucial transportation routes. They can similarly be honed to ensure cooperation with important regime goals such as winning elections or providing sufficient and affordable food for cities so that urban centers do not become tinder-boxes of collective action. By conditioning the favorable use of these tools on the behavior of rural subjects who need assistance, a government can gain advantageous coercive leverage that can be strategically deployed among critical constituencies during periods of heightened regime pressure.

I do not maintain that regimes typically calculate the political value of a property rights gap ex ante and then malevolently plan its every dimension and consequence to maximize their coercive leverage over the countryside. The argument that I am forwarding operates mainly in equilibrium as opposed to onset, once a property rights gap is opened up through initial land redistribution. A property rights gap that opens through land redistribution without extending property rights can first occur because a regime has other goals that conflict with property rights or ideological views about the pernicious consequences of certain forms of property rights. Or it can originate for more prosaic reasons tied to focusing on first completely eliminating rival landed elites or dedicating resources to maximizing the number of immediate land beneficiaries. In select cases, however, some members of a regime may indeed recognize certain political advantages of initially withholding property rights and act to pursue those advantages.

Regardless of the very initial origins of a property rights gap, governments normally realize its political advantages relatively quickly and then intentionally maintain the gap or even grow it larger, sometimes for decades. This dynamic occurs among a wide range of politicians across ideological lines, sociological origins, and political backgrounds. It is an equilibrium that snatches governments and economies even when politicians initially have good intentions with regard to designing property rights over redistributed land.

The choice for rural dwellers that live under the equilibrium of a property rights gap is clear: toe the regime line and gain assistance or forego benefits and face a rural life riddled with the market distortions and complications that arise from lacking property rights. This stark choice binds land reform beneficiaries that lack property rights to an incumbent regime by making the regime, and the state apparatus the regime controls, central to citizens' strategies for economic survival.

Encouraging this repeated interaction with the state also renders land reform beneficiaries more "legible": the regime comes to know who land reform beneficiaries are and where they live – and how to extract political support from them at low cost. And by providing rural individuals with property that lacks rights, the difficulties associated with selling land and protecting it from counterclaimants encourage land reform beneficiaries to remain in rural areas where populations are dispersed and collective action barriers are high.

Granting property without property rights is not merely an oversight or a political blunder when viewed through this lens. Quite the opposite: it is one of the most politically valuable policies that land redistribution makes possible. And it can be accomplished in a plethora of ways. These range from the more extreme, such as forcing land beneficiaries into collective farms or cooperatives, or nationalizing land and then granting beneficiaries usufruct rights, to the mundane, such as withholding formal land titles or failing to link titles to any property register or land cadaster.

The insight that political actors can benefit by manipulating property rights over land has been observed in other contexts. Boone (2014), for instance, demonstrates how, against a backdrop of rising competition for land in Africa, politicians that preside over statist land tenure regimes back new settler communities in rural areas with long-settled populations. Politicians then leverage powerful linkages to local political spheres to mobilize new settlers for political ends by taking advantage of their reliance on the state for their tenuous land rights.[15] A similar dynamic can occur in states that seek to

---

[15] In Boone's context, and in a departure from the main thesis in this book, political incentives to politically manipulate property rights in Africa have grown in recent decades with the emergence of multiparty electoral competition. However, and more consistent with the conclusions here, electoral competition in many of these cases is not entirely free and fair. Incumbents systematically leverage the power of the state over land and other resources to their political advantage. There are a number of other important differences in the historical background conditions of land ownership in sub-Saharan Africa that also lead to patterns of property rights provision that diverge from those in this book, most prominently the nature of colonial rule and widespread customary authority over land, as well as low person–land ratios and relatively weak states that do not have the capacity to conduct land redistribution in the way many countries in other regions have done so over the last century. See Chapters 2 and 3 for further discussion.

secure their frontiers by allocating land in a contested and controversial fashion to new settlers in areas dominated by ethnic minorities that are viewed as supportive of a cross-border hostile power (McNamee 2018).

Furthermore, scholars of urban informality have also recognized the political utility in underproviding property rights over land. Take for example Collier's (1976) classic work on illegal urban settlement formation in peripheral Lima in the mid-twentieth century. Collier demonstrates that the elite and their political allies supported informal settlement in which settlers lacked legal land titles not only as a way to facilitate evictions from inner-city slums but also in order to link the urban poor to the state and win their political support. Elites and their allies used the marginal status of settlers to shape the nature of their political activity and demand-making. More recent evidence supports the notion that lacking a land title can make urban slum residents more vulnerable to clientelistic exchanges since politicians can condition ongoing land occupation on political support (Holland 2017; Larreguy et al. 2018). This taps into the underlying fears of eviction among the undocumented.[16]

Closing Property Rights Gaps

Democracies are most often responsible for closing property rights gaps that previous authoritarian regimes generated. Democracies tend to close property rights gaps because of an asymmetry in how pluralistic political systems process popular demands against the violation of powerful minority interests.

Policymaking in democracy grinds to a halt when powerful and vocal minorities throw up resistance to threatening reforms, as landed elites do with land redistribution. Democracies are consequently unlikely to successfully conduct significant land redistribution. But there is rarely a powerful and vocal minority that opposes securing property rights in the land reform sector.[17] Property holders that lack complete property rights stand to gain from these efforts unless their claims are contested. And individuals with contested claims are likely to be more dispersed and much less powerful than the landed elites that had to be physically displaced through land redistribution.

Absent well-organized resistance from powerful minority interests, democracies can channel popular demands into the political system and will act on them with greater fidelity than dictatorships. Securing incomplete property rights is often one of these demands when a wide swathe of rural dwellers lacks them. There are plenty of reasons why securing property rights for land beneficiaries who lack them can be popular. Land reform beneficiaries who gain greater property rights protection can benefit from higher land prices and more liquid land markets, can more easily secure loans and credits by using

---

[16] With the growth of urban centers in the developing world, there is increasing recognition of the political importance of urban tenure insecurity and land regulation (Auerbach et al. 2018).

[17] The same is not necessarily true outside of the land reform sector. See Chapter 3 for a discussion.

their land as collateral and thereby reap returns to investment in their land, and are less likely to be forced into a position of political and economic dependence on an incumbent government.

Democracy provides a range of paths for land reform beneficiaries that lack property rights to stump for them. Land reform beneficiaries can support politicians that promise greater rule of law and property security. They can elect legislative representatives that pursue legislation and funding for land titling and other property rights–enhancing programs. Furthermore, independent judiciaries may rule in favor of greater property rights security by formalizing the legal basis of a previous land reform and requiring the legislature and bureaucracy to provide legal protections to reform beneficiaries. The process of extending property rights need not be strictly technocratic; it is often inherently political.[18]

Closing a property rights gap is particularly likely under democracy when political competition and coalitional formation draws peasants directly into the ruling coalition. Placing peasants in the driver's seat supercharges incentives to both redistribute property and extend property rights over property. While the former is typically foreclosed by the institutional constraints of democracy, reforms that secure property rights are more likely to be implemented.

However, there remain exceptional circumstances in which there is a concentrated set of losers to securing property rights and those losers capture an important veto point. This typically occurs when a residual set of landed elites survives land redistribution or when political winds shift toward democracy before landed elites are entirely ruined and dispersed. In these cases, landed elites may organize to capture a veto point from which to oppose efforts to secure property rights if there are aspects of securing property rights that harm them, such as cementing in the new status quo distribution of property. Often they organize through the legislature, which has historically been a redoubt for landed elite interests that gather through conservative parties.

There is one additional circumstance conducive to closing a property rights gap in the countryside that transcends political regime type: foreign pressure. All countries periodically face economic crises generated by financial panics, debt servicing, currency imbalances, or reversals in economic growth. Crises of sufficient severity can force a country to seek the help of international financial institutions such as the International Monetary Fund and World Bank. In the post–World War II era, these institutions demand economic and political reforms in exchange for lending support. Privatization and greater security of property rights are typically core conditions for receiving support. A yawning property rights gap that prevails over the countryside is a prime target. Foreign pressure can close rural property rights gaps in this fashion.

---

[18] This point is consistent with Boone's (2018) conclusions from land titling in the Ivory Coast in recent decades.

1.8 CONSEQUENCES OF PROPERTY RIGHTS GAPS

Property gaps have ruled the countryside in many places over the last century. Around one-third of countries across the world created substantial property rights gaps, following Paths B or C of the property rights gap as depicted in Figure 1.2. In some countries, like Mexico and Russia, property rights gaps swallowed up half or more of all agricultural land for many decades. Quickly closing a property rights gap is a rarity. Some countries, such as Cuba, followed Path C and continue to preside over large property rights gaps that they generated many decades ago.

That hundreds of millions of individuals living in the rural sector have spent their lives farming land that they received from the government but that lacks property rights has fundamentally shaped trajectories into modernity for them and the countries they reside in. For one, the underprovision of property rights to land reform beneficiaries sapped any positive effects of equalizing land ownership on economic growth and dynamism. Large landowners in many countries long reigned at the top of rigid and hierarchical social relations and systematically opposed policies such as industrialization and democratic reforms that threatened to drain cheap rural labor from their estates or politically empower traditionally marginalized social groups. Rather than replacing this landowning class with a set of dynamic and empowered rural workers with the tools and property rights protections that could facilitate creating a robust and modern agricultural sector, land redistribution often paved the way for a weak peasantry that suffered from a lack of property rights and ultimately struggled to stay afloat.

Governments threw these peasants a life preserver that just barely kept their heads above water through providing a stream of necessary but paltry annual benefits. But they never brought them into shore. Agricultural productivity consequently drifted as investment, mechanization, and the adoption of new farming technologies lagged. Regimes that faced the resultant passive and weak rural populations that languished under a property rights gap then tilted public policy in favor of cities. Basic public goods and services such as primary education and health, as well as comfortable state jobs, were targeted to urban centers.

The inability of land recipients to alienate their most valuable asset or to accumulate significant wealth stunted urban transformation in countries with large property rights gaps and kept land reform beneficiaries dispersed across the countryside. These limitations also delayed rural human capital formation. This fueled growing inequality over time as the countryside increasingly fell behind cities.

Property rights gaps eviscerated the advance of rural political power. The star of urban political power rose as rural populations remained dispersed and the countryside remained underdeveloped. Urban restiveness became more threatening than rural rebellion and the economic payoffs for cultivating relatively productive urban centers were bright. Urban primacy became urban political power, enabling demands on the state even under authoritarianism. Property rights gaps also set the stage for rampant clientelism to replace the old social hierarchies between landowners and peasants. Incumbent parties quickly learned to reap the advantages of their iterated interactions with geographically fixed rural dwellers and tilt the political playing field in their favor by calling land beneficiaries to heel during elections.

To be sure, while some of these dynamics further entrench government control over the countryside, these efforts are not always successful. The initial spark of peasant support from land redistribution can fade over time against this difficult backdrop. Some governments that need or want support may adjust accordingly. But in most cases the development train has already left the station; reversing it is not easily done.

Table 1.1 summarizes how the three canonical paths of property rights gaps map onto the outcomes in this discussion. Provided that land reform occurs at all, Path A represents a path to prosperity.[19] Path B, by contrast, is a path to delayed development. And Path C is a path to stubbornly stagnant underdevelopment.

In short, characterizing the extent and duration of property rights gaps aids in understanding many dimensions of economic, social, and political life in the countryside.

1.9 ROADMAP OF THE BOOK

The rest of the book proceeds as follows. Chapter 2 provides a broad descriptive overview of the historical evolution of property rights gaps in Latin America. It does so over a long period stretching to the early twentieth century. This requires translating the conceptual notion of a property rights gap into concrete empirical measures. Chapter 2 therefore examines the broad distinctions in forms of property holding over time, spanning from private, individual holdings to government property, informal ownership, and collective and communal ownership. It also distills key insights from the property rights literature to create a set of distinctions among property rights over property and then classifies yearly and cumulative property rights gaps in accordance with these distinctions. Armed with these original metrics of property rights gaps, Chapter 2 provides the first panoramic view of the evolution of property rights and property rights gaps in the rural sector of Latin America.

Chapter 3 begins with an overview of major prevailing explanations for a lack of property rights in some countries. None are fully sufficient to understand the widely varying patterns in property rights gaps. Chapter 3

---

[19] If no land reform occurs, Path A economies will retain unequal countrysides. The path to prosperity in these cases is narrower, and requires countries to develop through modernization that draws workers to cities and renders agriculture relatively less important.

TABLE 1.1 *Economic, social, and political consequences of the property rights gap*

Property rights gap path	Land reform contribution to agricultural productivity and economic growth	Urbanization	Urban policy bias	Rural/urban inequality	Rural political power	Clientelism	Examples
Path A	Positive	Fast	Limited	Relatively stable	Significant	Limited	Colombia, Uruguay
Path B	Neutral or negative; could flip after gap closes	Slow then increasing	Substantial then wanes	Grows	Weak	Substantial	Peru, Mexico
Path C	Neutral or negative	Slow	Substantial	Grows	Weak	Substantial	Cuba, Dominican Republic

then provides a novel theory of why governments generate, maintain, and close property rights gaps. It examines how the main political actors that determine these outcomes – ruling political elites, landed elites, the rural masses, and international actors – interact with one another in pursuit of their preferred outcomes. The chapter lays out the logic whereby governments sometimes redistribute land but withhold property rights from land reform beneficiaries in order to enmesh them in relations of dependence on the state, providing the state with critical coercive leverage over the countryside. It provides an overview of the mechanisms that governments can use to withhold property rights from land reform beneficiaries, the distortions that this generates in the rural economy, and how these very distortions are used as handles to intervene in rural life in order to ensure social quiescence and political support. Chapter 3 then outlines under what conditions governments close property rights gaps by extending more secure property rights to former land reform beneficiaries without further redistributing property.

Chapter 4 empirically tests the theory's main implications. It does so by examining patterns in original data on yearly and cumulative property rights gaps in Latin America from 1920 to 2010. This period in Latin America is particularly fruitful for testing the theory. Nearly every country in the region began this period with high levels of landholding inequality, but there was strong divergence in how governments addressed it. Political regimes and institutions as well as the composition of ruling coalitions varied widely. And many countries interacted sporadically with international financial institutions and faced pressure from these institutions.

Chapter 4 documents that authoritarian governments in particular redistribute land but withhold property rights from land reform beneficiaries. Coalitional splits between ruling political elites and landed elites drive patterns of land redistribution under dictatorship. But a logic of rural control drives authoritarian regimes to withhold property rights from land reform beneficiaries, often for decades at a time. It is democracies rather than dictatorships that typically close a prevailing property rights gap. This is especially likely when peasant groups are politically empowered and any remaining large landowners are either unopposed or politically unorganized. But foreign pressure, particularly in the wake of severe crises that require turning to international financial institutions, can also force governments into closing a property rights gap. This operates on both authoritarian and democratic regimes. These findings are not driven by state capacity, economic trends that correlate with waves of democracy, historicized legacies of redistribution and property rights, the strength of party systems, US pressure, or political ideology, though some of these factors do have an important independent impact on the property rights gap.

Chapter 5 turns to the consequences of property rights gaps. Millions of rural dwellers in Latin America have lived large parts of their lives, and in some cases, their entire lives, in a state of limbo in which they receive property but few if any rights over that property. This shapes many basic contours of their lives and livelihoods. And it has broader economic, political, and social repercussions. This chapter demonstrates using an array of evidence that understanding property rights gaps is like shining a spotlight into the dark: it helps to explain a host of pervasive problems and critical dynamics at the heart of rural life that scholars have long sought to explain.

Chapters 6 and 7 take a complementary approach to Chapters 4 and 5 by examining in depth a single country case. These chapters focus on Peru, where a military regime generated an enormous cumulative property rights gap starting in the late 1960s. Property rights were strengthened under democracy in the 1980s, but the property rights gap did not seriously begin to close until a return to dictatorship and external pressure in the face of a major structural economic adjustment program in the 1990s. Through a process-tracing exercise that tracks the key theoretical factors outlined in Chapter 3, Chapter 6 details the economic and political conditions that led to the origins and closing of Peru's property rights gap, taking it along canonical property rights gap Path B. This chapter draws on primary and secondary documents and interviews in examining the theory's causal mechanisms.

Chapter 7 then turns to a wealth of localized original data on land reform in Peru as well as data on property rights and metrics of development to investigate how the creation of local-level property rights gaps shaped subsequent economic and social outcomes linked to development. Together, these localized cumulative property rights gaps formed Peru's large national-level cumulative property rights gap. The analyses utilize a geographic regression discontinuity design that takes advantage of Peru's regional approach to land reform through zones that did not entirely map onto major preexisting administrative boundaries. Consistent with the theory and with Chapter 5, this chapter finds that local property rights gaps in Peru drove a slower shift away from agricultural labor, underpinned lower agricultural productivity and educational attainment, and fueled higher rates of inequality and poverty. Chapters 6 and 7 therefore ultimately help to demonstrate the theory's internal validity as well as its utility in understanding variation in development outcomes within as well as across countries.

Chapter 8 turns to property rights gaps outside of Latin America in order to put the region's experience in comparative perspective. The principal aims of the chapter are threefold. First, the chapter examines the historical prevalence and nature of property rights gaps around the globe by generating an original account of the principal features of property rights over land that governments have granted to beneficiaries in the course of all major redistributive land reform programs since 1900. Second, the chapter investigates whether the factors that have generated and closed property rights gaps in much of Latin America operate in a similar fashion in other regions. Finally, this chapter examines property rights gaps in two countries with very different histories and development trajectories outside of Latin America: Portugal and China.

Process-tracing exercises in each of these cases demonstrate further support for the causal mechanisms that typically guide the creation and closing – or in China's case, modification – of property rights gaps. These cases also help to demonstrate the usefulness of the theory for helping to better understand cases that are typically viewed through the lenses of ideology and limited state capacity.

The concluding chapter begins by discussing the book's implications for the influential debate on long-term economic and political development in Latin America. The theory and evidence presented here call for a reinterpretation of received wisdoms on development in the region.

This chapter also examines limitations and alternatives to the property rights paradigm. Property rights as they are typically conceived of by neoliberal policymakers are not a cure-all for rural development. But land tenure security is indeed critical for rural inhabitants. There is an emerging consensus around the need for more nuanced and context-specific property rights and a new set of international guidelines regarding how to respect, record, and strengthen such rights. This chapter outlines how the theory impinges on the implementation of these guidelines and details some of the potentially unintended consequences that might result.

The conclusion then demonstrates how the book's theory speaks to the broader relationship between politics and markets. The creation of markets and management of property rights is a general problem in all developing country scenarios. The argument has implications for property rights in other realms aside from land and divorced from a first step associated with redistribution. States can generate new markets or enable the rise of new markets, or new markets can arise organically. A government can then choose whether, and how, to delineate and protect property rights for actors that operate in those markets. Subsequent governments can maintain this status quo or upend it.

Like with rural property rights gaps, understanding the nature and composition of a country's political institutions as well as government coalitional dynamics and foreign pressure can help to make sense of broader property rights regimes. The conclusion develops these insights systematically and then applies them to the evolution of subsoil property rights over oil in Mexico since its independence from Spain, subsoil mining rights for minerals in the United States since the Gold Rush, and property rights in the banking sector in Venezuela in recent decades. The discussion illuminates in new ways several broader puzzles about states and markets, such as why governments would unilaterally erode property rights in certain markets and why governments would ever extend property rights to what seem to be relatively weak social actors.

2

Conceptualizing and Measuring the Property Rights Gap

A critical first step toward building and testing a theory of the property rights gap is constructing a measure of the gap and gathering comparable data on that measure. This is no small feat. It represents one of the largest hurdles to understanding the enormous transformations that have occurred in the rural sector around the world over the last century. In practice, rural dwellers hold a wide panoply of rights over their property – rights that have been at times solidified and at other times radically upended or redefined. Measuring the property rights gap is complicated in good part due to this wide world of property rights.

In highly developed Western countries, the most common prevailing form of private property rights entails individual, formal ownership with few restrictions on the ability to alienate property or to capture rents or benefits from that property. This is coupled with clear property delineation. But this scenario is hardly the norm from a global perspective. Governments also own land. In some cases, they own all of a country's land and merely lease it to individuals or grant usufruct rights over it. Many landowners around the world hold property collectively or communally rather than individually. In many countries with a private sector, the vast majority of landholders have informal property ownership.[1] These landholders either lack title to their property – they may have customary rights to property or simply be de facto owners or squatters – or they hold disputed, restricted, or encumbered titles that are not predictably recognized or upheld in courts. Many private landowners face a web of restrictions to alienability in the form of restrictions on the ability to sell, lease, or mortgage property or to use it as collateral for obtaining loans.

Scholarship on property rights reflects this wide variation in property rights. Numerous authors across disciplines as widely varied as economics, law, anthropology, and political science have grappled with making sense of differing property rights regimes and their consequences. Unsurprisingly, therefore, the study of property rights and the definitions that are employed are not monolithic.

---

[1] The World Bank estimates that perhaps only 30 percent of the world's population has legally registered title to their land (Muñoz 2017).

32

The task at hand, however – to systematically measure and gather data on the property rights gap – is a positive rather than a normative one and therefore requires making concrete coding decisions. This in turn requires deciphering a set of common, observable, and consequential distinctions among property rights that are theoretically relevant. In short, it requires identifying a North Star and then using it to draw a map for guidance.

The goal of this chapter is precisely this: to analytically differentiate among property rights over property and then classify property rights gaps according to these distinctions. While coding many distinct dimensions of property rights and gathering data along these many dimensions would be a herculean task and risks losing the forest for the trees, drawing a mere binary distinction between complete and incomplete property rights is both insufficient and unsatisfying. I pursue a middle path that relies on the fact that property rights are a "bundle of rights" (see, for instance, Becker 1977; Munzer 1990) and elements within that bundle are frequently correlated.

I focus on several key aspects of property rights in constructing my measures: land formalization, defensibility, and alienability. These core aspects of property rights have been at the center of intense study and theorization of property rights for more than half a century. Focusing on them enables the construction of measures of complete property rights, partial property rights, and an absence of property rights. Property that is not formalized in any way, is indefensible, or is inalienable indicates an absence of property rights. At the other end of the spectrum, land with formal, registered title that has few consequential restrictions on alienability reflects complete property rights. Partial property rights indicate incomplete or imperfect formal ownership, consequential restrictions on alienability, or serious limits to defensibility.

The definitions I employ do not require property to be held individually for property rights to be complete. But if land is held collectively or communally, the group as a whole must at least have the *option* to decide whether or not its members can alienate their land.

Armed with these definitions, I detail data on both the redistribution of landed property and the property rights held by the beneficiaries of land redistribution for all countries in Latin America over the period from 1920 to 2010. I collected data on land redistribution and property rights separately from one another because property rights over land can and do change over time. These data enable the construction of various, comparable measures of the property rights gap over redistributed land for the first time. They yield the first systematic picture of rural land ownership and property rights to date for any large grouping of countries over a substantial time period.

The coding scheme that I develop for measuring the property rights gap is not unique to the land tenure structure or landholding patterns that prevail in Latin America. In fact, it can be broadly applied to countries around the world. Chapter 8 discusses property rights gaps and their consequences outside of Latin America.

2.1 THE DRAMATIC EVOLUTION OF PROPERTY RIGHTS IN LATIN AMERICA

Most Latin American countries entered the twentieth century with rural sectors guided largely by private property rights regimes. Land inequality was extreme and shaped broader social and economic inequalities. To a large degree, this was a legacy of colonial-era land grant and forced labor practices such as the *hacienda, encomienda,* and *repartimiento* systems. The hacienda system extended ownership to land to a small number of powerful colonizers through grants sponsored by viceroys, governors, and town councils or through purchases from the Crown or indigenous groups. The encomienda and repartimiento systems granted the use of massive pools of indigenous labor to colonizers. Early nineteenth-century independence movements disrupted these systems with varying degrees of success in selected areas. But in many cases the military officers who fought for independence appropriated or were assigned rights to enormous colonial tracts of land (Griffin 1949, 179).[2]

Frontiers and the share of publicly owned land simultaneously shrank in the nineteenth century. Public lands distribution moved largely in tandem with economic development and population growth as it has in many countries since the nineteenth century (Barbier 2010).

Figure 2.1 is a map that displays a public land concession to a private citizen in the eastern part of the department of Cusco in Peru. As Peru's population grew in the nineteenth and twentieth centuries, especially in the more populated regions of the Andes, individuals started pushing farther and farther down the slopes of the Andes into less settled areas. This dynamic also transpired in Bolivia, Colombia, and Ecuador.

Figure 2.1 shows a land concession in the area of Pilcopata, Peru. The plot of interest, labeled *terrenos de Isona* ("Isona's lands"), is bordered by several other private landholdings. Those to the left of Isona's land in the map belonged to a landowner named Ollanta. Land next to Isona's at the bottom of the map belonged to a landowner named Pelayo. Bordering Isona at the top and right-hand side of this map are state-owned lands (*terrenos del estado*). Isona was, therefore, located at the frontier of private and public land. These types of grants pushed frontiers farther out over time, often in a sequential, cascading manner as occurred here in Pilcopata, and played an important role in privatizing public lands.

The trend of distributing public lands to private individuals was reinforced by state weakness in parts of Latin America. Several wars, such as the War of the Pacific and the La Plata War, broke out among young Latin American states over boundary disputes, typically in sparsely settled areas. States consequently

---

[2] The disruption was greatest outside of the most populous areas and was particularly severe in New Granada (especially Venezuela), parts of Mexico, Chile, and Uruguay (Griffin 1949, 176).

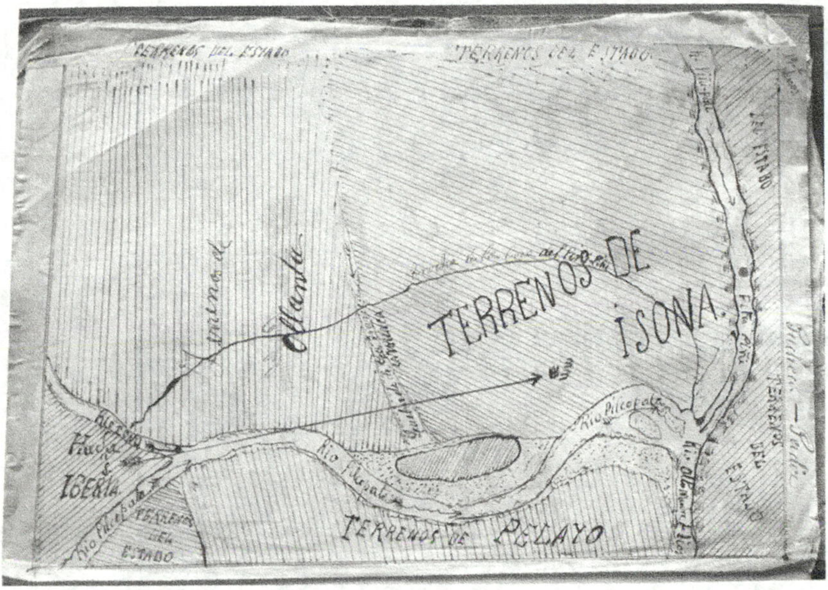

FIGURE 2.1 Public land grant in Pilcopata, Peru
Note: Map accessed at the Archivo Regional de Cusco, Cusco, February 2018.

sought to settle these areas as buffer zones against their neighbors by granting or auctioning off public tracts of land to private individuals.[3]

States also expropriated the Catholic Church and lands held in mortmain at a massive scale in the nineteenth century. The church was a key part of the colonial project and became an enormous landholder in Latin America, allying with or even comprising an important segment of the landed elite (Gill 1998). In some countries such as Mexico, it was the single largest landowner by the mid-nineteenth century (Otero 1989). Liberal politicians attacked the role of the church in the state in the mid-late nineteenth centuries. The key weapon in their arsenal was expropriating church land (Albertus 2015, Ch. 2; Gill 1998, 65). In most cases, such as Mexico, governments sold off church lands to private individuals. In a few cases, like Ecuador, it initially retained a substantial portion of these lands and rented them out to private individuals.

Figure 2.2 displays a map of the extent of church lands expropriated in the canton of Cayambe in the highlands of Ecuador. These lands, in the shaded areas, covered

---

[3] Distributing lands to private individuals in sparsely populated border regions can stimulate settlement and production, making foreign incursions more costly and foreign claims of cross-border territorial ownership more complicated. This strategy is not unique to Latin America. It also occurred in the United States and Canada in the nineteenth century (e.g., Frymer 2014). And it continued into the twentieth century in Latin America, such as in Bolivia and Paraguay in the wake of the Chaco War.

FIGURE 2.2 Expropriated church lands in Cayambe, Ecuador
Note: Map is from *Municipio de Cayambe* (1970). Shaded areas are former church lands.

nearly half of the canton's land area. Expropriations began in 1908 under President Eloy Alfaro's Ley de Manos Muertos. The government confiscated clerical property and initially rented it to wealthy farmers (Haney and Haney 1987, 2). The 1918 Civil Code abolished debt peonage and tied labor a decade later. The state came to control nearly 20 percent of the Sierra as a consequence of these reforms. It held the land in haciendas comprising what was known as the Asistencia Social. Older, feudal labor relations were primarily transformed into the more flexible, semifeudal *huasipungaje* system, whereby tenants received usufruct rights to a subsistence plot of land in exchange for a work obligation on the hacienda. Later, in the 1960s, these lands began to be distributed through land reform programs.

In some countries, particularly those where indigenous populations were large, such as Mexico, Peru, and Bolivia, private property regimes existed alongside substantial communal property structures that had evolved from precolonial systems such as the *ejido* or *allyu*. The predominantly indigenous communities that lived under these structures were progressively pushed to the margins of their economies. Landholding inequality actually became more extreme in the late 1800s as a major commodity boom spurred private landowners to appropriate indigenous lands that were increasingly valuable due to growing transportation links to external markets (Coatsworth 2008). This dovetailed with the spread of ranching on extensive tracts of land to meet the growing European and North American demands for meat consumption and clothing. Ranchers pushed numerically smaller and sometimes seminomadic indigenous groups off more sparsely populated grasslands and wetland regions such as the Pampas of Argentina and the Pantanal in Brazil.

Figure 2.3 is a map that exemplifies haciendas pressing in on indigenous lands. The map displays the bimodal distribution of land in the districts of Urubamba, Yucay, and Huayllabamba in the Peruvian department of Cusco in the mid-1960s. Large haciendas ran up and down the valley in a fashion typical of the time, flanking the road that bisected them (haciendas are indicated with the abbreviation "Hda." in the map). Narrowly squeezed between these haciendas were disparate indigenous communities (labeled "comunidades" and abbreviated "com.") and smaller properties (labeled *pequeñas propiedades*). Members of these communities and smaller properties were part and parcel of the hacienda economy. Their livelihoods, security, and freedom of movement were impacted by the hacienda owners. Other communities were physically encircled by or incorporated within hacienda land.

To be sure, the private property rights that prevailed across much of Latin America at the outset of the twentieth century were often poorly documented and enforced by powerful landholders rather than courts. This is in part because many powerful private landholders had obtained or expanded their lands in the nineteenth century by appropriating and enclosing the lands of indigenous communities (Saffon 2015). Private smallholders in most countries had relatively weak protections of their property rights or merely had de facto possession of state-owned land or private land held by larger landowners.

Beginning in the early twentieth century, however, numerous countries in Latin America undertook enormous programs of land reform that radically shifted the distribution of property ownership and upended prevailing property rights regimes. Land reform accelerated during the Cold War and in the wake of President Kennedy's 1961 Alliance for Progress.

The most high-profile land reform programs centered on land redistribution: the undercompensated or uncompensated expropriation of land from the private sector and its redistribution to the land-poor. Regimes such as postrevolutionary Bolivia, Chile under Allende, Cuba under Castro, Mexico under the Institutional Revolutionary Party (PRI), and Peru in the 1970s under military rule seized the

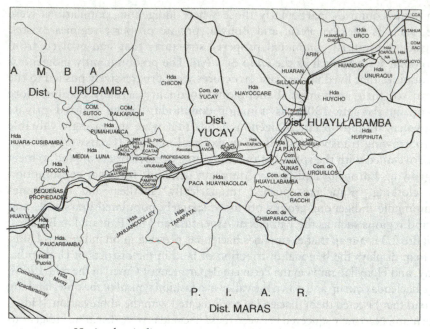

FIGURE 2.3 Haciendas, indigenous communities, and small private properties in Cusco, Peru

Note: Map is a reproduction of the original, which was produced by the *Ministerio de Agricultura, Oficina de Ingeniería y Catastro*. Accessed from the *Centro Bartolomé de las Casas*, Cusco, June 2014.

property of large landowners and redistributed it to peasants. Several other governments implemented less radical programs of land negotiation: the acquisition of land from the private sector with market-value compensation or above and its subsequent transfer to the land-poor. Examples include Brazil after 1993, Costa Rica beginning in the 1960s, and Venezuela from the 1960s to the early 1990s. Still others, such as Colombia and Ecuador, focused on public land distribution: the state-directed transfer of state-owned land to settlers.

Many governments implemented several types of land reform simultaneously. For example, Colombia purchased a significant amount of privately owned land for redistribution alongside its larger program that distributed public lands.

Programs of land redistribution and land negotiation induced the biggest shock to existing property rights in Latin America. Part of this is due to their scope. Between 1920 and 2010, 167 million hectares of land transferred hands through these two types of land reform. This represents 9 percent of Latin America's total land area. But because most land redistribution and negotiation focused on cultivable regions, as opposed to, say, jungle land deep in the Amazon or arid deserts, the total amount of land transferred through these two reform policies comprises approximately 43 percent of *all cultivable land in the region*.

Of equal importance, however, land reform programs introduced new property rights regimes on a massive scale. In most countries this entailed an enormous spike in informal ownership and a sort of property rights twilight zone. The private property rights regime that prevailed among large landowners was quickly wiped out but not immediately replaced by clear, stable systems of property rights. Instead, a host of provisional, partial, or informal forms of ownership and usufruct arose.

When governments put in place more stable property rights regimes, they often deviated substantially from the property rights regimes they replaced. What were these new property rights regimes? In broad terms there were four principal types: cooperative ownership with some degree of local control, communal ownership structures, direct state ownership and management with individual shares in production or wage labor, and individual ownership either without formal title or with provisional title.

Land reform beneficiaries that lived in cooperatives engaged in joint production and received a share of joint profits. Cooperative rules determined activities and benefits, and these rules in turn were created by cooperative members, the state, or both. Land could not be bought and sold by individuals within these cooperatives. In many cases, cooperatives had limited influence on precisely who constituted their membership. If the state, for instance, demanded that a cooperative incorporate new members, it was often compelled to do so. One example is the cooperatives created by Peru's military regime in the 1970s from the land they expropriated from private landowners. Another example is the *asentamiento* cooperative structure that emerged in Chile from the land reform under presidents Frei and Allende.

Communal ownership structures differed from cooperatives in that land itself was held communally and its use and allocation were determined by the community. This meant that in some communities the bulk of land could be exploited individually with all or part of those profits kept individually. Typically, however, some portion of land was reserved for community use for activities like grazing animals or common farming. Land and profits could be reallocated through community decision-making. And in most cases, informal norms governed farming and other activities, such as the sharing of labor during harvests and the requirement to give a portion of time toward community service. One example of this arrangement was the *ejido* system in Mexico under the PRI.

In contrast to these previous scenarios, at times the state took direct ownership of private land acquired through land reform and directly managed this land with little input or decision-making from private individuals. Land reform beneficiaries in these cases were individuals who were employed on state farms and either were given some share of production revenue or were paid a wage for their labor. Examples include Cuba's state farms created in the wake of the Cuban Revolution and the state farms created in the early 1980s by the Sandinista government in Nicaragua.

In another set of cases, land reform paved the way for individual ownership but without formal title or with provisional title. Sometimes land reform beneficiaries received land without receiving any sort of title. Other times they received land with a certificate or property title that was not linked in any way to a property registry or land cadaster. Still other times they received a provisional title that could only be converted into a formal title without liens or encumbrances after a certain time period had elapsed (typically several decades) or after they had paid a certain amount to the state for their property. Many times individuals did not comply with these regulations and transferred their land in informal markets, rendering the new owner fully to the informal sector. One example of individual land grants without formal title is Venezuela's land reform program in the 1960s and 1970s.

Even among these broadly different types of ownership there was often blending and evolution over time. In some cases, states held the formal title to cooperatives, and in other cases, cooperative members held formal or provisional title. Sometimes title was transferred between them. States at times managed cooperatives or manipulated their membership or production decisions even when cooperatives held title. In many cases of communal ownership, communities lacked formal title to their lands. Furthermore, if and when cooperatives and communal ownership structures were broken up by the state, members often transitioned into holding land informally. Individuals in many of these cases later bought and sold land without titles.[4]

In several cases, such as Colombia, the property of expropriated private landowners was transferred to land reform beneficiaries along with private property rights. But governments more typically granted former land reform beneficiaries private property rights years or decades after these individuals had initially received land – if they did so at all. In some countries, the shift of the land reform sector toward private property rights occurred after the initial land reform recipients had died off or moved to growing urban centers. In other cases, like Peru in the 1990s, informal rural transfers had occurred and states remained weak so that they had trouble extending property rights to former land reform beneficiaries. In still other cases, like Mexico in the 1990s and 2000s, property rights were strengthened but there was never a broad shift to more individual forms of ownership.

2.2   IDENTIFYING AND DEFINING RELEVANT DIMENSIONS OF PROPERTY RIGHTS

The previous section points to many different forms of property rights over redistributed land as well as changes to these property rights over time. How can we make sense of these trends in a parsimonious manner?

---

[4] Informal land transfers also occurred even in some cases of cooperative and communal ownership where individuals or groups were able to lay de facto claim to specific plots of land.

The key to making headway is to distill several discernible and distinct dimensions of property rights that will both capture key dynamics of the theory and aid in building empirical measures of property rights and the property rights gap. Toward that end, I now turn to unpacking the different relevant dimensions of property rights distinctions conceptually. The property rights distinctions and definitions I utilize are common and built from a longstanding literature including authors such as Demsetz (1967), Feder and Feeny (1991), Libecap (1993), and Ostrom (1990).[5] It is important to note, however, that these definitions are hardly monolithic, as important scholarship in fields such as law, sociology, and anthropology makes clear (see, for example, Ellickson 1993; Netting 1981; Radin 1987; Rose-Ackerman 1985; Stark 1996). Neither have the definitions I employ always been historically dominant.[6]

Nonetheless, coding and comparison requires that I use clear definitions and rules. It is also important from an empirical perspective not to change my property rights definitions over time. Doing so could bias empirical tests of the theory. While notions of property rights and their completeness have shifted over time, ideas regarding what constitutes "full" property rights as I engage with them have been around since before the beginning of the time period of analysis. The political consequences of incomplete property rights have also been present throughout the period regardless of how politicians form or project ideas about rights.

I begin by following Commons (1968) and define a property right as an enforceable authority to undertake particular actions in a specific domain. Property rights define the actions regarding a specific item that individuals can take in relation to other individuals. The rights of certain individuals entail commensurate duties on the part of others to observe that right (Ostrom 2003).

The specific item of interest here is land among land reform beneficiaries. Property rights over land vary in several key dimensions that this chapter will explore in depth: whether rights are privately or publicly held, whether rights are formal and defensible, whether rights are alienable, and whether rights are collective or individual in nature. To be sure, these are hardly the only dimensions of property rights over land. Rights can also vary in other ways such as how long they endure (Barzel 1997), the degree to which they generate externalities by encouraging certain forms of resource use (Libecap 1993), and whether enforcement is centralized or decentralized (Ostrom, Schroeder, and Wynne 1993b).

Nonetheless, I focus on the key dimensions previously enumerated for two reasons. First, these dimensions of property rights are central to the theory and

---

[5] One area in which there has been more disagreement within this literature is on whether property rights need to be individual to be complete. As I discuss later in the chapter, I follow recent work, which builds in part from Ostrom's seminal contributions, on how collectives can hold a full bundle of property rights in equal form to private individuals.

[6] Ostrom (2003) provides an important overview of a wide range of literature on both the various forms of property rights across distinct societies and the historical development of property rights.

to assessing it empirically. Second, these dimensions of property rights have been debated and discussed for many decades and are at the core of some of the most influential scholarship on property rights.

Private Versus Public Ownership

A first and critical dimension over which property rights vary is whether property and the rights over it are vested in the government or in private individuals. Public ownership prevails when the government formally owns land either by constitutional stipulation or formal title and has the authority to conduct a full range of activities over land including accessing land, managing who else has access and what that access entails, withdrawing resources, and regulating and managing use. By contrast, full private ownership prevails when private individuals or groups of individuals have formal title, possess this range of rights, and have the authority to sell or lease these rights. Private property need not be held by private individuals in order to possess a full range of rights: private land can be held collectively by communal groups or cooperatives as well.

The distinction between government and private property should not be confused with public versus private goods or resources. Different types of property regimes at times have similar operational rules with respect to resource access and use (Feeny et al. 1990). At the same time, a single type of good or resource can be governed and managed under different property regimes. Common-pool resources, for instance, can be owned and managed by government, private individuals, communal or cooperative groups, and voluntary associations (Bromley et al. 1992).

The rights of private owners, even if "complete," are never absolute or unbounded. They have responsibilities to avoid harming the rights of others at a minimum (Demsetz 1967). More typically, there are additional restrictions such as the necessity of ceding property for the purposes of eminent domain. Restrictions go even further in some cases without causing direct injury to private property holders. For instance, as in contemporary South Africa, a government may legislate that the state has a right of first refusal when certain groups of private owners (such as large landowners) sell land without impinging upon the ability of sellers to name their price.

Although the distinction between public and private property is a clear one theoretically, the lines can blur at times as governments and private citizens tussle over, ignore, or encroach upon the property rights of one another. Sometimes private landowners effectively have their property rights stripped by the state. Take for instance Cuba. The government passed two major agrarian reform laws in 1959 and 1963 in the wake of the Cuban Revolution. These laws nationalized foreign-owned land, led to the state purchase of other private lands, and expropriated millions of hectares of other privately owned land and redistributed it to a new set of small private landowners. The private plots that land beneficiaries received, however, were not divisible and could only be sold to the state or transferred by inheritance (Thomas 1971), effectively dismantling private property rights. Another example is Venezuela's ongoing land reform program. Individuals who successfully apply for land grants are given provisional title over their land subject to submitting a production plan to the land reform agency and undergoing a follow-up assessment that the plan has been put into place (Albertus 2015b). However, in many cases the bureaucracy does not conduct a timely assessment, leaving land reform recipients in a state of legal   limbo vis-à-vis the government for years.

In other scenarios, private property rights are effectively extended over state lands – and at times evolve into "complete" private property rights. States themselves can encourage this transformation by setting policies to privatize state lands through adverse possession or through grant-making or auction procedures. One example comes from Colombia. Colombia used frontier settlement of public lands (*baldíos*) beginning in the 1800s to relieve pressure on established landholdings in the Andes and Caribbean coast by encouraging surplus landless laborers and the land-poor to claim property by cultivating virgin lands. From 1900 to 2012, the state granted nearly 23 million hectares of land to petitioners through some 565,000 adjudications (Villaveces and Sánchez 2015, 23–24).

However, in some cases individuals squat on or enclose public lands illegally and over time exert effectively private property rights over such lands. This is especially common where states are weak and either cannot enforce their own property rights or cannot distinguish them. Alongside legal public land settlement in Colombia, land speculators and large landowners systematically and illegally enclosed public lands in frontier regions dating at least back to the mid-nineteenth century. They did so by leveraging their resources and political clout to illicitly obtain private land titles (LeGrand 1986; Saffon 2015). Subsequent titles have built on these.

A similar dynamic played out in Brazil. There was no law regulating land access between Brazil's independence in 1822 and 1850. The result was widespread frontier land squatting and land claiming. Brazil passed a major land law (the *Lei de Terras*) in 1850, which gave legal titles to all land privately occupied by 1854, including pre-independence land grants. The law simultaneously mandated that all land not yet occupied by private parties would "devolve" back to the state. Land policy was decentralized to Brazil's newly created states when the country became a republic in 1889. Policy was thereby handed to gubernatorial administrations, which were effectively in cahoots with local agricultural elites. Many states incorporated land policy laws similar to the 1850 Land Law into their constitutions (Silva 1996). In practice, however, large, politically connected landowners continued to occupy new land that was meant to have devolved back to the state. Local power holders (*coronels*) selectively enforced the land law with the help of corrupt state officials and fake land titles. They prevented new smallholders from obtaining land while at the same flouting the law by occupying public lands and resisting the establishment of functioning land cadasters. Brazil's states have at times struggled in recent decades with separating public versus private lands (via *ação discriminatória*) for the purposes of land reform. In some exceptional cases, such as São Paulo in the mid-1990s, state governments attempted to acquire and distribute longtime "private" lands that were judged as *terras devolutas* by the courts through "reclamation" (Meszaros 2013, 47), to which landowners raised quick and stiff resistance.

For the purposes of measuring the property rights gap and building and testing the theory, I seek to determine whether the beneficiaries of land redistribution programs have private property rights over their land or whether these rights are vested in, consequentially infringed upon, or withheld or underprovided by the state. This task is more straightforward than discriminating between state and private ownership over lands that have long been occupied through dubious or corrupt means outside of the land reform sector.

Importantly, when the state withholds or infringes upon the property rights of private citizens, it gains leverage over them. Activities such as investing in land, selling harvests, passing land down to heirs, obtaining loans, and even maintaining land access can all come to depend on the cooperation and support of the state – which often comes with a political price.

Formalization and Defensibility

A second dimension of variation in property rights is whether property holdings and the rights tied to them are formalized. Formalization is at the root of many conceptions of property rights, especially in economics (De Soto 2000; Feder and Feeny 1991; North 1981). The formalization of land gives it legal recognition and delineates in a clear-cut fashion the nature and delimitations of property as well as the rights associated with it. This diminishes uncertainty and risk around alternative claimants or rights that may or may not be associated with holding property, such as withdrawing resources or making improvements.

Formalization is closely tied to property rights in part because of the historical and conflicting panoply of entitlements that characterize land possession and use in most countries. As the United Nations and World Bank frame it, there are often overlapping claims between the "statutory or customary, primary or secondary, formal or informal, group or individual" rights of individuals and communities to land as well as state "ownership" claims of lands for which the government itself may not fully know the extent, location, or actual use (FAO et al. 2010, 2–3). These institutions advocate sorting out and reconciling these claims through a process of adjudication and formalization, which includes "(i) the identification of all rights holders" and "(ii) legal recognition of all rights and uses, together with options for their demarcation and registration or recording" (FAO et al. 2010, 2).

The most common mechanism for formally delineating and enforcing property rights is a system of land titling supported by a public land registry and a land cadaster. Formal land titles are legal documents that serve as evidence of ownership and that delineate the physical boundaries of a parcel and the rights associated with it. Delineating and enforcing ownership also requires ensuring that more than one party does not have a legal claim to the same plot of land. Land registries address this issue by systematically recording land titles and relevant details associated with a property such as the owner's name and the property's location and size.

Cadasters take land registration one step farther by systematically and exhaustively cataloging both public and private landholdings and landowners through establishing and adjoining in a single record (i) the location and boundaries of landholdings and (ii) interests in landholdings, including rights and obligations. Most modern cadasters are cartographic, meaning that they record landholdings in maps. These records make land parcels and associated property rights legible to the state (Scott 1998, 35–36).

Some of the earliest cadasters were constructed to distinguish state lands from private ones, to identify resources for making potential improvements, and to interest possible land purchasers (Kain and Baigent 1992, 332–33). But the broader development of the cadaster in many European countries was closely associated with the emergence of capitalist landowning and more individualized agrarian systems.

Much of the literature considers the establishment of land cadasters as expensive, complicated, and dependent on state capacity (Onoma 2009; Soifer 2013). Some scholars have suggested using the extent and quality of land cadasters as a proxy for state capacity (e.g., D'Arcy and Nistotskaya 2017). But in perhaps the broadest and most systematic review of land cadasters, Kain and Baigent (1992) demonstrate that land cadasters are actually quite old and can be created with relatively simple tools. Even the Roman Empire had created a fairly comprehensive cadaster. Partial cadasters were fairly widespread in Europe in the seventeenth and eighteenth centuries and the systematic mapping of rural lands was completed in the eighteenth and nineteenth centuries. As these authors write, "Though possession of the technical capability to survey and map individual properties at a large scale is an obvious prerequisite of state mapping, there is no case reviewed in this book where mapping was prevented by lack of skilled personnel or equipment" (Kain and Baigent 1992, 342).

Linking property registers to land cadasters and keeping both up to date is much more administratively complex and costly. It entails coordination between local and central administrators and a system for recording and updating ownership as land is bought, sold, subdivided, and otherwise transferred or reclassified. As Onoma (2009, 36) puts it, "Once these [cadastral] surveys are carried out, hiring, training, and paying professionals with the technical ability to register and keep proper and easily accessible records on titles and deeds is... expensive. Creating tribunals to adjudicate land disputes and marshaling institutions to monitor and enforce rights across a country are also costly." To a much larger degree than creating a cadaster in the first place, this requires infrastructural state power – the ability to penetrate society and implement policy evenly across territory (Mann 1984).

Land titles need to be not only clear but also defensible for land formalization to provide property rights security and effectively diminish uncertainty and risk associated with holding and transferring property. Those who hold legally recognized land titles need to be able to effectively call on the state for the enforcement of their rights. This requires the state to be a responsive and effective enforcer, a role it may not be able or willing to play (Holland 2017). It also requires disputants to recognize the legitimacy of the state as a third-party arbiter. As Feder and Feeny (1991, 137) put it, "If private property rights are not viewed as being legitimate or are not enforced adequately, de jure private property becomes de facto open access."

The gap between legality and legitimacy is part of the reason why informal property enforcement mechanisms can sometimes be equally or even more effective than formal ones at protecting landholders (Goldstein and Udry 2008).[7] This is typically the case where customary ownership is longstanding and uncontested, communities are tight-knit and stable, the state is a distant, new, or inconstant presence, and land transactions are limited. For instance, in many sub-Saharan African states where customary ownership is the norm, a relatively stable lineage of chiefs may rule in a particular area and reinforce patterns of land use. This likely helps to account for the finding that formal land titling has muted social and economic effects in many parts of Africa (Brasselle, Gaspart, and Platteau 2002).

Longstanding and uncontested informal ownership is empirically rare in Latin America. Indigenous landholders were uprooted and expropriated at a massive scale during the colonial era. This process continued, and in some places accelerated, in the postcolonial era with events such as the late nineteenth-century commodity boom and railroad penetration. Consequently, it is implausible to assume any quick reinstallation of credible, stable, and predictable informal property rights on the back of both the longstanding violation of those rights in preceding centuries followed by the violation of the rights of private landowners who were expropriated for the purposes of land redistribution back to the putatively original owners.[8]

---

[7] For further discussion of the tensions between legality and legitimacy linked to land titling in Africa, as well as the sometimes contentious and partisan nature of titling, see Boone (2018).

[8] In some cases of major land redistribution, such as Peru in the 1970s, the chief beneficiaries were not the original indigenous landowners that had been displaced in the colonial and postcolonial periods but rather "middle class" mestizo peasants who directly labored on large estates. In the

Land titles may also lack defensibility for more pedestrian reasons. Sometimes titles are not linked to a land registry; sometimes land registries are incomplete or multiple in number and partially overlapping but not updated; sometimes land registries are not linked to a land cadaster; and sometimes a land cadaster does not exist. These are abiding issues throughout much of Latin America. The question in these cases is not only one of *whether* the state will enforce a property right but also *how* the state will enforce that right. For instance, if an individual holds a land title that is not linked to any land registry, then whether it is valued more highly than any other piece of paper depends on how local courts or recorders will view it.[9] If property registers are local but there are disputes over administrative boundaries, then partially overlapping land registries can proliferate. Landowners may be subject to claims by individuals who are recorded in an alternative registry as possessing the same land if registries are not kept up to date. If land titles and land registries rely on the physical description of boundary demarcations such as trees and streams rather than on maps with geographic coordinates or simply on survey coordinates, and if the trees in question die or a stream is rerouted, then property boundary disputes can more easily arise.

This discussion suggests that land formalization and defensibility are to some extent a matter of degree. Individuals or groups in Latin America during this time tended to have private property rights that are formal and secure, rights that are imperfectly formal or that provide some degree of security while not eliminating significant uncertainty and risk, or a lack of property rights due to a lack of land title, the lack of a connection between a land title and any recording system, or the lack of any property rights enforcement.

Partial property rights, informal property rights, and indefensible property rights all provide hooks for states that seek to manage and manipulate land reform beneficiaries. The promise of economic security tied to newfound land ownership can be quickly rendered chimerical by a state that chooses not to enforce one's property against a counterclaimant. By contrast, toeing the party line can bring complementarities to property ownership such as more predictable enforcement, agricultural credits and loans through government programs that could not be accessed through a private bank given impartial property rights, and preferential access to improvement projects such as irrigation systems.

Peruvian highlands, for instance, many indigenous groups had been pushed out of the valleys and further up into the hills and mountains upon dispossession. While these groups can now gain formal recognition of informal and often communal landholdings, these landholdings comprise a smaller and more marginal portion of agricultural land.

[9] There is also variation within Latin America regarding the institutional infrastructure for defending property rights against the state or other private parties. In some cases, such as Mexico, there are agrarian courts nested within the executive, whereas in most cases the judiciary handles property rights disputes.

Alienability

Alienability gives landholders the flexibility to transfer or leverage their property for a wide range of purposes. I follow Ostrom (2003, 250) and define alienability as the right to sell or lease exclusion, management, or withdrawal rights. What are these subsidiary rights? Exclusion rights to land entail the right to determine who can or cannot gain access to land, what the nature of that access encompasses, and how that right may be transferred. Management rights entail the right to regulate internal land use patterns such as production decisions and to transform property by making improvements, such as building fences or irrigation systems. Withdrawal rights entail the right to obtain products from the land such as harvests.

The *right* to alienate land does not imply that individuals will *exercise* this right. Landowners may choose to retain their land and pass it down to the next generation rather than sell it. These same landowners, however, may want to leverage their property in ways that would not be possible without the right to alienate it. For instance, a landowner may want to migrate abroad temporarily or work elsewhere on a seasonal basis and lease their land while they are away. Or a landowner who has a bad harvest may face depleted savings and want to turn to a bank for a loan to buy seed and fertilizer or to make improvements for the next year. Land is a particularly attractive form of collateral because it is immobile and does not easily depreciate rapidly. These activities would not be possible without alienation rights over land.

Alienability facilitates liquid land markets by enabling individuals and groups to sell and lease their land. It can also contribute to wealth accumulation (Alston, Libecap, and Mueller 1999; Libecap 1993) as land can be leveraged for investing in improvements and transferred to individuals who will exploit it efficiently (Demsetz 1967).[10]

Alienability can also pose risks to property holders. Some land recipients may prefer inalienability as a protection from dispossession by wealthier actors or savvy competitors (see, for example, Boone et al. 2019b; Saffon 2015).[11] And in some group-based settings, a property transfer can harm others more than it benefits parties to the transaction (Ellickson 1993, 1376).

Nonetheless, strict inalienability renders land reform beneficiaries subject to potential state manipulation. Inalienability can debilitate rural land markets as land reform beneficiaries that want to either sell or lease their land must forego

---

[10] This latter point assumes that land will be transferred to those who will put it to its highest valued use. This depends on a large number of factors (Larson and Bromley 1990), and is rarely, if ever, fully realized.

[11] This point is consistent with Rose-Ackerman (1985, 931), who writes that "inalienability turns out to be a very complex concept, and one whose legitimate uses can be clarified through economic analysis combined with a sensitivity to noneconomic ideas – most notably ideas of citizenship and distributive justice." It also intersects with the contemporary debate on "global land grabbing" and rural smallholder dispossession (see Borras Jr. and Franco 2012).

this opportunity, simply abandon what they have, or try as many do to illegally sell or lease their property in informal markets (Deininger 2003). Inalienability also prevents land reform beneficiaries from using their land as collateral to obtain private-sector loans. This can stunt private credit markets and generate underinvestment in agricultural production and improvements to land with attendant negative consequences for agricultural earnings (Deininger 2003). These problems, which can mean the difference between making ends meet and absolute poverty for rural families, encourage land reform beneficiaries to turn to the state to resolve these issues for them. The state can then condition the resolution of these problems on political reciprocity or quiescence. Consequently, in many cases, land reform beneficiaries who received inalienable lands later sought the advantages of alienability when they had the option to do so.

Individual Versus Collective Ownership

Land can be held either individually or collectively among groups of individuals such as communities. Many conceptions of property rights, especially in economics, view individual ownership as a more "complete" property right than collective ownership (e.g., De Soto 2000). This view builds from a long and influential literature detailing issues linked to moral hazard and resource appropriation associated with common property regimes (Demsetz 1967; North and Thomas 1973). Individual ownership, by clearly delineating who owns what, defining what rights that ownership entails, and enabling individuals to make determinative choices over decisions such as alienation or withdrawal, endows owners with a more complete and enforceable set of rights than collective ownership.

This view, however, has been successfully challenged in a host of literature. As Ostrom (2003) makes clear, common property resources and collective property rights should not be conflated. Collectives can hold a full bundle of property rights in equal form to private individuals. It is the status and organization of the holder of property rights, as opposed to the rights themselves, that differ between private individuals and collectives.

In practice, individuals and groups often weigh the scale of property rights to land against factors such as production possibilities and risks. Ellickson (1993), for instance, shows how environmental and personal security risks impacted the conversion of jointly held land to individual land at different rates in New England, Bermuda, and Utah. In a similar vein, Netting (1976, 1981) shows in a study of Swiss peasants that "the attributes of the resource affected which property-rights systems were most likely for diverse purposes." A single peasant community would often divide agricultural land into distinct family-owned parcels while simultaneously organizing grazing lands on the steep Alpine hillsides into communal property systems. In short, collective ownership may be more efficient than individual ownership under certain circumstances.

The upshot is that there is not a clear mapping between the scale of ownership and how "complete" a property right is.[12] To be sure, many forms of collective ownership have historically prevented their members from exercising full property rights. But this need not be the case. In the data I have collected I can distinguish among differences in the degree of property rights held by collectives.

One illustrative example of variation in property rights despite stasis in the collective scale of ownership comes from the *ejido* system in Mexico. *Ejido* lands distributed to communities as a whole by the PRI prior to 1992 had highly incomplete property rights. These lands were not formally titled with their distribution and *ejidatarios* could not legally sell, lease, partition, or mortgage their property, even with support from the community as a whole. Land could be reallocated among members of the community with sufficient community support.

The Mexican government began a land titling effort in 1992 through the Program for the Certification of Ejido Rights and Titling of Urban Plots (PROCEDE). PROCEDE granted formal and complete property rights to *ejidatarios*, even for the vast majority of those in *ejidos* who decided to maintain collective ownership of their land. It offered *ejidos* registration, plot delineation, and separate title to members over house plots, farm plots, and a share in the value of common lands. PROCEDE allowed *ejido* lands to be sold within the *ejido* and leased to members within or outside the *ejido*. It also recognized *ejidos* as legal bodies able to enter into contracts and joint ventures and it allowed for the full privatization of *ejido* land through a two-thirds vote of the *ejido*'s General Assembly. Given these advantages, the vast majority of *ejidos* voted to join PROCEDE.

2.3   DATA SOURCES FOR LAND REFORM AND PROPERTY RIGHTS

I collected data on land redistribution, initial property rights over redistributed land, and subsequent changes in property rights through land titling and associated programs. I gathered these data directly from land reform agencies through fieldwork and from primary and secondary sources. Every country in

---

[12] Even international development agencies such as the World Bank now reflect this consensus and have shifted from the previous paradigm of individual land titling to supporting a continuum of property rights. This has yielded, among other changes, a shift in how indigenous land rights around the globe are recognized and demarcated. For more details on the international community's current approach to property rights provision and protection that covers legitimate versus legal tenure rights, the potential multiplicity of rights over land, and the scale at which rights may operate, see the Voluntary Guidelines on the Responsible Governance of Tenure developed by the Food and Agriculture Organization of the United Nations. The Principles for Responsible Agricultural Investment, developed by the World Bank, the Food and Agriculture Organization, the International Fund for Agricultural Investment, and the United Nations Conference on Trade and Development, also reflect this more nuanced view of property rights.

Latin America has had at least one land reform agency or other government entity such as a Ministry of Agriculture dedicated to land reform. Land reform agencies typically collect very detailed data on land transfers and the nature of land titling. Importantly, the land titling data I collected match the theoretical focus of this book in that they capture the titling of and property rights over land allocated via land reform rather than overall land titling.[13]

For some countries – Bolivia, Chile, Colombia, Ecuador, Mexico, Peru, and Venezuela – I collected individual-level land transfer and titling data or disaggregated data at the provincial or municipal level directly from land reform agencies through fieldwork. I obtained similarly detailed transfer-level data from Brazil through an official data request to its national land reform agency. In Bolivia, Colombia, Ecuador, and Venezuela, fieldwork entailed working directly with bureaucrats in existing land reform agencies to learn about the process of land reform and the nature of the data that they manage and to make official data requests.[14] In Chile, Mexico, and Peru, I collected data from land reform archives housed in contemporary ministries of agriculture and agencies devoted to either property formalization or agrarian reform. In these latter cases, I met many career bureaucrats working in the land reform archives who had formerly worked for either the country's land reform agency or Ministry of Agriculture and were therefore intimately familiar with the nature of the land reform data and the process of land grant-making.

These are the countries that had the most active and longstanding land reform programs and that consequently merited the most careful attention to data collection. Together they comprise 84 percent of all of the land redistribution recorded in Latin America from 1920 to 2010. Land reform was smaller scale and more episodic in nature elsewhere in the region, often occurring in a short, well-documented burst preceded and followed by no land redistribution at all.

For the other countries in Latin America, I collected national-level statistics or sub-national statistics from land reform agencies and ministries of agriculture, agency publications, or other government publications. This was accomplished through an official data request for Uruguay. In other cases,

---

[13] There are two cases where data on titling cannot be directly linked to previous land reform: Chile starting with Pinochet (due to the murky nature of auctions) and Guatemala starting around the late 1990s. This is mainly because in each case, formerly redistributed land was returned to former owners or reassigned from the initial beneficiaries to new owners. This circumstance was anomalous during this period.

[14] This includes information such as how land petitions are made, how they are processed by the land reform agency, how landholdings are acquired, how land is physically redistributed, the legal proceedings around redistribution and petitioning, what information the land reform agency gathers on land reform beneficiaries, and what the ongoing relationship between land beneficiaries and the agency entails.

I obtained government documents through a wide range of libraries and archives.

Data from countries where I collected disaggregated statistics enabled comparison to national-level data in order to verify the aggregate data generation process. Finally, I used secondary sources in all cases to check the validity of government publications.

The raw data on land redistribution and land titling, while paramount, are rarely sufficient in themselves to construct measures of the property rights gap. This is because information on the nature of property rights is often embedded in law. Raw data on land transfers or land titling themselves are often not enough to assess whether those who are receiving land are also gaining each of several key property rights tied to land: formalization, defensibility, and alienability.

Generating data on property rights gaps therefore required reading and assessing legal documents associated with property rights over land. Information on the nature of property rights to land reform beneficiaries is enshrined in most cases in land reform laws that guide land redistribution and sometimes land titling. These laws may outline limits to alienability for land reform beneficiaries, may vest ownership in the state, in collective structures, or in individuals, and can outline any number of other aspects of property rights. In other cases, property rights may be defined in associated legislation. And subsequent legislation and law can of course change the nature of property rights for former land reform beneficiaries.

Creating metrics of the property rights gap also required reading literature on the role of the state in rural areas. Land beneficiaries may receive formal property rights that are serially ignored by the state, eroding defensibility. Property rights may not be registered or property registries may be highly incomplete or not linked to a land cadaster. In short, tracking the property rights of land reform beneficiaries over time requires attention to disparate types of evidence.

The data employed here represent the first systematic coding of land transfers and property rights over transferred land in a way that is cross-country comparable and which spans a considerable time period. Later in the chapter, I provide several specific examples of how I translated the data I collected into the construction of property rights gap metrics.

2.4   CONSTRUCTING THE PROPERTY RIGHTS GAP

I construct two main measures for the property rights gap. One is annual and the other marks cumulative gaps over time. Each measure distinguishes between two broadly different degrees of property rights in the data: (i) the property rights gap between distributed land and *at least* partial property rights (i.e., partial or complete rights) over that land, as well as, separately, (ii) the gap between distributed land and complete property rights over that land. As discussed previously, property need not be individually held under the property rights definitions I employ. Full property rights can also be established over collectively held lands.

This section proceeds in several steps. I first turn to distinguishing between an absence of property rights, partial property rights, and complete property rights. I also explain why, for this period in Latin America, focusing on a partial property rights gap is more relevant than a complete property gap. Next, I detail the construction of the partial and complete property rights gap variables (annual and cumulative) and the constituent component variables that comprise these property rights gap measures: land redistribution and land titling. The latter variable, land titling, captures not only the formalization of property rights but also the set of rights that titles endow their owners. Along the way, I provide a summary and overview of the data as well as a classification of where each country in Latin America fits into the three canonical paths of property rights gaps.

Coding Degrees of Property Rights over Redistributed Land

Consider first an absence of property rights. Land that is distributed but not titled is coded as not having either partial or full property rights. The same is true of titles that are not recognized or legally defensible. One example would be titles that are not linked to any property registry or cadaster. I also code land with titles that do not allow individuals or collectives to rent, lease, sell, or mortgage their lands under any circumstances as having an absence of property rights.

Next consider partial property rights. Partial property rights entail a formal land title from the state that endows recipients with specified rights. But these titles are often imperfect or incomplete. Property may not be entirely alienable, and instead face consequential restrictions on the ability to sell, lease, partition, or mortgage property. For instance, land sales may be prohibited for a certain period of time within receiving the land or until recipients pay a specified amount for the land. Alternatively, property may be alienable but the lack of an orderly property registry or land cadaster makes it difficult in practice to defend land claims or use land as collateral. For instance, a land cadaster may not exist and property registries may be outdated or decentralized, giving rise to a panoply of overlapping land claims.

Finally, consider complete property rights. Land titles are formal and property is alienable in this case. Property is registered by the state. Property delimitations are generally clear and land titles rarely overlap. These latter stipulations are typically achieved by cadastral mapping, and often by linking cadasters with property registries.

Partial property rights over distributed land are much more common historically in Latin America and elsewhere than complete property rights over land. This is in part due to decentralized and disorderly land registers (for instance, registers that are partially overlapping, outdated, or incomplete) and land cadasters that failed to clearly and consistently delimit property in coordination with registers. And it is in part due to the wide range of restrictions to property rights for land reform beneficiaries.[15] Partial property rights provide some degree of independence from the state – though hardly complete independence – to beneficiaries. Given these considerations, I construct separate variables that capture the property rights gap between distributed land and *at least* partial property rights (i.e., partial or complete rights) over that land, and the property rights gap between distributed land and complete property rights over that land.

Constructing an Annual Property Rights Gap Measure

I create two principal variables, one annual and one cumulative, that capture the property rights gap using data on partial and complete property rights. Both of these variables focus on the establishment of property rights over land that the state has redistributed. The first variable is the Yearly Titling Gap. This is a "flow" variable that captures the annual difference between the amount of land redistributed and the amount of land over which partial or, separately, complete property rights are established.

The constituent components used to construct the annual property rights gap variable, as well as the cumulative property rights gap variable defined later in the chapter, capture the extent of land redistribution and land titling. These building blocks therefore merit discussion first in order to better understand how the property gap measures are constructed and what they capture.

Land redistribution data are constructed according to the physical area (in hectares) of private landholdings acquired by the state in a given country-year for redistribution to the land-poor. Land redistribution in Latin America, as elsewhere, has often been implemented through land ceilings that set thresholds for the maximum legal size of property holdings, or through the requirement that property serve a "social function" defined by efficient exploitation criteria and the prohibition of certain forms of tenure relations. I code the redistribution of all private land regardless of compensation structure. This encompasses both land redistribution and land negotiation (see Albertus 2015). In most cases, such as Cuba under Castro, Nicaragua under the Sandinistas, and Peru under military rule in the 1970s, redistributed land was expropriated at much less than market value or wholesale confiscated. In other cases, such as Brazil after 1993,

---

[15] As mentioned in Chapter 1, all countries in the region had land registries by the early twentieth century but they were often not unified and faced problems with disorder and with outdated entries. Nearly every Latin American country had a cartographic land cadaster that covered between three-quarters and all of the national territory prior to the generation of property rights gaps (D'Arcy and Nistotskaya 2017), but these again faced issues with completeness and clear property delimitations.

market prices were paid to landowners. Both policies have been redistributive in nature, even if to a different degree.

As Chapter 3 outlines, the process of land reform is similar for land redistribution with full compensation and for land redistribution without compensation or with below market compensation. While the latter may entail more coercion to obtain property, both processes are institutionally exacting and require executive, legislative, judicial, bureaucratic, and often military support. And at the end of the day, such reforms require physically dispossessing landowners and often require the organized settlement of new laborers on former landowners' property.[16]

Land redistribution with full compensation can reduce landowner resistance. But there are still many cases in which large landowners resist such reforms.[17] This is because landholding can deliver large landowners benefits that extend beyond simply possessing a valuable asset. Historically, large landowners were able to use their position at the pinnacle of rural social relations to manipulate and pressure workers to vote for favorable candidates (thereby delivering favorable policy) and to suppress rural wages (thereby increasing landowners' income) (Moore 1966; Huber and Safford 1995; Rueschemeyer, Stephens, and Stephens 1992; Ziblatt 2009). At the same time, the wealthy have often used landholding as a hedge against inflation in unstable economies (Ellis 1992). Consequently, land expropriation – even with full compensation – can spur lengthy and costly legal battles and trigger substantial short-term (and in some cases long-term) disruptions to income on the part of landowners.

I do not include the distribution of public lands in the construction of the land redistribution data. This is because the colonization of public lands is guided by a different theoretical logic than the one that will be detailed in Chapter 3. Land colonization does not have strong redistributive implications and does not involve seizing property from large landowners. It therefore faces less resistance from large landowners than the redistribution of private land, and it is administratively and institutionally easier to implement as a result (see Albertus 2015).[18] Governments may also pursue land colonization to grow the tax base or to populate frontier zones to protect against foreign incursions. Finally, land colonization often requires less direct interaction between the state and beneficiaries and occurs in frontier zones where state power is more peripheral by definition, giving the former fewer opportunities to exert credible leverage over the latter through the underprovision of property rights.[19]

[16] See Albertus (2015, Ch. 4) for more details. The main empirical results in Chapters 4 and 5 are similar when focusing only on redistributed land compensated at sub-market values.

[17] One illustrative example is Brazil since the 1993 constitutional amendment mandating market compensation for land expropriations.

[18] Landed elites may at times even support land colonization as a way to relieve pressure from the landless on the property of large landowners (Albertus 2015, Ch. 5).

[19] Of course, this dynamic differs if a country first nationalizes all land, making it effectively public, and then redistributes that land. This did not occur completely anywhere in Latin America in the

Since countries have different sizes and geographical topographies, and therefore different endowments of land that may be used for agricultural purposes, the land redistribution variable is normalized by total cultivable land to generate comparable cross-country data. Cultivable land area data is taken from the Food and Agriculture Organization (2000). Land redistribution is therefore ultimately measured as the percentage of cultivable land redistributed in a calendar year. Land redistribution ranges from 0 percent to 62.84 percent (the latter corresponding to Nicaragua in 1979). It has a mean of 0.90 percent and a standard deviation of 3.76 percent.

To better illustrate how the land redistribution variable is coded, consider the cases of Mexico and Colombia. In Mexico, the National Agrarian Registry (RAN), housed within the Agrarian Reform Secretariat (SRA) and centered in Mexico City, manages a detailed database called the *Padrón e Historial de Núcleos Agrarios* on all of Mexico's over 30,000 land reform communities that received land communally as *ejidos* dating back to the time of the Mexican Revolution. For each *ejido* there are data on the date the community received its land grant from the government, its location, land area, the size of the community holding the land, the amount of land dedicated to housing versus personal family plots versus commonly used areas, and other information tied to *ejido* changes such as whether a community split into two or acquired additional adjacent land.

I used these data to calculate annual figures for the number of hectares of privately held land that were expropriated and granted to land reform petitioners. Because the theoretical focus in this book is on property rights over land that the government grants anew to land reform beneficiaries, I do not include the recognition or confirmation of what were typically indigenous communities that already had de facto, relatively autonomous control of their property. I also exclude the colonization of public lands. Between the revolution and 2010, Mexico's government redistributed 51 million hectares of land.[20]

Land reform in Colombia, in contrast to Mexico, has long centered on the distribution of vacant national lands (*tierras baldías*) to settlers (Albertus 2019). However, the Colombian government has also engaged in a series of land redistribution programs dating back to the 1930s. Based in part on Law 74 of

---

period of study, although some countries nationalized significant portions of land (e.g., Cuba). The focus here is on whether governments first displaced relatively stable forms of private ownership over land prior to distributing that land. For a recent treatment of the effects of land colonization in the United States via the 1862 Homestead Act, which provided some short-term limitations to property rights, see Matteis and Raz (2019).

[20] Redistribution is closer to 85 million hectares when including the recognition or confirmation of communities that already had de facto, relatively autonomous control over their land (*reconocimiento* or *confirmación y titulación de bienes comunales*). Data on recognitions and confirmations are also included in the RAN database. Based on data from the National Institute of Statistics and Geography and the Agrarian Reform Secretariat, there were also nearly 15 million hectares of public lands distributed to settlers during this period.

1926, the government began a small parcelization program in the early 1930s to purchase productive estates affected by property or work contract disputes and divide them between the tenants and squatters on the estate (LeGrand 1986, 137–141). Land purchases for subsequent parcelization continued in the 1940s in areas with particularly acute land conflicts, albeit at a slower pace, and even into the 1950s during *La Violencia*, a brutal social upheaval that pit Liberals against Conservatives and left 200,000 people dead.

Data on the extent of land redistributed through these programs on an annual basis are garnered from various sources prior to the establishment of a land reform agency in Colombia, including LeGrand (1986) for the early 1930s, annual publications of the Ministry of Industry's *Anuario estadístico* covering 1934 until 1940, records of the Banco Agrícola Hipotecario from the early 1940s, Machado (2009) for the late 1940s, and Sánchez (1991) for the 1950s. This range of sources reflects the institutional instability of land redistribution programs and the lack of a dedicated land reform agency. The administration of the parcelization program changed frequently, from the Ministry of Agriculture in the 1930s to the Ministry of National Economy to the Institute of Parcelization, Colonization, and Forestry, to the Institute of Colonization and Immigration in the mid-1950s and then to the Caja Agraria in 1956. In most years during this period, the government would purchase a small number of relatively large private properties for redistribution, making these data fairly easy to track and verify despite institutional turnover.

The Social Agrarian Reform Act of 1961 (Law 135) established Colombia's first land reform agency, the Colombian Institute for Agrarian Reform (Incora). Incora mainly dedicated its efforts to the continued colonization of public lands. But it also conducted measured land redistribution. There were two chief modes: land expropriations from the private sector (*expropiaciones*) and negotiated purchases from the private sector (*adquisiciones/compras directas*), both dedicated for subsequent redistribution. There were also two other modes of land acquisition that I do not include in my data because they either do not entail direct state action in redistribution or because they do not involve reallocating land from private landowners to the land-poor. The first are donations and grants from private individuals and corporate or legal entities to the government (*cesiones*). These are in any case very small in number. The second are property reversions to the state (*extinción de dominio*). These can occur when a landowner does not exploit their land in accordance with the law. Most property reversions occur on formerly public lands that are granted to but then abandoned by settlers or on privately held lands that are abandoned (Machado 1994, 106). In a small number of cases reversions occur when land is seized from armed groups that are using it illicitly. These lands revert to the national land bank as public lands.

Annual data on land redistribution from the 1960s through the 1990s are from Incora's records. The government briefly shut down Incora in the early 2000s and restarted the agency as the Colombian Institute of Rural

Development (Incoder). Annual data on land redistribution in the 2000s, mainly through the purchase of private properties for subsequent redistribution, are from Incoder. I conducted several episodes of fieldwork with Incoder to better understand the nature of the data that they manage and made data requests accordingly. Colombia's government redistributed approximately 2.3 million hectares of land from the 1930s, when the parcelization program began, until the end of the 2000s.

What about the broader panorama of land redistribution in Latin America? Bolivia, Brazil, Chile, Cuba, the Dominican Republic, El Salvador, Guatemala, Mexico, Nicaragua, Panama, Paraguay, Peru, and Venezuela all redistributed more than 20 percent of land relative to cultivable land area. Some of these countries, such as Cuba, Bolivia, Nicaragua, and Peru, redistributed considerably more than 20 percent. Argentina, Costa Rica, Ecuador, and Honduras all redistributed less than 10 percent of cultivable land area. Every country implemented some land redistribution. Land redistribution also exhibits considerable temporal variation. Far from being simply a Cold War phenomenon, numerous countries engaged in land redistribution prior to the Cold War (for example, Mexico and Paraguay) and others redistributed land well after the close of the Cold War (for example, Brazil and Venezuela).

The second building block for the property rights gap variables is land titling. Land titling captures the annual percentage of cultivable land, previously or concurrently redistributed only, that is titled with either partial or, separately, complete property rights. For instance, if 5 percent of cultivable land was redistributed, and it is then all titled, land titling would take a value of 5 percent. This variable has a mean of 0.45 percent and a standard deviation of 2.23 percent.

To illustrate how this variable was coded in greater detail, return to the examples of Mexico and Colombia from above. These cases demonstrate the importance of analyzing the legal framework around land redistribution and land titling in order to assess the nature of property rights that land reform beneficiaries hold as well as how those rights fit into the conceptual framework of property rights laid out earlier in the chapter.

Mexico's 1917 constitution embedded land reform in Article 27. While *ejidos* were granted communally to villages as a whole, Article 27 initially opened the door to the possibility that subsequent laws could enable splitting up *ejido* lands and perhaps even alienating them.[21] But such laws did not transpire in the following decades. To the contrary, the first complete Agrarian Code that was established in 1934 legislated the complete inalienability of *ejido* lands by proscribing sales and rentals.[22] *Ejido* members

---

[21] Article 27 initially prescribed common ownership "until such time as the manner of making the division of the lands shall be determined by law."

[22] This is contained in articles 117 and 140 of the 1934 Agrarian Code. Article 27 of the constitution was amended in accordance in 1937.

that did not personally work their plots for two consecutive years would lose their land.[23] And *ejidos* were not permitted to use lands as collateral for mortgages.[24] In addition to these significant limitations to property rights, the vast majority of *ejido* members also lacked any formal land title certificates.[25]

On top of the fact that many *ejido* members violated the agrarian code by renting their parcels to other *ejido* members or hiring help to work their land for personal or economic reasons (Morrett 1992, 81–88), risking land forfeiture per the law, the lack of title contributed to the indefensibility of landholding. Indefensibility was further compounded by the fact that the Agrarian Code authorized various government entities such as the Agrarian Department, the Secretary of Agriculture, and the Agrarian Bank to directly intervene in numerous *ejido* affairs, including land disputes.[26]

Government control over property rights in the land reform sector became hard-wired into federal policy. Laws regulating *ejidos* were vested in the federal government and *ejidos* were registered in the Agrarian National Registry. The lack of property rights in the land reform sector was not reflective of an overall ideological antagonism to property rights in Mexico. Private property was guided by state-level civil codes and registered in state-level property registers and notary archives. At the same time that the government tightened its grip over the land reform sector by hobbling property rights, it simultaneously engaged in efforts to generate a more robust, parallel property rights regime in the private sector by granting some private landowners safeguards against expropriation via *certificados de inafectabilidad* starting in 1938, shortly after the passage of the Agrarian Code.

Limitations to alienability, formalization, and defensibility hampered property rights in the land reform sector and endured from the time of Mexico's revolution until the early 1990s. Legislation in the intervening period, such as the 1971 Federal Law of Agrarian Reform, did not change fundamental property rights restrictions. I consequently code zeroes for the land titling variable in Mexico throughout this period.

Mexico began granting secure and complete property rights to *ejidos* and their members beginning in the 1990s under PROCEDE. This followed from a major 1992 modification of Article 27 of Mexico's constitution and the passage of the 1992 Agrarian Law to replace the 1971 federal agrarian law. Both laid the legal groundwork for providing former land reform beneficiaries with greater property rights. PROCEDE then offered *ejidos* formal land registration in an orderly, centralized registry, plot delineation, and separate title to members over house plots, farm plots, and a share in the value of

---

[23] This is contained in article 144 of the 1934 Agrarian Code.

[24] This is contained in article 138 of the 1934 Agrarian Code.

[25] Fernández y Fernández (1964, 15) indicates that only roughly 5% of *ejido* members in *ejidos* that had received final land grants held any sort of title.

[26] See, for instance, articles 20, 21, 27, 28, 35, 38, 173, 174, 213, and 216 of the Agrarian Code.

common lands. It allowed *ejido* lands to be sold within the *ejido* and leased to members within or outside the *ejido*. PROCEDE also recognized *ejidos* as legal bodies able to enter into contracts and joint ventures and allowed for the full privatization of *ejido* land through a two-thirds vote of the *ejido*'s General Assembly.

I accessed data from the Agrarian Reform Secretariat on the number and physical land area of *ejidos* that received formal legal certification through the PROCEDE program on an annual basis in order to construct the land titling variable figures for Mexico beginning in the 1990s. I code the property rights granted through PROCEDE as complete property rights.

The property rights granted to land reform beneficiaries in Colombia contrast sharply with those granted to land reform recipients in Mexico. From the outset of land redistribution in Colombia in the 1930s, the government granted land to individuals rather than collectives. Property delimitations were surveyed and recorded and individuals were given property titles as part of the administrative procedure granting land itself.

Land grants did, however, come with some restrictions. Starting with Law 200 of 1936 and continuing with Law 100 of 1944, Law 135 of 1961, and Law 1 of 1968, recipients of redistributed private lands were required to repay the government for the costs of land acquisition, surveying, and any land improvements that the government made.[27] Once the payments were completed, typically over a period between 10 and 20 years, land beneficiaries would no longer face encumbrances to the title of their land. There were further property rights restrictions following Law 135 of 1961. For example, land beneficiaries needed to clear land sales and rentals, and in some cases mortgaging, in advance with the land reform agency Incora.[28] Violations of these stipulations could enable Incora to repurchase the farm from its owner at the appraised value if it chose to do so, though there are few well-documented cases of this occurring. Several of these restrictions were loosened over time, especially following Law 160 of 1994, which dropped many of the circumstantial restrictions on selling or transferring land provided that the land received was smaller than a specified threshold (one "agricultural family unit"). In short, while land reform beneficiaries always had a path to alienate their land if they chose, it was not always a clear, easy, and immediate path.

Property rights for land redistribution grant recipients faced one additional, and perhaps more important, set of limitations: the defensibility of their land. Dating back to the early twentieth century, many landowners faced problems with vague definitions of plot boundaries tied to formal titles, issues with

---

[27] See, e.g., articles 71, 82, and 83 of Law 135. The government also required land recipients to pay for land in the parcelization program of the early 1930s, but many considered the land they received as public rather than private and refused to pay (see LeGrand 1986, 139–41).

[28] See articles 51, 53, and 81 of Law 135, amended by articles 10 and 25 of Law 1 of 1968. See also the discussion in Findley (1972, 893–97).

overlapping land claims stemming from disorderly local property registers and corruption, and limited state presence to consistently uphold legal property claims (Albertus and Kaplan 2013; LeGrand 1986; Peña Huertas et al. 2014; Restrepo and Morales 2014). This applies just as well to land reform beneficiaries. Land registration became more transparent and standardized beginning in 1970 through Decree 1250. This decree generated a centralized registry system with branches in each department capital. Property ownership and delimitations advanced further with updates to the land cadaster system in 1983 and a shift from manual to digitized records in the early 1990s.

In light of these considerations, which were based on discussions with Incoder bureaucrats, archival research, and reviewing primary documents and the secondary literature, I code land grants transferred through land redistribution in Colombia as receiving partial property rights dating back to the beginning of the period. I code grants as receiving full property rights starting in 1970. This means that the land titling variable that records at least partial property rights in the case of Colombia is equal to the land redistribution variable for Colombia. Colombia consequently followed canonical property rights gap Path A (see Figure 1.2). It did not open up a property rights gap with its limited extent of redistribution.[29]

How do the experiences of Mexico and Colombia with land titling fit with other countries in the region? Bolivia, Ecuador, El Salvador, Nicaragua, Panama, and Peru all made major efforts to strengthen property rights over formerly redistributed land through land titling. Many large-scale land titling programs were rolled out in a frenzy in the 1990s and 2000s. Others date back to the 1960s or even earlier. Unlike land redistribution, not every country has granted at least partial property rights to beneficiaries in the reform sector. Cuba is particularly notable in this regard, though Brazil and Paraguay have similarly been major titling laggards.

Figure 2.4 displays country-by-country trends in both land redistribution and land titling across Latin America from 1920 to 2010. Land titling in this figure is coded according to the distribution of formal titles with *at least* partial property rights (i.e., partial or complete rights).

Note that the y-axis scales differ across countries in Figure 2.4 given the widely varying intensity of land redistribution and land titling by country. In some countries, such as Argentina and Ecuador, neither land redistribution nor land titling ever exceeded much more than 1 percent of cultivable land in any single year from 1920 to 2010. By contrast, in countries like Chile, Cuba, and Nicaragua, there were years in which at least one of these variables exceeded

---

[29] While there are not clear data indicating whether former land reform beneficiaries that received partial property rights ever had these rights further secured, Muñoz-Mora et al. (2018) indicate that state programs to verify, reconfirm, and strengthen existing land titles are rare in Colombia. One did occur late in the period from 1997–2002, however, with support from the Inter-American Development Bank.

50 percent of cultivable land. Adjusting the scale by country enables a clear picture of yearly fluctuations for each country that would be dwarfed by using a common scale.

In several cases displayed in Figure 2.4 – Argentina, Colombia, Costa Rica, and Uruguay – the dashed line indicating land titling very closely or perfectly tracks the solid line indicating land redistribution, making them hard to distinguish. These lines are superimposed because these countries never opened up a property rights gap. Comparing these country graphs to those in the next figure following Figure 2.4 will help illustrate this point. Recall, for instance, the previous discussion of how the coding of land redistribution and land titling coincide in Colombia. There are also other countries with superimposed lines for shorter periods of time. One example is Brazil since the 1980s. But these are generally exceptions rather than the rule. Again, comparing Figure 2.4 with the following figure will help illuminate these cases.

Differencing the land redistribution and land titling variables on an annual basis yields the first property rights gap variable: the yearly titling gap. This variable can take positive or negative values. This measure registers a large positive value if a lot of land is redistributed but little is titled. By contrast, if little land is redistributed but a lot of formerly redistributed land is titled, then this variable registers a large negative value. This variable has a mean of 0.43 percent, a standard deviation of 4.25 percent, and ranges from –47.86 percent to 62.84 percent.

The governments that engaged in some of the largest land redistribution programs were systematic land titling laggards. Bolivia, Brazil, Chile, Cuba, the Dominican Republic, El Salvador, Guatemala, Mexico, Nicaragua, Panama, Paraguay, Peru, and Venezuela all failed to quickly title the enormous numbers of land beneficiaries that received land through redistributive land reform programs. This generated large and positive yearly titling gaps. In many of these same cases, later governments engaged in major land titling efforts over the reform sector without simultaneously redistributing new land, generating large negative titling gaps. Recall the case of Mexico discussed previously, which fits this pattern. Mexico generated a parade of large, positive yearly titling gaps between its revolution and the early 1990s. This gap turned negative as land reform slowed to a trickle and PROCEDE began giving property rights to former land reform beneficiaries.

In a few cases – Argentina, Colombia, Costa Rica, and Uruguay – land titling kept pace with land redistribution and consequently these countries did not generate a yearly titling gap. Land redistribution was very minor in Argentina at just over 1 percent of cultivable land cumulatively. But land redistribution came to exceed 5 percent of cultivable land in Costa Rica and it reached nearly 15 percent of land in Colombia and Uruguay over the course of many decades, placing many thousands of families on quality farmland.[30] In Costa Rica, for

---

[30] Recall that given how this chapter defines land redistribution, these figures comprise the redistribution of private lands separately from any public lands that may have been distributed.

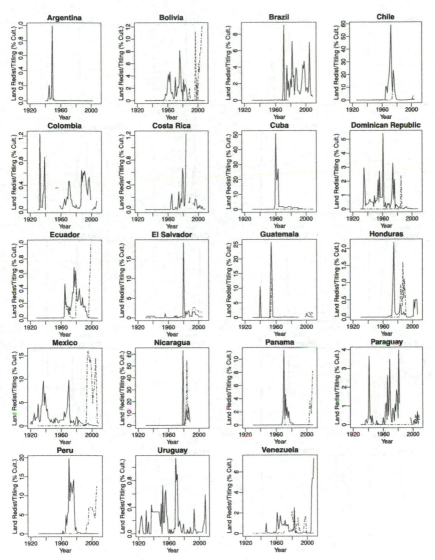

FIGURE 2.4 Land redistribution and land titling in Latin America, 1920–2010
Note: Solid lines indicate land redistribution as a percentage of cultivable land. Dash-dotted lines indicate land titling as a percentage of cultivable land.

instance, the government in the late 1960s began purchasing productive farms in established regions and settling peasants on them under what was known as the Río Cañas model (Seligson 1980, 133–34). Similarly in Colombia and dating back to the 1930s, the government selectively purchased productive private farms in areas of peasant pressure and then granted plots to peasants.

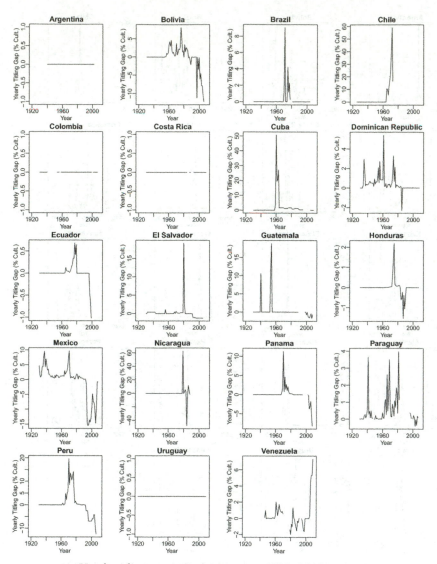

FIGURE 2.5 Yearly titling gap in Latin America, 1920–2010
Note: Solid lines indicate the yearly titling gap as a percentage of cultivable land.

There are also many years in which countries engaged in neither land redistribution nor land titling, again generating no annual titling gap. Examples include Argentina since the 1960s and Honduras and Panama prior to the 1960s.

Figure 2.5 displays the country-by-country yearly titling gap trends. The yearly titling gaps in this figure capture the annual gap between distributed land and *at least* partial property rights (i.e., partial or complete rights) over that land. Comparing Figure 2.5 with Figure 2.4 also helps to illuminate circumstances where land redistribution and land titling precisely track each other.

The Cumulative Property Rights Gap Measure: Construction and Classifying Cases According to Canonical Property Rights Gap Paths

The second property rights gap variable is the cumulative titling gap. This is a "stock" variable that captures the annual difference between the cumulative amount of land redistributed since 1920 and the cumulative amount of land over which partial or, separately, complete property rights are established. It therefore helps to capture delays in establishing property rights and policies that do not widen the gap. A regime that takes power on the coattails of another redistributive regime that did not grant property rights over redistributed land may, for instance, similarly avoid providing property rights because it is in their political interest. Whereas the yearly titling gap would register as zero if this new regime neither redistributed nor titled land, the cumulative titling gap would register this new regime as a titling laggard. The cumulative titling gap has a mean of 19.68 percent and a standard deviation of 36.19 percent.

The cumulative titling gap measure enables mapping Latin American experiences with land redistribution and property rights over land into the three canonical paths of property rights gaps that the first chapter outlines. Recall from Figure 1.2 that countries that trace Path A never open up a property rights gap in the countryside. Countries that follow Path B generate a property rights gap but later close it. And countries that tread Path C generate a property rights gap but never close it.

Figure 2.6 displays the cumulative titling gap country-by-country trends. The cumulative titling gaps shown in this figure register the cumulative gap between distributed land and *at least* partial property rights (i.e., partial or complete rights) over that land. The figure categorizes countries by whether they followed property rights gap Path A, Path B, or Path C.

Several countries in Latin America have followed Path A and never generated a cumulative titling gap. Others spent decades without a cumulative titling gap. Most country-years that do not register cumulative titling gaps across the dataset are characterized by neither land redistribution nor land titling. This is true, for instance, for most of Argentina's history between 1920 and 2010 with the exception of a few years. In several Path A cases, however, land titling kept pace with longstanding and active redistribution, albeit somewhat limited on an annual basis, foreclosing the generation of a cumulative titling gap. Colombia, Costa Rica, and Uruguay are illustrative examples.

In contrast to the Path A cases, governments in the Path B and Path C cases generated cumulative titling gaps as they implemented major land redistribution programs but withheld property rights from land reform beneficiaries. Yearly titling gaps stacked up in these cases. Cumulative titling gaps became large in

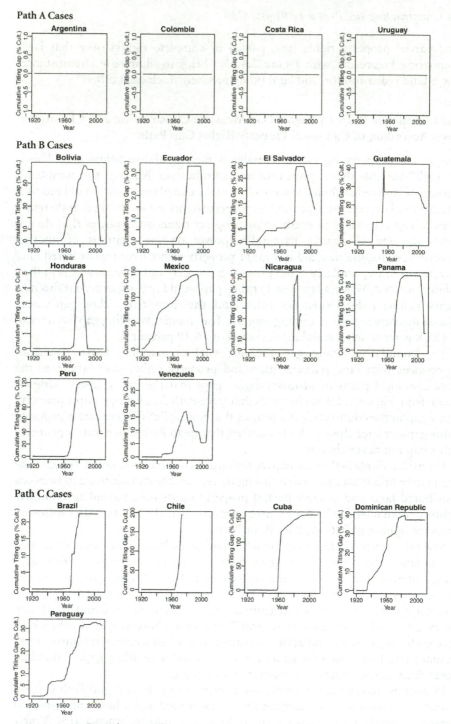

FIGURE 2.6 Cumulative titling gaps in Latin America by property rights gap path, 1920–2010

Note: Solid lines indicate the cumulative titling gap as a percentage of cultivable land. In some cases where marginal, not easily cultivated lands are also redistributed, the titling gap can exceed 100 percent of cultivable land (e.g., Cuba, Mexico).

Bolivia, Brazil, Chile, Cuba, the Dominican Republic, El Salvador, Guatemala, Mexico, Nicaragua, Panama, Paraguay, Peru, and Venezuela.

Cumulative titling gaps eventually exceeded half of all cultivable land in the country in Bolivia, Chile, Cuba, Mexico, Nicaragua, and Peru. And in the exceptional cases of Chile, Cuba, Mexico, and Peru, where rural populations were large and land reform incorporated substantial tracts of marginally productive lands, cumulative titling gaps exceeded the total amount of cultivable land.

Take Chile, which generated the largest, albeit short-lived, cumulative titling gap: nearly double the amount of cultivable land in the country by the end of Salvador Allende's rule. Chile's land redistribution program ballooned under Salvador Allende in the early 1970s as he pledged to "eliminate the hacienda." Land expropriations outpaced Chile's cultivable land area as the government set landholding ceilings based on a standardized threshold of 80 basic irrigated hectares that was used to assess productivity.[31] The government expropriated not only high-quality land but also marginal lands in excess of the threshold that were not as productive on a per hectare basis. This included more arid areas of the coast and northern *altiplano* as well as mountainous areas (Garrido 1988, 174). Most peasant beneficiaries were then incorporated into *asentamientos*, a type of rural cooperative in which beneficiaries lacked individual titles and other core property rights.

Similarly in Mexico, it became increasingly common to distribute marginal, low-quality land over time (Sanderson 1984). This was particularly true in the more arid north of the country. Because land beneficiaries lacked property rights prior to the 1990s, Mexico's cumulative titling gap eventually grew to outpace its stock of cultivable land.

Where land redistribution occurred rapidly without titling, as in Nicaragua, governments quickly generated cumulative titling gaps. Slower land redistribution programs that were not following with titling instead gradually built formidable titling gaps. Examples of this more gradual trajectory are the Dominican Republic and Paraguay.

Substantial cumulative titling gaps endured in most Path B cases for at least as long as the governments that created them. In many cases they endured even longer. A large cumulative titling gap in Bolivia that grew from the 1950s until around 1980 was only eliminated during the 1990s and 2000s after the fall of dictatorship and a turn toward democracy. The same general pattern occurred in Ecuador and Panama. The PRI in Mexico built an enormous cumulative titling gap over the course of decades and only tackled it beginning in the 1990s in the wake of major structural adjustment and with international assistance. In the Path B cases, however, governments eventually closed cumulative property rights gaps, even if they endured for significant time periods.

---

[31] A basic irrigated hectare was a standardized unit detailed in the law used to assess productivity, with reference to irrigated land in the Melipilla area of the province of Santiago.

One somewhat anomalous case grouped in Path B is Venezuela. Venezuela initially opened and then largely closed its cumulative property rights gap. But in a reversal, the property rights gap began to grow again in the mid-2000s as President Hugo Chávez started redistributing substantial amounts of land without property rights. This gap remains open under President Nicolás Maduro, who has widened it even further.

In contrast to the Path B cases, governments generated cumulative property rights gaps in the Path C cases and these gaps remained stubbornly persistent. Massive land redistribution under Fidel Castro in Cuba still has never been followed by substantial efforts to secure property rights. In cases like the Dominican Republic and Paraguay, governments that created large cumulative titling gaps fell but their successors chose to maintain those gaps rather than close them. In Brazil, new yearly property rights gaps were eliminated starting in the 1980s (see Figure 2.5), but the government never returned to systematically title those who had received land in the time of the country's military dictatorship.

The one country that is anomalous in the Path C group is Chile. The available evidence suggests that Chile actually followed more of a Path B pattern, closing its cumulative property rights gap partly under the rule of dictator Augusto Pinochet and further after the return to democracy. But verifying this with credible land titling data linked to former land reform is difficult. Some formerly redistributed land was returned to prior owners; other lands were auctioned in a murky fashion to new landowners, some of which were politically connected to the Pinochet regime; still others remained with the initial beneficiaries.[32] The Pinochet regime implemented a land registration program in the early 1980s to reduce the number of rural families without land titles, regularizing slightly more than 100,000 land titles (World Bank 1992, 74). In the meantime, however, many peasants who received land had to sell it due to a lack of government technical support and credits and a requirement to repay past production credits, increasing land transactions in the 1970s and 1980s (Thiesenhusen 1995, 110). This complicates linking subsequent land titling with former land redistribution. Land titling progressed further after the return to democracy as some rural groups began to lobby the government for property rights again (Labarca 2016, 145). Several programs sought to regularize titles for rural individuals, including those who had been granted land but no titles by past supreme decrees (Siclari 2006, 13; 23–24). Some of these regularization programs continue (such as the program *Un pedacito de Chile*). But it is not always straightforward to link titling to former land reform beneficiaries.

The countries within each of the three paths of property rights gaps displayed in Figure 2.6 are clustered in ways that deviate from most conventional narratives of Latin American development or history. Countries like Cuba

---

[32] For discussion, see, for instance, Lapp (2004, 81) and Thiesenhusen (1995, 109).

and Paraguay that followed Path C are very different when it comes to colonial settlement patterns, geographical endowments, and economic and demographic history. But these countries both share a history of strong and longstanding authoritarian rule in which rulers sought to control their rural populations.[33]

In a similar fashion in the Path B cluster, countries as disparate as Peru and Panama are rarely thought to have much in common. They differ dramatically in their topographies, natural resources, colonial history, and ethnic composition. But they share some consequential political similarities: both were ruled by military juntas drawn from outside the traditional political class beginning in the late 1960s and both subsequently transitioned to democracy. Bolivia and Mexico share a similar political trajectory in terms of the rise of an outsider political elite that ruled in an authoritarian fashion, albeit in a very different mode of rule and for much longer than the juntas in Peru and Panama, before transitioning to democracy. These latter countries were also hit hard by economic crises in the 1980s and 1990s.

Path A gathers together some more conventional bedfellows, though again not without surprises. Argentina and Uruguay share a similar history of colonial settlement in which large numbers of Europeans were attracted to plentiful farmland with productive soils. Costa Rica is also often viewed as "exceptional" within Latin America, tied in part to relatively egalitarian rural settlement in its early history. Colombia, however, is wildly different from all three in terms of settlement, geography, and economic development. But Colombia shares with Costa Rica and Uruguay an interesting political history that was rare in Latin America: longstanding postcolonial oligarchic rule that enabled democracy to grow early roots. These countries all suffered authoritarian reversals at least once since 1920, but landowners were never on the sidelines of politics for any significant time during dictatorship. Costa Rica and Uruguay eventually became two of Latin America's shining democratic stars over decades. Argentina suffered much more pervasive cycling between democracy and dictatorship, but there too landowners were almost always a strong force in politics regardless of regime type.

This discussion provides some initial hints regarding what matters for the evolution of property rights gaps starting in the twentieth century. These gaps are not simply shaped by the colonial past or immediate postcolonial aftermath. Nor are they a deterministic function of geographical endowments. More important is the role of politics once Latin American populations had grown, economies had begun to diversify, and states had begun to strengthen. The next chapter will elucidate in greater depth the specific political factors that are critical to generating and closing property rights gaps.

---

[33] Brazil, the Dominican Republic, and Paraguay are all Path C cases in which property rights gaps persisted under democracy after the eventual replacement of longstanding authoritarian rule. Chapter 4 discusses how other elements of the theory beyond regime type help to make sense of these more recent patterns.

2.5 CONCLUSION

This chapter charts a new path in making sense of and visualizing property rights gaps. Property rights over land are widely divergent. Land can be held by individuals, groups, and governments, ownership can be formalized or informal in various ways, and property rights can face a diverse array of restrictions. All of this complicates conceptualizing and measuring the property rights gap.

But this chapter demonstrates that it is possible to unpack important distinctions in property rights, to differentiate among them, and also to ultimately classify property rights according to these distinctions in a way that can be comparably applied to a broad range of cases. I hone in on several critical components of property rights in constructing my property rights gap measures: land formalization, defensibility, and alienability. I use these aspects of property rights to construct measures of complete, partial, and absent property rights.

This chapter outlines and then visualizes the data used to construct measures of the property rights gap based on these definitions. The picture of rural land ownership and property rights that emerges is a fascinating one that confirms key elements of received wisdom while also adding new insights. Property rights gaps emerged and grew in nearly every country in Latin America since 1920. In some countries, these gaps have persisted, in others they have shrunk, and still others, they have been eliminated. The next chapter builds a theory of the conditions that determine these changes.

3

The Political Origins of the Property Rights Gap

Why do governments that distribute land to their citizens often withhold property rights from the recipients, presiding over widespread property informality in the countryside for years or even decades at a time despite the manifest economic and social problems this generates? And why do the governments that grant more secure property rights over land often withhold from redistributing land as well, even if there is popular demand for it?

There is little existing work that directly addresses this set of puzzling empirical regularities. But this book is hardly the first to examine why governments sometimes do not extend property rights to their citizens and protect those rights. There are several prominent prevailing explanations for the more general lack of secure property rights in some countries. These include government policy myopia, ideology, and insufficient state capacity. This chapter begins with an overview of these explanations. Each has merits and each clearly operates in or even drives certain cases of property rights gaps. But they are not themselves sufficient to account for the wide variation in the opening and closing of property rights gaps over time across countries. Alone they miss too many cases and leave a trail of discrepant evidence. They also fail to account for a critical political logic that lies at the heart of shifts in property rights gaps.

The chief task of this chapter is therefore to advance and develop a new theory that more comprehensively and faithfully accounts for the origins, persistence, and demise of property rights. The theory also aids in understanding a host of major consequences of a property rights twilight zone. Why do some countries remain relatively rural and develop slowly while others urbanize, grow, and transform rapidly? And why are corruption, inequality, and clientelism widespread across the countryside in some countries and not others?

Critical to understanding these questions are political regimes. Democracies and dictatorships fundamentally differ when it comes to generating, upholding, and eliminating property rights gaps. Authoritarian regimes tend to redistribute land from large landowners to the land-poor but withhold property rights from beneficiaries. Democracies, by contrast, often grant property rights to beneficiaries of previous land reforms but do not redistribute any additional property on their own. This consequential difference is driven by how political regimes empower or disempower different groups in society, by differences in institutional powers and constraints, and by the incentives that flow from incumbency and political competition.

But political regimes are not deterministic of property rights gaps. Authoritarian regimes frequently have the institutional capacity and political authority to redistribute property without rights, but they also have to have incentives to do so. This occurs when landed elites are excluded from the ruling governing coalition and pose a potential threat to the incumbent regime. Democratic regimes, by contrast, are typically so saddled with checks and balances that any attempts to redistribute property will be stopped in their tracks by powerful landed elites who capture veto power through the legislature or judiciary. Democracies can, however, translate popular demands into policy when these demands do not strongly harm powerful minority interests. This implies that democracies are more likely to grant property rights to former land reform beneficiaries that lack rights. Closing a property rights gap is especially likely under democracy when peasants are incorporated in the ruling coalition and can push for property rights protection. But it is still not guaranteed. Most prominently, landed elites can seek to block property rights reforms through the legislature – historically a redoubt for landed elite interests – if they are threatened by them.

There is one additional circumstance conducive to closing a property rights gap in the countryside that transcends political regime type: foreign pressure. All countries face periodic economic crises driven by financial panics, currency imbalances, debt servicing, or negative shocks to economic growth. Crises that are sufficiently severe can force a country to turn to international financial institutions for help. These institutions have frequently demanded economic and political reforms in exchange for lending support in the post–World War II era. Privatization and greater security of property rights is typically a core condition for support. This can close rural property rights gaps. Both democracies and dictatorships yield to foreign pressure in the face of a severe crisis, albeit in somewhat different ways.

This chapter develops these arguments in several steps. It details the conditions under which governments redistribute land on a large scale. It then examines why the same conditions conducive to the redistribution of land are also associated with the withholding of property rights from land reform beneficiaries. The discussion explores the political benefits of a property rights gap from the perspective of incumbent rulers along with the myriad ways it complicates the lives of land beneficiaries and renders them more easily subject to coercion by the government. Finally, the chapter outlines the conditions most conducive to closing a property rights gap and the economic and social consequences of doing so.

3.1 PREVAILING EXPLANATIONS FOR THE UNDERPROVISION OF PROPERTY RIGHTS

Previous work does not examine the chief puzzle that this book takes on: why it is that governments create property rights gaps through policies that redistribute land and then withhold rights over that land from beneficiaries. But existing scholarship does offer explanations for why some countries lack secure property rights. These explanations can be organized into three main groups: government myopia, ideology, and insufficient state capacity. Understanding the origins of these explanations, as well as their strengths and weaknesses, provides an important backdrop for developing and assessing a new theory of the property rights gap.

Myopia

A first explanation for a widespread lack of property rights is government myopia. Perhaps governments simply did not know that underproviding property rights would generate perverse economic and social consequences or that they could shape property rights in a more productive way. After all, the principle of providing greater legal security for property rights, despite being a longstanding practice dating back to the enclosure movement in England and colonial settlement in the Americas, and reflected in the work of prominent thinkers such as John Locke, did not emerge as a commonly shared plank of policy advice by powerful international financial institutions such as the International Monetary Fund (IMF) and World Bank until the 1980s. Scholarship on the evolution of property rights regimes long emphasized exogenous factors such as population pressure and resource abundance (Feder and Feeny 1991), technological change (Demsetz 1967), and production possibilities and risks (Ellickson 1993; Netting 1981).

The new institutional approach to development economics, encapsulated and catalyzed by North's (1990) seminal work, emphasized that property rights are not exogenously given but rather evolve in response to political and economic forces and form a critical institutional pillar of an economy. One of the most prominent advocates of secure and formalized property rights, Hernando de Soto, published his influential book *The Other Path* in 1986. *The Other Path* argues that insecure and inadequately documented property rights choke off development by denying citizens access to the structures and institutions that they need to flourish economically.[1]

---

[1] One of de Soto's implications was that because property rights informality was driving underdevelopment in Peru, it was also providing fertile ground for the type of social and political instability linked to the contemporaneous Shining Path insurgency. De Soto's later book *The Mystery of Capital* (2000) built from *The Other Path* to argue that informal and insecure property rights stymied development by preventing underlying assets from being converted into

A related explanation holds that perhaps governments in previous decades recognized the importance of property rights and their ability to shape them but simply blundered into underproviding them by choosing cheap or ineffective methods of provision, such as linking land to property registers that were not self-updating and consequently quickly became outdated (Yoo and Steckel 2016).

There can be little argument that external pressure for securing domestic property rights has been ratcheted up in recent decades – a point that I directly address in this book's theory. Furthermore, the tools and expertise to deliver secure property rights became more available in the last several decades as the importance of property rights became incorporated into the neoliberal economics mantra.

But several pieces of evidence cast doubt on this as a complete stand-alone explanation for the property rights gap in many countries. First, governments in some countries that redistributed land as early as the 1920s and 1930s, such as Colombia and Uruguay, granted land reform beneficiaries complete property rights from the beginning of their land reform programs and continued to do so amid program changes over nearly a century. Second, other governments recognized that withholding property rights from beneficiaries in the course of land redistribution was generating economic stagnation and other economic and social distortions but continued to withhold property rights anyway. Later in this chapter I will discuss the case of Mexico, which created a parallel private property rights regime while withholding property rights from the land reform sector in order to counterbalance the negative effects of land reform on economic growth.

Finally, external pressure and financing for land formalization and the distribution of land that was purchased from large landowners for redistribution to the landless with complete property rights dates at least back to President John F. Kennedy's 1961 Alliance for Progress in Latin America (Kapstein 2017). But few Latin American governments implemented land reform programs consistent with Alliance for Progress guidelines and those that did had uniformly small programs (Lapp 2004). The bulk of governments that engaged in land redistribution ignored Alliance for Progress guidelines.

A more plausible explanation that ties underproviding property rights to government myopia stems from the recognition that governments often pursue a variety of goals and these goals can at times conflict with one another. Many governments in the early and mid-twentieth century across the developing world sought to overcome underdevelopment by addressing persistent social and economic ills that had roots in the colonial era. Tackling economic and social inequality, deep-seated poverty, and the alienation of rural and other

capital, traded outside of narrow groups where people know and trust one another, and used as collateral for loans.

disadvantaged groups from political life were at the heart of efforts toward "internal decolonization" (see, for example, Casanova 1965; Quijano 2000).

Given the necessity of maintaining living standards and enhancing output, many policymakers feared that converting a countryside dominated by large estates into a fractionalized patchwork of privately held small properties would generate short-term scarcity if land beneficiaries shifted to subsistence agriculture (see Pryor 1992). This threatened to push marginalized populations deeper into poverty as economies of scale in agriculture were eliminated. Equally dangerous was the possibility that private property rights could engender land reconcentration if beneficiaries could alienate their land and were forced to do so during negative economic shocks or by more powerful agents in the countryside.

Finally, some governments sought collectivization, cooperatives, or nationalization as a way to extract rural surplus for the purposes of industrialization and managing growing urban populations (Lipton 2009).[2] Indeed, the primacy of domestic industry over agriculture, supported by overvalued exchange rates, agricultural price controls, and the lion's share of state subsidies, was an important component of the import substitution industrialization developmental policies that ruled the day in many Latin American countries in the mid-twentieth century (Baer 1972).

Of course, how a government weighs policy goals against one another, weighs goals against risks, and determines national priorities is often filtered through ideas and ideology – a related explanation that I take up next.

Ideology

A second explanation for the widespread lack of property rights in the rural sector of some countries is linked to ideology. Prior to the neoliberal era, there was a broad and influential debate about the origins of land concentration and the forces that tended toward concentration in the developing world that informed theories of the reallocation of land and the types of property rights that should be exercised over that land.[3] These theories, in turn, impacted strategies of development through political ideology and through broader political competition. One particularly prominent manifestation of this dynamic was the Cold War rivalry between US capitalism and Soviet communism and associated pressure in Latin America and developing countries in other regions for specific developmental strategies (Haggard and Kaufman 2008; Hirschman 1968; Montgomery 1984).

---

[2] For an overview of the discussion and debate about the importance of agricultural surplus in industrialization, see Mellor (1986).

[3] See, e.g., Goodman and Redclift (1982) for an overview of some of the key elements of this debate from a Marxist perspective as it pertains to Latin America and Europe, Kay (1974) for a comparison of the development of the European manorial system and the Latin American hacienda system, and De Janvry (1981, ch. 1) for a general overview.

A host of scholars dating back to the early twentieth century challenged Western notions about the plausibility and benefits of smallholding agriculture in a capitalist economy. One strain of thought was captured in Polanyi's classic and influential work *The Great Transformation*. Polanyi argued that the introduction of "free" markets can bring with it harsh volatility that wreaks havoc on those who are the least prepared and have the fewest resources to resist negative shocks (Polanyi 1944). In the countryside, this erodes risk-insulating social relationships and reciprocity and can give way to land concentration, peasant dispossession, and labor repression. Polanyi links these destabilizing market forces to Europe's wars and revolutions of the early twentieth century.[4] And, of course, they can generate popular backlash and leverage for leaders to frame their solutions to these problems that restrict property rights, such as land inalienability or collectivization, as a way to avoid the negative consequences of free markets.

Scholars in the Marxist tradition similarly recognized the pernicious consequences of capitalism but conceived of them in a different manner. Marxist scholars viewed the concentration of land across much of the developing world as a consequence of the spread of capitalist production (Bartra 1993; Kay 1974; Paré 1977). Marx argued that a process of "primitive accumulation" would separate direct peasant producers from their means of production as capitalism takes root (Marx 1967 [1867], 723). This historically took place through the expulsion of peasants from their land, which in many cases was farmed communally at least in part, and the appropriation of that land by capitalist landowners.[5] Capitalist market forces drove laborers into relations of personal dependence on landlords, mediated by powerful social hierarchies. The final result was landlessness and rural instability.

In a related but distinct vein, dependency theorists viewed land concentration as a consequence of first-world demands for primary commodities. This resulted in market pressures for land monopolization and the use of peasant labor as "shock absorbers" against cyclical demands in agriculture (e.g., Frank 1969).[6] Exceptionally large properties such as *latifundios* in Latin America were not simply an anachronistic vestige of the colonial era in this view but rather a function of markets and the broader world economy.

---

[4] The concerns with smallholder dispossession and the acquisition of large tracts of public lands by powerful actors have again been heightened in the contemporary era of globalized investment and agricultural supply chains. This is reflected in the ongoing debate on "global land grabbing" (see, e.g., Borras Jr. and Franco 2012 and Wolford et al. 2013 for reviews) and in the UN and World Bank's development of the Principles for Responsible Agricultural Investment.

[5] Lenin (1964 [1899]) argued that this may not take place as rapidly as Marx's thesis implies, but can also occur slowly and in diverse ways.

[6] One of the more influential dependency theorists in Latin America was Raúl Prebisch, whose work as an early director of the Economic Commission for Latin America helped to bring structuralist economics into mainstream policymaking in the region.

Another set of scholars examining land issues from a Marxist perspective emphasized the ability to extract rents and natural resources from large tracts of land without significant investment (Bunker 1988; de Janvry 1981). This supported an equilibrium of land concentration that was relatively immune to pressure for development, capital improvement, and enhanced living standards for peasant workers. And given the historical circumstances in which large landowners acquired large tracts of land at low cost, they had weak incentives later on to engage in productivity-enhancing investment (Edelman 1992).

These ideas percolated into policymaking through domestic political ideologies and foreign influence. The critics of capitalism and private agricultural smallholding viewed the solution to landholding concentration as twofold. First, it was necessary to eliminate extensive tracts of privately held land. Second, it was necessary to prevent their reconstitution through the dispossession of the beneficiaries of land reform.

Import substitution industrialization and a heavy state hand in the economy, including in the redistribution of land, replaced liberal policies in many developing countries (see, for instance, Hirschman 1973). Furthermore, leftist and especially socialist governments under the influence of Cold War pressure often sought to organize land reform beneficiaries collectively. Part of the drive to collectivize was tied to ideological and developmental desires to collectivize the means of production. But it was also viewed as a safeguard against peasant dispossession of their newfound land access, whether by remaining large or middle landowners or by especially savvy or ambitious small-scale farmers. This manifested in different ways, ranging from creating cooperatives to collectives to nationalizing land. In many cases it entailed restrictions to land alienability. It is worth noting, however, that as Lipton (2009, 191) concludes in a wide-ranging analysis of collectivization around the world, "Collectivisation hardly ever stems from demand by poor rural families. What they want is land of their own." In other words, state goals and projects did not necessarily reflect popular demands.

Leftist ideology in Latin America, and communism in particular, grew stronger in the wake of the Russian and Mexican revolutions and under the influence of Marxist economists who built from Walras' general equilibrium theory to fashion proposals for planned economic models in opposition to the unchecked inequality that was associated with Adam Smith's principles of spontaneous order promoted by the "invisible hand" of the market.[7] Politicians and development economists from both the West and the Soviet bloc pushed for redistributive policies coupled with statist economic policies as a way to kick-start underdeveloped and unequal economies. The influence of economists such as Oskar Lange and the award of the Nobel Prize to economists Tjalling Koopmans and Leonid Kantorovich in 1975 reflected and promoted the power of socialist ideas. And land reform experiences from Eastern

---

[7] See, e.g., Machovec (1995) on the twentieth-century ideological evolution of economic thought.

European socialist countries, such as Yugoslavia, came to serve as models for Latin American countries.

The Cold War and the Cuban Revolution, on the other side, encouraged the proponents of private property and capitalism to push harder to translate their ideas into policy. Perhaps most prominent was United States President John F. Kennedy's promotion of social and economic development in Latin America through the 1961 Alliance for Progress. As the historian Arthur Schlesinger, who was one of the Alliance for Progress architects, described it, the Alliance "represented a very American effort to persuade developing countries to base their revolutions on Locke rather than Marx" (Schlesinger 1965, 589). The Alliance for Progress supported land reform that privileged the distribution of publicly owned land where possible, sought to raise productivity and efficiency over redistribution, and encouraged respect for private property through the compensation of any landowners that were expropriated and the allocation of land to private owners rather than collectives or state-run farms (Kapstein 2017; Lapp 2004).

The Latin American debt crisis in the 1980s and the fall of the Soviet Union ultimately discredited alternatives to capitalism and ushered in the neoliberal era, which favored privatization and individual property rights. Early experiments in neoliberalism in the region include infamous examples such as the Chicago Boys economists overhauling the Chilean economy under Augusto Pinochet. Major international financial institutions, especially the IMF and the World Bank, came to espouse and promote economic orthodoxy by the 1980s and played a critical role in promoting it throughout Latin America in the context of the debt crisis and subsequent currency and financial crises.

There is little doubt that ideology played a role in the redistribution of property without property rights that this book documents.[8] Consistent with this, I find an impact for left-wing ideology in the empirical analyses of the property rights gap in Chapter 4.

But it is important to underscore that ideology is far from determinative of property rights gaps. Some countries, such as the Dominican Republic and Paraguay, redistributed land without property rights before the Cold War under ideologically conservative authoritarian rulers. Even during the Cold War, avowedly anticommunist regimes, such as the military regime that ruled

---

[8] Ideology has also factored into state policies over urban land titling and informality in Latin America. Collier (1976), for instance, demonstrates in the context of illegal urban settlement formation in peripheral Lima from the late 1940s to 1970s that the authoritarian and condescending way in which export-oriented elites and urban commercial interests in Peru viewed and cultivated illegal urban settlers was deeply rooted in their ideological conception of the way political relationships in society should operate. For example, some of these elites saw the relatively cheap policy of allowing the free appropriation of marginal urban land as a way to undermine more radical left-wing political alternatives such as the American Popular Revolutionary Alliance (APRA). State policies toward urban informality shifted with the ideological orientations and biases of different elite groups whose political influence and relationship with the central government waxed and waned over time.

in Peru from 1968 to 1980, distributed land without property rights. Other countries, such as Colombia and Uruguay, flipped between left and right rule for many decades but continued to grant full property rights to beneficiaries of land redistribution across these ideological shifts.

These are not the only trends that seem anomalous from the perspective of an ideology-based explanation of the property rights gap. Some countries in the post–Cold War era, such as Venezuela and Zimbabwe, started new programs of land redistribution that withheld property rights from beneficiaries. Other countries with right-leaning governments that quickly jumped aboard major guidelines of the Washington Consensus, such as Paraguay, have barely reduced their property rights gaps in recent decades.

Insufficient State Capacity

A third major explanation for prevalent insecure and incomplete property rights in some countries is that states, as the central actors in establishing and enforcing property rights, do not always have the capacity to provide complete property rights (Besley and Persson 2009; Dincecco 2017). After all, extending complete property rights can be costly and require significant infrastructural power (D'Arcy and Nistotskaya 2017; Onoma 2009).

At the root of providing property rights in the countryside are systems of information over land that maintain information on the location and extent of property holdings and who has interests in those holdings. Land registries achieve this aim by recording and documenting the possession of land, typically through land titles, along with information on the holder's name and the property's location and extent. Land cadasters take land registration a step farther through the systematic and exhaustive cataloging of landholdings and landowners by adjoining the location and boundaries of landholdings with the interests in those landholdings, typically in cartographic form. This requires physically surveying land and recording and documenting its holders in registers that are created by or accessible to the state.[9] To remain complete over time, land information systems have to avoid excessive "drift," whereby the failure to record transactions and recalibrate registries can lead to a disjuncture between registries and the social reality of land possession.[10] This requires administrative capacity in the form of some degree of technical competence, bureaucratic professionalism, and coordination. This capacity needs to reach across a country's territory.[11]

---

[9] As (Kain and Baigent 1992, 342) point out, land surveying has a very long history and can be done with fairly simple tools. In many countries, surveys used to construct land cadasters were conducted by both state agents and private parties.

[10] For a broader theoretical discussion of institutional drift, see Thelen and Streeck (2005).

[11] A substantial literature dating back to the work of Max Weber emphasizes the importance of bureaucratic autonomy and professionalism and the control of corruption as critical to state capacity. While these were highly imperfect in the Latin American countries under study, the

Most Latin American states had substantial land information systems by the time the property rights gaps analyzed in this book arose. All countries in the region had land registries by the early twentieth century, even if they were not unified or entirely well ordered. And prior to the generation of property rights gaps, nearly every Latin American country had a cartographic land cadaster that covered between three-quarters and all of the national territory (D'Arcy and Nistotskaya 2017).[12]

Almost all countries in Latin America had also conducted agricultural censuses prior to the generation of any significant property rights gap. This entailed the enumeration of all rural properties and enabled calculating figures such as the number of properties above a certain size threshold, the prevalence of certain land tenure relations, or landholding inequality at very localized levels that could be used for policymaking. These censuses imply significant information about both smallholders and larger landowners. They also collected data on land ownership versus tenancy, farming techniques, crop types and productivity, and labor relations in many cases. This should not be particularly surprising given the immobility of land and the desire of individuals or groups to claim it as their own.[13]

This is not to say that Latin American states were Leviathans that could easily extend and protect property rights during the period of this study. To the contrary, as Chapter 2 indicated and as Chapter 4 will elucidate in greater detail, complete and well-protected property rights over rural land in Latin America have remained relatively elusive in part due to limitations in state capacity.[14] And I find empirical evidence that the strongest states are most associated with property rights stability. But states across the region have long provided a degree of property rights protection when it was a goal. And most have long had much greater capacity to provide property rights than they have at times actually deployed.

Aside from the fact that property rights gaps in the region have typically been preceded by land registries, cadasters, and agricultural censuses, consider that the creation of a property rights gap first requires the physical redistribution of land, which also requires substantial state capacity (Soifer 2013). If

---

broader motivating question of this book is why governments with sufficient capacity were often unwilling, as opposed to unable, to protect property rights.

[12] Two exceptions are the Dominican Republic and Guatemala, which did not achieve this level of coverage until 1949 and 1971, respectively.

[13] Of course, fear of the use of land documentation efforts to aid taxation, track citizens, or even aid dispossession can at times encourage rural dwellers to oppose the documentation of land interests and encourage drift (Scott 1998, 48; Mangonnet 2020). In Latin America, land taxation has historically been very low (Bird and Slack 2004; Engerman and Sokoloff 2002), largely due to the opposition of large landowners.

[14] Land registry drift can be significant even in advanced economies. This is why markets for tools such as property title insurance often exist. In some cases, such as California's Proposition 13 of 1978, laws can be drafted that encourage considerable property registry evasion.

a government can successfully marshal the state apparatus to physically redistribute massive tracts of private property from some of society's most powerful individuals to its broader citizenry and enforce the new status quo, then it is much more likely – though hardly guaranteed – to have the capacity to provide property rights to the recipients of that property.

Furthermore, there can never be a better time to grant property rights to rural dwellers than when conducting land redistribution. The physical process of land redistribution by definition means that governments have to interact with beneficiaries. In most land reform agencies, the processes tied to valuating property, determining the suitability of property for expropriation, conducting expropriation proceedings, collecting information on potential and actual beneficiaries, assigning beneficiaries to property, and then often aiding those beneficiaries with setting up production make it hard *not to get to know* beneficiaries. If rural populations are not legible to the government prior to land redistribution, they certainly become more legible in its course. This makes assigning property rights relatively easier in the context of land redistribution than divorced from it. And while maintaining and updating property rights is never a simple administrative task, it is typically facilitated in the wake of land reform by virtue of the fact that many governments that redistribute land follow up to monitor land beneficiaries and interact repeatedly with them to negotiate subsidies, credits, farming inputs, and political support.

Of course, as this book explores, many governments decide instead to withhold property rights from the beneficiaries of land redistribution. Land beneficiaries often receive property rights over their land decades later, if at all. Ironically, by the time property rights are extended, populations are sometimes far less legible than at the time of land reform. This is particularly true if, as was often the case in Latin America, intervening economic or other crises force state retrenchment from the countryside and informal rural land transactions creep along. Nonetheless, when states get serious about property rights reform, they are often able to roll out major initiatives to grant property rights. This is frequently true even if they have a weak grasp on their rural populations.

The timing of the extension of property rights to beneficiaries of land redistribution across Latin America also casts doubt on the notion that state capacity is the determinative factor driving the provision of property rights. Recall, for instance, that countries such as Colombia and Uruguay provided property rights to the beneficiaries of land redistribution as early as the 1920s and 1930s. Yet countries like Mexico in the 1980s or Brazil in the 1970s engaged in land redistribution while withholding property rights from beneficiaries. Mexico and Brazil in the latter part of the twentieth century vastly outstripped the state capacity of countries such as Colombia and Uruguay in the early twentieth century by any reasonable measure of state capacity.

Rather than state incapacity or institutional weakness, I find that the creation of property rights gaps is more closely related to the concept of forbearance, whereby politicians engage in intentional and revocable nonenforcement of property rights of land reform beneficiaries. Like Holland (2017), states that fail to enforce property rights tolerate informality as a way to generate rents. But unlike the cases Holland studies, governments that maintain this equilibrium do not do so beneficently or to signal favorability to constituents. The withholding and nonenforcement of property rights instead facilitates the exercise of control over rural dwellers.

3.2 POLITICAL DETERMINANTS OF REDISTRIBUTIVE LAND REFORM

Myopia, ideology, and state capacity all contribute to an understanding of why governments may sometimes withhold property rights from their citizens. The evidence for them in certain cases is undeniable. But they are insufficient explanations in and of themselves. They cannot entirely explain why incomplete rural property rights often fester for years on end. Nor do they fit the patterns of the upending of property rights through land redistribution without granting property rights to land beneficiaries in as neat a fashion as a convincing explanation should. And all of them miss a critical political logic that is rooted in extending rural social control and channeling support.

This chapter builds out this political logic for the property rights gap. It begins with the first step to creating such a gap: land redistribution. In prior work, I have outlined the conditions under which the redistribution of land occurs (see Albertus 2015). This is a critical antecedent to building a property rights gap. I briefly describe previous findings and then focus the rest of this chapter on theorizing why governments would withhold or extend property rights to land beneficiaries and under what conditions property rights gaps are likely to be elongated or closed.

Major land reform that reallocates the distribution of private property is a complex political undertaking. Land redistribution requires the sustained cooperation of a wide range of political actors and sufficient administrative capacity. A wide range of institutional actors is required to operate together to pass and implement land reform. The opposition of a small number of actors can jeopardize reform: if the executive opposes reform, the legislature cuts off funding, the judiciary raises legal barriers, or the bureaucracy is corrupt or unorganized, redistributive land reform efforts will fail. The land reform process is consequently quite protracted and involved.

Political regimes therefore play a critical role in conditioning the likelihood of successful land reform. Although both democratic executives and autocratic rulers at times have political incentives to pursue land redistribution, the onerous institutional cooperation necessary to pass and implement land reform implies that regimes with more institutional constraints – typically democracies – are less likely to implement redistributive land reform programs. Democratic institutions typically build a larger number of veto points into government that require outsized coalitions to support major policy changes. A greater number of veto points enable the empowerment of more heterogeneous interests within the legislature, executive, bureaucracy, and judiciary. Large landowners can scuttle land reform by influencing *any* of these actors to obstruct reform.

By contrast, a ruling political elite that faces few veto points and is motivated by their political coalition to displace traditional landed elites is better able to coherently leverage state resources to conduct land redistribution. These conditions typically obtain under dictatorship or foreign occupation. If large landowners in a legislature seek to block land redistribution in an authoritarian regime, the regime can threaten them, strip their seats, usurp legislative authority on the issue, or even disband the legislature. If judges block concerted efforts at land redistribution, an authoritarian regime can selectively replace judges, refashion the judiciary, or lean harder on judges on the bench. Finally, an authoritarian regime can populate the bureaucracy and military with individuals who will faithfully adhere to the demands of executive power lest their livelihoods, or even their lives, be put at risk. These actions eliminate pressure points that landowners could otherwise use to forestall land reform.

Not all authoritarian regimes or foreign occupiers conduct land redistribution. Those that do so must have powerful political incentives. These incentives derive from the coalitional composition of the ruling coalition, and in particular splits between ruling political elites and landed elites.

A ruling political elite is composed of key military players and civilian politicians as well as important political appointees and is normally headed by an elected executive under democracy or a dictator or junta under autocracy. Ruling political elites share the power and organizational capacity to run the government. They control the state apparatus and therefore wield a credible threat of violence. This enables them to redistribute property and to grant, withdraw, and modify property rights. They also have broad policymaking influence that affects citizens' welfare and economic choices. Political elites seek primarily to remain in office or to obtain greater power and autonomy for the institutions they represent. There can be substantial variation in the social origins and diversity of ruling political elites.

Landed elites, by contrast, are large landowners who own land as a livelihood, as a form of wealth holding, or for leisure, and who derive elevated social or economic status as a result. Landed elites seek first and foremost to maintain their land and protect their property rights. Cohesion within this group is underpinned by a shared interest in preventing land redistribution.

Landed elites in most Latin American countries, and in many other developing countries outside the region, have been small in number but command substantial economic power through extensive landholdings and the control of rural labor. Table 3.1 displays rates of landholding inequality

TABLE 3.1 *Landholding inequality in Latin America*

Country	Year	Landholding Gini
Argentina	1952	86
Bolivia	1950	94
Brazil	1920	82
Chile	1936	94
Colombia	1950	85
Costa Rica	1960	78
Cuba	1945	79
Dominican Republic	1950	79
Ecuador	1950	86
El Salvador	1950	83
Guatemala	1950	86
Honduras	1952	76
Mexico	1930	96
Nicaragua	1950	76
Panama	1960	73
Paraguay	1960	94
Peru	1960	93
Uruguay	1950	81
Venezuela	1950	94

Note: Figures for Argentina, Bolivia, Chile, Cuba, the Dominican Republic, Ecuador, El Salvador, Guatemala, Honduras, and Nicaragua are from the World Bank (1978). Remaining figures are from Bhattacharya and Ulubasoglu (2010), with calculations based on decadal reports of the World Census of Agriculture published by the Food and Agriculture Organization of the United Nations.

across Latin America using the earliest available data within the period of study.[15] Inequality is measured with a Gini coefficient that ranges from 0 (complete equality) to 100 (complete inequality). Landholding inequality was high across the board. In many countries it was extreme. For comparison, the Gini coefficient of land inequality in countries such as Canada, France, and the United Kingdom around this time was in the 50s or 60s. Landed elite power in the early to mid-twentieth century approached that in Latin America in a number of other developing countries in East and Southeast

[15] Earlier landholding data are not available for many countries in the region because they did not conduct full agricultural censuses that would enable the calculation of landholding statistics for prior years. However, the figures in Table 3.1 are all calculated either prior to or at the outset of major programs of land redistribution (see Chapter 2 for the timing of these programs).

Asia, the Middle East, and North Africa as well (Griffin et al. 2002). This relative dominance of large landowners in rural areas contributes to their social cohesiveness and ability to act collectively. While there may be overlap between landed elites and ruling political elites, such overlap is rarely complete.

The regimes that are most strongly motivated to conduct land redistribution are those that rise to power in countries with a strong landowning class, but whose ruling political coalitions do not draw on landowner support to either seize power or run the state once in office.[16] One example is a narrow military regime installed by junior officers that hail from the hinterlands. Examples include Egypt under the Free Officers and Peru under General Velasco. Another is a regime that is launched into power via peasant mobilization and that incorporates peasants in the ruling coalition. This can occur through a social revolution, as in Bolivia, Cuba, China, and Nicaragua, or at the ballot box, as in Venezuela under Rómulo Betancourt or Guatemala under Jacobo Arbenz.[17] A third example, albeit a less common one, is foreign occupation or invasion in which the occupying authority does not partner with landowners to rule. Examples include the Kuomintang after it fled to Taiwan during the Chinese Civil War, the Soviet Union in Afghanistan, or the United States occupation of Japan after WWII.[18]

Rival elite landowners who do not comprise the ruling coalition and are not closely allied to it can pose a host of threats to incumbent regimes. These rival landowners can fund coups, deliberately fail to deliver rural quiescence, tilt their workers to vote against the incumbent regime, withhold local tax revenue and critical foreign exchange from export sales, and block food distribution to cities. Furthermore, landed elites around the world have historically provided a blanket of basic services to rural laborers: basic education, credits and loans during economic downturns, access to markets, and even local policing. Powerful landowners in these cases have a strong and independent social and material base that binds local populations directly to them rather than to the state for critical services. These circumstances give ruling political elites strong incentives to crush rival out-groups composed of large landowners through land redistribution. Eliminating rivals can also serve as credible signal of the ruling political elite's exclusive reliance upon their support coalition. This helps to consolidate insider support.

---

[16] For a discussion of the circumstances that can give rise to splits between ruling political elites and landed elites, such as drives for state autonomy, a diversifying economy, ethnic difference, and foreign occupation, see Albertus (2015, Ch. 2).

[17] Coalitional incentives for land redistribution can consequently arise under democracy as well as dictatorship. Democracies, however, are typically too institutionally constrained to successfully implement land redistribution.

[18] Most episodes of major land redistribution, however, are determined domestically (Albertus 2015, 268–278). Foreign occupation in support of land redistribution did not transpire in Latin America during the period of study. Part of this is because of the influence of the United States in the region as a foreign power along with its general antipathy toward large-scale land redistribution.

3.3   GENERATING A PROPERTY RIGHTS GAP: GRANTING PROPERTY
WITHOUT RIGHTS

Land redistribution is a valuable strategic tool that rulers can deploy to destroy powerful elite rivals and win insider support. But it also provides regimes with a political opportunity vis-à-vis society: to bind mass populations to the regime. Granting land acquired via land reform to the landless can bind recipients to an incumbent regime by making the regime, and the state apparatus it controls, the center of citizens' "strategies of survival": the sets of practices and expectations that help ordinary people locate and secure the basic goods and services they need to flourish (Migdal 1988).[19]

This is attractive to a ruling regime because the rural masses vastly outnumber either ruling political elites or landed elites and can pose threats to political stability, economic extraction, and social control. In Latin America, 21 percent of the entire population remained rural in 2010. This figure was more than 50 percent before 1961. A substantial majority of rural laborers are relatively poor.[20] The rural masses are fairly diverse. Smallholders, renters, squatters, sharecroppers, day laborers, indigenous communities, and peons can simultaneously coexist in a single national agrarian economy. But they are united by a common and powerful goal: to improve their well-being via increased access to land. The rural masses therefore typically support land reform in substantial majorities, even if their electorally expressed preferences may at times be somewhat different due to factors such as clientelism.[21]

The rural masses also prefer to have land tenure security and flexibility around property use if and when they possess land, even if they do not always seek individual ownership – a point that was examined in-depth in Chapter 2. This implies that the rural masses that lack land will not only support land redistribution but also prefer to have property rights over their land.[22] For the subset of the rural masses that have received land through a land reform

---

[19] A similar strategy can be pursued with respect to permitting or encouraging urban land settlement without providing titles to settlers. Existing literature provides evidence of the political utility of urban informality in terms of shaping citizen claim-making (Collier 1976), exerting political dominance and establishing clientelism (Collier 1976; Larreguy et al. 2018), and gaining an edge in elections (Holland 2017).

[20] Circa the mid-twentieth century in Latin America, for instance, it was not uncommon for 60–70 percent of the smallest landowners in a country to hold less than a tenth of the land (FAO 1981).

[21] This is even true when ongoing land reforms have problems or shortcomings that disadvantage peasants over the longer term. For instance, Mexico's 1988 national agrarian survey (*Encuesta nacional agropecuaria ejidal*) demonstrates overwhelming support for continued land redistribution despite manifest problems linked to the PRI's manipulation of peasant voters through land reform. See also, e.g., Albertus et al. (2016).

[22] This point is consistent with Ansell and Samuels (2014), who argue that smallholders will support institutional constraints on governance in order to enhance the protection of their property rights.

program in the past but did not receive property rights over that land, they will seek greater property rights security.

The fact that the rural masses will typically support land redistribution and property rights security does not, of course, imply that they will be able to act effectively or that these outcomes will occur. There are a host of barriers to rural collective action. Chief among these are geographic dispersion and paternalistic and repressive land tenure relations. Clientelism and mechanisms of state or landlord control over information, basic needs, and even freedom of movement can further complicate collective action.

While the collective action problem facing the rural poor can often only be overcome by mobilization from above, coordination points, exogenous shocks, and organizational innovations can at times enable the poor to act collectively. This can come in the form of rural strikes, road blockades, and uprisings. It can also manifest as the systematic organization of political activism through the formation of social movements, protests, marches, and even lobbying. These movements can become longstanding rural tools of pressure and mobilization. For instance, Bolivia, Brazil, and Ecuador have large and sophisticated peasant organizations that continue to pressure for both land redistribution and greater property rights security.

For the typically authoritarian regimes that successfully redistribute land, control over mass rural populations is far preferable to facing an autonomous and organized peasantry, even if that peasantry helped to launch the regime into power via a social revolution. After all, such regimes typically seek to stay in power and extract from society. These feats are more easily accomplished without having to periodically face down either coup-mongering rival landed elites or mobilized and autonomous peasant groups.

Enmeshing land reform beneficiaries in relations of dependence on the state is much easier if regimes grant property to beneficiaries *without property rights*. Simply providing one-time land grants with complete property rights can render beneficiaries more self-sufficient and independent from the state. It may even enable an entrepreneurial subset of new small-scale farmers to begin to accumulate more land and position themselves as a new set of rural powerbrokers that could threaten the regime in the future. This is not to say that smallholders with property rights are not vulnerable in any way to state policies towards agriculture, or that they cannot fall prey to clientelism. But they are relatively less vulnerable than land beneficiaries that lack property rights and manipulating them is relatively more complicated and costly.

This is self-undermining from the perspective of a regime conducting land redistribution that needs to forestall the rise of new challengers and ensure economic cooperation and elicit political support, whether to crush rebel movements, signal popular support through elections or mass demonstrations, or maximize extractive revenue. Even everyday forms of pressure from organized and autonomous peasant groups such as roadblocks, work strikes, and withholding food distribution can make completely ignoring rural demands costly.

Authoritarian regimes that engage in land redistribution instead usually grant property *without* attendant property rights. This strategy activates a set of additional political mechanisms that provide an opportunity to build peasant dependencies and manipulate beneficiaries in an effort to ease the pacification of the countryside and create a politically pliable and dispersed support base. Granting property without property rights is rarely an oversight or political blunder. To the contrary, it is one of the most politically valuable policies that land redistribution makes possible.

Granting incomplete property rights is not always initially or explicitly designed to render beneficiaries politically dependent. Sometimes governments initially underprovide property rights because they are focused on other national goals tied to development, productivity, or equality. In other cases, they withhold property rights due to political ideologies rooted in collectivism or the expectation that capitalism will yield land reconcentration. In still other cases, states may have weak administrative capacity and struggle to provide well-defined and enforceable property rights.

Furthermore, government efforts at rural social control do not imply that they do not also seek rural support. Government messaging around land reform and rural assistance indicates that peasant support is often a goal. Land redistribution is advanced as social justice and liberation from oppression and is typically quite popular. Certain forms of withholding property rights, such as collectivization or the formation of cooperatives, is billed as social solidarity or a means to protect gains against reactionary elites. Subsequent rural policies such as agricultural credits, subsidies, the provision of inputs, or product purchasing are promoted as a reflection of the importance of supporting the countryside. This is hardly surprising. Governance is easier when subjects are supportive rather than just controlled or manipulated.

But once a government recognizes how the underprovision of property rights to land reform beneficiaries binds peasants to it and presents valuable political advantages, then it will intentionally retain and even grow the property rights gap for political gain. This realization that can occur relatively quickly. Often it happens under the same leaders that initiate land redistribution. Shortly after land redistribution begins, a property rights gap typically settles in as an equilibrium that suffocates the countryside but that serves the political interests of the incumbent regime. New leaders that encounter such an equilibrium therefore typically retain it unless, as will be discussed later in the chapter, the political equilibrium radically changes (usually through a democratic transition) and leaders either no longer benefit from a property rights gap or are forced to close it by land reform beneficiaries.

Peasant support for government often withers under this equilibrium over time. Former supporters become disaffected. Sometimes this can drive periodic backlashes if an event enables land beneficiaries to overcome collective action problems. But more frequently it generates apathy and a turn inward as helplessness and disappointment mount.

Figure 3.1 illustrates two different modes of regime interaction with rural constituents in the wake of land reform. In Figure 3.1a, the regime distributes land to rural dwellers along with complete property rights. This renders beneficiaries economically and politically independent. They therefore have greater capacity to organize autonomously at a national or regional level. They can also move more easily to urban areas to position themselves better in a changing economy. Once in towns and cities, they can interact directly with one another more easily than when they are dispersed in rural areas.

In Figure 3.1b, the regime distributes land to rural dwellers but withholds property rights. This fixes beneficiaries in the countryside in a dispersed fashion. The property rights gap also enables the regime to interact with individual beneficiaries in an iterated manner. The hub-and-spoke system of state-beneficiary interaction provides the state with more information about rural dwellers over time as well as coercive leverage that can be used at critical moments to sustain the regime.

Figure 3.2 illustrates the two main paths that governments can take once land has been redistributed without property rights, generating complications for land beneficiaries. A government can choose to either close the property rights gap or uphold it. This has critical consequences for former land reform beneficiaries and for the incumbent government itself.

The remainder of this section develops in greater detail the logic that encourages many of the authoritarian regimes that redistribute property to withhold property rights from beneficiaries for long periods. The following

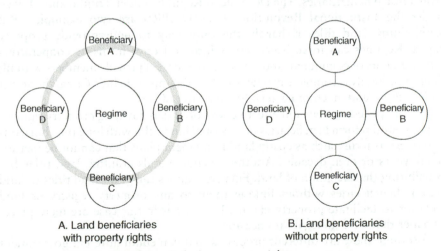

A. Land beneficiaries
with property rights

B. Land beneficiaries
without property rights

FIGURE 3.1 Regime–beneficiary links by property rights

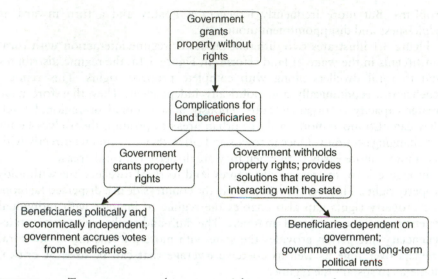

FIGURE 3.2 Two responses to the property rights gap and attendant consequences

section will address why democratic regimes that take their place often close the property rights gap.

Common Ways to Underprovide Property Rights and Consequences for Property Holders

One common tactic in underproviding property rights is to withhold land titles from reform beneficiaries. The Dominican Republic under Trujillo and Mexico under the Institutional Revolutionary Party (PRI) are two examples. But withholding land titles is hardly the only way to underprovide property rights. Regimes can force beneficiaries into collective farms or cooperatives with elements of communal land ownership and then provide members with ill-defined or highly incomplete property rights. Examples include Cuba, the Soviet Union, Peru, and much of Eastern Europe after WWII.

A more pedestrian but still effective way of underproviding property rights is to grant land reform beneficiaries provisional land titles with long time horizons and onerous terms such as costly land repayment plans that cannot be met for many years or even decades. Another avenue entails granting land titles but prohibiting the alienation of land. Finally, regimes can grant land titles to land reform beneficiaries without linking them to any property registry or land cadaster to facilitate property claims. Land titles in this case are mere pieces of paper that have no legal ramifications.

Although these are different processes that can entail different government actions or inaction, they have a common consequence that is of core theoretical interest: land beneficiaries lack property rights. Receiving land that lacks property rights engenders a predictable and shared series of complications for land beneficiaries regardless of the path that brings them to that point.

First, a lack of property rights makes it difficult if not impossible to use land as collateral to obtain loans or credits from private banks. That makes it harder to independently muster the funds to finance agricultural inputs such as seeds and fertilizers that are critical to production. It is even more difficult to fund high-expense capital improvement projects such as irrigation systems and access roads and to buy expensive but productivity-enhancing mechanized equipment. Consequently, underinvestment in the land is commonplace.

Second, highly incomplete property rights make it harder to sell, lease, partition, or mortgage property. Potential buyers are more likely to be wary about counterclaims on a property and banks are unlikely to help finance transfers or accept land as collateral. Rural land markets therefore become highly inefficient and in some cases they completely seize up.

Finally, the absence of a formal title makes it more difficult for landholders to protect against encroachment on their property from neighbors, land squatters, or even enclosures by larger landowners. Proving ownership to local police or courts is difficult and gives the latter leverage for extracting bribes or eliciting regime support. This also makes landholders wary of migrating to urban areas for employment lest their vacancy invite land invaders. It therefore fixes beneficiaries in the countryside.

Political Returns to Underproviding Property Rights

All of the "complications" faced by land reform beneficiaries without property rights appear at first glance to be inefficient from an economic or even from a social perspective. Incomplete property rights can stunt long-term economic growth by inhibiting accumulation, production, and economic dynamism (Acemoglu et al. 2001; North 1990). Widespread property informality can scare off foreign investors and capital (Songwe and Deininger 2009).[23] And it can generate contestation over ill-defined and poorly documented property delimitations (Deininger 2003).

Regimes that create a property rights gap in the countryside, however, accrue a panoply of political rents by exploiting the lack of property rights to enmesh land beneficiaries in dependence on the state for their everyday needs. Regardless of how a property rights gap is created, its existence enables an incumbent regime to exert leverage over land beneficiaries by stepping in to provide a common set of solutions for the problems generated by a lack of property rights.

---

[23] Customary forms of land access and common property rights, however, have also been exploited by foreign actors in order to acquire land at a large scale that they would otherwise be prohibited from acquiring (Wolford et al. 2013).

These solutions are often designed to require beneficiaries to repeatedly interact with the state over time. First, the state can step into the private banking void in the countryside and act as a monopoly provider of credits and agricultural inputs. Second, state agents can facilitate orderly land transfers among loyal beneficiaries, marshaling the coordination of state banks, local notaries, and a land reform agency – though they often do not support land beneficiaries transferring their land in order to move to urban centers. Finally, the state can protect the new status quo distribution of property by deploying the police to expel squatters, resolve local disputes, and deter land enclosures.

These activities establish the state as the indispensable purveyor of life's necessities in rural areas.[24] Furthermore, they constitute a repertoire of tools that the regime can use strategically at critical points in time to elicit support. A regime that presides over a large property rights gap can dole out scarcely available credits and inputs in the lead-up to a critical election or use them to co-opt opposition groups. It can also wield an ever-present coercive threat to withdraw support and render beneficiaries vulnerable to the market distortions the regime created. In this way, one-time land transfers are transformed into a continuous reliance on state programs and resources to access the inputs and services needed to cultivate land.[25] When these programs and resources flow freely – at least to some recipients – they can generate genuine support.

Table 3.2 provides a summary of the ways regimes can underprovide property rights, the complications this generates for land beneficiaries that lack property rights, and "solutions" that can be deployed to address these complications shy of simply granting property rights to land beneficiaries.

Regimes that preside over a property rights gap can also benefit from having a geographically fixed and dispersed base of politically pliable rural clients. Land reform beneficiaries that lack property rights are more likely to remain in rural areas where barriers to collective action are steep. This keeps them from

[24] These interventions can also be complemented by other state policies such as price supports or the guaranteed purchase of certain agricultural products. Both of these policies become relatively more important when producers face limited options for financing inputs, investment, and insurance as well as limitations to pursuing an alternative livelihood because of property rights restrictions.

[25] This account complements and builds out Yashar's (2005) argument about the nature of citizenship, autonomy, and rights in rural areas in new ways. Yashar (2005) argues that state-led and hierarchical corporatist citizenship regimes of mid-twentieth-century Latin America that extended social rights (including land access) unwittingly provided space for the reemergence of indigenous leaders, the reconstitution of communities, and the institutionalization of indigenous community practices and identities at the local level even where states tried to convert indigenous groups into "peasants." But in the land reform areas that this book examines, rural autonomy was at best segmented; to the extent that it flourished, it did so in spaces such as those Yashar analyzes tied to identity and interests that did not challenge the fundamental economic and political projects of incumbent regimes.

TABLE 3.2 *State tactics for and solutions to the underprovision of property rights*

Ways to underprovide property rights	Complications for land beneficiaries without property rights		State-provided "solutions" short of granting property rights
(1) Withhold land titles	(i) Cannot use land as collateral to obtain loans and credits for inputs and investment	→	(i) Create monopoly agencies to provide agricultural loans, credits, and subsidies
(2) Grant titles without linking them to a property register or cadaster			
(3) Force beneficiaries into collectives or cooperatives	(ii) Cannot formally sell, lease, divide, or mortgage land	→	(ii) Facilitate land transfers and inheritance with a land reform agency and local notaries
(4) Grant provisional titles with long time horizons and onerous repayment terms	(iii) Cannot protect against counter-claimants or prove ownership	→	(iii) Use police and courts to resolve boundary disputes and protect against encroachment
(5) Prohibit alienability of land			

migrating to urban political tinderboxes. They can also be used as a political counterweight to cities, which often serve as the most critical threats to incumbent regimes, especially those that are authoritarian (Wallace 2014). And they can provide a consistent food supply to urban centers, rendering them less volatile.

Land reform beneficiaries are a particularly tempting source from which to extract political support at low cost because beneficiaries become more "legible" to the government in the process of first doling out land. The government can therefore interact with them more efficiently and at less cost in the future. Withholding property rights further bolsters the hook into land reform beneficiaries by causing rural land markets to seize up. In these cases, if the government needs to go knocking on doors to demand support or call in favors, it is more likely that the same family opens the door.

The reduced mobility of land reform beneficiaries that lack property rights helps to explain why an alternative rural strategy is unlikely to be as effective for an incumbent regime: redistributing land with complete property rights and then attempting to control markets, and in turn peasants, by monopolizing credits and rural financing. It is incompatible to simultaneously grant property rights over land while substantially restricting rural land markets and rural mobility. Doing so would imply some limitations to property rights. A regime could, however, grant land beneficiaries property rights and try to accrue political rents by monopolizing rural credits, loans, and subsidies. But this is an expensive strategy unless the private banking sector is weakened or eliminated, which entails a set of restrictions to property rights in a different sector. To be sure, the state could compete against a weak private sector, but this is a costly strategy that has serious limitations relative to withholding property rights over rural land.

Two Illustrative Cases: Mexico and Peru

To illustrate several tactics and dynamics tied to the granting of property without property rights, I turn to two prominent cases that traced canonical Path B from Figure 1.2: Mexico and Peru. Authoritarian regimes in both cases generated large property gaps in the countryside that endured for decades before they were closed. I provide a brief account of how these property gaps were opened and the political equilibrium that set in as a result.

The Property Rights Gap in Mexico

Plutarco Calles became president of Mexico as the hand-picked successor of Álvaro Obregón in 1924, shortly after the Mexican Revolution toppled the longstanding rule of Porfirio Díaz. Calles consolidated his support and, in 1929, founded what became the hegemonic PRI by inviting influential generals, regional elites, nascent industrialists, and labor bosses to join his new political party. Each of these groups brought along a vast network of political supporters.[26]

The PRI took up the Mexican revolutionary mantle in the 1930s and held power in an authoritarian fashion until Mexico's transition to democracy in 2000. Its ruling coalition largely excluded traditional landed elites that had been powerful prior to the Mexican Revolution, particularly, though not exclusively, those from Central and Southern Mexico.[27] Consequently, for decades, the PRI systematically harassed and expropriated large landowners without compensation and granted their land to Mexico's peasants. Over the course of its rule and including postrevolutionary land redistribution in the lead-up to the PRI's formation, Mexico redistributed 51 million hectares of land. This constitutes over a quarter of Mexico's land area and more than the total of cultivable land.[28]

Many scholars emphasize that land redistribution in Mexico was a key component of the PRI's programmatic vision grounded in social justice that emerged from the Revolution, although imperatives for economic growth, social articulation, and industrialization at times impeded equity considerations in the countryside (see, for example, Bartra 1993; Ibarra Mendivil 1989). The Mexican government sought peasant support, and for several decades among a large portion of the peasantry, won it. Even so, other scholars suggest that land reform served as an instrument of peasant control or regime "legitimation" (Esteva 1980; Warman 1972).

One revealing window into the early design of Mexico's land reform stems from a conflict over the nature of land redistribution and property rights in the early 1920s between Chihuahua governor Ignacio Enríquez on the one hand and President Plutarco Calles and his predecessor, Álvaro Obregón, on the other. Enríquez faced federal pressure from Obregón to redistribute several large haciendas in the northern state of Chihuahua, such as the prominent Terrazas estate, and to grant the land communally to local groups of peasants following a prerevolution model of indigenous rural community known as the *ejido*. Enríquez dragged his feet and mooted an alternative: to colonize public lands and carve off portions of haciendas by selling them to peasants, members of the middle class, and even generals who would then work the land as autonomous producers (Domínguez Rascón 2003, 74). Enríquez thought this would reactivate the local rural economy, catalyze land markets, attract

---

[26] Calles built political support during his rule among three main factions that had jockeyed for power during the revolution: small farmers from central Mexico who had lost their land during the Porfiriato, the fledgling labor movement that had formed through Díaz's promotion of mining, railroads, and manufacturing, and a contingent of merchants, mine owners, and ranchers from Mexico's northern states who were followers of Alvaro Obregón.

[27] The PRI did incorporate, however, a group of northern ranchers and mine owners. These elites played a greater role in ruling coalitions beginning in 1940.

[28] Redistribution is closer to 85 million hectares including the recognition or confirmation of communities that already had de facto, relatively autonomous control of their property.

investment, and spur modernization, all while avoiding the creation of communal *ejidos* and retaining powerful landowners as local investors.

Obregón resisted Enríquez's proposal for the alleged reason that its principal danger was the incapacity of the state to control the mass of peasant land beneficiaries (Domínguez Rascón 2003, 74). Calles was even more forthright and told Enríquez in a conversation: "The ejido is the best method of controlling these people [peasants] by merely telling them: If you want land you have to support the government; if you are not with the government, you won't get land" (quoted in Tobler 1990, 439).

Calles ultimately steamrolled Enríquez's plan. Calles and all of his successors that governed under the PRI in subsequent decades stripped large landowners of their land and social position in much of the countryside and redistributed privately held land as *ejidos* to villages as a whole. Groups of peasants had to petition for land grants from the government, which would begin an onerous application process that engendered uncertainty and lengthy bureaucratic delays as well as repeated peasant interaction with authorities (Sanderson 1984).

Peasants that were successful in this process acquired land as villages and the right to use and work it individually or collectively. But they were not granted full property rights and did not receive formal land titles. Peasants were not permitted to leave their plots idle for more than two consecutive years and were not allowed to rent individualized plots. This generated incentives to remain in the countryside where the PRI had greater leverage over them. Furthermore, neither villages nor individual peasants could sell the land or use it as collateral to access commercial loans.

The property rights restrictions that land beneficiaries faced stunted rural land markets and engendered a dearth of privately provided credit. Peasants were forced to rely on state subsidies and credits for seeds, insurance, fertilizer, and other inputs – typically obtained through official petitions (Thiesenhusen 1995, Ch. 2). The PRI created and controlled a proliferation of agrarian federal agencies to monopolize peasants' survival strategies. FERTIMEX distributed fertilizer, CONASUPO bought harvests, Banco Ejidal (later BANRURAL) granted credits, and the Ministry of Agrarian Reform settled land use conflicts and boundary disputes. These agencies could threaten the denial of benefits if peasants failed to support the party at election times.

The distortions created by property rights restrictions led to the undercapitalization and decline of the *ejido* sector over time relative to private farm enterprises (Sanderson 1986). Peasant support for land redistribution was not replicated in the same straightforward way for many of the land reform's consequences and associated programs. Yet the PRI's greatest political strongholds long remained in rural areas such as Oaxaca and Chiapas. And rural populations remained large: urbanization was stunted for Mexico's level of development given the imperative of peasants to remain on the land to maintain it.

Enríquez moved into public opposition of the regime after leaving his post as Chihuahua's governor and acerbically criticized the land reform and the *ejido* model. He argued that the government "has turned the agrarian problem into a weapon in the hands of political candidates . . . [P]oliticians prefer to preserve a state of agitation and uncertainty among ejidatarios, with respect to the possession of their parcels, in order to make them submissive to the government and to use them as weapons in their electoral battles . . . " (quoted in Domínguez Rascón 2003, 75). To Obregón and Calles, "the ejido had the primordial function of controlling the rural masses," and this control was vital for the consolidation of the new regime (Domínguez Rascón 2003, 75). Tobler (1990, 439) concurs, writing that for these leaders, "the economic and social objectives of the agrarian reform were less important than their political function, which is to say, their pacifying and stabilizing effects."

These assessments are consistent with the conclusions of many Mexico specialists who argue that the PRI used its control of land to sustain its patronage networks (Eckstein 1968; Sanderson 1986; Silva Herzog 1959; Simpson 1937).[29] Albertus et al. (2016) reach a similar conclusion that land redistribution served to underpin regime stability based on empirical evidence that land redistribution was greater during election years and in places where the threat of rural unrest was most elevated.

It is important to acknowledge, however, that the PRI did not initially design the concept of the *ejido* or tailor its impartial property rights from the outset with a clear vision of precisely how this would cultivate peasant dependence on the state. To the contrary, the *ejido* stems from a prerevolution model of indigenous rural communities rooted in self-government, local autonomy, and inalienable access to land (Kourí 2015). Many peasants demanded that the PRI constitute *ejidos* and viewed collective landholding and inalienability as a safeguard against future land dispossession and a way to protect the community integrity that had been serially violated in the colonial period and the nineteenth century.

This dovetailed favorably with the communist ideological leanings of a considerable contingent of the PRI in the 1930s, who viewed the *ejido* as a prelude to the collectivization of agricultural production. Pragmatists viewed group-based land redistribution as more efficient and rapid than individual redistribution and nationalists saw the *ejido* as a unique and venerable link to Mexico's great indigenous civilizations (Kourí 2015). The PRI also viewed the *ejido* as a manageable way to supply cheap food and raw materials to urban centers to promote development (Gordillo et al. 1998).

---

[29] In an analogous fashion, numerous Mexico scholars argue that the PRI's neglect of urban land titling enabled it to generate dependence among those who lacked titles to plots of land or homes (Davis 1994; Ward 1999). More recent scholarship indicates that land titling in Mexico has served to reduce clientelism by making voters less susceptible to threats and more free to vote according to their policy preference (Larreguy et al. 2018).

But the PRI did adjust the *ejido* model in its favor and built a formidable and hierarchical bureaucratic structure to link *ejidos* to the regime. Early on, it shifted the traditional mode of *ejido* land distribution to collective distribution, as opposed to individual distribution within collectives, and vested itself rather than communities with protecting *ejido* rights (Otero 1989). And in the 1930s, the PRI created the National Peasant Confederation (CNC) and compelled all *ejido* members to join, giving it greater supervisory power over *ejidos*.

Furthermore, there is substantial evidence that the Mexican government purposely withheld property rights – including any type of formal title, contrary to community demands – for a long period of time once it realized that this had the politically useful effect of generating peasant dependency. Especially after 1940, once the PRI had settled into an equilibrium of stable authoritarian rule, it recognized and decided to maintain and even enhance certain features of the agrarian reform such as the prohibition on rentals and sales that gave them greater leverage over land beneficiaries (de Janvry et al. 2014). The negative economic consequences of a lack of property rights on agricultural investment and production stacked up over time and became hard to ignore (Albertus et al. 2016).

Peasant communities that were supportive of land redistribution bridled under the smothering weight of stasis and government control. Some peasants organized to demand greater juridical security to their landholdings (Encinas and Rascón 1983, 130). Several business interest groups such as the Comité Coordinador Empresarial similarly advocated for clearer and more secure property rights for *ejidos* and their members (Arriola 1976, 475). Many more peasants sought to skirt property rights restrictions and turned to informally renting or selling their plots despite the risks (Cockburn 1987; Gordillo et al. 1998).[30] Some peasants saw a dim future and emigrated out of *ejido* communities, leaving their most valuable but least fungible asset – land – behind (Astorga 1985; Paré 1977).[31] As populations grew and the first generation born into the newly formed *ejidos* came of age, there was a great deal of conflict within households, between households, and against *ejido* bosses. This generated a push for changing the system to improve land access and secure greater protections against *ejido* bosses (Gordillo et al. 1998, 159).

But rather than address these concerns by enhancing property rights protections for land reform communities and their members, the PRI maintained the structure of *ejidos* and instead sought to shore up a parallel,

---

[30] As I discuss later in the chapter, *ejidos* overwhelmingly voted to join the land formalization program PROCEDE in the 1990s to shore up their property rights once they were allowed to do so.

[31] Because of the implications of an entire family losing land access, migrants were frequently members of a larger household, though not heads of household who held agrarian rights within the *ejido*.

secure property rights track in the countryside. It began issuing some private landowners guarantees against expropriation via *certificados de inafectabilidad* so that agricultural production as a whole would not crater. And in reaction to burgeoning peasant mobilizations and protests in the 1960s and 1970s, it did not extend property rights and tenure security but instead revitalized its corporatist arrangements and doled out more land (Gordillo et al. 1998, 160).

The Property Rights Gap in Peru

Peru, like Mexico, generated an enormous property rights gap in the countryside under military rule from 1968 to 1980 despite the fact that Peru's dictatorship had very different origins and institutions than Mexico's PRI. A coup led by junior military officers that hailed from the hinterlands seized power in Peru in 1968 under General Velasco. Velasco declared a sweeping land reform in 1969 that directly attacked the most powerful landed elites – a longtime political rival to the military – and eventually expropriated and redistributed half of all private agricultural land by 1980. As General Velasco stated in a national speech on June 24, 1969 that promulgated the land reform law, agrarian reform was "of decisive importance for national development" and would lead to "social and economic transformation that would make the country free, just, and sovereign."

The government, however, did not grant land reform beneficiaries property rights over their land. It instead converted large estates into collectives or cooperatives of former workers. The regime also withheld titles from cooperative members, maintained co-ownership of cooperatives until the mortgage on the land was paid, and prohibited land sales, leasing, and the use of assets as collateral for loans.

The official motive in doing so was to retain economies of scale in production and agricultural output critical for urban food consumption. General Velasco underscored this in his 1969 speech introducing the law: "The Law of Agrarian Reform has to affect the totality of the business of large estates. But this does not mean that large properties will be divided and fragmented, because that would result in a damaging decline in agricultural productivity. Consequently, the law seeks to maintain large properties under a different and fair property regime [the cooperative]." Scholarship on the regime's inner workings indicate that this played a critical role in the decision (Cleaves and Scurrah 1980).

The Velasco regime was also influenced by the work of the prominent Peruvian intellectual José Carlos Mariátegui (Mayer 2009, 246fn2). Mariátegui's 1928 essay entitled "The Land Problem" pointed out how indigenous rural communities could be transformed into socialist cooperatives and also argued that large coastal sugar and cotton estates mainly exported their products to serve foreign demands and did not sufficiently contribute to Peru's domestic food demands.

But beyond these influences and the hopes of winning peasant support through reform, the regime also clearly sought to control the peasantry and to cultivate a small number of clear local leaders that they could interface with to meet the regime's goals (Matos Mar and Mejía 1980; Mayer 2009; McClintock 1981). This militated toward forcing beneficiaries into aggregate production units and limiting their political and economic autonomy.

Many peasants opposed this arrangement and tried to push back. As Lastarria-Cornhiel (1989, 142) writes, "There was pressure from the beneficiary families from the beginning for more individual production and less collective land." Mayer (2009), de Celis (1977), and many others document peasant complaints about the cooperative structures and demands to disband them.

The government ignored this pressure and instead pushed beneficiaries into the National Agrarian Confederation (CNA), a peak agricultural-sector organization that established corporatist control over peasant actions. As Pasara (2015, 61–62) describes it, "The state, through institutions [like the CNA], vertical and hierarchical, selectively channels popular demands stemming from the most organized sectors and gives them benefits accompanied by political control; in this way it seeks to avoid class consciousness and organization and win political loyalty from beneficiaries." Together with the state-run Agrarian Bank and the Agricultural Development Bank, the CNA was used to provide compliant and active peasant groups with the bulk of credit, inputs, and investment (McClintock 1981, 42).

The military regime sent bureaucrats into the cooperatives to directly aid in managing them. It also deployed agents from its "social mobilization" agency, SINAMOS, to agitate for and monitor peasant groups. Consequently, the regime knew which peasants were supportive and which opposed to the regime, joining rival groups like the independent Peasant Confederation of Peru (CCP). As Mayer (2009, 6) writes, "The threat of the military boot was always palpable."

General Velasco's prime minister, General Francisco Morales Bermúdez, pushed him out of office in 1975. Morales at first continued land redistribution at a large scale but then curtailed it dramatically in the late 1970s as his regime took a conservative shift and sidelined many of the Velasco-era radicals. But Morales never moved to extend property rights to land beneficiaries. And when the military was finally forced out in 1980, it was at the hands of urban strikes and protests rather than rural ones.

3.4 CLOSING THE PROPERTY RIGHTS GAP: GRANTING PROPERTY RIGHTS WITHOUT PROPERTY

The theory so far indicates that democracies should be less likely to engage in land redistribution than nondemocracies. Because democracies typically have relatively high institutional constraints to rule, powerful landed elites threatened by redistribution can block it via aristocratic parliaments, independent judiciaries, or other democratic institutions. This is true even if the executive has strong political incentives to pursue land redistribution.

In contrast, however, democracies are *more likely* to extend and protect property rights – albeit without granting property – for individuals in the land reform sector that have incomplete property rights or none at all. Democracies are therefore more likely to follow the left-hand-side path depicted in Figure 3.2. This is consistent with a range of neo-institutional accounts of the state (for example, Levi 1989; North 1990; Olson 1993). It is due to an asymmetry in how pluralistic political systems process popular demands against the violation of powerful minority interests. Before examining how this operates, however, it bears recalling why rural dwellers would demand property rights in the land reform sector to begin with.

Demands for Property Rights in the Land Reform Sector

The discussion of land reforms in Mexico and Peru suggests that beneficiaries of land redistribution prefer to have land tenure security and flexibility around the use of their new property rather than face the twin barriers of (i) a rigid set of government-imposed mandates regarding how property must be used and held; and (ii) a dense thicket of damaging and distortionary rural market failures that spawn a labyrinth of bureaucratic agencies, rules, and procedures that must be heeded in order to survive. Land reform beneficiaries typically stand to gain from property rights protections.[32]

Property rights security makes it more difficult for an incumbent government to force land beneficiaries into a position of political and economic dependence. Property rights therefore hold the promise of greater independence and autonomy. They can also provide protections against property encroachment by counterclaimants or the state. This gives land beneficiaries greater flexibility in their residence and labor allocation. For instance, beneficiaries can more reliably migrate seasonally to supplement their income with off-farm labor and expect that their land will not be appropriated when they return. They can also choose to fallow their land without concerns that it will be appropriated. This facilitates long-term planning and production. Property rights that enable the transfer of land also ensure that beneficiaries can leave their land to future generations without either having that land revert to the state or forcing the next generation into informality and its attendant uncertainties. And under the right policy and regulatory circumstances, secure property rights can help protect against land dispossession, can support higher land prices and more liquid land markets that are advantageous if land beneficiaries decide to change occupations or move to urban centers, and can facilitate securing loans and

---

[32] This can be true even where communities prefer collective ownership. In Mexico, for instance, many *ejidos* simultaneously pushed for collective titles via PROCEDE and the ability to determine whether to retain collective ownership of land (which most chose to do).

credits through the use of land as collateral, enabling land beneficiaries to reap greater returns to investment in their land and to better afford to send their children to school.[33] These are some of the most common reasons that can undergird popular demand for property rights among land reform beneficiaries that lack them.

Reflecting this demand, there are numerous examples of former land reform beneficiaries with weak property rights demanding, petitioning, or organizing to pressure for greater property rights under democracy. Consider several examples from Latin America. In El Salvador, soldiers from the insurgent group Farabundo Martí National Liberation Front (FMLN) and land reform beneficiaries that lacked property rights allied to demand property rights during the early 1990s peace negotiations (Thiesenhusen 1995, 157–158). In Bolivia, the Unified Confederation of Rural Workers of Bolivia (CSUTCB) broke from the regime-controlled peasant federation toward the end of dictatorship in 1979 and organized in subsequent decades to push for greater property rights protections. Mid-sized producers in Venezuela who had received land with weak property rights petitioned for land titles in greater numbers starting in the mid-1970s (Delahaye 2003, 102–106).

In Peru, the National Smallholder's Association (ANAPA) sought titles for former cooperative workers who had received land when cooperatives broke up in the 1980s but lacked property rights. They partnered with the Peruvian Peasant Confederation in a series of strikes and mass meetings in an effort to achieve their aims (Moreno 1994, 58). Some land reform beneficiaries that lacked property rights in the Dominican Republic organized into a National Council of Agrarian Reform Beneficiaries in the 1980s and petitioned the government to issue them land titles. In Mexico, the demands of *ejidos* for collective and layered titles to the lands they had previously received continued in force after the transition to democracy. By 2005, over 95 percent of *ejidos* had voted to join the government's titling program Program for the Certification of Ejido Rights and Titling of Urban Plots (PROCEDE).

The Landless Workers' Movement (MST) in Brazil has been at the forefront of social movements pushing for both land redistribution and greater property rights security since the country's return to democracy in the 1980s. In Ecuador, the Confederation of Indigenous Nationalities of Ecuador (CONAIE) has played a similar role since the mid-1980s. Although its chief aim has been state recognition of ancestral territorial claims and greater autonomy and recognition for indigenous groups, CONAIE also partnered with peasant

---

[33] For further discussion and evidence, see, for instance, Besley and Burgess (2000); Deininger et al. (2004); Galor et al. (2009), and the discussion in Chapter 1. There is a large literature on the background conditions under which property rights will or will not yield these advantages. For an introductory overview, see Fermin-Sellers and Sellers (1999); Brasselle, Gaspart, and Platteau (2002); Deininger and Feder (2009), and the discussion in Chapter 2.

groups that were beneficiaries of former land redistribution to pressure the government for land titles.

The popular demand for greater land rights under democracy in some Latin American countries in recent decades has dovetailed with the organization of indigenous movements and mobilization of indigenous identities. As Yashar (2005) details, the rise of neoliberal citizenship reforms around the time of democratization in many Latin American countries in the 1980s and 1990s sparked indigenous movements that sought greater recognition by the state, more political autonomy, and new forms of representation (Yashar 2005). Sometimes these movements incorporated or allied with previous land reform beneficiaries that lacked property rights. They were largely distinct from them in other cases.

I do not assert the stronger claim that rural dwellers more generally beyond the land reform sector necessarily demand greater property rights security through land formalization, though this can also occur, especially among the less powerful. There is a substantial literature demonstrating that certain populations can at times oppose land formalization or are indifferent to it. The conventional wisdom is that rural elites should be particularly opposed to widespread land titling (Lipton 2009, 151). For instance, Honig (2017) demonstrates in a study of customary law settings in Senegal and Zambia that individuals with substantial customary privileges gain advantages from maintaining customary rights. Onoma (2009) similarly concludes that chiefs in Ghana benefit from weak property rights regimes that they help to create and uphold. In China, Mattingly (2016) finds that lineage heads discourage strong property rights such as land titles in order to control local populations. Mangonnet (2020) finds that rural elites in Brazil resist land registration and regularization to maintain the benefits of illegibility. And in Kenya, Boone et al. (2019a) describe how a cluster of insider elites that illicitly allocated land titles to themselves over decades opposed reform to the corrupt Ministry of Lands and a popular push to distribute titles much more widely and transparently.[34]

There is evidence in some of these very same settings that less powerful individuals, which form a considerable majority of the population, actually support greater property rights security. Honig (2017), for example, shows that individuals with lesser customary privileges in Senegal and Zambia exhibit greater demand for adopting state land titles over retaining customary rights. Similarly in Kenya, land activists and civil society groups pushed for the new 2010 constitution and a new land policy that would wrest control of land titling, registries, and resettlement from the Ministry of Lands and advance land titling in Kenya's settlement schemes and property rights security more broadly (Boone et al. 2019a).

---

[34] This example shows how rural elites that oppose widespread land titling may simultaneously favor selective titling that allocates land in their favor illicitly or irregularly.

But there are also cases in which weaker rural actors are indifferent or even opposed to land titling or putative improvements in property rights security. Indifference can stem from marginality or weak state presence whereby rural individuals anticipate that land titles would be of little utility or would not be easily defensible.[35] Opposition can arise among rural individuals that view formalization as a Trojan Horse for dispossession by more powerful actors, as a degradation of their practiced relations with land, or as a challenge to elements of their broader repertoire of political and social rights. For example, Hetherington (2009) demonstrates how many Paraguayan peasants opposed legislation strengthening their formal property rights for fear that this legislation would be bundled with favorable treatment for large landowners that could in turn attempt to dispossess them. In northwest Vietnam, many villagers opposed a land registration initiative that would have increased their legal land rights because these rights did not accommodate villagers' multiple layers of social control over land (Sikor 2006). In Ivory Coast, surveys of rural villagers indicate varying preferences for titling, with opposition particularly consistent among those who viewed titling as a threat to their other political and social customary rights (Boone et al. 2019b).[36]

This discussion suggests at least three circumstances where demand for titles can be low. One is settings where land access and tenure are guided by customary authority, particularly where customary authorities can circumvent the ability of individuals with lesser privileges from expressing demands for formal titles. These settings are not particularly relevant to the main focus of this book for two reasons. First, the focus here is on property rights gaps in the land reform sector. Customary authority is less salient in post–land reform settings than in communities where landholding was not already disrupted by redistributive state intervention.[37] State-led land reform not only disrupts or dissolves customary authority but also orients claim-making for land-related issues against the state and rewires state–citizen relationships as the state adopts roles and functions previously held by local traditional authorities. Second, the main empirical focus of the book is Latin America, where customary authority in rural areas was disrupted and uprooted at a massive scale during the colonial era. This contrasts with much of sub-Saharan Africa and parts of Oceania where customary land tenure is still predominant.

---

[35] Relatedly, rural dwellers may be indifferent to property rights where land pressure is low and therefore challenges to de facto claims are rare (e.g., Feeny 1988).

[36] Boone et al. (2019b) also documented titling opposition among villagers with concerns of dispossession by wealthier actors through distressed sales, villagers worried about taxation, and some women and youth where titles went to individual male heads of household. At the same time, there was titling support in areas with in-migration, where collective certification was seen as a potential option, and where investment was significant.

[37] Of course, customary tenure systems can themselves be reinforced or in some cases even imposed in a specific fashion by states (Boone 2014).

Another circumstance in which demand for land titles can be low is where existing informal land rights are more capacious than the rights and tenure security that are offered through a formal land titling program. For instance, multiple users may hold rights to a single resource and land titles may not accommodate this complexity (Bromley 1989). Relatedly, demand can be low where informal land rights are fundamentally bundled with other informal political and social rights that would be challenged through a land formalization program. These scenarios are most likely to be true in contexts of customary land tenure arrangements or where land tenure has been relatively stable and autonomous from the state over the course of generations. Again, this is not typically the case in aftermath of land reform. Even in many – though not all – customary tenure systems, law has evolved over time to grant increasingly narrow and more specific rights to landholders (Bates 1989; Migot-Adholla et al. 1991), making land titling relatively easier and more attractive.[38]

A third circumstance in which demand for land titles can be low is where the state or the rule of law is weak and citizens do not anticipate titles being valuable or defended. The conventional wisdom is that formal property rights are worth little when not supported by credible state protection (Feder and Feeny 1991; Deininger and Feder 2009). Titles confer legal protection that is more valuable when institutions can reliably prevent the government from reneging on protection and prevent outsiders from infringing on property rights.

Even if this is true, some scholarship challenges the premise that demand for formalized rights is predicated on credible state protection. Scholars that study human rights and social movements argue that rights can also serve as powerful symbols that motivate engagement and mobilization (Tarrow 1994; Simmons 2009). Consistent with this, Kopas (2020) finds evidence for popular demand for land titles both in areas with strong state institutions and with weak institutions, and furthermore demonstrates that land rights empower citizen engagement more where they are weakly enforced. Furthermore, individuals

---

[38] The increasing displacement of communities with customary tenure through large-scale land acquisition by foreign actors (Wolford et al. 2013) and growing land pressure through population growth (Boone 2014) may dovetail with the evolution of customary tenure systems to increase the attractiveness of land formalization in these settings in the future. A shift away from the naïve one-size-fits-all era of neoliberal property rights advocacy by international actors and toward a more nuanced view of fitting property rights to context, for instance as expressed in the 2012 Voluntary Guidelines on the Responsible Governance of Tenure developed by the Food and Agriculture Organization of the United Nations, could do the same. Even if these factors may not shift demand for formal land titling in the short term, they provide reasons to consider creating "shadow property rights" as a backstop for individuals and groups that rely exclusively on customary authority for land access, as well as motivation to consider how various property rights (e.g., to a house, to grazing rights, to agricultural plots, to extraction from the commons, and/or to a share in community profits) can be "layered" to meet the realities of land use and the desire of communities while also enabling individuals that suffer abuses or want to opt out to obtain protections and mobility. See the concluding chapter for further discussion.

may desire land titles in weakly institutionalized contexts even if they do not fulfill all of their ostensible functions. For instance, land titles may not secure legal protections for their holders but still could be desired as symbols of an individual's effective occupation of land, as was the case in a land formalization program in Cameroon (Firmin-Sellers and Sellers 1999). Regardless, to the extent that the demand for property rights varies in part with credible state protection, this hypothesis can be separately interrogated by examining the explanatory power of state capacity on the property rights gap as outlined previously in this chapter.[39]

How Democracies Process Concentrated Land Redistribution Losers Versus Dispersed Land Titling Losers

Assuming that there is a baseline degree of demand for property rights among land reform beneficiaries, why would democracies be associated with property rights provision? Recall that democracies struggle to redistribute land at a significant scale because of large landowner opposition. But unlike land redistribution, any losses from land titling in the land reform sector are comparatively small and the losers more dispersed.

The losers from land redistribution are large landowners who are few in number and have a lot at stake – the forfeiture of their very valuable property – if they are targeted with redistribution. By virtue of their small numbers, economic power, and common interests, they can often solve their collective action problem and organize to block redistributive reform by capturing veto points in a pluralistic political system.

There is not typically a comparable set of concentrated losers in land titling in the land reform sector.[40] Most land reform beneficiaries who lack property rights or have incomplete rights do not lose anything through land titling. To the contrary, subject to the caveats in the previous discussion, they stand to gain from tenure security.

As previously, I do not maintain that this assumption necessarily holds outside of the land reform sector, though there are plenty of examples of broader rural populations that lack property rights over their land benefiting from titling programs. Particularly in contexts where land contestation is considerable and ownership is informal, such as in frontier areas or regions with a history of migration or population displacement, land titling can be used

---

[39] Chapter 4 examines this empirically against the main theory. To the extent that the demand for property rights varies instead with the rule of law, with greater institutional constraints to rule (associated with democracy) conferring greater benefits to land titles, then the demand side of property rights and its association with democracy would dovetail theoretically with the supply side of property rights described previously.

[40] As discussed in the previous section, however, there may be rural elites outside of the land reform sector that could lose in a broader land titling effort.

for political or redistributive ends to favor certain constituents over others (Boone 2018). This can operate more akin to land redistribution.

The main potential losers from titling in the land reform sector are those whose land claims are contested with others. This may be due to overlapping claims from a land redistribution program or from illegal postreform occupancy achieved clandestinely or through force. These losers are much more dispersed and less individually powerful than the landed elites that were physically displaced through redistribution, making any resistance to titling easier to overcome. And they frequently prefer a favorable titling resolution rather than no titling at all.

Relatedly, whereas legal challenges to the seizure of property can strike at the heart of the legality of an entire land redistribution program, particularly when property rights are constitutionally protected, challenges to property titles among land reform beneficiaries are more likely to be ad hoc and unthreatening to the legality of the titling process as a whole. It is therefore unlikely to spur judicial blockage.

What about the potential for resistance from former landed elites who lost their land through a land redistribution program? Given the very different political conditions under which land redistribution and titling occur and the fact that they are typically separated by years or even decades, former landed elites are often dispersed, ruined, and politically discredited by the time land titling programs are initiated. They do not pose strong opposition under these circumstances. Elites that can still organize typically do so to seek compensation for lost property rather than to oppose subsequent titling processes. Consider the powerful and tight-knit landed elites in Peru or Zimbabwe after land reform in these countries. The process of land reform weakened and dispersed landed elites in both cases. Years later a subgroup of former elites organized to seek compensation for their expropriated property, albeit unsuccessfully. In Peru, where major land titling later occurred, elites did not expend their resources on opposing titling efforts.

It would be a step too far, however, to argue that there is never a concentrated and powerful opposition to land titling in the land reform sector. This scenario – an exception rather than the rule – is most likely when efforts at granting property rights to land reform beneficiaries occur shortly after land redistribution and landed elites were not destroyed via land redistribution. Landed elites that retain power may push against strengthening property rights for land beneficiaries in order to avoid entrenching the new status quo. Furthermore, remaining large landowners may benefit from widespread weak property rights in order to impoverish peasants and force them to work for low wages on their estates (Fergusson 2013).

El Salvador is an illustrative example. A military junta composed of junior officers seized power in 1979 and implemented a major land redistribution program in 1980 by expropriating and redistributing 472 estates in excess of 500 hectares (McElhinny 2006, 283). The junta converted these estates into cooperatives that inscribed peasant workers but did not grant them property rights or titles over the land. Land redistribution slowed dramatically by 1982 when the Christian Democrats took control of the Ministry of Agriculture after an election. The Christian Democrats also formed a coalition with right-wing parties (the Nationalist Republican Alliance and the Party of National Conciliation) in the constituent assembly to draft a new constitution. These parties dominated legislative elections from the return of democracy in 1984 through the 1991 elections. The subsequent conclusion of El Salvador's Civil War brought the rebel group FMLN into mainstream party politics.

Large landowners seized the initiative during the early 1980s political reversal to oppose both further land redistribution and efforts at granting property rights to land reform beneficiaries that threatened to cement in the status quo. Representatives tied to landed interests in the Constituent Assembly successfully pushed to temporarily freeze land titling in 1982, a move that was reversed under foreign pressure. They then supported new constitutional statutes limiting further land redistribution. Landowners that had already been expropriated intentionally spread misinformation among cooperative workers that the reforms were no longer in effect, hoping they would forfeit their claims (Strasma 1989, 410). Large landowners and oligarchs also employed paramilitary squads to intimidate and attack potential beneficiaries of land redistribution and of land titling in an attempt to dissuade them from seeking to join cooperatives or applying for titles (Mason 1986, 508–512).

El Salvador's process of land titling, however, was in part more contentious than most under democracy because land redistribution continued at a low level alongside titling. This spurred collective resistance against redistribution by landed elites that spilled over into titling. Eventually, following the Civil War settlement in 1992 and in partnership with the World Bank, El Salvador created the National Registry Center, which sought to unify all property records and extend land formalization efforts. The country also continued land titling through the program *El Salvador, País de Propietarios*.

Democratic Representation as a Conduit for Channeling Popular Demands into Policies

The typical lack of a concentrated and powerful set of land titling losers in the land reform sector implies that, vis-à-vis land redistribution, institutional constraints pose less of an obstacle to policy implementation. But why would democracy be *positively* associated with granting property rights? Although democracy is generally effective at protecting vocal and politically powerful minorities such as large landowners when institutional constraints are high, it is also effective at channeling popular demands into the political system and acting on those demands *in the absence of opposition from powerful minority interests*.

The previous discussion provides reasons for why land reform beneficiaries will typically support property rights protections. Importantly, demands for property rights can be channeled into the political system under democracy regardless of the makeup of the executive's ruling coalition. Whereas there are no formal venues through which rural dwellers that lack property rights can effectively push for land titles in an uninstitutionalized regime in which they are excluded from the ruling coalition, such venues do exist when there is a plurality of political institutions. Rural dwellers with weak or impartial property rights are likely to support politicians that promise greater rule of law and property security (Ansell and Samuels 2014, 8–11). They can elect representatives to the legislature that pursue legislation and funding for land titling programs. And independent judiciaries may rule in favor of greater property rights security by recognizing and formalizing the legal basis of a previous land reform, requiring the legislature and bureaucracy to provide legal protections to reform beneficiaries. This need not be a technocratic process. It can also be political and partisan as politicians use land formalization to curry favor among valued constituencies and build winning coalitions (Boone 2018).

Closing a property rights gap is particularly likely under democracy, however, when peasants are incorporated into the ruling coalition. When the executive office is freely and fairly contested, as under democracy, politicians must compete with one another regularly. This necessitates seeking broad coalitions that could directly include rural dwellers. Because peasants are direct beneficiaries of redistributive land reform programs, the inclusion of peasants in the ruling coalition under democracy generates strong incentives both for redistributing land and for granting property rights over redistributed land.

Although land redistribution itself is often foreclosed under democracy due to institutional constraints, the provision of property rights over formerly redistributed land is more politically feasible. And the incentives are strong when peasants are incorporated into the ruling coalition.

To be sure, democratically elected politicians may, like authoritarian rulers, benefit from a property rights gap. This is particularly true where clientelism is rife. After all, a property rights gap facilitates dependency on state programs and can therefore be used to cheaply swing votes in the run-up to elections as politicians pump spending on rural programs or dole out favors in rural areas. In Venezuela, for instance, the main political parties, Democratic Action (Acción Democrática, or AD) and the Social Christian Party (COPEI), strategically distributed land without titles from the 1950s–1970s and then used investment in rural infrastructure and inputs to sway the critical rural constituencies that helped win national elections (Albertus 2013).

These arrangements can sometimes be sustained for years or even decades in democracy. But they cannot be sustained forever. Untitled individuals can switch their political allegiances to politicians favoring stronger property rights without facing major retribution, protected by the secret ballot and courts. This provides incentives for new political entrants to promise greater property rights. The same is not true under dictatorship. Authoritarian regimes route survival strategies directly through them with no alternatives, making citizens less likely to deviate.

Consequently, democracies should be associated with a "property rights surplus." Aside from exceptional circumstances, democracies can extend property rights even though they are hamstrung when it comes to granting property.

Elite Presence in Legislative Chambers: The Graveyards of Property Rights Reform

The discussion in the previous section indicates that, while rare, organized opposition to land titling can surface under democracy. What circumstances might systematically facilitate the blockage of land titling under democracy that is pushed forward by a government that incorporates peasants into its ruling coalition?

The key to answering this question lies in understanding how interests are institutionally represented under democracy. Peasants that are incorporated into the ruling coalition in a parliamentary democracy will hold substantial sway in both the executive and the lower chamber of the legislature. Peasant influence over the executive under presidentialism may also translate into representation in the lower chamber, especially if, as in most of Latin America, legislative and presidential elections are held concurrently and the electoral system has a degree of proportionality. Neither of these scenarios, however, forecloses the possibility that the legislature retains a concentrated and sufficiently powerful set of land titling losers that can muster enough votes to scuttle reform. Landed elites in Latin America have historically gained outsized representation in legislative chambers and used their position to block unfavorable legislation (Albertus 2015). Losers in the extension of property rights to former land reform beneficiaries could use a position in the legislature to block land titling or legislation to secure property rights if indeed there are harmful aspects to them.

Upper legislative chambers are especially prone to elite capture. Landed elites have historically had a disproportionately large presence in upper chambers through conservative parties. Peasant-based parties that win strong electoral victories, capturing the executive and lower chamber, may not be able to vanquish oppositional forces in the upper chamber. This is made even more complicated by the fact that many upper chambers require supermajority thresholds to pass policy. Residual fractionalization in the upper chamber is indicative of the presence of oppositional forces to the executive, or at least diverse political groupings, including landed elites, that could block major policy initiatives through obstruction. This complicates passing land titling legislation that benefits peasants.

Consider the history of extending property rights to land reform beneficiaries in the Dominican Republic. The strongman Rafael Trujillo redistributed private, underutilized land to peasants between the 1930s and his 1961 assassination. He also legalized certain forms of squatting and nationalized some private sugar enterprises. But recipients of these lands did not receive formal property rights and were manipulated for political ends by the regime. The same was true when the land of Trujillo and his associates was redistributed in the early 1960s, and for land initially redistributed under the Dominican Agrarian Institute (IAD) in the 1960s and 1970s.

Land invasions and pressure for agrarian reform mounted after a 1966 shift toward partial democracy. But "the elitist politics of the past endured. The government found itself searching for detente with the landed groups; by the late 1960s, little land was being redistributed" (Stanfield 1989, 311). Remaining large landowners opposed securing the property rights of land reform beneficiaries. Doing so was off the table given the strong position of parties tied to landed elites in the Senate in particular, which was dominated by the rightist Social Christian Reformist Party from 1966 until the 1978 elections that brought full democracy to the country. As Gil (1999, 164) writes, "From the beginning of the Agrarian Reform there was a market for land inside the settlements. The successive administrations of the IAD attempted to stop this market, but it was impossible due to the political implications." Large landowners preferred an absence of titling in the reform sector so they could illegally accumulate reform-sector land at below-market prices. Once acquired, reform sector land was legalized to the new owners through official institutions such as the Land Court (Gil 1999, 165).

Extending property rights to land reform beneficiaries only began when Salvador Jorge Blanco of the Dominican Revolutionary Party was elected in 1982 following a split within the party. Jorge Blanco was supported largely by the middle and lower classes, including the rural poor (Wiarda and Kryzanek 1983, 545). Facing popular pressure to break up land reform collectives, the legislature, which was dominated by the Dominican Revolutionary Party in both chambers, passed Law 269 in 1985 permitting the creation of "associative *asentamientos*." Production in these settlements would occur in individual parcels (Stanfield 1989, 332). Formal land titling also began in this year, though it was quickly scaled back to meet the minimum tied to the tepid pace of land redistribution after the 1986 election brought large landowners back into governing coalitions and into political domination of the upper and lower chambers through an alliance with the Social Christian Reformist Party. Land titling thereafter briefly crawled along in part at the behest of international lenders such as the IMF in the wake of an economic stabilization program. This partnership, however, was also scuttled before the end of the 1980s.

There is one more institutional venue under democracy that powerful land titling losers could try to influence or capture to oppose the extension of property rights to former land reform beneficiaries: the judiciary. But the judiciary is unlikely to serve as a bulwark against extending property rights. Extending property rights to land reform beneficiaries almost uniformly occurs following the legislation of a land titling program. And because land titling protects property rights rather than violating them as with land redistribution, there is not likely to be a constitutional or statutory basis on which to strike down a land titling program. Whereas judiciaries have struck down land redistribution legislation under democracy on the basis of violating property rights in countries such as Brazil in the mid-1980s and again in the 1990s, South Africa in recent years, and Venezuela in 2004, there are few such examples of judiciaries shuttering land titling programs.

To summarize, an array of institutions under democracy provides the untitled more opportunities to populate them and to appeal to them to advance their interests vis-à-vis dictatorship. Extending property rights is particularly common when peasants form part of the ruling coalition. Aside from exceptional circumstances in which there is a concentrated set of losers to land titling and those losers capture an important veto point – typically the legislature – democracies should be able to more easily extend property rights over property than dictatorships.

Bowing to International Pressure: Granting Property Rights under Structural Adjustment Programs

So far the theory indicates that while democracies are often too constrained to redistribute land, they are much more likely than dictatorships to grant property rights to land reform beneficiaries that lack them. That is because democracies are more effective at channeling popular demands into the political system and, in the absence of strong opposition from concentrated minority groups, can respond to those demands. A "property rights surplus" should be especially likely when peasants are incorporated to the ruling coalition and when any landed elites that survived land redistribution do not have the capacity or wherewithal to organize opposition by retaining a choke hold on the legislature.

There is one more circumstance that is propitious for closing property rights gaps by granting property rights to land reform beneficiaries that lack them: external pressure from international actors in the context of major structural adjustment. Although foreign actors only occasionally intervene in land redistribution, they more frequently play a critical role in property rights reforms and must be taken into account as an independent actor separate from ruling political elites, landed elites, and the rural masses.

All countries suffer periodically from major financial, debt, banking, currency, or other economic crises. An increasingly common response in the post–WWII era has been to turn to international financial institutions such as the IMF and World Bank for assistance in the form of loans and stabilization programs. In exchange for assistance, these institutions require not only collateral but also political and economic reforms that encourage privatization, reduce the role and size of government in the economy, stoke investment (including foreign investment) and production, and protect private property rights.[41]

Pressure to strengthen rural property rights where they are weak or absent can be included in this suite of reforms. Efforts to bolster rural property rights typically come through land formalization and titling programs. In Latin America, a host of countries such as Guatemala, Mexico, and Peru conducted large-scale land titling as part of structural adjustment programs implemented in the wake of currency, debt, and banking crises that rocked the region in the 1980s and 1990s. The same transpired in much of Eastern Europe in the wake of the collapse of communism. Given an incumbent government's alternative to accepting these demands – further macroeconomic chaos that can threaten to unseat it – international lenders are often in the driver's seat to shape reforms when they are called upon.

Both democracies and dictatorships bow to this pressure, but they do so in different ways. Dictatorships accept conditionality tied to property rights reforms in order to ensure regime survival and forestall the most imminent threats that stem from popular backlash to economic crisis. Extending property rights to rural areas can weaken a regime's coercive grip on the countryside, portending greater rural mobilization and independence in the future. But the most pressing threats in rapid economic crises typically stem from cities as urban workers with the greatest capacity for collective action face the threat of unemployment and rapidly deteriorating living conditions. This is an authoritarian regime's worst nightmare. Given the severity of this threat, most authoritarian regimes will reluctantly swallow a bitter rural reform pill and strengthen rural property rights and conduct other unsavory reforms with the goal of living to see another day. To be sure, their responsiveness to foreign pressure can be ratcheted up significantly if external actors offer carrots in the form of development assistance to entice reform. But such assistance is not typically a sine qua non for reform.

Of course, authoritarian regimes that are forced to seek external assistance in times of economic crisis do not always survive. These crises can cause authoritarian regimes to crack and give way to democracy (Albertus and Menaldo 2018). This can give rise to dual transitions toward both democracy and the market, including strong property rights protections. This occurred dramatically in Eastern Europe with the demise of the Soviet Union against the backdrop of the Washington consensus and it also played out in parts of Latin America and Asia (Przeworski 1991; Haggard and Kaufman 1995).

Structural adjustment under democracy can also stir contentious internal political dynamics. These political dynamics typically differ from those under

---

[41] The nature and scope of conditions required for assistance also extend to a host of other macroeconomic policies such as trade and currency devaluation but depend on the nature of the crisis and the government requesting assistance.

dictatorship. Much of this is driven by competitive elections. A major economic crisis followed by the necessity to implement structural adjustment in order to receive international assistance is often a kiss of death to the incumbent party. Opposition parties that can credibly claim innocence in the origins of the crisis can tar incumbents with mismanagement and a trail of damaging policies. A severe economic crisis can even bring down the party system as a whole if several major parties share the blame for generating it. These dynamics unleash strong and sometimes unpredictable domestic political contestation. Opposition parties often rise to power from the ashes on promises to turn the page on old policies, to push for a better deal with international lenders, or even to eschew the policy prescriptions of international lenders.

But once they reach office, former outsiders may do an about-face and accept international assistance given the lack of appealing alternatives and armed with an electoral mandate that can outlive short-term pain (Stokes 2001). This is most likely when assistance packages are quite substantial. Dovetailing with this dynamic, domestic contestation and churn can generate greater bargaining power for democracies to win hefty development assistance to pay for property rights reforms and land titling programs. And it can cause international lenders to provide associated development assistance to help prop up a crisis-stricken democracy that is teetering in the face of popular discontent.

Regardless, democracies are less likely than dictatorships to merely accede to foreign pressure. They may demand and win substantial development assistance amid a crisis. Or the political leadership may only have the cover to bow to foreign pressure when the payoffs are quite high and can be readily observed by voters. Such assistance can then be used in part to engage in extending more secure property rights to land reform beneficiaries and other rural dwellers when property rights protection is one of the stipulations of international aid.

Four Illustrative Cases of Closing Property Rights Gaps: Nicaragua, Ecuador, Bolivia, and Mexico

To illustrate the different paths outlined above to granting property rights without further redistributing property, I briefly present how this played out in the cases of Nicaragua, Ecuador, Bolivia, and Mexico. All of these countries first conducted land redistribution under authoritarian rule while withholding property rights from land beneficiaries. Each country then traced one of four separate routes that the theory envisions will bring a close in the property rights gap.

Nicaragua, Ecuador, and Bolivia closed the property rights gap under democracy. Nicaragua did so with peasants incorporated into the ruling coalition and without landowners capturing legislative veto points. This was in part because Nicaragua was a nascent democracy with relatively few institutional constraints when it began to close the property rights gap. This enabled it to simultaneously continue land redistribution at a low level. In Ecuador, popular pressure for more secure property rights over untitled land that was redistributed under military rule generated a major land formalization program. This occurred despite the lack of a direct peasant presence in the ruling democratic coalition. Ecuador therefore demonstrates how democracy can channel popular demands for property rights into policy in the absence of significant resistance by landed groups. In Bolivia, a neoliberal government without a peasant coalitional base closed the property rights gap under pressure from the IMF and World Bank. Popular demands for land formalization aided in quickly implementing property rights reform and in receiving substantial development assistance to aid in land titling.

Mexico closed a large portion of its property rights gap in the twilight years of the PRI's dictatorship. In the wake of a major debt crisis followed by a currency crisis, it pursued land formalization as part of a series of structural reforms initiated by IMF and World Bank intervention. In acceding to the demands of foreign lenders, the PRI sought – but ultimately failed – to stave off the threat that economic crisis posed to the regime's ability to maintain political control.

Nicaragua: A Government Based on the Peasantry Closes the Property Rights Gap under Democracy

Major land redistribution in Nicaragua transpired after the Sandinista National Liberation Front (FSLN), a guerrilla group that recruited from the peasantry, violently toppled the Somoza regime in a 1979 revolution. The FSLN leadership sought to eliminate the Somoza threat and other large landowners while not risking economic instability. It immediated expropriated Somoza and his cronies' holdings – a total of 800,000 hectares in 1,500 estates – in 1979 under Decree 3 and Decree 38 (Kaimowitz 1989, 385). These were held by the state and administered by the newly created Nicaraguan Agrarian Reform Institute (INRA). The government feared that production would decline if these large, modern farms were broken up. It also worried that recipients would shift from cultivating export crops to basic crops for domestic consumption and in doing so destroy export earnings (Kaimowitz 1989, 385).

Peasant groups were dissatisfied that they had not directly received their own land from the Sandinistas. They consequently began to organize and invade private holdings. The government responded with a new agrarian reform law that was passed in 1981 via Decrees 760 and 782. The new law set landholding ceilings and subjected landowners with holdings larger than the region-specific thresholds to expropriation for underutilization, sharecropping, disinvestment, or location in an agrarian reform zone.

The ruling FSLN held elections in 1984 that led to an FSLN victory along with a democratic opening.[42] The FSLN also held a supermajority in the

---

[42] There is some disagreement about the nature of Nicaraguan democracy in the mid-late 1980s. Whereas Boix, Miller, and Rosato (2013) classify Nicaragua as a democracy, Mainwaring and Pérez-Liñan (2014) classify it as a semidemocracy prior to 1990.

legislature. With few institutional constraints, it continued redistributing land, albeit at a slower pace than prior to election. But it also became more responsive to peasant demands for stronger property rights given that peasant voters were a cornerstone of its coalitional basis.

One plank of this became a third phase of agrarian reform that expanded from its initiation in late 1983. The government shifted its focus in this phase to small individual producers given the large numbers of rural families that had either been unwilling to join production cooperatives or who lived in areas where large areas of land were unavailable for cooperatives (Kaimowitz 1989, 387–388). This pivot was induced both by peasant pressure for individual farming and by a belief that peasants would better defend their own land than cooperative land in the face of attacks by counter-revolutionary *contra* forces (Thiesenhusen 1995, 130). The government titled a large number of peasant families under this phase of reform. It also solidified the focus of land redistribution from state farms and cooperatives to individual families.

Ecuador: Democracy Channels Popular Demands to Close the Property Rights Gap

The traditional hacienda was the typical production unit in Ecuadorian agriculture until the 1940s on the coast and until the 1960s in the highland Sierra. The democratic election of President Velasco Ibarra in 1960 brought promises of land redistribution, but little action was taken after the commission he appointed to study agrarian problems encountered concerted opposition from landholding interests (Redclift 1978, 23). Opposition was particularly strong among representatives in the Senate, including the president of a regional Chamber of Agriculture, and members on executive commissions (Handelman 1980, 6).

A narrow military junta seized power in 1963 and declared a limited reform in 1964 that targeted idle lands and those worked under oppressive forms of land tenure for redistribution. A portion of these lands were titled, but redistribution outpaced titling. General Rodríguez Lara seized power in 1972 and in 1973 initiated a stricter land reform law. Land reform increased still further once another set of officers pushed Lara from office in 1976. Unlike in the 1960s, beneficiaries of land redistribution starting under General Rodríguez Lara did not receive titles to their land.

The country elected Jaime Roldós Aguilera in 1979 to head its first democratically elected government in decades. Roldós assumed office under a new constitution that replaced Ecuador's longstanding bicameral legislature with a unicameral chamber. While redistributive land reform continued (albeit at a reduced pace), the split within President Roldós' own party as well as opposition from several other parties and the Cámaras de Producción suppressed attempts by the left to strengthen agrarian reform. However, the 1980–1984 National Development Plan sought to consolidate property rights over land being used for agricultural production. For the first time since the beginning of land redistribution in Ecuador, peasants receiving land through the trailing land redistribution program received formal titles to their plots. Yearly property rights gaps were thereby eliminated starting in 1980.

Former land reform beneficiaries and other groups with informal property rights also began organizing to seek land titles with the return to democracy (Alexander 2007, 209). Groups formed cooperatives and joined in government discussions through local organizations to increase pressure (Lehmann 1986, 616). There was an indigenous uprising in 1990 and large-scale protest by CONAIE demanding the recognition of indigenous territories in the Amazon and a continuation of the agrarian reform. Some of the land reform beneficiaries partnered with CONAIE in the push to extend property rights to the broader indigenous rural community. Another indigenous uprising in 1994 succeeded in winning national recognition of the ancestral territories of indigenous communities.

In the same year, 1994, congress passed the Law of Agrarian Development, effectively ending what was by then a very tepid pace of land redistribution. The focus shifted to land titling and formalization programs in response to popular demand. Larger landholders and conservative agricultural groups came to support this demand since the country's disorganized legal tenancy framework left owners at risk for security breaches and titling disputes (Fausto 2004, 298). Property rights were therefore extended at a broad scale under a series of centrist governments beginning in the late 1990s and continuing into the 2000s to former beneficiaries of land redistribution and other groups that lacked formal titling. Titling was overseen by the National Institute of Agrarian Development within the executive branch and local officials of the Notary Public and Municipal office within the judicial branch. The property rights gap was closed by the time Rafael Correa came to office.

Bolivia: Foreign Pressure Closes the Property Rights Gap under Democracy

Beneficiaries of Bolivia's longstanding land reform that started in 1953 and ran through the 1970s did not receive land titles or secure property rights for the land that the government redistributed to them from large landowners. Titles were instead conferred to unions affiliated with the National Confederation of Peasant Workers (CNTCB), which was politically controlled by the Revolutionary Nationalist Movement (MNR) party that dominated politics in a mostly authoritarian fashion after the Bolivian revolution (Bottazzi and Rist 2012).[43] Seeking political autonomy and stronger (collective) property rights, reform-sector peasants broke off from the CNTCB in 1979 and created the CSUTCB to advance their interests. Separately, the Confederation of Indigenous Peoples of

---

[43] The MNR was a complex party that changed in character over time. But nearly all major regime type datasets classify Bolivia as authoritarian from 1953 until the late 1970s. One exception is Mainwaring and Pérez-Liñan (2014), who classify Bolivia as a semidemocracy for the brief period from 1956–1963.

Bolivia (CIDOB) initiated a push for property rights for indigenous groups with longstanding but informal ties to the land, particularly in the lowland territories (Bottazzi and Rist 2012).

Peasant pressure for both more land redistribution and greater property rights continued in the 1980s. But land redistribution ground to a halt shortly after Bolivia became democratic in 1982. A key turning point was 1985 when, facing hyperinflation, a reformed MNR under President Paz Estenssoro adopted a rigid structural adjustment program at the behest of the IMF dubbed the New Economic Policy. The emphasis of agrarian reform shifted toward land titling due to the New Agrarian Policy applied at the outset of 1986 (CNRA 1987, 12–13).[44] Bolivia began to shrink rather than grow its property rights gap for the first time since the early 1950s revolution when land redistribution began. Progress on closing the property rights gap advanced in the late 1980s, spurred in part by a major infusion of development assistance that came to exceed 10 percent of GNI by 1989. But land titling came to a halt in 1992 as the key land reform agencies were charged with corruption and their activities put on hold. Stories proliferated of elites with government connections steering land titling and public land grants in their favor.

A new wave of neoliberal structural reforms began under the government of Gonzalo Sánchez de Lozada in 1993 with the help of the IMF and World Bank to try to jolt the Bolivian economy out of a low-growth state. The World Bank partnered with Bolivia in 1993 to fund the National Land Administration Project (PNAT). Land titling resumed as part of a broad array of policies prescribed by the World Bank and IMF in exchange for loans and other aid. This dovetailed with popular pressure for greater property rights security from CSUTCB and CIDOB. Both of these groups participated in the negotiations that led up to the 1996 INRA land titling initiative and mobilized their members for a march that culminated with the passage of the law. INRA sought, among other goals, to regularize the formal titling of land to strengthen property rights. The extension of property rights to former land reform beneficiaries and other indigenous groups with informal landholding status skyrocketed under INRA. This shrank the property rights gap even more rapidly than during the late 1980s. Meanwhile, foreign development assistance to Bolivia remained very high.

Evo Morales was elected in 2005 and promised an "agrarian revolution" to expedite the process of land redistribution and the extension of titles and to uphold the INRA laws in force (Urioste 2006). But despite the 2006 passage of the Community-Based Re-Launching of the Agrarian Reform, Morales faced serious difficulties in implementing his agrarian reform plans given strong opposition from large landowners in Santa Cruz who rejected the redistribution of unproductive property. Land redistribution was essentially

---

[44] The New Agrarian Policy also encouraged the continued distribution of state-owned land, greater agricultural productivity, and the prevention of the parceling of small properties.

blocked, turning the primary focus of the land reform to titling longstanding land claims by indigenous groups and the distribution of state-owned land.

Mexico: Foreign Pressure Closes the Property Rights Gap under Dictatorship
Unlike Nicaragua, Ecuador, and Bolivia, Mexico began closing its property rights gap under dictatorship rather than democracy, albeit in the twilight years of the PRI. Like Bolivia, however, this shift came in response to foreign pressure.

Circumstances began to favor the closing of the property rights gap in the wake of the 1982 debt crisis. Mexico was shut out of borrowing in international markets and had to turn to the IMF for loans when it defaulted on its debt in 1982. In exchange, the IMF required that Mexico engage in economic adjustment and structural reform. Major reforms aside from reining in public spending included trade liberalization and privatization of key banking functions in the wake of the nationalization of the banking sector. The government also privatized several of the state-owned companies that had critical ongoing coercive leverage over land beneficiaries in the agricultural sector, including those that provided seed and fertilizer, grain storage, and marketing of coffee, sugar, and tobacco (Yúnez-Naude and Barceinas 2006, 218). It also began the elimination of the National Company of Popular Subsistences (CONASUPO) in the mid-1980s, which had supported producer prices for a host of basic crops by processing, storing, and distributing them. Land redistribution slowed to a trickle.

But as foreign investment lagged and unemployment skyrocketed, incoming president Carlos Salinas de Gortari promised a new round of structural reforms in an effort to stave off growing popular discontent by stoking economic growth. Salinas privatized the banking system in 1991–1992, deregulated the economy, initiated negotiations for the North American Free Trade Agreement (NAFTA) in 1991, and, facing imminent agricultural competition with food imports due to NAFTA, amended the constitution in 1992 to formally end land redistribution and begin a transition to complete property rights for land that had already been redistributed.

The extension of property rights occurred under PROCEDE, which was drafted under World Bank guidance beginning in 1990. As de Ita (2006, 148) writes, "Profound agrarian reform in twentieth-century Mexico began with the revolution of 1910 and ended with the World Bank." PROCEDE offered *ejidos* registration, plot delineation, and separate title to members over house plots, farm plots, and a share in the value of common lands. It allowed *ejido* lands to be sold within the *ejido* and leased to members within or outside the *ejido*. PROCEDE also recognized *ejidos* as legal bodies able to enter into contracts and joint ventures and allowed for the full privatization of *ejido* land through a two-thirds vote of the *ejido*'s General Assembly.

PROCEDE started out slowly but gained major steam in 1994 and continued at a rapid clip. This year coincided with more IMF and World Bank intervention on the back of a major currency crisis that sparked the devaluation of the peso along with a spike in inflation and capital outflows. International lenders sought rapid progress in further deregulation of the economy and privatization along with stricter bank capitalization requirements, clearer accounting standards, and other reforms.

The vast majority of *ejidos* voted to join the PROCEDE program given its advantages. By 2005, 96 percent of agricultural households had registered their land rights and 89 percent had received titles (Castellanos 2010). Among other things, receiving property titles and entering the property registry allowed land beneficiaries to take out loans against the land to make investments. This implicitly relies on a legal right to alienate land. Some *ejidos* voted to allow *ejidatarios* to leave the *ejido* for longer periods of time without losing their plots while providing for a mechanism to transfer land that was not returned to within that time frame. But few *ejidos* voted to entirely disband. In other words, most *ejidatarios* preferred some form of collective ownership and wanted the benefits of rights formalization conferred with alienability, but many did not want to actually exercise their rights to alienate their land per se.

3.5 CONNECTING THE THEORY TO THE THREE CANONICAL PATHS OF PROPERTY RIGHTS GAPS

This chapter sheds light on why countries trace each of the three canonical paths of property rights gaps over time. Figure 3.3 provides a summary of how the theory maps onto each of these canonical paths.

A country that traces Path A never generates a property rights gap over rural land. This could be because a country never redistributes land to begin with or because property rights are granted along with all land that is redistributed. The theory anticipates that the former circumstance – never redistributing land to begin with – can occur under either democracy or under dictatorship where landed elites are incorporated in the ruling coalition. The latter circumstance – redistributing land and concurrently granting property rights over that land – should be rare. Regimes that redistribute land are typically authoritarian in nature and withhold property rights from land beneficiaries. But in exceptional circumstances, a democracy is able to avoid suffocating elite institutional blockage and redistribute land at a measured scale. Such a democracy will also grant property rights to land recipients given popular demand.

More common than Path A is Path B. A country that follows Path B first generates a property rights gap in the countryside by redistributing land but withholding property rights over that land. The theory anticipates that this will typically occur under an authoritarian regime in which landed elites are excluded from the ruling political coalition.

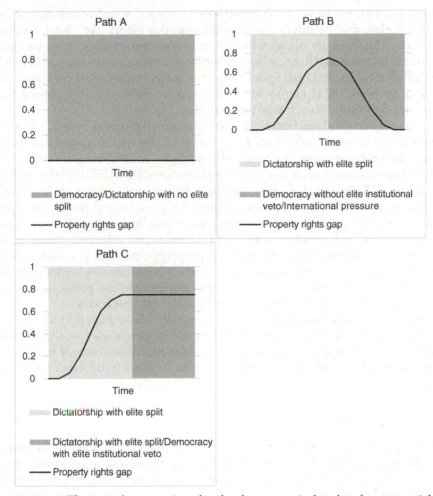

FIGURE 3.3 Theoretical expectations for the three canonical paths of property rights gaps

Note: The y-axis in each graph indicates the proportion of a country's land under a property rights gap.

A country that follows Path B later closes the property rights gap. This can happen under two broadly different circumstances. First, there may be a transition to democracy in the country. Driven by the incorporation of peasants into the ruling political coalition or simply by popular demands from land reform beneficiaries that lack property rights over their land, a new democracy will close the property rights gap. This occurs provided that there is not a residual component of landed elites with an interest in blocking the extension of property rights that have institutional position – often membership in the legislature – to do so. Alternatively, a regime, whether democratic or authoritarian, can be driven to close the property rights gap under foreign pressure. This typically occurs when a severe economic crisis forces a country to turn to international financial institutions for stabilization assistance. In these circumstances, international institutions may force a regime that presides over a large property rights gap to shore up property rights security, closing the property rights gap, in exchange for assistance.

A country that follows Path C, like one that initially follows Path B, starts by generating a property rights gap. This property rights gap is created under the same circumstances as at the outset of Path B: by an authoritarian regime in which large landowners are not integrated into the ruling political coalition. But a country following Path C does not close the property rights gap. It instead maintains it for a very long period of time. This can occur because the same regime remains in power. Once the regime hits an upper limit on land redistribution, redistribution halts, but there is no effort to grant land beneficiaries property rights. Stasis in the property rights gap in a Path C case can also occur if there is a transition to democracy but remaining landed elites or those that lost their property have a vested interest and the political clout to block the extension of property rights to land reform beneficiaries.

A country that follows Path C could *eventually* follow Path B by closing its property rights gap. Depending on the regime in power, this would require either regime change or an erosion in the institutional position of remaining landed elites. Or it would require major foreign pressure in the face of a severe crisis.

3.6 CONCLUSION

Property rights gaps in rural areas are a widespread regularity in many developing countries. Governments that attack longstanding land inequality through land redistribution often relegate a vast swathe of land beneficiaries to the informal sector. This generates a host of economic, social, and demographic distortions, not to mention resentment on the part of land beneficiaries. By outlining a theory of why some governments redistribute land without accompanying property rights over that land, this chapter provides a new framework for understanding why property rights gaps are commonplace. This chapter also offers an explanation for why some governments – typically a very different set than those that generate a property rights gap – grant property rights over formerly redistributed land without redistributing additional land.

Key to understanding these dynamics are political regimes. Authoritarian regimes tend to redistribute land from large landowners to the land-poor when their rule is not based on the coalitional support of large landowners. But these regimes also withhold property rights from beneficiaries. Democracies, by contrast, often grant property rights to beneficiaries of previous land reforms but do not redistribute any additional property on their own. This can occur regardless of the makeup of the ruling coalition under democracy. But it is especially likely when peasants are integrated into the ruling coalition and when any remaining landed elites will not be harmed by solidifying the new status quo of property rights, or if they are, do not capture key legislative veto points to block property rights reform. Foreign pressure for structural economic reform, including extending security of property rights, can also force both democracies and dictatorships to close the property rights gap when a crisis is sufficiently dire.

4

Evidence on the Rise and Fall of Property Rights Gaps in Latin America

The theory in Chapter 3 holds that political regimes, political coalitions, and external pressure are key to generating, upholding, and eliminating property rights gaps. This chapter employs the property rights gap data and coding scheme developed in Chapter 2 to empirically test whether this is the case and to what extent. The chapter focuses on Latin America in the twentieth and early twenty-first centuries.

This period in Latin America was rife with political turbulence. Political transitions in many states brought shifts from dictatorship to democracy and back again. Some countries, such as Peru and Argentina, shifted repeatedly back and forth between political regimes. These regimes varied widely in institutional constraints, modes of rule, and duration. Political elites with widely divergent support coalitions and agendas rose and fell from power. Ruling political elites at times allied with landed elites and at other times came into direct conflict with them. In some cases, peasant groups formed a cornerstone of ruling parties. Toward the end of the twentieth century, a host of Latin American countries were slammed with economic, financial, or debt crises – and in some cases all three.

This range of political and economic variation provides ideal circumstances for testing the theory in this region. It also helps in assessing the impact of alternative explanations that in more stable political environments can be difficult to reject, such as the trend in many countries outside of the region to simultaneously and slowly become more democratic while developing higher state capacity.

I find strong evidence in support of the theory that property rights gaps are generated by authoritarian regimes where the ruling coalition of political elites does not overlap with landed elites. Countries that embark on the canonical property rights gap Path B or Path C follow this path to opening a property rights gap. In contrast, property rights gaps are typically closed by democratic regimes, especially when peasants are in the ruling coalition and legislative fractionalization does not give opposition lawmakers a chance to block reform. Property rights gaps are also closed by both authoritarian regimes and democracies when countries are forced into structural adjustment programs. These circumstances drive a divergence between countries that follow Path B, closing the property rights gap, and those that follow Path C, maintaining the property rights gap.

The main results hold both in the descriptive statistics and in a host of regression models regardless of the specification of the property rights gap. The findings are also robust to accounting for prominent rival explanations and using instrumental variables estimation to account for potential endogeneity in political regime type.

This chapter ends by enumerating and testing several additional observable implications of the theory. One implication is that the typically authoritarian governments that redistribute property without rights should also undertake complementary policies such as distorting crop prices that hobble the capacity of land reform beneficiaries to succeed as independent producers. This further renders them dependent on government services and inputs and in doing so makes them more vulnerable to state coercion. A second theoretical implication is that governments that redistribute property in the rural sector but withhold property rights do so for strategic reasons: they seek to eliminate rival elites and create pliable and dependable rural constituencies. Property rights enforcement and violation in other sectors of the economy should therefore not necessarily mirror that of the rural sector. I find empirical support for both of these implications.

4.1 RESEARCH DESIGN AND MEASUREMENT STRATEGY

To examine how political regimes, the composition of ruling coalitions and opposition forces, and economic factors impact the property rights gap variables outlined in Chapter 2, it is necessary to create measures for these key independent variables. We must also identify other variables that may have an independent impact on the property rights gap. This section outlines the variables I use as part of an original panel dataset that covers all Latin American countries from 1920 to 2010.

Property Rights Gaps and Constituent Components

The main dependent variables capture property rights gaps in several ways as well as the constituent components used to construct the property rights gap variables. In terms of property rights gaps, I focus on the two main measures detailed in Chapter 2: the Yearly Titling Gap and Cumulative Titling Gap. Each of these variables is constructed using data on land redistribution and land titling. I also conduct several analyses of the determinants of the variables Land Redistribution and Land Titling on their own. Across the board, the land titling data match the theory in that they capture the titling of land allocated via land reform rather than overall titling.

Since countries have different sizes and geographical topographies, and therefore different endowments of land that may be used for agricultural purposes, each dependent variable is normalized by total cultivable land to generate comparable cross-country data.[1] Cultivable land area data are taken from the Food and Agriculture Organization (2000). The dependent variables are therefore ultimately measured as percentages of a country's cultivable land.

Table 4.1 contains descriptive statistics for the dependent variables and other variables used in the analyses. The yearly titling gap measure varies from –47.86 percent to 62.84 percent of cultivable land. The latter value corresponds to Nicaragua in 1979 when the Sandinistas expropriated the holdings of Anastasio Somoza and his cronies. The former value corresponds to Nicaragua in 1984 when the Sandinistas started granting large numbers of titles with limited property rights, mainly to squatter families that had inhabited land through land invasions that the state recognized as legitimate through land reform laws. The cumulative titling gap varies from 0 percent to 195.51 percent. The latter value corresponds to Chile at the end of Salvador Allende's rule as discussed in Chapter 2.

Figures 2.4–2.6 in Chapter 2 display detailed graphs of each of the property rights gap variables and their constituent components for every country in Latin America from 1920 to 2010.

Key Independent Variables

The first key independent variable is regime type. The theory indicates that democracies should be less likely to generate a property rights gap. I measure democracy with the Polity IV index, which ranges from –10 (least democratic) to 10 (most democratic). I use this over other measures of democracy because it incorporates information on electoral competition as well as on institutional constraints to rule, which the theory anticipates are key channels driving property rights gaps and surpluses. The Polity index is also one of the most widely used measures of democracy. I label the variable as Polity Score and scale the measure to run from –1 to 1 for ease of interpretation in the analyses that follow.

The Polity IV index contains five main components. Three are tied to the structural characteristics that govern the nature of access to executive power and the exercise of that power: the degree of competitiveness in executive selection, the extent to which executive recruitment is open to a wide range of members of society, and the extent of institutional constraints on the executive. The remaining two components capture political participation: the extent to which participation is regulated by binding rules over who can participate and when and how they can do so, and the degree to which political participation is competitive (such as via elections).

Although the Polity IV index is the main measure of regime type in the empirical analyses in this chapter, the results are also similar using other

---

[1] Results are similar using nonnormalized data.

TABLE 4.1 *Descriptive statistics*

Variable	Mean	Std. Dev.	Min.	Max.	N
Land redistribution	0.90	3.73	0	62.84	1421
Land titling	0.44	2.22	0	54.64	1387
Yearly titling gap	0.42	4.23	−47.86	62.84	1342
Cumulative titling gap	18.07	35.8	0	195.51	1648
Yearly titling gap (full PR)	0.58	4.08	−15.44	62.84	1355
Cumulative titling gap (full PR)	20.34	36.72	0	195.51	1648
Polity score	0.08	0.65	−0.9	1	1721
State capacity	0.74	0.44	0	1	1729
Rural pressure	6.26	0.73	3.23	7.79	1517
Left ideology	0.22	0.42	0	1	1694
Percent urban	22.47	15.35	0	62.26	1725
Revolutions	0.31	0.69	0	9	1613
Age of land cadaster	51.06	44.65	0	180	1729
Years of prior land conflict	6.95	8.71	0	34	1729
Years of democracy	13.79	16.52	0	71	1729
Prior land redistribution	29.63	51.94	0	257.32	1710
Prior land titling	7.36	19.13	0	155.03	1710
Prior land titling (full PR)	3.89	15.19	0	155.03	1710
Sum Polity score in region	0.4	2.03	−3.8	5.2	1702
Previous transitions to dictatorship	0.67	0.96	0	4	1729
Democracy (binary)	0.44	0.5	0	1	1729
US aid (log 2011 USD per capita)	16.37	4.58	−4.61	21.49	1216
Military regime	0.1	0.31	0	1	1317
Party linkages	−0.56	1.22	−2.99	3	1692
Party switching	9.80	7.93	0	46	1677
Landowners excluded	0.43	0.49	0	1	1680
Peasants included	0.23	0.42	0	1	1523
Upper chamber fractionalization	0.53	0.25	0	0.9	534
Structural adjustment	0.39	0.69	0	4	448
ODA (log net, % of GNI)	−0.64	1.91	−6.05	4.28	599
Agricultural prices	−0.04	0.17	−0.52	0.43	350
Bank/natural resource expropriations	0.02	0.14	0	1	1501

common regime measures. I discuss a simple binary measure of democracy that centers on political contestation later in the chapter.

The second set of key independent variables captures the composition of ruling coalitions. Although the theory anticipates a baseline relationship between regime type and the property rights gap, coalitions should condition the effects. A split between ruling political elites and landed elites under dictatorship generates strong incentives for the redistribution of land away from landed elites to rural dwellers, but without attendant property rights. These conditions should generate a large property rights gap. On the other hand, the inclusion of peasants in the ruling coalition under democracy generates strong incentives for redistributing land with property rights. Although land redistribution is unlikely under democracy, titling formerly redistributed land can indeed occur. This is especially likely if the legislature does not serve as an elite redoubt that can be used to block land titling. These conditions should close any existing property rights gap.

When ruling political elites are landed elites, are appointed by landed elites, or their rule is fundamentally materially supported by landed elites, I code Landowners Excluded as a "0"; it is otherwise coded as a "1." In this latter case, the ruling political elite is often actively avoiding alliances or significant material support from landed groups. I code Landowners Excluded using a host of country-level primary and secondary sources.[2] Landowners are excluded from the ruling coalition in 43 percent of country-years.

It is important to recall the definitions of ruling political elites and landed elites in order to best understand how the political exclusion of landowners is coded in practice. Chapter 3 defines ruling political elites as key military players and civilian politicians and important political appointees. This group is normally headed by an elected executive under democracy or a dictator or junta under autocracy. Ruling political elites share the power and organizational capacity to run the government. I restrict the focus on civilian politicians to the executive branch given its primacy in land reform initiatives. Key political appointees include those that occupy cabinet positions and the appointed leadership of the main agencies, if indeed these individuals are appointed. Top military officers may also constitute political elites – most often, though not exclusively, under dictatorship – if they are critical political players that have considerable policy influence. Chapter 3 defines landed elites as large landowners who own land as a livelihood, as a form of wealth holding, or for leisure, and who derive elevated social or economic status as a result. Landed elites often command substantial economic power through extensive landholdings and influence over rural labor markets. They seek first and foremost to maintain their land and protect their property rights.

To code the exclusion of landowners from the ruling political elite, I first examine whether ruling political elites are themselves landed elites or whether they are appointed by landed elites (for instance, if the head of state is indirectly elected by a legislature dominated by landowning interests). I code the coalitional exclusion of landowners as being absent if this condition is met. If the first condition is not met, I next determine whether landed elites provide

---

[2] See the online appendix for sources and details.

substantial financial, logistical, repressive, or other material support that fundamentally bolsters the ability of political elites to rule in office. I code the coalitional exclusion of landowners as being absent regardless of the first condition if this second condition is met. By contrast, landowners are coded as excluded if neither the first nor the second condition is met. Evidence that the ruling political elite actively avoided alliances or significant material support from landed groups aids in coding the presence of landowner political exclusion.

One particularly useful piece of information in constructing the landowners excluded variable aside from whether the executive is a member of the landed elite is the composition of the cabinet. A strong landed elite presence in the cabinet, where they take on the role of ruling political elites, signals the lack of the exclusion of landowners. One illustrative example is Argentina from 1910 to 1940, during which 40 percent of all cabinet appointments went to members of the Rural Society, the organization of large landowners (Teichman 2002, 509).

Cabinet composition aids in coding instances when landed elites are excluded from the coalition of ruling political elites but it is not deterministic. Large landowners can gain status as political elites if they are appointed to important agencies that lack cabinet portfolios or are simultaneously powerful military players that intervene directly in governing. Landed elites may also ally with political elites in more informal ways, such as through financial contributions or logistical support of key government functions such as the maintenance of order (see Albertus 2015, Ch. 2).

One example of landed elite political exclusion is Paraguay under longtime ruler and Colorado Party leader Alfredo Stroessner (1954–1989). Stroessner constructed a narrow cabinet composed primarily of military figures with few regional interests or coherent substantive economic interests (Lewis 1980, 115). Stroessner selected them on the basis of loyalty. Chapter 6 will detail another prominent example of the exclusion of landowners during military rule in Peru from 1968 to 1980. But landed elite exclusion from the ruling political elite is far from unique to military regimes. Landed elites have also faced exclusion from personalist regimes such as the Trujillo regime in the Dominican Republic and from party-based regimes such as under Castro in Cuba and the PRI in Mexico.

Elite splits also occurred in many democratic regimes where leaders were elected from political parties that excluded landed elites and then appointed ministers and agency heads within the executive largely to the exclusion of powerful landowners. Examples include Morales in Bolivia, Arévalo and Arbenz in Guatemala, Ortega in Nicaragua, and Lula in Brazil.

The coding of the variable Landowners Excluded sheds light on the construction of a second coalitional variable of interest: the inclusion of peasants in the ruling coalition. When ruling elites have peasant origins, are appointed by peasant movements, or their rule is fundamentally materially supported by peasants, I code Peasants Included as a "1." It is otherwise coded "0." As with the variable Landowners Excluded, I code the variable Peasants Included using a host of country-level primary and secondary sources.[3] Peasants are included in the ruling coalition in 23 percent of country-years.

The variable Peasants Included focuses on the political inclusion of the rural masses, and in particular those who are relatively poor. Recall from Chapter 3 that the rural masses can be quite diverse. Smallholders, renters, squatters, sharecroppers, day laborers, indigenous communities, and peons can simultaneously coexist in the rural sector of a single country. But these individuals share in common farming as a principal and direct occupation, often pursued to meet their basic needs.[4] They typically hold positions of low social status.

In a manner analogous to coding the variable Landowners Excluded, in order to code Peasants Included I first examine whether ruling political elites are themselves members of the rural masses. I code peasants as included in the ruling political coalition if this condition is met. If the first condition is not met, I next determine whether the rural masses provide substantial logistical, repressive, or other material support that fundamentally bolsters the ability of political elites to rule in office. I code peasants as included in the ruling political coalition regardless of the first condition if this second condition is met. Peasants are coded as excluded if neither the first nor the second condition is met. Cabinet composition aids in coding instances when peasants are included or excluded from the coalition of ruling political elites. But as with Landowners Excluded, cabinet composition is not deterministic of the coding of this variable since alliances between ruling political elites and the rural masses can be forged outside of cabinet membership.

In some cases, such as Bolivia and Nicaragua, social revolutions mobilize peasants to topple the state and are a central element of postrevolutionary ruling coalitions. Take for example Nicaragua in the 1980s after the Sandinista National Liberation Front, a guerrilla group that recruited from the peasantry, violently toppled the Somoza regime in a 1979 revolution. Authoritarian leaders forge crucial alliances with groups or parties that incorporate sectors of the peasantry in other cases. A military junta that ruled in the Dominican Republic in 1962–1963 did this, bringing in civilian partners to help rule that had the backing of the Dominican Revolutionary Party, which in turn drew its support in part from peasants. Elected leaders rise to office on the back of strong support from the rural masses in still other cases. This is true, for instance, of a series of Venezuelan leaders from the political party Acción Democrática.

---

[3] See the online appendix for sources and details.

[4] This is therefore a broader group than peasants per se, who typically engage in nonwage labor and make autonomous production decisions (see Kearney 1996, Ch. 3).

It is important to underscore, however, that the inclusion of peasants in the ruling political coalition does not itself imply that peasants are the dominant political force and can therefore unilaterally dictate policy. The expression of peasant political power can vary within ruling coalitions that incorporate peasants. Peasants may, for instance, be politically incorporated but still face barriers to exercising their power in certain ways due to a lack of direct access to the coercive tools of the state, obstacles to collective action, or manipulation by other coalition partners that do not inherently share their interests.[5]

The variables Landowners Excluded and Peasants Included together constitute several possible formations of ruling coalitions: large landowners and peasants can both be excluded from government, landowners can be included and peasants excluded, or peasants can be included and landowners excluded. In no instances during the period of study were both landed elites and peasants incorporated within the same ruling coalition.

The next key independent variable captures a critical factor that can mute the effect of peasant incorporation on the property rights gap under democracy. When the rural masses gain power as part of the executive ruling coalition, they do not always simultaneously win sweeping control of the legislature as well. Landed elites have historically had a disproportionately large presence in legislative chambers. This is especially true of upper legislative chambers. As the winds of political change tilt against elites, party fractionalization in the upper chamber when the rural masses are incorporated in the ruling coalition is indicative of the ability of elites and other diverse political forces to maintain a toehold in politics. This can complicate passing land titling legislation that benefits peasants – and even more so given that many upper chambers require supermajority thresholds to pass major policy reforms.

I use a measure of upper legislative chamber political fractionalization to operationalize this hypothesis. Upper chamber fractionalization also has the benefit of having greater distance from a country's democracy score than broader measures of veto points or lower chamber fractionalization. Nonetheless, alternative measures like these behave similarly to upper chamber fractionalization in the statistical analyses.

I measure Upper Chamber Fractionalization as the probability that two random draws of members from the upper chamber will be from different parties. Data are from Henisz (2002), with data updated through 2010.[6]

The final set of key independent variables capture the one remaining condition for which the theory anticipates property rights gaps are likely to be closed: under foreign pressure. A financial or debt crisis of sufficient severity

---

[5] Furthermore, while this variable is coded at the national level, there can be regional differences, whereby peasant groups from one area are more politically powerful than those from another. One example of this is postrevolutionary Mexico.

[6] To test the robustness of the findings to lower chamber fractionalization and a broader measure of veto points, I also used data updated from Henisz (2002) for these variables.

may impel a country to turn to international financial institutions for a lifeline. If this occurs when the country has an existing property rights gap, international financial institutions are likely to force the country to close it and institute property rights reforms as part of a structural adjustment program in exchange for lending support.

Dictatorships that have few electoral constraints but face the threat of popular backlash due to crisis swallow these programs hook, line, and sinker. Democracies, by contrast, have to sell structural adjustment programs to domestic constituencies. This makes them pickier about cooperating with foreign actors under pressure and can give them leverage with international lenders and donors. Property rights reforms through large-scale land titling are consequently most likely to occur during structural adjustment under democracy when international donors grant substantial development assistance to pay for property rights reforms and land titling programs. Structural adjustment should be linked to land titling in dictatorships at much more moderate levels of development assistance. This is not to say that dictatorships are not also more responsive to foreign demands for property rights reform when development assistance is dangled to them as a carrot. But they will also more readily accede to foreign pressure even in the absence of considerable assistance.

I measure the variable Structural Adjustment as the implementation of major structural reforms to financial sector liberalization in the previous five years. Data on financial reforms are from Abiad et al. (2010) and span the years 1973–2005. These authors constructed an index that is widely used and takes integer values from zero (no reform) to twenty-one (fully reformed). The index varies depending on policy changes with respect to credit controls, reserve requirements, interest rate controls, entry barriers, state ownership, policies on securities markets, banking regulations, and restrictions on capital accounts. The average score within Latin America during this period was just under nine.

The data on financial reforms capture actual policy changes. This differs from mere "stroke of the pen" reforms that shift the status quo on paper but not on the ground, generating an implementation gap like many of the adjustment policies that Van de Walle (2001) studies in the context of Africa in the 1980s and 1990s. Financial reforms in the database capture important changes to factors like credit controls, the exercise of interest rate ceilings on demand deposits, state ownership over the banking sector, and actual restrictions on international financial transactions, such as imposing multiple exchange rates on various international transactions. Many Latin American countries have undertaken radical structural adjustment reforms in recent decades, even if there has been variation in response to external pressure (Pop-Eleches 2008).

Major structural reforms are coded as "1" when the financial reform index increases by more than two points within a year. This follows the threshold that Abiad et al. (2010) use to characterize large structural reforms since they are especially consequential and relatively rare. Such large reforms constitute approximately 5 percent of the country-years that Abiad et al. (2010) include in their full dataset and 7 percent of country-years in the Latin America subsample. Structural reforms that meet this threshold are major episodes of reform that typically occur in the wake of IMF or other international lender intervention. Examples include Peru's structural reforms in the early 1990s, Chile's reforms under Pinochet in the mid-1970s, and Bolivia's reforms in 1985 and 1992. I construct a five-year moving lag of major structural reforms given that there can be a lag between the implementation of such reforms and associated external pressure on the one hand and property rights reform progress on the other hand.

I construct the variable Official Development Assistance in order to capture the potentially different conditions under which democracies and dictatorships respond to external pressure through structural adjustment. I measure development assistance using net official development assistance as a percentage of gross national income (GNI). These data are available beginning in 1976. I log this measure to normalize its distribution. Data are from the World Bank's World Development Indicators.

Control Variables Capturing Major Existing Explanations for the Property Rights Gap

The statistical analyses also include a set of control variables. The controls can be divided into two groups. The first group captures major existing explanations for the property rights gap that are described in detail in Chapter 3: government myopia or conflicting goals that compete with agriculture, ideology, and state capacity.

Myopia is difficult to measure since it relies on intentions and information. A range of evidence discussed in Chapter 3 – from the historical timing of the provision of property rights over land to the fact that some regimes created parallel secure and insecure property rights regimes – casts doubt on its explanatory power when narrowly construed. But a related alternative is more plausible: governments pursue a variety of goals and these goals can at times conflict with one another. Of particular importance during this period in Latin America were growing urban constituencies and the drive to industrialize. Some governments may have generated property rights gaps through the creation of land reform collectives, cooperatives, or land nationalization as a way to extract rural economic surplus for the purposes of managing growing urban populations that were viewed not only as the economic engines of the future but also a potential threat given the greater capacity for collective action in cities. To address this explanation, the models therefore include Percent Urban to proxy for a political and economic counterweight to the countryside that competes for preferential policies. Data are from the Correlates of War project. In other words, urbanization proxies for urban over rural importance and the power of urban interests that, if myopically attended to, could place the countryside at a disadvantage.

A second major existing explanation for the underprovision of property rights is ideology. Whether based on theories of developmental strategy, driven by an interpretation of the historical origins of landholding concentration, or coaxed by the twentieth-century geopolitical rivalry between socialism and capitalism, ideologically left-wing governments in particular may be more motivated to redistribute land but not land titles. I therefore include a dummy variable, Left Ideology, for left-wing executives. Post–WWII data are available from Huber et al. (2012). I garner pre-1945 data from the Ideology of Heads of Government dataset.

A third existing explanation for underproviding secure property rights is linked to state capacity. Some states may simply lack the administrative or infrastructural capacity to provide complete property rights in the context of land reform. Some may lack the capacity to implement land reform at all. To account for this, I include State Capacity, a time-varying measure of whether a country has conducted a comprehensive census within the previous ten years. This variable proxies for the capacity of the state to penetrate into society and conduct large-scale administrative duties. The data build from Soifer (2013) by using his data covering the period 1945–2005 and his coding rules to extend the measure temporally both prior to 1945 and up until 2010.

Additional Control Variables

The regressions also include a second set of control variables. These controls do not fit into the three major alternative explanations for the property rights gap. But they may nonetheless impact land redistribution or the granting of property rights and therefore their omission could confound the results.

I include a control for latent rural pressure from below since this may increase land reform (Thiesenhusen 1995). Rural Pressure is measured by value-added agriculture per dweller in the agricultural sector. The size of the agricultural sector is measured in millions of constant 1970 dollars and is taken from the Montevideo-Oxford Latin American Economic History Database. Agricultural population size is taken from Vanhanen (2009). This measure taps land pressure and should be lower when the amount of land and the value of agriculture are high relative to rural labor force size. I invert this measure so that higher values indicate higher land pressure and log it to normalize its distribution.

I also include several proxies for rural mobilization. Years of Prior Land Conflict measures the number of years of land-related conflict and large-scale rural protests since 1910. It captures active land redistribution demand. Data are constructed based on Albertus (2015, 43–44). As Acemoglu and Robinson (2006) indicate, popular unrest may yield concessions in the form of redistribution. I also include a measure of revolutions to tap active, broader popular threats. Revolution may result in large-scale redistribution and reduce institutional constraints to rule. Data are taken from Banks' Cross-National Time-Series Data Archive.

I include several variables capturing a country's background historical circumstances that can condition later policymaking. Age of Land Cadaster is a control for the number of years that a country has had a land cadaster with mapping coverage of at least 75 percent of the national territory. An older cadaster signifies greater capacity to delimit and determine ownership over land. Data are constructed from D'Arcy and Nistotskaya (2017). Years of Democracy controls for the duration of prior democratic spells. This can impact property rights security that later regimes face.

Finally, the models include Prior Land Redistribution and Prior Titling. These variables are measured as the cumulative percentage of land redistributed or land titled, respectively, since 1920. Further land redistribution or land titling may be influenced by past activity. A regime that follows a redistributionist dictatorship that opens up a large property rights gap may be less likely to redistribute land and more likely to title it if there is little land left to distribute but high demand for property rights.

4.2 POLITICAL AND ECONOMIC PATTERNS TIED TO THE PROPERTY RIGHTS GAP

Figure 4.1 begins by displaying the cumulative titling gap and democracy score for each country in Latin America. The figure is split up by whether a country followed canonical property rights gap Path A, Path B, or Path C. Recall that land redistribution and land titling diverge as the cumulative titling gap grows, with redistribution outpacing titling. As the cumulative titling gap shrinks, titling outpaces redistribution. When the cumulative titling gap is flat and positive, a government is maintaining an existing property rights gap. Two circumstances could occur when the titling gap is flat and takes the value of zero: either there is no land redistribution and no land titling or land redistribution and land titling are equivalent.[7]

The countries in Figure 4.1 that follow Path B or Path C show that land redistribution typically outpaces titling under dictatorship when the democracy index is low. A commonly used threshold separating democracy from dictatorship on the Polity IV index is a score of 0.6. Of course, not all dictatorships generate property rights gaps under these conditions. Property rights gaps are especially likely to grow when landowners are excluded from the ruling coalition. Examples include Bolivia after the 1952 revolution, Peru under military rule in the early 1970s, and Nicaragua after the Sandinistas took power in 1979.

---

[7] There are, however, no cases of large-scale land redistribution with equivalent titling.

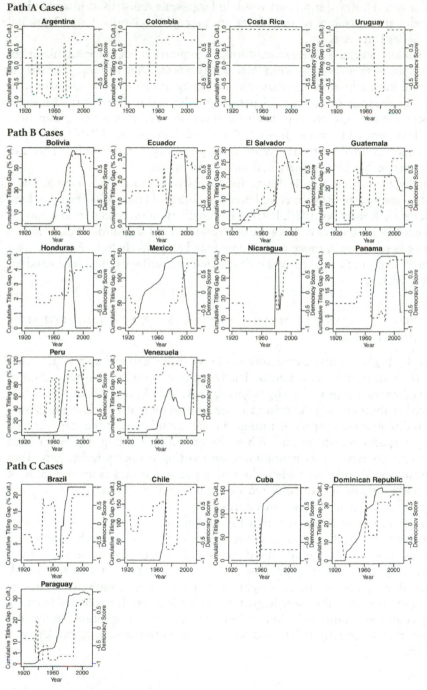

FIGURE 4.1 Cumulative titling gaps and democracy, 1920–2010
Note: Solid lines indicate the cumulative titling gap as a percentage of cultivable land.
Dashed lines indicate a country's democracy score.

The Path B and Path C cases in Figure 4.1 contrast with the Path A cases in countries do not generate a property rights gap. Several of the countries that followed Path A were largely democratic during the period. Examples include Colombia and Costa Rica. But in each Path A case, episodes of dictatorship, if they occurred at all, failed to line up with ruling coalitions in which landed elites were sidelined from power. For instance, military regimes in Colombia in the mid-1950s and Uruguay between the 1970s and mid 1980s did not rule to the political exclusion of landed elites.

The property rights gap tends to close, by contrast, under democracy. Figure 4.1 indicates that there are very rarely significant shifts in property rights *just before* democratization. The property rights gap instead tends to close *after* democracy is instituted. But there are several notable exceptions, such as Peru under Fujimori in the mid-1990s and Mexico under the PRI in the mid-1990s.[8] Both of these property rights gap closings occurred in the wake of major structural adjustment and financial reform programs that brought in international lenders that pressured for stronger property rights through cadastral and property registry reform as well as land titling. These patterns in the raw data are consistent with the theory.

Figure 4.1 also displays several Path C cases in which property rights gaps persisted for years despite the introduction of democracy. This transpired in the Dominican Republic, Brazil, and Paraguay. Other elements of the theory beyond regime type again help to explain these cases.

Consider the Dominican Republic. Successive democratic governments since the 1980s largely sat on an existing property rights gap that was created by the longtime dictator Rafael Trujillo and several subsequent governments. This was not merely due to lack of popular pressure for greater property rights from land reform beneficiaries. Some former land reform beneficiaries organized themselves by the 1980s into a National Council of Agrarian Reform Beneficiaries and petitioned the country's land reform agency to issue them land titles. In 1985, under popular pressure, Congress broke up collective farms and converted them into associations whose members held individual parcels (Meyer 1989, 1226). This enhanced property rights, and indeed, the government began a land titling program in this year that granted property rights to some land reform beneficiaries for the first time. This dovetailed with pressure from the IMF for economic reforms at the outset of a structural adjustment agreement. But titling was slow. Most land beneficiaries still lacked property titles and continued to pressure for them.

---

[8] Chile is likely another exception. The evidence available suggests that it began closing its property rights gap under Pinochet and continued under democracy. But as Chapter 2 indicates, land-titling data that can be linked to former land reform is hard to come by for Chile. Consequently, Chile is missing property rights gap data beginning in the mid-1970s and it drops from the empirical analyses for this period.

Several factors stymied a swift delivery of more complete property rights since the mid-1980s. The first was the political power of remaining large landholders. These landholders benefited from the absence of titles because it enabled them to illegally accumulate reform-sector land at below-market prices (Gil 1999, 164–165). Landholding interests, initially through an alliance with the Social Christian Reformist Party, captured positions in the Dominican Republic's legislature, including the upper house. This enabled them to block property rights initiatives that would contravene their interests. Second, the government prematurely cancelled its agreements with the IMF twice in the 1980s and eventually charted its own path out of economic crisis. This undercut the leverage that international lenders could have used to exert more pressure for property rights reforms. Meanwhile, clientelism and vote buying were rife under the country's new democracy and the major political parties all played the game. This further undermined translating popular preferences into policy.

But these forces could not hold out forever under democracy. The government began new efforts to close the property rights gap as the country's democracy consolidated and foreign pressure for titling ramped up. Leonel Fernández reformed land courts, passed a property registration law, and created new regulations to strengthen cadastral measurement after his election in 2004. This occurred shortly after the collapse of the presence of the Social Christian Reformist Party, one of the parties tied most closely to landholding interests, in the Senate. Fernández also won financial support in 2007 from the Inter-American Development Bank to strengthen land tenure security and land administration. The property rights gap consequently began to close further in the 2010s after the Figure 4.1 graphs end.

Like the Dominican Republic, the property rights gap in Brazil that was created under dictatorship persisted for years after its transition to democracy. This is in spite of property rights reforms beginning in the 1980s that granted new land redistribution beneficiaries property rights, ensuring no new yearly property rights gaps and an end to the growth of the cumulative property rights gap. It is also in spite of the growth of a well-organized social movement, the Landless Workers' Movement, that pushes for both land access and land tenure security for peasants.

The political position of large landowners and a lack of effective foreign pressure played a permissive role in initially ignoring a fix for Brazil's military-era property rights gap, similarly to the Dominican Republic. Many large landowners survived the military's land redistribution and joined forces through the Rural Democratic Union (UDR) to limit further redistribution under Brazil's 1988 constitution (Payne 1992). These landowners remain one of Brazil's most powerful congressional blocs, known as the *bancada ruralista*. They have used a barrage of lawsuits and illicit means such as organizing violent paramilitary groups to defend their property and appropriate land from weaker actors that lack secure property rights (Albertus et al. 2018; Bruno 2003). This was made easier by Brazil's notoriously fragmented coalition politics and society after democratization (Weyland 1996). Until the rise of the Workers' Party in the 2000s, which has close ties to the Landless Workers' Movement, there was no decisive actor or political party to take the initiative vis-à-vis closing the property rights gap.[9]

At the same time, Brazil did not experience the same breadth of structural adjustment as some other countries in Latin America since the 1980s. Periodic economic crises in Brazil have invited pressure from international lenders for reforms tailored to specific economic policies. But the sheer size of Brazil's economy and domestic market has shielded it to a greater degree from broad-based international pressure for sweeping policy reforms that could include issues like property rights reforms that address problems from decades hence.

The Workers' Party took up the mantle of property rights reform upon sweeping into Brazilian politics at the national stage in 2003. It won substantial funding in 2005 from the Inter-American Development Bank to start systematically registering untitled land and linking plots to a rural land cadaster. This included land formerly redistributed during the military's rule. But initial progress on titling in the former land reform sector was slow and hard to distinguish from broader land titling. Data on land titling in Brazil are therefore missing starting in 2005 in Figure 4.1. Nonetheless, the initiation of the closing of Brazil's military-era property rights gap in 2005 was an important political development, and one anticipated by the theory.

Paraguay differs from the Dominican Republic and Brazil in that it transitioned to democracy later and in less significant fashion. The authoritarian-era Colorado Party continued to win the presidency until 2008 despite the fact that the longtime dictator Alfredo Stroessner was toppled in 1989. And it continued its dominant position as the largest party within both houses of congress up until the present. Given how large landowners entrenched themselves within the party over time, especially after Stroessner's personalist stripe of authoritarian rule ended, it is no surprise that they have opposed most efforts to close the property rights gap. Remaining property informality represents an opportunity for large landowners to appropriate land and labor cheaply or illicitly and to push agricultural policy in their favor given the obstacles that untitled smallholders currently face to organizing to advance their interests (Viladeslau 2003). Paraguay's relatively low levels of indebtedness simultaneously enabled it to largely avoid pressure from

---

[9] Fernando Henrique Cardoso, Brazil's first strong two-term president since its 1985 transition to democracy who was in office from 1995 to 2002, did pass the Land Information and Registry Law (Law 10,267) in 2001. This law sought to increase property rights security via a new cadaster and land regularization, as well as to integrate the rural cadaster with the public land registries. It was not targeted specifically at the land reform sector and did not make significant progress until Cardoso had left office.

TABLE 4.2 *The yearly property rights gap by key theoretical conditions*

Regime type	Condition	Average yearly titling gap (%)	Total observations
Dictatorship	–	0.72	894
	Landowners excluded	1.62	415
	Landowners not excluded	–0.06	473
	During structural adjustment	–2.18	17
	No structural adjustment	1.44	49
Democracy	–	–0.17	448
	Peasant coalition and high upper chamber fractionalization	2.94	59
	Peasant coalition and low upper chamber fractionalization	–1.74	24
	During structural adjustment	–0.91	56
	No structural adjustment	–0.90	207

Note: Democracies are defined as regimes with a Polity IV index score of 0.6 or greater; dictatorships have a Polity IV index score of 0.5 or lower. High upper chamber fractionalization is coded when fractionalization exceeds 0.58, the median of this variable; otherwise, fractionalization is coded as low. The variables used to define the other conditions are defined in the text.

international lenders for major structural reforms that could have included property rights reforms during Latin America's debt crisis and in the 1990s.[10]

Paraguay elected its first non-Colorado president in over 60 years, Fernando Lugo, in 2008. Lugo built a political coalition that included rural peasants. He garnered Inter-American Development Bank funds to begin a program in 2011 to regularize rural property rights. But he was impeached in a controversial and bitterly partisan fashion by the Colorados in 2012.

Table 4.2 presents the relationships between another important metric of the property rights gap – the yearly titling gap – and the full set of key explanatory variables in the theory in tabular form. The table divides country-years in the dataset into bins that correspond to different conditions where the theory anticipates the yearly property rights gap to be relatively high or low.

Consider first that, as Table 4.1 indicates, the average yearly titling gap across the dataset is 0.42 percent of cultivable land. That this value is positive reflects the fact that some countries that created property rights gaps have yet to close them. Looking across regime type, dictatorship is associated with positive yearly property rights whereas democracy is linked to negative yearly property

---

[10] Paraguay entered its first IMF program in 2003. The country was already rebounding from a recession at the time. The government's position in initiating the program enabled it to have more control over structural reforms, which it mostly limited to economic reforms. The World Bank had a series of programs in the country in the 1980s and 1990s but eventually pulled back due to unsatisfactory progress on economic and governance reforms.

rights gaps. Yearly property rights gaps are particularly high under dictatorship when there is a coalitional split that excludes landed elites from the ruling political elite. Yearly property gaps are otherwise close to zero. Yearly property rights gaps are large and negative under dictatorship under one condition: in the wake of major structural economic adjustment. Note that because data on structural adjustment programs are only available since 1979, the data are sparser in these categories.

The bottom half of the table turns to democracy. Yearly property rights gaps among democracies are particularly negative when peasants are incorporated into the ruling coalition and upper legislative chamber fractionalization is relatively low. The gaps are positive when upper chamber fractionalization is high. This latter raw statistic contrasts with theoretical predictions, but subsequent analyses demonstrate that it does not hold up when introducing control variables, country fixed effects, and time trends. Like dictatorships, democracies tend to close property rights gaps more quickly during structural economic adjustment programs. But these programs have a much more muted effect on democracies than on dictatorships.

These bivariate relationships on the whole provide support for the main theoretical arguments in Chapter 3. However, a host of other factors may also influence property rights gaps. Ignoring these factors may confound the inferences that are drawn from the basic bivariate patterns in the data.

4.3 STATISTICAL ANALYSES OF THE PROPERTY RIGHTS GAP

I next conduct a series of regressions to more rigorously examine empirical support for the theory. The regressions that examine the titling gaps employ ordinary least squares (OLS) models. They address heteroskedasticity, serial correlation, and contemporaneous correlation using Driscoll-Kraay standard errors with a Newey West adjustment for serial correlation. I employ tobit models when the dependent variable is Land Redistribution or Land Titling since these variables are left-censored at zero. The tobit models address heteroskedasticity and serial correlation by clustering standard errors by country.

All of the models include linear, quadratic, and cubic time trends to control for common shocks and secular trends in land titling and land redistribution. Cold War pressures and global conditions during the 1960s and 1970s were more conducive to autocratic rule and import substitution industrialization strategies that favored industrial interests and supported land redistribution. Conditions shifted by the 1980s and 1990s toward support of democratization and neoliberal property reforms. These trends were correlated with broad shifts in political regimes and political coalitions in the region, first to greater dictatorship and the political exclusion of large landowners and then toward democracy and the inclusion of landowners. Time trends therefore help to guard against the possibility of attributing a causal role to the impact of political regimes or political coalitions on the titling gap that instead reflects secular shifts due to other factors like development trends, popular ideas regarding what constitutes full property rights, or Cold War–era policies such as foreign aid or Kennedy's 1961 Alliance for Progress (Kapstein 2017).[11]

Political Regimes and Competing Existing Explanations

The first set of regression analyses seeks to highlight the baseline relationship between political regimes and the property rights gap and to put this relationship into context against the other major existing explanations for the underprovision of property rights: conflicting state goals that compete with agriculture, ideology, and state capacity. Demonstrating that political regimes can help account for the property rights gap even after taking into account these alternatives will provide the groundwork for subsequently examining in more detail how and when regimes matter for property rights gaps in terms of the political coalitions they empower, the political constraints that they may face, and how they manage property rights when confronting challenging economic circumstances.

This first set of analyses proceeds in three steps. It begins by examining determinants of the yearly titling gap and cumulative titling gap. In a second step, it turns to the constituent components of the property rights gap: land redistribution and land titling. It then examines potential endogeneity between political regimes and property rights gaps in the final step.

Figure 4.2 presents the findings for the main variables of interest: democracy, percent urban, ideology, and state capacity. The figure presents the estimated coefficients for these variables along with 90 and 95 percent confidence intervals. Each row of the figure represents the findings from a different regression. Figure 4.2 does not present the coefficients from the additional control variables discussed previously. However, with the exception of prior land redistribution and prior titling, the other controls are not consistently strong predictors of property rights gaps.[12] The complete results are in Appendix A at the end of the book.

The first eight rows of Figure 4.2 present the main coefficients from regressions that examine the yearly titling gap and the cumulative titling gap as outcomes. These regression models employ OLS and include country fixed effects to control for unobserved heterogeneity that could drive a titling gap and be correlated with political regimes. For instance, initial geographic endowments could have impacted property rights protection, institutional quality, and land concentration (Engerman and Sokoloff 2002), later impacting land redistribution or titling.

Rows 1–4 focus on partial property rights gaps. The regression used to generate the results in Row 2 drops country-years that witnessed neither land redistribution nor land titling. It therefore separates two circumstances: country-years where there is no land redistribution and no land titling, and country-years where land redistribution and land titling are equivalent. Both of these would yield a yearly titling gap of zero. Yet the former observations may be characteristically different

---

[11] The results are also robust to including country-specific time trends.
[12] Unsurprisingly, prior land redistribution is generally positively linked to property rights gaps and prior land titling is negatively linked to property rights gaps.

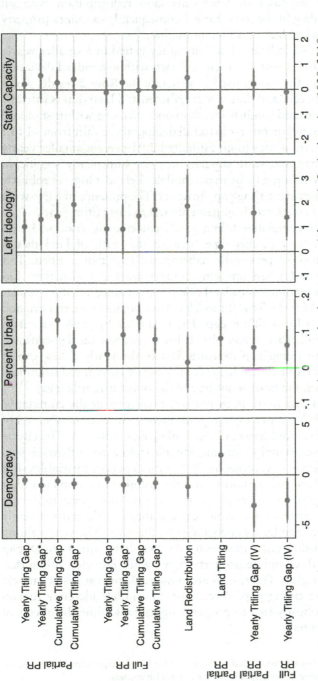

FIGURE 4.2 Political regimes and competing existing explanations for the property rights gap in Latin America, 1920–2010

Note: Figure presents the point estimates, 90 percent confidence intervals (thick lines), and 95 percent confidence intervals (thin lines) for the variables indicated from a series of regressions where the dependent variables are indicated in the rows on the left. Additional coefficients are estimated but not displayed.

* Selected observations are dropped. Rows 2 and 6 drop observations where there is no land redistribution or land titling. Rows 4 and 8 drop observations where there has been no previous land redistribution or land titling since 1920.

from the latter, for instance if there is no demand for redistribution or titling. Importantly, there are *no cases* of large-scale land redistribution with an equivalent amount of titling in the data. Row 2 consequently examines property gaps that are different in size but not different in kind.[13]

The results in Rows 1–2 indicate that democracy is tied to a smaller yearly titling gap. This is consistent with the theory. A two within-standard deviation increase in democracy in the model used to generate the Row 2 results yields a smaller yearly gap between land that is redistributed and land that is titled by 1.16 percent of cultivable land (slightly less than one-third of a within-standard deviation). Moving from full dictatorship to full democracy, a shift from –1 to 1 on the democracy scale, translates to an estimated 2.01 percent smaller yearly titling gap. Percent urban and state capacity are not statistically significant predictors of the yearly titling gap in these models. Left ideology is robustly and positively tied to the yearly titling gap, however. The presence of a left-wing executive is linked to an estimated 1.34 percent larger yearly titling gap.

Rows 3–4 turn to the cumulative titling gap. Democracy is associated with a smaller titling gap in Row 3, this time between the stock of land that is redistributed and the stock of previously redistributed land that is titled. This effect strengthens in Row 4 when dropping country-years in which there has been no previous land redistribution or land titling activity since 1920 for similar reasons as those outlined for the Row 2 model. A two within-standard deviation increase in democracy yields a titling gap that is smaller by 0.96 percent of cultivable land in Row 4. This model also helps to address the left-censored nature of the cumulative titling gap measure. Unlike the yearly titling gap in which titling of formerly redistributed lands could outpace current redistribution, generating negative values, the same is not true of the cumulative titling gap.[14]

Ideology and percent urban are both positive predictors of the cumulative titling gap in Rows 3–4. A ten percentage point increase in a country's level of urbanization is linked to a 0.62 percent larger titling gap in Row 4. The effects of state capacity, however, remain indistinguishable from zero in Rows 3–4.

Rows 5–8 replicate Rows 1–4, respectively, but the dependent variables shift to differences between land redistribution and the granting of complete rather than partial property rights. Complete property rights are empirically more rare than partial property rights in Latin America. But they should most strongly undermine the dependence of land beneficiaries on the state. The yearly titling gap and the cumulative titling gap variables for the complete property rights gap only consider titling with complete property rights while ignoring titling that grants partial property rights. The results are similar. Democracy is negatively tied to the creation of a titling gap. Percent urban and left ideology remain positively and mostly robustly tied to property rights gaps while the effects of state capacity remain muted.

---

[13] Results are similar dropping cases where redistribution and titling are equivalent and positive.
[14] The results for the cumulative titling gap are similar using tobit models.

Rows 9 and 10 examine the constituent components of the property rights gap: land redistribution and land titling. These models therefore speak to the question of whether the findings for the property rights gap may be driven by one rather than both of its components. These regressions employ tobit models given that the outcome variables are left-censored at zero. Because tobit models suffer bias when using unit-level fixed effects, these models introduce region fixed effects for Central America, the Caribbean, the Andes, and the Southern Cone.[15]

The coefficient on democracy is negative and statistically significant in Row 9. A two within-standard deviation decrease in democracy yields more land redistribution by an estimated 1.3 percent of cultivable land (roughly one-third of a within-standard deviation). Left ideology is also associated with more land redistribution. The effects of urbanization and state capacity, by contrast, cannot be distinguished from zero.

Democracy has an opposite and slightly larger effect on land titling in Row 10. This is as anticipated. A two within-standard deviation increase in democracy yields more land titling by an estimated 2.29 percent of cultivable land (roughly one within-standard deviation). Percent urban is tied to more land titling. And left ideology loses its statistical significance, as expected.

Rows 9–10 together suggest that the relatively unconstrained regimes with the greatest capacity to deliver equalizing reforms through property redistribution are the same regimes that are least likely to grant rights over that property. By contrast, democratic regimes with more institutional pluralism clean up their mess, titling but not redistributing.

The final two rows of Figure 4.2 examine whether the results are robust to accounting for potential endogeneity. Reverse causality could drive the findings if a greater property rights gap prompts landowners and other key actors to install a favorable but institutionally unconstrained dictator. A property rights gap could also simply further erode institutional constraints and representativeness in an existing regime's rule. On the other hand, large landowners that are threatened by land redistribution and a widening property rights gap could push for greater institutional constraints to rule via a negotiated pact for democracy that protects their interests.[16] It is thus unclear a priori whether reverse causality inflates or works against the empirical estimations.

I conduct an instrumental variables analysis to address endogeneity concerns. A valid instrumental variable must satisfy the exclusion restriction: its effect on the dependent variable should work exclusively through the potentially endogenous right-hand-side variable of democracy. I identify two instrumental variables that, theoretically, should only affect the property rights gap in this indirect manner.

---

[15] See Albertus (2015) for how these regions are defined.
[16] For more elaboration of this logic as well as examples, see Albertus (2017) and Albertus and Gay (2017).

I follow empirical research on the determinants of democracy in order to capture exogenous variation in democracy. The first instrument is the sum of the Polity score of countries in a given country's neighborhood. This follows research on the diffusion of political institutions. The logic is that democratic regimes are more likely to emerge and survive in an environment where there are a greater number of democracies (Gleditsch and Ward 2006). I use the sum of a country's previous transitions to dictatorship as a second instrument. Many authors have documented persistence in regime cycling whereby previous democratic breakdowns are harmful for pluralistic politics (for example, Przeworski et al. 2000). Crucially, and conditional on the assumption that one of the excluded instruments is exogenous, statistical tests of the overidentifying restrictions suggest that these instruments satisfy the exclusion restriction and are thus valid ways of capturing exogenous variation in democracy.

Row 11 reports the main coefficients of interest of the second-stage results from a regression in which the yearly titling gap capturing the partial property rights gap is the dependent variable. Figure 4.2 does not report the coefficients on the instruments from the first-stage regression, where democracy is the dependent variable. But those results conform to theoretical expectations. The sum of the Polity score of countries in the region is strongly positively tied to democracy whereas previous transitions to dictatorship is strongly negatively tied to democracy. Furthermore, the F-statistic is 14.48 in the first stage, above the commonly used threshold of ten separating strong from weak instruments.[17]

The Row 11 results confirm the other results displayed in Figure 4.2. Democracy is negatively tied to the partial property rights gap. Percent urban and left ideology are again positively tied to the partial property rights gap as in previous models. Importantly, a Hansen-J test of the overidentifying restrictions returns a chi-square of 0.49 (p=0.48); it therefore fails to reject the hypothesis that these instrumental variables are exogenous conditional on the validity of one instrument. The magnitude of the democracy variable in Row 11 increases vis-à-vis the OLS estimates displayed in Rows 1–8. This suggests that the failure to account for possible endogeneity leads to an underestimate of the effect of democracy on the titling gap. One potential reason is offered earlier: a widening property rights gap could actually induce large landowners to push for greater institutional constraints to rule.

Row 12 again analyzes the yearly titling gap, but now turns to the complete property rights gap as the dependent variable. The underlying regression model uses the same instruments as for Row 11. The coefficients on the instruments are strong and in the expected direction.[18] The second-stage results again support

---

[17] See Staiger and Stock (1997).

[18] The F-statistic is 16.11 in the first stage. Furthermore, the Hansen-J test of the overidentifying restrictions fails to reject the hypothesis that these instrumental variables are exogenous (p=0.12) conditional on the validity of one instrument.

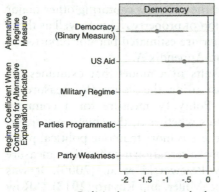

FIGURE 4.3 Political regimes and the property rights gap when accounting for alternative explanations

Note: Figure presents the point estimates, 90 percent confidence intervals (thick lines), and 95 percent confidence intervals (thin lines) for the regime type variable from a series of regressions that are similar to the Row 1 specification of Figure 4.2, but diverge in the ways indicated in the rows on the left. Additional coefficients from these regressions are estimated but not displayed.

the previous results: democracy is a strong predictor of the complete property rights gap. The same is true of urbanization and ideology.

Alternative Explanations for the Finding on Political Regimes

The results displayed in Figure 4.2 establish a robust baseline relationship between political regimes and the property rights gap. This is consistent with a principal component of the theory laid out in Chapter 3. At the same time, Figure 4.2 indicates that leftist ideology and conflicting state goals that compete with agriculture, which typically rear their head as cities rise as a political counterweight to the countryside, also typically play an important role in driving property rights gaps.

There remain, however, several possible alternative explanations for the link between political regimes and the property rights gap in Figure 4.2. If confirmed, these other explanations would suggest a different interpretation of the results that are not entirely consistent with the theory.

Figure 4.3 presents the key findings from a series of regression models that explore these alternative explanations. The figure presents only the estimated coefficients for the relevant democracy measure along with 90 and 95 percent confidence intervals. Each row of the figure represents the findings from a different regression. All of the underlying regression models used to construct the figure are similar to the Row 1 specification of Figure 4.2, which uses the yearly titling gap and the partial property rights measure as the dependent variable. This is the most relevant year-over-year property rights gap measure given the historical prevalence of partial over complete property rights in Latin America.[19] Coefficients for the variables capturing other major existing explanations for the underprovision of property rights as well as those for the additional controls discussed earlier are estimated but not reported in Figure 4.3. The full results are presented in Appendix A.

Row 1 of Figure 4.3 presents the results of a model that examines the sensitivity of the regime type results to using the Polity IV measure of democracy. This model substitutes the Polity IV measure for a common binary measure of democracy that captures whether (i) the chief executive is elected; (ii) the legislature is elected; (iii) there is more than one political party competing for office; and (iv) there is political alternation in office. This measure was initially constructed and coded by Przeworski et al. (2000). It was subsequently revised and updated by Boix, Miller, and Rosato (2013).[20] Row 1 of Figure 4.3 indicates that this binary measure of democracy, like the Polity IV measure, is negatively associated with a yearly titling gap. Shifting from dictatorship to democracy on this measure yields a smaller yearly gap between land that is redistributed and land that is titled by an estimated 1.21 percent of cultivable land.

Rows 2–5 of Figure 4.3 return to the main Polity IV measure of democracy and test the robustness of this variable when sequentially adding in a series of additional control variables that could account for the link between regime type and the property rights gap.

Row 2 examines the robustness of the democracy variable to accounting for influence from the United States. Recall that the time trends should pick up broad shifts in foreign influence across the region to a degree. But country-level and time-varying influence, particularly via US aid, may also impact land redistribution or land titling. Foreign aid, and especially President Kennedy's Alliance for Progress, helped finance land reform offices and studies of land reform need (Kapstein 2017). It also sought to prop up favorable political regimes – especially, though not exclusively, democracies. US aid made up the bulk of foreign aid to Latin America during this period (Lapp 2004). Only later during episodes of structural economic adjustment did international donors and lenders come to play a more important role.

The regression model underlying the Row 2 results introduces a control for log US aid per capita in constant 2011 dollars. Data are taken from the US Agency for International Development's "Greenbook" dataset and are available since 1945. Foreign Aid is negative and statistically insignificant. This is perhaps not surprising given that only a small amount of US aid actually went to land reform (Lapp 2004). Meanwhile, the coefficient on Democracy remains negatively tied to yearly property rights gaps.

---

[19] Results are largely similar using the yearly titling gap with full property rights.
[20] These authors add one additional criterion for a regime to be coded as democratic: that at least half of the adult male population is enfranchised.

Rows 3–5 examine other important characteristics of polities that could be correlated to regime type and drive the findings: whether a regime has military or other origins, the degree to which governments are clientelistic or programmatic, and whether political parties are strong or weak. Data on the military origins of regimes, or alternatively personalist or single party origins when a regime is authoritarian, are binary measures from Geddes, Wright, and Frantz (2014). Data on party programmaticness and the strength of political parties are from the V-Dem database. The programmaticness variable measures the main form of major political party linkages to their constituencies and is scaled to be continuous. It varies from entirely clientelistic (–3) to entirely programmatic (3). Party strength is measured as the percentage of members of the legislature that change or abandon their party between elections.

Democracy remains a negative and statistically significant predictor of the property rights gap in Rows 3–5, whereas the coefficients from these additional variables are consistently statistically insignificant. This supports the argument that regime type per se is key for driving a property rights gap.

Ruling Coalitions, Crises and External Pressure, and the Property Rights Gap

The findings in Figures 4.2 and 4.3 indicate that political regimes directly impact the property rights gap. But the theory when fully specified also points to additional driving mechanisms: the composition of political coalitions and external pressure in the face of structural economic adjustment. First, consider political coalitions. Land redistribution should be more likely when powerful landed elites are excluded from the ruling coalition. This generates incentives for landowners' political rivals to attack and destroy them – a task more easily accomplished under dictatorship when landowners have little recourse to institutional safeguards to block redistribution. These conditions, however, do not increase the likelihood of titling. They should consequently be tied to a greater property rights gap.

On the other hand, the inclusion of peasants in the ruling coalition under democracy generates incentives for both redistributing land and extending property rights. Institutional constraints typically prevent land redistribution under democracy. But the same is not true of titling formerly redistributed land provided that the legislature does not enable elites to block such a policy. These conditions should therefore close an existing property rights gap.

Finally, property rights gaps are likely to be closed when a financial or debt crisis strikes and forces a country to turn to international financial institutions for a lifeline. These institutions have historically demanded property rights reform in exchange for lending support. Dictatorships readily accept these conditions to survive and forestall popular backlash. The more contentious process of structural adjustment under democracy often means that democracies will only respond to foreign pressure for property rights reforms and land titling programs when they have access to high levels of development assistance to help pay for such programs.

I test these hypotheses in two steps. I first examine the generation of large property rights gaps through land redistribution and the growth and maintenance of these gaps. I then examine support for the theoretical claims regarding the closing of property rights gaps.

Following Property Rights Gap Paths B and C: Opening and Maintaining the Property Rights Gap

Figure 4.4 presents the main findings from a series of regressions that use land redistribution, the yearly titling gap, and the cumulative titling gap as dependent variables. Because the focus is on opening, growing, and maintaining property rights gaps, the figure presents the estimated coefficients and confidence intervals for the key variables that the theory links to these outcomes: democracy, landowners excluded, and an interaction between these variables. Each row of Figure 4.4 represents the findings from a different regression where the dependent variable is listed on the left. Coefficients for the control variables – the same set used in the analyses underpinning the Figure 4.2 results – are estimated but not reported in Figure 4.4. The full results are in Appendix A.

As the theory anticipates, Row 1 of Figure 4.4 indicates that the exclusion of landowners from the ruling coalition is tied to more land redistribution. Land redistribution increases by an estimated 3.26 percent of cultivable land when landowners are excluded from the ruling coalition and the democracy index is 0. This value corresponds to dictatorship. The interaction between landowners

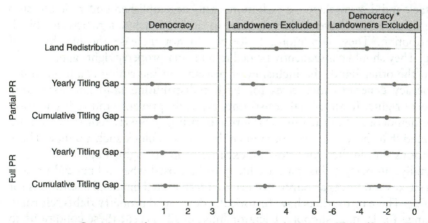

FIGURE 4.4 Opening and maintaining property rights gaps: The effects of political regimes and ruling coalitions

Note: Figure presents the point estimates, 90 percent confidence intervals (thick lines), and 95 percent confidence intervals (thin lines) for the variables indicated from a series of regressions where the dependent variables are indicated in the rows on the left. Additional coefficients are estimated but not displayed.

excluded and democracy indicates that as a country's level of democracy increases, the coalitional exclusion of landowners has a more muted impact on the property rights gap. Land redistribution is entirely eliminated at the highest levels of democracy even when landowners are excluded from the ruling coalition. This finding is consistent with the findings from Figure 4.2.

The uninteracted democracy term in Row 1, interpreted as a county's level of democracy when landed elites are included in the ruling coalition, is statistically insignificant. This is again consistent with the theory: when large landowners are politically powerful within the ruling coalition, they can block land redistribution regardless of the level of democracy. Reform will simply be dead on arrival to the executive.

Figure 4.5 plots the marginal effect of the exclusion of landowners from the ruling coalition on land redistribution as the democracy index varies in order to facilitate the interpretation of the Row 1 results. Using the Row 1 coefficients, the marginal effect of an elite split on land redistribution is positive until the democracy index exceeds 0.9, which is close to the maximum for this variable. It is only statistically distinguishable from 0 at the 95 percent level, however, until the democracy index reaches 0.5. While elite splits are positively linked to land redistribution, their effect on land redistribution therefore declines as a country's level of democracy increases. The absence of landed elites from the top echelon of executive power cannot prevent them from stalling reform through other venues such as the legislature in countries that meet the threshold of democracy at 0.6 and above.

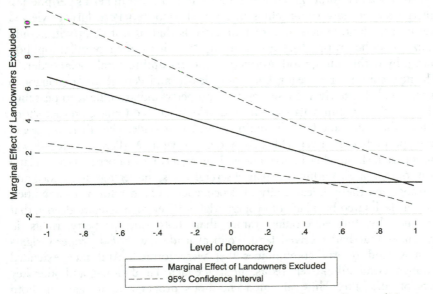

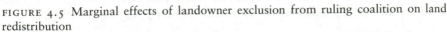

FIGURE 4.5 Marginal effects of landowner exclusion from ruling coalition on land redistribution
Note: The y-axis indicates land redistribution as a percentage of cultivable land.

Rows 2–3 of Figure 4.4 turn to examining how regime type and the political exclusion of landowners impact the yearly and cumulative property rights gaps. These rows examine property rights gaps using the partial property rights measures. Ruling coalitional dynamics operate on the property rights gaps in the same way as for land redistribution. The exclusion of landowners from the ruling coalition under dictatorship is strongly linked to growing the property rights gap through yearly titling gaps and through maintaining larger cumulative property rights gaps. Democracy, by contrast, is not associated with growing or maintaining a large property rights gap whether large landowners are politically excluded from the ruling coalition or not.

Rows 4–5 examine property rights gaps on an annual and cumulative basis using the complete property rights measures. The results are similar to those displayed in Rows 2–3. The uninteracted term for democracy, however, gains statistical significance in these models. But the estimated coefficients are substantively weak. For instance, increasing a country's democracy score by one-quarter of the democracy index from 0.5 to 1 – a significant jump – yields an increase in the yearly titling gap of less than 0.5 percent of cultivable land.

The findings displayed in Figure 4.4 echo the Chapter 3 discussion of the generation of property rights gaps in Mexico and Peru. Both postrevolutionary Mexico and military-ruled Peru in the 1970s were highly authoritarian countries. Mexico's ruling coalition was heterogeneous and spanned the rural – urban divide but it largely excluded traditional landed elites that had held sway prior to the revolution – especially those from central and southern Mexico. Peru's military regime was run by junior military officers that had mostly been born and raised in middle- and lower-middle-class families in Peru's peripheries. Furthermore, the new ruling elites in both Mexico and Peru largely viewed powerful large landowners as threatening rivals that, if not dealt with, could organize to either topple the government or at least turn popular opinion against it by withholding food production and disrupting rural social order.

The new authoritarian regimes in both Mexico and Peru therefore sought to eliminate landed elite rivals by seizing their property and granting it to peasants. But both of these regimes also sought to develop their economies, prevent short-term food shortages, and limit disruption in the countryside. They therefore began granting property collectively (Mexico) and in cooperatives (Peru) in a top-down, authoritarian fashion while intervening in the everyday lives of beneficiaries in land reform communities. Within the span of several years, the regimes in Mexico and Peru recognized the political utility of dependency in land reform communities, which was facilitated by a lack of property rights. They then acted to deepen that dependency by further eroding rather than bolstering property rights in communities that had received land. Political leaders withheld property rights from new land reform communities that were formed. And they extended government domination over credits, inputs, de facto landholding, and other key aspects of rural life. This generated enormous property rights gaps in both countries and led them definitively away from property rights gap Path A.

Contrast the cases of Mexico and Peru with a Path A case such as Colombia that never opened up a property rights gap. Colombia was a democracy for most of the period between 1920 and 2010. But during periods of authoritarianism, the ruling coalition incorporated landed elites. This foreclosed the political incentives for opening a property rights gap.

Colombia was effectively an oligarchy with limited enfranchisement until the 1930s. Power rotated between Liberals and Conservatives in the early twentieth century. But both parties incorporated contingents of large landowners and therefore had limited incentives for land redistribution (Zamosc 1986).[21] Land reform instead centered on the distribution of vacant national lands to settlers. Landowner domination survived the turn to democracy in the 1930s and through the 1940s. Partisan conflict spun out of control in the late 1940s and early 1950s as a period of conflict known as *La Violencia* spread across the country. Both traditional parties openly supported the military's seizure of power in 1953 in order to reestablish order. But they later united to help overthrow ruling General Rojas Pinilla after he sought to increase his power and build a populist support base (Palacios 2006, 132). Liberals and Conservatives joined forces to reestablish democracy through the National Front agreement. This was a political pact in which these parties agreed to rotate power and exclude other parties over the subsequent 16 years (Zamosc 1986, 15–16).

The National Front unity government passed the Social Agrarian Reform Act in 1961, which also established Colombia's land reform agency. Leaders were wary of the example of the recent Cuban revolution and faced the real threat of insurgency with the formation of peasant "independent republics" and new communist guerrilla groups such as the FARC and ELN in the mid-1960s. But the power of large landowners in government kept the focus of land reform on the distribution of public land over private land. Land redistribution was measured and consisted mostly of selective purchases from the private sector for transfer to peasant beneficiaries. Beneficiaries received land titles and registration with their plots.

The only time Colombia's ruling coalition excluded landed elites to a substantial degree was during the Lleras Restrepo administration (1966–1970). He was supported by an alliance of some sectors of the bourgeoisie and also attempted to broaden his popular base of support to peasants (Zamosc 1986, 47–51).[22] Lleras Restrepo promoted peasant organization, tried to establish a direct corporatist link between the peasantry and the state, and sought to increase land redistribution. But his policy efforts were thwarted by the resistance of large landowners from both parties that used their positions in the legislature and judiciary to scuttle reform

---

[21] This is true even during López Pumarejo's (1934–1938) rule during the "Liberal Hegemony" when he implemented the "Revolución en Marcha" (see also LeGrand 1986).

[22] Zamosc (1989, 114–115) argues that this was in part to undercut the rise of populism in cities and to support the expansion of industry by gaining the political support of peasants, and perhaps even to build a rural base of electoral support for a future presidential bid after the end of the National Front.

(Dugas 2000, 91). Landowners within the subsequent administration of Misael Pastrana were decisive in squelching more radical attempts at land reform. Landowners struck an agreement with politicians in 1972 under the Chicoral Pact to halt further attempts at land redistribution (Albertus and Kaplan 2013).

Where Property Rights Gap Paths B and C Diverge: Closing the Property Rights Gap

The results displayed in Figure 4.4 and the discussion of Mexico, Peru, and Colombia provide strong support for the theory's predictions regarding how coalitional dynamics and regime type drive the opening and maintenance of property rights gaps. But are the theoretical predictions regarding the full range of factors that act to drive down or eliminate the property rights gap similarly borne out in the data?

Property rights gaps are closed by granting property rights to the beneficiaries of land redistribution that never received property rights over their land. Figure 4.6 therefore presents the main findings from a set of regression models that use land titling as the dependent variable. The figure presents the estimated coefficients and confidence intervals for the key variables that the theory links to closing the property rights gap. In a departure from Figures 4.2 and 4.4, however, each box in Figure 4.6 represents a different regression. The rows associated with each box represent the findings for the variable indicated. The sample used in each regression is indicated above each box. As previously, coefficients for the control variables – the same set used in the analyses underpinning the Figure 4.2 and 4.4 results – are estimated but not reported in Figure 4.6. Full results are available in Appendix A.

The results in the first box of Figure 4.6 indicate that political regime type rather than the position of large landowners vis-à-vis the ruling coalition drives land titling. Democracy is associated with higher levels of land titling in this model. Increasing a country's democracy score by one-quarter of the democracy index from 0.5 to 1 yields more land titling by an estimated slightly greater than 1 percent of cultivable land on an annual basis. Decreasing a country's democracy score from –0.5 to –1 yields less land titling by 1 percent of cultivable land. This contrasts with the land redistribution findings in Row 1 of Figure 4.4, in which the coalitional exclusion of large landowners is an important factor in driving redistribution.

The first findings in Figure 4.6 are reflected in the case of Ecuador, which was discussed at the end of Chapter 3. Ecuador created a National Development Plan that sought to consolidate property rights over land being used for agricultural production quickly after its return to democracy in 1979. The residual small-scale redistribution program that was a remnant of authoritarian-era legislation slowed to a trickle. The beneficiaries of this program began receiving formal land titles for the first time in the face of peasant organization at the local level. This persisted for nearly two decades regardless of whether landed elites and peasant groups were excluded from the ruling coalition or not. The property rights gap was then effectively closed

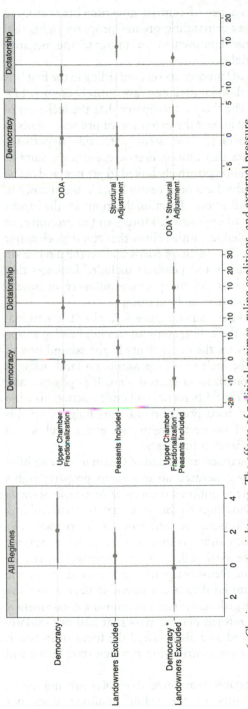

FIGURE 4.6 Closing property rights gaps: The effects of political regimes, ruling coalitions, and external pressure

Note: Figure presents the point estimates, 90 percent confidence intervals (thick lines), and 95 percent confidence intervals (thin lines) for the variables indicated. Each box presents estimates from a different regression model. The dependent variable in all models is land titling. The sample is indicated above each box. The first model includes all regimes; the second and fourth are restricted to democracies (observations where the democracy score is 0.6 or greater); the third and fifth are restricted to dictatorships (observations where the democracy score is less than 0.6). Additional coefficients are estimated but not displayed.

beginning in the late 1990s under a series of centrist governments that faced burgeoning rural popular movements demanding greater property rights that dovetailed with the desire of large landowners to mitigate the negative consequences of insecure property rights.

But the null effect of the exclusion of landowners on land titling in the first box of Figure 4.6 does not imply that coalitional dynamics are entirely unimportant for closing the property rights gap. The theory anticipates that the inclusion of peasants in the ruling coalition should impact the extension of property rights to those that lack them under democracy. Consistent with this hypothesis, the second box of Figure 4.6 indicates that among democracies in the sample, including peasants in the ruling coalition is positively linked to greater land titling by approximately 5 percent of cultivable land on a yearly basis in the absence of upper legislative chamber fractionalization. Fractionalization in the upper chamber is indicative of the presence of oppositional forces to the executive, or at least diverse political groupings, including landed elites, that could block major policy initiatives through obstruction. The negative coefficient on the interaction between upper chamber fractionalization and peasants included indicates that upper chamber fractionalization counteracts the positive influence of having peasants incorporated in the ruling coalition on land titling.

To facilitate the interpretation of these results, Figure 4.7a plots the marginal effect of the inclusion of peasants in the ruling coalition on land titling as the democracy index varies. This figure uses the coefficients in the second box of Figure 4.6. The marginal effect of the inclusion of peasants on land titling is positive until upper chamber fractionalization exceeds 0.6. It is positive and statistically distinguishable from 0 at the 95 percent level until fractionalization reaches 0.35. Therefore, while peasant incorporation into the ruling coalition is positively linked to the granting of property rights, its effect declines as a country's upper chamber fractionalization increases.

The case of Nicaragua that was discussed at the end of Chapter 3 exemplifies this finding. The Sandinistas initially generated an enormous property rights gap after forcibly seizing power from the authoritarian ruler Anastasio Somoza in 1979 by redistributing large landholdings to the peasantry but withholding property rights. But 1984 elections brought a shift toward democracy. The ruling Sandinistas then became much more responsive to growing peasant demands for stronger property rights. After all, peasant voters were a crucial cornerstone of its political coalition. Democracy muted the capacity of the Sandinista government to redistribute land to a considerable degree, but the party held a supermajority in the legislature. The government consequently began titling large numbers of land reform beneficiaries that had not initially received property rights over their land and also shifted the focus of its much smaller land redistribution program from distribution through state farms and cooperatives to individual families.

The third box of Figure 4.6 indicates that these dynamics are unique to democracy. The inclusion of peasants in the ruling coalition does not

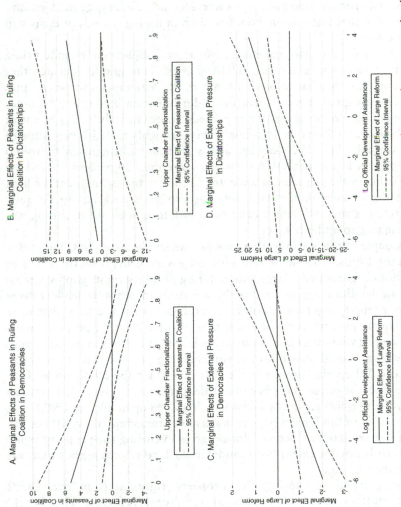

FIGURE 4.7 Marginal effects of peasant inclusion in ruling coalition and external pressure on land titling

Note: The y-axes indicate land titling as a percentage of cultivable land.

necessarily translate into greater land titling under dictatorship regardless of upper chamber fractionalization. This null effect may also indicate the lesser value of land titles in a regime where the rule of law and therefore property rights protection is weak. Figure 4.7b plots the marginal effect of peasant inclusion on land titling as regime type varies. The graph confirms these null findings.

Boxes four and five of Figure 4.6 turn to testing the final set of theoretical predictions regarding the effects of structural adjustment on land titling. Box four indicates that structural adjustment under democracy in the absence of any official development assistance has no discernible impact on closing the property rights gap through land titling. Democracies are not more amenable to extending property rights in the face of structural adjustment when they are forced to go it alone. The interaction term between structural adjustment and development assistance, however, is positive. Democracies engage in more land titling provided that international donors pitch in during periods of crisis and structural reform.

Figure 4.7c plots the marginal effect of structural adjustment on land titling as official development assistance (ODA) varies. This graph indicates that development assistance has to be significant to tilt democracies to act in times of crisis. The marginal effect of structural adjustment on land titling becomes positive when development assistance exceeds approximately 1.75 percent of GNI (slightly over 0.55 on the log scale). This is roughly the 75th percentile of the ODA variable. The effect only becomes statistically distinguishable from 0 at the 95 percent level when ODA surpasses more than 20 percent of GNI – a very high value. Although there is some imprecision in the estimates at the high end given the sparsity of the data, this suggests assistance has to be quite substantial for structural adjustment to translate quickly into closing the property rights gap under democracy.

One example of this scenario that was previously discussed in Chapter 3 is Bolivia in the 1990s. A string of authoritarian governments from the 1950s to 1970s in Bolivia generated a large and enduring property rights gap by seizing large private landholdings and redistributing them to peasants while vesting beneficiary property rights with politically affiliated peasant unions that were controlled by the government. The first serious effort to close the property rights gap came several years after democratization in the mid-1980s in the context of a rigid IMF-sponsored structural adjustment program that the government adopted to halt hyperinflation. For the first time since the 1950s under IMF policy pressure, the government began to title former land reform beneficiaries and the property rights gap inched down. Titling sped up in the late 1980s with a major infusion of foreign development assistance that crept above 10 percent of Bolivia's gross national income. But progress in closing the property rights gap halted with a major corruption scandal in the land reform agency that was decades in the making.

Bolivia returned to closing the property rights gap in the 1990s following another wave of neoliberal structural reforms. The World

Bank helped to design a new land administration framework that included titling as part of another infusion of development assistance. This coincided with growing peasant pressure for greater property rights. It resulted in a new land reform agency (INRA) and a titling initiative that made rapid progress in closing the property rights gap despite the lack of formal peasant incorporation into the government. The fact that much of the restructuring was funded externally – net official development assistance to Bolivia exceeded 10 percent of GNI at the time – smoothed its domestic reception. In addition to World Bank funding and technical support, the Inter-American Development Bank as well as the governments of Canada, Denmark, the Netherland, Sweden, and the United States helped to fund INRA and its land titling efforts.

Box five of Figure 4.6 examines the effects of structural adjustment on land titling under dictatorship. In contrast to democracies, structural adjustment under dictatorship is positively tied to land titling when log ODA is zero, which translates into 1 percent of GNI. This is the 60th percentile of ODA in the data. Dictatorships are therefore more directly responsive to the demands of international lenders for greater property rights protection when crisis hits. The conditions of structural adjustment appear to be close to sufficient for dictatorships to extend property rights through titling. But more development assistance can speed the process. The positive and statistically significant interaction term in box five of Figure 4.6 points to this. The magnitude of the interaction term is large, indicating that marginally more development assistance has a greater impact on land titling during structural adjustment under dictatorship than under democracy. The graph in Figure 4.7d bears this out: the marginal effect of structural adjustment on land titling becomes positive in dictatorships at lower levels of ODA than in democracies and the slope of the line is also steeper.

Mexico's elimination of the property rights gap under PROCEDE is a case in point. Chapter 3 details how, starting in the early 1990s toward the end of the PRI's authoritarian rule, Mexico made an effort to close the property rights gap by extending secure property rights to former land reform beneficiaries. The country was engaging in major structural economic reforms at the time and experiencing foreign pressure tied to the debt crises, NAFTA negotiations, and a currency crisis. Development assistance alone never became significant enough to spur land titling – it never exceeded 0.12 percent of GNI and was substantially lower on average from the 1980s through the 2000s. But the PRI feared the social consequences of economic crisis and unemployment and adopted a remarkably widespread range of reforms that contravened longstanding party economic policy in order to access international borrowing and attract increasingly important foreign investment. The apogee of land titling in Mexico ultimately coincided with a local maximum in development assistance to the country.

Analyzing Major Efforts to Close the Property Rights Gap through Survival Analyses

The Figure 4.6 analyses capture annual fluctuations in land titling as part of the effort to close property rights gaps. These analyses therefore investigate which conditions are most – or least – associated with significant annual extensions of property rights over land that lacks such rights. An alternative and complementary modeling approach is to focus on "the beginning of the end": when cumulative property rights gaps finally begin to close in a meaningful way. Are the conditions most conducive to embarking on tackling an existing property rights gap similar to those that account for the most significant reductions in property rights gaps?

I estimate a series of Cox proportional hazards models that calculate the "risk" of a property gap closing in order to examine this question. In a typical survival analysis, one measures the time to failure as a function of some observed or experimental factors (for instance, the time between initial lung cancer treatments to relapse as a function of smoking). Here, I examine the time it takes for a property rights gap episode to "fail" through the significant closing of the gap.

Of course, closing a property rights gap entails the existence of one to begin with. This analysis therefore focuses on countries that follow canonical property rights gap Path B or Path C. Countries that followed these paths opened up a property rights gap at some point. It is worth underscoring that survival models take into account right censoring, which is an important consideration given that some property rights gaps – those that follow canonical Path C – are ongoing. These gaps could close in the future but had not done so as of the end of the sample period.

One advantage of such an analysis is that it boils down the closing of the property rights gap to an intuitive and important outcome: a major effort to close the gap. This occurs at maximum once for each country that generates a property rights gap. Such an analysis, however, lacks the degree of granularity that the models used to generate Figures 4.4 and 4.6 exploit. Fifteen countries in the region generated a cumulative property rights gap during the period of analysis. Only ten – the countries that followed canonical Path B – made major progress in largely closing it. One Path C case, the Dominican Republic, made some progress closing the property rights gap in the 1980s but then halted. Because there are a small number of "failures" in which the property rights gap starts to shrink, statistical analyses will be relatively less powerful, making it difficult to account for the wide range of factors that can lead property rights gaps to inch down or up on a yearly basis.

I therefore use a simple approach to this analysis. I focus on each of the main theoretical predictors of the closing of the property rights gap in turn: regime type, external pressure in the face of structural adjustment, and the position of peasants in the ruling coalition under democracy.

I code the initiation of a property rights gap when at least 1 percent of a country's cultivable land has been redistributed without attendant property rights. The clock starts ticking from that moment. Governments can move to close the property rights gap, open it further, or retain an existing gap. I code "failures" in terms of a major effort to close the property rights gap, calculated as a reduction of at least 5 percent of the existing property rights gap in the span of three years.[23]

Figure 4.1 indicates that most cumulative property rights gaps tend to shrink fairly quickly once they begin to shrink at all. But there are exceptions. Consider the Dominican Republic. The cumulative property rights gap took a step down in the Dominican Republic in 1985. It shrank by 5.3 percent but then remained static in subsequent years.[24] The reduction occurred when, facing popular pressure to break up collective farms that had been previously established by the Dominican Agrarian Institute for land reform beneficiaries, Congress passed Law 269 to subdivide these lands into individual parcels (Meyer 1989). But the government retained other redistributed land under state ownership or otherwise withheld titles from former beneficiaries. The only other Path C case that chipped away at its property rights gap in the dataset was Paraguay. However, the property rights gap there only barely inched down in a fashion that was neither appreciable nor sustained.

Because no country in this sample generates more than one cumulative property rights gap, I pool the data to exploit both between and within variation. Robust standard errors are clustered by country to address heteroskedasticity and any intragroup correlation within countries.

Figure 4.8 presents the results. Each graph presents survival rates from a separate Cox proportional hazards model according to a key theoretical parameter linked to the closing of the property rights gap. I lag these variables by one period in order to capture conditions that prevailed as the property rights gap shrank. Curves that decline more quickly indicate that a particular condition is associated with a more rapid closing of the property rights gap.

Figure 4.8a examines a first key hypothesis that flows from the theory: that a country's regime type should impact the closing of a property rights gap. I again use the Polity IV index to measure regime type. Figure 4.8a plots two survivor functions for the property rights gap. The first captures estimated time to closing the property rights gap under democracy. The second captures estimated time to closing the property rights gap under dictatorship.[25] Consistent with the theory,

---

[23] Results are similar choosing a higher threshold of 10 percent. In Guatemala and Venezuela, property rights gaps were closed somewhat episodically rather than smoothly. The first year to reach the threshold for closing the property rights gap in Venezuela is 1981. In Guatemala, I code the year for reaching this threshold as 2002 in accordance with the second episode of closing. This is because the first significant reduction is due not to closing the property rights gap through providing property rights but rather through the quick return of a portion of redistributed lands to their original owners. This was an exceptional case that is different theoretically from the main focus here.

[24] Results are similar when eliminating the Dominican Republic as an episode of reducing the property rights gap and focusing strictly on the Path B cases.

[25] I use the median scores for democracy and dictatorship in the sample, with countries at or above a Polity score of 0.6 considered democracy. The median Polity score among democracies in the sample is 0.8 and the median Polity score among dictatorships is –0.3.

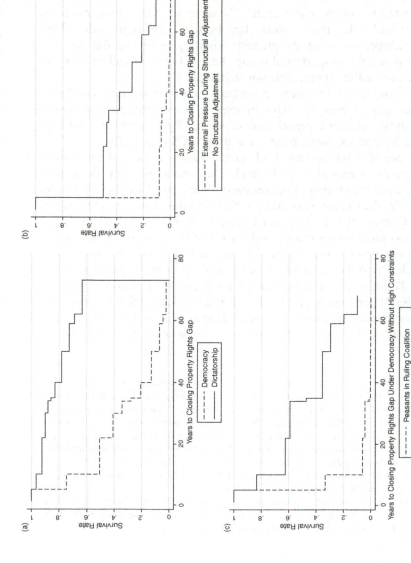

FIGURE 4.8 Survivor plots for time to closing a property rights gap

(a) Property rights gap survivor rate by regime type

(b) Property rights gap survivor rate by presence of external pressure during structural adjustment

(c) Property rights gap survivor rate in democracies without high political constraints by presence of peasants in ruling coalition

Note: These graphs of survivor rates are produced by estimating Cox proportional hazard rates of closing the property rights gap according to the key factor indicated in each graph.

democracies are predicted to make major efforts to close the property rights gap much more rapidly than dictatorships (p<0.01). It is rare for a democracy to preside over a property rights gap for a long time without addressing it.

Figure 4.8b examines a second important theoretical prediction: that external pressure during structural economic adjustment will force the closing of a property rights gap. This dynamic should operate on both democracies and dictatorships, even if they may respond in somewhat different ways. I use the same measure of structural adjustment as earlier in the chapter: the implementation of major structural reforms to financial sector liberalization in the previous five years. Again as the theory anticipates, external pressure during structural adjustment prompts rapid effort to close the property rights gap (p<0.05).

Figure 4.8c displays the results of a third theoretical prediction: that among democracies, property rights gaps are particularly likely to be closed when peasants are incorporated into the ruling coalition and opposition lawmakers do not have an institutional venue that they can rely on to block reform. The analysis relies on the same measure of peasant incorporation in the ruling coalition as previously. However, unlike with the panel data analysis earlier in the chapter, the small number of "failures" in which the property rights gap starts to shrink along with the restriction to democracies makes the data too sparse to estimate the role of upper chamber fractionalization alongside peasant incorporation. I instead turn to a broader measure of overall political fractionalization that serves as an institutional constraint to policymaking. Data for the measure are similarly drawn from Henisz (2002) and capture the number of independent branches of government with veto power over policy along with the distribution of preferences among the actors that inhabit these branches.[26] To operationalize the third theoretical prediction, I limit the analysis to observations of democracies that do not face high political fractionalization.[27] Again the results are consistent with the theory: peasant incorporation into the ruling coalition under democracy is conducive to closing the property rights gap when high political constraints do not enable an entrenched opposition to block such a policy (p<0.10).

4.4 OBSERVABLE IMPLICATIONS: COGNATE POLICIES OF RURAL CONTROL AND STRATEGIC RURAL TARGETING

The results so far support the core predictions of the theory advanced in Chapter 3 regarding the conditions under which property rights gaps are likely to be forged or eliminated. But the theory also implies several additional observable implications that have not yet been tested.

---

[26] The variable is PolconIII.
[27] I rely on the Boix, Miller, and Rosato (2013) data to classify regimes as democratic. There are too few observations to gain precise estimates using a Polity IV index cutoff of 0.6 or above to define democracy. I define high political fractionalization as PolconIII values at or above 0.5, which is roughly the 90th percentile of this variable among democracies in the sample.

Cognate Policies of Rural Control

One implication of the theory is that the typically authoritarian governments that redistribute property without rights should also undertake cognate policies that hobble the capacity of land reform beneficiaries to succeed as independent producers. This will render land reform beneficiaries even more dependent upon government services and thereby more vulnerable to state coercion. In other words, the political returns to underproviding property rights in the land reform sector can be supercharged if governments double down with other policies that weaken the autonomy and independence of rural dwellers.

The first box of Figure 4.9 presents the results of a regression model that examines whether the same political conditions conducive to the generation of a property rights gap – authoritarian government and a ruling coalition that excludes large landowners – also yield unfavorable distortions to crop prices for agricultural producers. Creating policy distortions to prices while withholding land titles would leave land beneficiaries with little room to chart an independent course.[28] The regression uses as a dependent variable Agricultural Prices, measured as a country's nominal rate of assistance (NRA) to total agriculture. The NRA is the production-weighted percentage by which domestic producer prices are above or below the border price of like products. It varies between negative one (when prices are reduced to zero) and any positive value (by which percentage prices are increased). Nominal Agricultural price data are available over the period 1955–2007 from Anderson and Valenzuela (2008). They are the most comprehensive and systematic data on agricultural prices available. Nonetheless, only eight Latin American countries have coverage in the dataset.[29]

The NRA measure covers a wide range of agricultural commodities and is not limited specifically to export commodities. Nominal rates of assistance are estimated for more than seventy different agricultural products in order to construct the measure. This coverage represents approximately 70 percent of the gross value of agricultural production in the countries in the database.

The first model displayed in Figure 4.9 is estimated via OLS using Driscoll-Kraay standard errors with a Newey West correction for serial correlation. It includes the same controls as those discussed previously and used in the models to produce Figure 4.2. The complete results are also in Appendix A.

The results are consistent with the theory. Dictatorship is associated with the suppression of agricultural prices, but only when large landowners are excluded from the ruling political coalition. The findings are consistent with Bates' (1981) influential argument in the context of sub-Saharan Africa that rulers penalize

---

[28] Unfortunately, systematic data on other relevant cognate policies such as the provision of agricultural credits and support for insurance markets are not available in a similar way to data on agricultural prices. Chapter 8, however, introduces a rough classification of agricultural credit and other input support for major cases of land reform around the globe.

[29] The countries covered by the dataset span property rights gap Paths A, B, and C: Argentina, Brazil, Chile, Colombia, the Dominican Republic, Ecuador, Mexico, and Nicaragua.

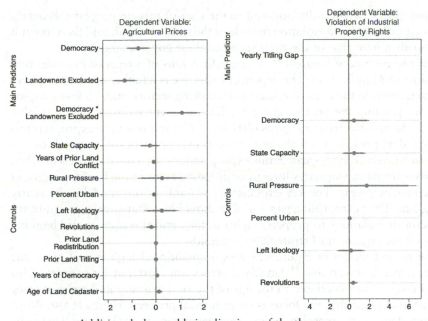

FIGURE 4.9 Additional observable implications of the theory
Note: Figure presents the point estimates, 90 percent confidence intervals (thick lines), and 95 percent confidence intervals (thin lines) for the variables indicated. Each box presents estimates from a different regression model. The dependent variable for each model is indicated at the top of the figure. Country fixed effects are controlled for via a within transformation in both models. Constants and time trends are not shown.

rural areas by distorting crop prices given the higher costs of urban collective action. But the findings add an important addendum: rural areas can avoid unfavorable crop price distortions when politically powerful landowners can either gain a foothold in the ruling coalition or push for institutional protections to resist policies that run counter to their interests. This occurs less frequently in Africa relative to Latin America in good part because, given different tenure relations and land – person ratios, large landowners in Africa have not historically been as powerful an elite group as in Latin America (see Albertus 2015, Ch. 8).

Strategic Targeting the Rural Sector

A second implication of the theory is that governments that redistribute property without property rights do so for strategic reasons tied to crushing rival elites and creating pliable and dependable rural constituencies. These governments are neither simply kleptocracies that seek to steal from the rich across the board to line their own pockets, nor they are merely run by ideologues that are broadly opposed to the idea of private property. Property rights enforcement and violation outside of the rural sector should therefore not necessarily mirror that of the rural sector in these governments.

The second box of Figure 4.9 presents the results of a regression model that examines this implication. The dependent variable is whether or not there were expropriations in the natural resource or banking sectors under a given regime episode spanning the year in question. Data on expropriations are available from 1930 to 2008 from Albertus (2015c).[30] Natural resource expropriations are coded as present when the government expropriates oil, mineral, or gas firms in a given country-year. Bank expropriations are coded as present when the government expropriates foreign or domestic firms in the banking sector in a given country-year. The key explanatory variable in this model is the yearly titling gap. The yearly titling gap variable should be a statistically insignificant predictor of violations to property rights in the natural resources and banking sectors if the argument of strategic titling holds.

The second model in Figure 4.9 uses a conditional logit model given the binary dependent variable.[31] Standard errors are clustered by country. This model drops controls related to the age of the land cadaster and years of prior land conflict given that the focus is on industrial property rights. It also drops previous democratic experience given that democracy is not hypothesized to be tied to incremental (lack of) expropriation in the industrial sector in the same way as democracy is tied to greater land titling over time.

The results support the notion of the strategic granting or withholding of property rights over land. The yearly titling gap is a far from statistically or substantively significant predictor of violations to industrial property rights. The only statistically significant predictor in this model is revolution, which unsurprisingly is often tied to more broad-based changes in property rights writ large.

4.5 CONCLUSION

This chapter provides strong confirmatory evidence of the book's main theoretical propositions. Authoritarian regimes generate the lion's share of property rights gaps in the countryside. This is particularly true when the ruling political coalition excludes landed elites. But authoritarian regimes have little appetite for granting property rights to land reform beneficiaries. They instead use property rights gaps as coercive leverage over peasant beneficiaries to maintain order and elicit support at critical times.

Property rights gaps are often closed by democracies. The likelihood of closing such a gap is highest when peasants have a core position in the ruling

---

[30] See Albertus (2015c) for further details.
[31] Following Carter and Signorino (2010), it also includes a cubic polynomial approximation to the hazard (not shown).

coalition and landed interests cannot organize through the legislature to oppose legislation that solidifies property rights across a broad group of property holders. Property rights gaps are also diminished under both dictatorships and democracies when severe economic crises force countries to undertake structural economic adjustment, including property rights reform, in exchange for a lifeline from international lenders.

5

Consequences of the Property Rights Gap

This chapter demonstrates how property rights gaps dramatically and fundamentally shape the lives and livelihoods of rural citizens who live under these gaps. Property rights gaps have important and wide-ranging economic, social, and political consequences. They affect demographic change and agricultural production in the countryside, shape the delivery of basic services such as education to rural areas relative to their urban counterparts, and impact the degree of income inequality and even the pace of growth in an economy. Property rights gaps structure the ability of rural groups to exercise political power relative to cities and shape the nature of the relationship between parties and voters.

There are, of course, exceptions to these trends, and countervailing policies can at times mitigate or even reverse these consequences. But longstanding cumulative property rights gaps cannot easily be papered over. Property rights gaps tend toward these consequences over time.

Why do property rights gaps have these effects? Property rights gaps generate demographic stasis by making it difficult to alienate land and to accumulate enough savings to either leave it behind or send children off the farm. This keeps land reform beneficiaries dispersed across the countryside working in agriculture, stunting urban transformation. Property rights gaps distort incentives to invest in farm improvements and inputs due to tenure insecurity, a lack of access to credit, and in some cases an inability to capture the marginal benefit of increased labor. Property rights gaps consequently lead to slower growth in agricultural productivity per worker over time. In addition, property rights gaps are linked to urban policy bias by disadvantaging rural dwellers from accessing the same basic services and opportunities for employment by the state that urban dwellers enjoy. This can retard human capital formation in the countryside.

These dynamics fuel growing economic inequality over time as the well-being of countryside dwellers increasingly falls behind that of their urban counterparts. And they sow the seeds of underdevelopment. Scholars have long hypothesized that land inequality is inimical to economic development because of how it stunts human capital accumulation and facilitates elite capture. Land redistribution should therefore catalyze growth by equalizing landholding. This chapter finds, by contrast, that the modal experience with land redistribution in Latin

America – which entails a lack of property rights provision over distributed land – has stunted growth over the long term relative to countries that have redistributed land with attendant property rights. The political conditions under which redistributive land reform occurs are much the same as those that encourage the underprovision of property rights to land beneficiaries, and these outcomes have countervailing effects on economic development.

Property rights also have direct political consequences that shape the nature of access to power, the ability to translate preferences into policy, and contestation within society. Property rights gaps tilt the political playing field in favor of those living in urban areas rather than rural areas. Political leaders that preside over large property rights gaps are often born and raised in major cities and give preference to the needs of urban constituents. Furthermore, because property rights gaps provide regimes with coercive leverage over land reform recipients, property rights gaps generate quiescent countrysides that are ripe for political clientelism and unfair electoral practices. They are linked to clientelistic rather than programmatic linkages between parties and voters. Dispersed land reform recipients that are fixed geographically and lack property rights while facing obstacles to acquiring necessary agricultural inputs and credits are the stuff of clientelist party fantasy. Property rights gaps therefore present incumbent political parties with overwhelming temptations to use state resources to supercharge their electoral prospects at the expense of their competitors.

This chapter unpacks these outcomes and then systematically assesses how countries that follow canonical property rights gap Path B or Path C (redistributing land without property rights and thereby generating a property rights gap at least for a time) compare on these outcomes relative to countries that follow property rights gap Path A (redistributing land with associated property rights). In other words, it evaluates whether Path A is indeed the path to prosperity, whereas Path B is a path to delayed development and Path C is a path to underdevelopment.

This chapter also presents three case studies to complement and further extend these insights. One of these case studies examines the effects of land redistribution with property rights in a Path A case (Costa Rica). The second examines the consequences of a property rights gap and its closing in a Path B case (Mexico). The third provides a deeper look at the results of a property rights gap that was opened and never closed in a Path C case (Cuba).

5.1 SOCIAL AND ECONOMIC CONSEQUENCES OF THE PROPERTY RIGHTS GAP

A property rights gap generally has broad downstream effects for how rural citizens live their lives and for the structure of society and the economy as a whole. This is due to the political origins of the property rights gap and its intended consequences in terms of the control and manipulation of land reform beneficiaries. Many of these effects are pernicious and can outweigh the positive consequences typically associated with land reform programs.

I do not contend that property rights are the only sole determinant of the outcomes that this chapter examines. Such a claim would be highly implausible given that many of the outcomes I examine are complex. A host of other policies contribute to them as well. Other policies can also exacerbate or compensate for a lack of property rights among land reform beneficiaries.[1]

At the same time, there is ample research that provides evidence that property rights themselves also structure long-term development outcomes. This chapter begins by putting this work in conversation with this book's theory to logically draw out a series of anticipated consequences of a property rights gap.

The first consequence of a large property rights gap is that land reform beneficiaries are likely to remain in the agricultural sector. Landholding inequality is often linked with the attempt by large landowners to prevent out-migration from the countryside in order to suppress rural wages and increase profits (Moore 1966, Rueschemeyer et al. 1992). By extension, the elimination of large landowners through land reform can free up labor mobility and encourage migration to places that offer the most attractive jobs. But receiving land through a land reform program without the property rights to alienate it at a fair value fixes most reform beneficiaries to the plot of land that they receive. Moving risks losing the plot of land when property rights are indefensible or only imperfectly defensible. Most beneficiaries consequently remain in rural areas where they often scrape by with government assistance. Although family members may migrate to urban areas or abroad for permanent or temporary work as families expand and land scarcity grows, households should be more likely to retain some family members on the land to protect one of their most valuable and vulnerable assets.[2]

To be sure, receiving land may enable land reform beneficiaries to capture more of the value of their productivity than when they worked for large landowners themselves. This enhances the possibility of eking out a living in the agricultural sector and therefore the attractiveness of remaining in the countryside provided that the government assists with critical inputs and supports that cannot easily be obtained due to a lack of property rights. In addition, there will always be incentives for some significant portion of the population to remain in the agricultural sector due to factors such as a comparative advantage in farming due to skills or knowledge and because of demand for agricultural products. But the choice to remain in agriculture

---

[1] I return to this point later in the chapter.

[2] Together with the fact that land without property rights cannot be easily transferred or divided, these dynamics suggest a corollary hypothesis: that rural households living under a property rights gap are more likely to stack up rather than split up. I find empirical support for this hypothesis using a similar analysis strategy to that detailed ahead for the other outcomes.

rather than join the urban workforce stunts lifetime and intergenerational income over time for many rural workers as economic dynamism in rural areas of Latin America has lagged behind that of urban areas (World Bank 2013).

Regimes that generate property rights gaps benefit from rural demographic stasis. Populations that remain in the agricultural sector are geographically dispersed. This makes collective action more difficult relative to urban areas with concentrated populations. Being fixed geographically also enhances legibility: the state can more easily locate these individuals and build information about them over repeated interactions.

Another consequence of a property rights gap is slow growth in agricultural productivity. Land reform has the potential to underpin growth in agriculture when governments conduct land reform but do not open up a property rights gap by granting property rights to land reform beneficiaries. Land redistribution can directly improve the livelihoods of land beneficiaries in the short term as they receive a major asset – land – that provides a degree of insurance against social and economic risk and that yields benefits into the future through production. Land reform can alter agency problems that often proliferate in tenancy contracts in unequal areas with rigid social hierarchies. This enables laborers to capture a greater share of agricultural surplus and can foster accumulation decisions that support growth (Besley and Burgess 2000). Furthermore, secure property rights can improve the dynamics of rural land and credit markets and in doing so facilitate an efficient distribution and use of land and the complements that make it productive (Alston, Libecap, and Schneider 1996; Deininger et al. 2004; Deininger, Ali, and Yomano 2008).

But land reform beneficiaries that lack land rights against the backdrop of a property rights gap cannot easily establish or enforce more efficient contracts. And they cannot use their land as collateral to access loans and credits from private banks. This stunts investment in production-enhancing technology such as mechanized farm equipment. In addition, it can induce shortages in the inputs necessary to cultivate productive harvests if rural dwellers have limited savings at the beginning of a new planting season. Insecure property rights over land can also yield a shift toward planting shorter-term crops as an individual's time horizons are curtailed (Do and Iyer 2008).

Meanwhile, agricultural populations will remain substantial under a property rights gap for reasons discussed previously. This is a recipe for stagnation in output in agriculture. A property rights gap that is sufficiently large and enduring can swamp the positive effects of the well-documented inverse relationship between farm scale and productivity: that, all things equal, small farms are often more productive per unit area than large farms (Deininger 2003).

Of course, the government can step in to provide loans, credits, and inputs when beneficiaries lack them, stoking agricultural productivity in the short run. Chapter 3 argues that this hook into rural communities is at the core of generating a property rights gap to begin with. But governments more often seek dependency and fealty among rural populations over the long term than autonomy and upward mobility. This implies that governments will more typically provide rural dwellers with the minimum assistance they require to scrape by rather than generous assistance that could enable them to save and send their children to school or to seek opportunity in urban areas. And, of course, rulers change over time and governments are faced by periodic economic headwinds. They are therefore likely to force rural dwellers into privation periodically – and more so than urban dwellers given the state's greater capacity to monitor and control geographically fixed and dispersed populations.

A third consequence of a substantial property rights gap is urban policy bias. Rural populations facing a property rights gap are ripe for divide and conquer by the central state. Rural demographic stasis and geographic dispersion help to neuter the threat of unrest and policy pressures that simply cannot be kicked down the road. This contrasts with urban populations among which restiveness is harder to contain and can more quickly threaten centers of state power.

Furthermore, recall that a property rights gap foments headwinds to agricultural production. Economic growth in Latin America in the time this book focuses on was driven to a much larger degree by cities serving as the economic engine.

Faced with steeper risks to alienating urban populations and greater economic prospects from cultivating relatively productive urban centers, most regimes that preside over rural property rights gaps make the easy choice and cast their lot with cities.[3] This decision is manifested in a wide range of policies and political processes that favor cities. Regimes facing passive and more dependent rural populations that are under the thumb of a property rights gap are more likely to shunt basic public services such as primary education, health, and security toward urban centers. They will draw state employees from more educated urban populations that better understand urban issues and they will contract with urban-based businesses. Urban populations will therefore enjoy greater effective political power and more rapid human capital formation. They will also be able to more successfully make demands of government. This is not to say that rural property rights gaps generate state retrenchment from the countryside. To the contrary, land reform often paves the way for greater state involvement in the countryside (Grindle 1986). But this state involvement is of a particular, often political, stripe, as suggested in Chapter 3. I return to the nature of this involvement in the following section.

Because the property rights gap traps land recipients in rural areas over generations, slows agricultural productivity, and delays access to basic services

---

[3] This explanation therefore shares some affinity to but is not the same as Lipton's (1977) classic treatment, in which urban bias is attributed to the inherent power of a small contingent of convergent interest groups such as industrialists, urban workers, and large farmers.

that enable human populations to thrive, it generates a fourth important consequence: growing rural–urban inequality. Workers in cities gain more marketable and remunerative skills that underpin upward economic mobility. Their rural counterparts fall behind. Paltry support from the state, an inability to access private banking, stagnating productivity, and a lack of access to basic services cause substantial numbers of rural inhabitants that lack property rights over their land to linger in poverty. This contributes over generations to a yawning gap in well-being and livelihoods between cities and the countryside.

A final economic consequence of the property rights gap is muted economic development. From the perspective of this book's theory and the discussion of other social and economic implications of the property rights gap, it would be surprising if the property rights gap accelerated economic development. But the notion that land redistribution can actually stunt development is a more provocative claim when framed within the longstanding debate on whether reductions to land inequality via land reform spur economic growth.

A host of scholars argue that high landholding inequality stunts economic development. The theoretical mechanisms are legion but can be roughly divided into two distinct sets of hypotheses. The first is that land inequality induces a political battle in which poorer agents seek to tax the wealthy and implement progressive government services. This is analogous to other forms of inequality in the distribution of income and capital (Meltzer and Richard 1981). The resultant contestation introduces economic distortions that in turn stymie economic growth.

A second set of hypotheses instead emphasizes the economic distortions created by large landowners themselves when landholding inequality is high. Large landowners that tower over smallholders and the landless will seek to avoid taxes and undermine the provision of education at the local level in order to maintain a workforce that fails to meet literacy requirements to vote and that has little alternative marketable skills (Baland and Robinson 2008; Galor et al. 2009). They are also more likely to capture the banking system and use it to underprovide credit to smallholders and the landless in an effort to capture rents from surplus labor and to purchase land from distressed smallholders during negative economic shocks (Rajan and Ramcharan 2011).

Land reform should be an efficiency-enhancing reform from the perspective of this literature regardless of the precise form that it takes provided that it equalizes landholding. Land reform can pave the way for economic growth by reallocating assets to those who have strong incentives to use them and by removing rural elites that commandeer the state to their own ends. Consistent with this, Alesina and Rodrik (1994) suggest that a relatively egalitarian distribution of land is critical for the mobilization of savings and investment that makes economic growth possible. Land reform can also eliminate landowners who oppose growth-enhancing investments in human capital via education, which increases the productivity of labor in industrial production more than in agriculture and consequently drains the countryside of labor while raising rural wages (Galor et al. 2009).

The poster children for the growth-enhancing effects of land reform are South Korea and Taiwan (Haggard and Kaufman 1995; Rodrik 1995). Time and again scholars have emphasized these countries' post–WWII land-to-the-tiller reforms as laying the foundation for spectacular subsequent economic growth. Similarly, Indian states with more intense land reform witnessed higher economic growth and reduced poverty (Besley and Burgess 2000). And redistributive land reform during Japan's Meiji Restoration and again in the post–WWII period catalyzed growth through investments in education and a shift toward urbanization and industrialization (Galor et al. 2009).

But this book's theory regarding the property rights gap over redistributed land and the Chapter 4 findings raise critical questions about the generalizability of the growth-enhancing effects of land reform. Redistributive land reforms that reduce landholding concentration overwhelmingly occur under authoritarian regimes that face landed elite rivals. These regimes have incentives to withhold complete property rights from land beneficiaries. They can more easily manipulate land beneficiaries and extend political control over the countryside if land reform recipients face tenure insecurity and become dependent on the state for loans and agricultural inputs rather than turning to private sector businesses. Authoritarian regimes that redistribute land therefore frequently generate a property rights gap in the reformed sector by distributing land without defensible property titles. This gap has been large and enduring in many countries, and when it has been closed, it has been almost always closed under subsequent democratic regimes.

By providing land reform beneficiaries with incomplete property rights, equity-enhancing dictatorships can stunt the long-term economic development prospects of a more egalitarian distribution of property. Incomplete property rights over land can lead to underinvestment, sluggish rural land markets, and economic distortions in the allocation of labor (Deininger et al. 2004). Consider the example of untitled collective property with heavily restricted rights, which was introduced in many cases of major land reform such as Mexico and Peru. Collective ownership that is poorly regulated and unresponsive to the needs and realities of community members can create problems of moral hazard that have enormous economic implications over time (Lipton 2009; Ostrom 1990). And the lack of any formal ownership title, whether for individuals within collectives, for collectives as a whole, or both, typically prevents the ability to leverage land for credits and loans that can be used to invest in property improvements, training, and expensive but valuable inputs such as mechanized equipment.

Greater equality of access to land, in short, does not itself necessarily bolster economic growth. Property rights are part of the equation.[4] Furthermore, incomplete property rights regimes over distributed land work *directly*

---

[4] This observation is consistent with Lipton's (2009) findings regarding how collectivization sapped the life from agricultural production and investment in a host of communist countries ranging from Eastern Europe to Southeast Asia.

opposite to the positive hypothesized effects of more egalitarian property ownership.

Assessing Social and Economic Consequences of the Property Rights Gap

How can we assess these hypotheses regarding the broad social and economic consequences of the property rights gap? I do so by comparing data on outcomes between two fundamentally different groups of countries: those that trace canonical property rights gap Path A and therefore never generate a property rights gap through land reform, and those that trace Path B or Path C and therefore do generate a property rights gap through land reform.

Of course, countries have implemented land reform at varying points in their histories. Comparing outcomes between the Path A and Path B/C groups from the beginning of the time period in 1920 therefore makes little sense if some countries have lived with land reform or a property rights gap for a long time whereas others have done so for a short time in the more recent past. Furthermore, the Path B countries that generate property rights gaps later close them. This may cause their outcomes to diverge from Path C countries. Whereas Path B countries may experience delayed development, Path C countries should be on a path to persistent underdevelopment.

To address these issues, I generate the comparison between Path B/C countries and Path A countries as follows in order to assess the consequences of the property rights gap. I build from the setup of the survival analyses in Chapter 4 and code the beginning of a property rights gap in the Path B/C cases (the "treatment" group) when at least 1 percent of a country's cultivable land has been redistributed without attendant property rights. This marks the starting line for these cases. I examine outcomes within this group from that starting line moment until there is a major effort to close the property rights gap (if there is one at all). I consider a major effort to close the gap as a reduction of at least 5 percent of the existing property rights gap in the span of three years. The Path B cases consequently drop from the treatment group after they begin closing the property rights gap. The Path C cases that do not close the property rights gap remain in the sample until the end of the period. This approach is therefore faithful to the anticipated divergence between the delayed development outcomes in the Path B cases and the persistent underdevelopment in the Path C cases.

For the benchmark comparison group of Path A countries (the "control" group), I code the starting line as the beginning of any land redistribution rather than the beginning of the time period. Recall that property rights are granted over land that is distributed to land reform beneficiaries in these cases. This builds a counterfactual of what outcomes in Path B/C cases could have been had these countries granted property rights to land beneficiaries and followed the Path A path to prosperity. I code the finish line for these cases when no land redistribution has occurred for five consecutive years. This implies that countries can drop from the comparison group due to inactivity. Argentina, for instance, engaged in a short-lived bout of land redistribution from 1944 to 1954; it would consequently drop from the comparison group in 1959.

The comparison is therefore an intuitive one: once a property rights gap is opened, how do the economic and social outcomes of interest evolve in the Path B/C countries relative to the Path A countries that implemented land redistribution with property rights, *after the same number of years since the beginning of reform in each of the two groups*?

One advantage of constructing the comparison in this fashion is that it implicitly accounts for variables with strong time trends. Factors like population tend to grow over time across the board and analyzing the two groups against one another helps to net out underlying trends. Furthermore, because property rights gaps in the Path B and Path C cases opened at varying times and the redistribution of land with property rights in the Path A cases also began at differing times, the trends are unlikely to be driven by a set of factors such as development strategies or ideology that impacted one set of these countries at a certain time but not the other set.

The comparison I present is a basic one that does not necessarily demonstrate causality. But the differences hold in a more rigorous regression framework that uses the cumulative titling gap from Chapter 4 as the key independent variable and that includes time trends to account for secular shifts in the property rights gap and various outcome variables, country fixed effects that capture unobserved and time-invariant country-level factors such as culture or proximity to markets, and important time-varying factors that could separately impact social and economic outcomes and be correlated to the presence and size of a property rights gap. These include political ideology, state capacity, overall economic well-being, and urbanization.[5] The robustness of the findings to including these factors is important given the reality that the outcomes of interest are not monocausal: they can be affected by a spectrum of time-varying and country-specific factors as well. The regression results are in Appendix B at the end of the book. They are also robust to controlling for the key factors from Chapter 4 that drive the generation of property rights gaps to begin with: regime type, the exclusion of large landowners from the ruling coalition, and an interaction between these variables.

Although a regression framework returns the same results as the basic comparisons I present here, both are still unable to fully account for the effects of other government policies that can also impact the outcomes of interest such as the provision of agricultural credits, various price supports and subsidies, and support for insurance markets. Systematic data on these policies are simply not available during the time period of analysis. To the extent that these policies are correlated with development trends, property rights gap paths, state capacity, or political regimes, or if they systematically

---

[5] The results are also robust for controlling population growth. The property rights gap was growing at the same time that many countries were experiencing large population growth.

vary by country, then the regression framework will capture them to a degree. But the broader role of states providing background conditions for land and property rights to support development cannot be entirely accounted for here. However, the research design for the developmental effects of localized property rights gaps in Peru in Chapter 7 can more effectively control for these omitted factors. That chapter will demonstrate very similar consequences to those that follow in this chapter. This suggests an important role for the property rights gap on development.

A final consideration in interpreting the results that follow is whether they might be driven not by differences in the property rights gap but rather by differences in land reform itself. Some of the Path A cases, particularly Argentina, had minor land reforms, and some of the Path B and Path C cases had very large reforms. If land reform per se drives negative development outcomes, then this could account for a divergence from cases that experienced less land reform.

I examined this possibility in several ways. First, I tested the robustness of the findings to dropping Argentina, which had the least amount of land redistribution in Latin America at just over 1 percent of cultivable land. Second, I dropped all countries in which land redistribution was less than 10 percent of cultivable land over the period 1920–2010. This includes another Path A case, Costa Rica, as well as two Path B cases, Ecuador and Honduras. The findings are similar under each of these alternative specifications. Finally, while none of the Path A countries in Latin America conducted land reform at the scale of say Mexico or Peru, making it difficult to know for certain from these data how very large-scale land redistribution with associated property rights would have impacted development, other countries such as Estonia, South Korea, and Taiwan have done just that. These Path A countries undeniably followed the path to prosperity. Chapter 8 examines them in more depth.

Data and Measures for Outcomes

The analysis examines five different social and economic consequences of the property rights gap. The first outcome is the percentage of the economically active population that works in the agricultural sector. Data for this variable are from the Montevideo-Oxford Latin American Economic History Database and span from 1920 to 2010, though most countries in the sample do not have data that span this entire period. The average of this variable is 41.4 percent. This speaks to the importance of agriculture in Latin America during this period despite its declining value added within the economy as a whole.

The second outcome is agricultural productivity per rural worker. Data on the value of total agricultural output are from the Montevideo-Oxford Latin American Economic History Database. This data source harmonizes and standardizes raw figures across countries over time by converting them into constant 1970 US dollars. The size of the agricultural population is from Vanhanen (2009). The underlying population data are from country population censuses reported in volumes such as the FAO's *Production Yearbook*. I calculate productivity as the value of agricultural output in thousands of constant 1970 dollars per dweller involved in the agricultural sector. The mean of this variable is 2.57. I generate a five-year moving average of this variable to smooth short-term volatility in productivity.

The third outcome is urban policy bias. This variable captures the extent to which public policy and decision-making is biased in favor of urban areas over rural areas and is taken from the V-Dem dataset. Urban bias is greater in proportion to the extent that rural individuals are denied access to public services or participation in public life based on their status as a dweller in the rural rather than urban sector. It is an index ranging from 0 to 1 and is formed by taking the point estimates from a Bayesian factor analysis model of the indicators for access to public services (such as primary education, clean water, healthcare, and security provision) by urban–rural location, access to state jobs by urban–rural location, access to state business opportunities by urban–rural location, political power distributed by urban–rural location, and urban/rural parity in respect for civil liberties. The average index value is 0.66. This indicates that policy is typically slightly biased toward urban rather than rural areas.

The fourth dependent variable is income inequality. This variable is measured using the Gini index. The index runs from 0 to 100 where 0 represents perfect equality and 100 represents perfect inequality. Data are from the World Development Indicators and begin in 1979. The average level of inequality in the Latin America sample is 51.4. Unfortunately, there are no available comprehensive data that specifically capture rural–urban income inequality. However, it is well documented that poverty in rural areas of Latin America is systematically higher than in urban areas and has remained stubbornly persistent while economies have grown overall (World Bank 2013). This dynamic underpins inequality as a whole within society.

The final dependent variable is income per capita. This variable captures a country's level of economic development. Income per capita is measured in 2000 international dollars and is constructed primarily from the Penn World Tables with missing data filled in from Maddison Historical Statistics and the World Bank Development Indicators. The annual per capita income measure has a mean of $4,553 with a standard deviation of $2,582.

Analysis Results

Figure 5.1 presents the findings on how the property rights gap differentially impacts outcomes that follow from land reform with property rights in Path A countries on the one hand and land reform without property rights in Path B or C countries on the other hand.

Figure 5.1a indicates that the economically active population working in agriculture persists at higher levels for longer in the Path B and Path C countries that generate and retain a property rights gap relative to the Path A countries that redistribute land while granting property rights to land reform beneficiaries.

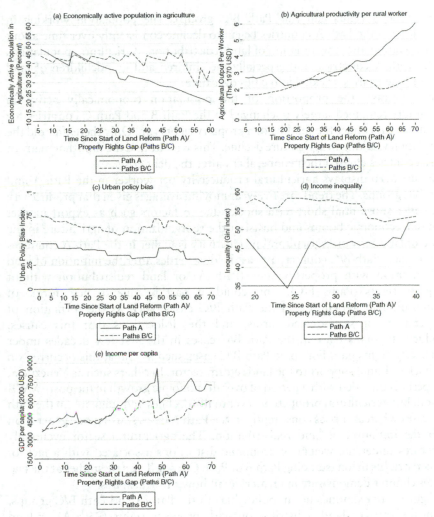

FIGURE 5.1 Social and economic consequences of the property rights gap
(a) Economically active population in agriculture
(b) Agricultural productivity per rural worker
(c) Urban policy bias
(d) Income inequality
(e) Income per capita

This is as anticipated. Property rights gaps encourage land reform recipients that lack property rights to remain in the countryside and work in agriculture. Countries that follow Path A and those that follow Path B or Path C began with approximately 45 percent of their populations working in agriculture shortly after the initiation of land redistribution that delivers property rights (the Path A group) or a property rights gap (the Path B/C group). The population working in agriculture in the Path A countries began to decline consistently over time about one generation after the initiation of land redistribution. Agricultural populations in the Path A countries, and especially the children and grandchildren of land reform beneficiaries, trickled into cities over time.

By contrast, the proportion of the population economically active in agriculture remained largely unchanged in the Path B and Path C countries for about 50 years under the shadow of a property rights gap. Only thereafter did the population working in agriculture decline. This was around the time that many of these countries entered the neoliberal era after the debt crisis.

Figure 5.1b displays agricultural productivity per worker in the Path A and Path B/C groups. The trends are five-year moving averages given that productivity can suffer substantial short-term shocks due to factors such as export market demand, economic booms and busts, or the reorganization of agriculture in the wake of land reform. Agricultural productivity is higher in the Path A countries than in their Path B/C counterparts as the dust settles after the initiation of land redistribution with property rights (Path A) or land redistribution without property rights (Paths B/C). This could in part be due to new forms of organization in agriculture in the Path B/C cases, such as the formation of cooperatives or state-owned farms, and the dislocations that this causes. Productivity snaps back in the Path B/C cases in the first few decades under a property rights gap. For some Path B/C cases such as Cuba, this occurred on the back of initial support to the land reform sector. In others such as Venezuela, this period coincided with a period of overall economic growth in the post–WWII period. But agricultural productivity eventually declines and stagnates in the Path B/C cases whereas it rises consistently in the Path A cases starting one generation after the initiation of land redistribution. The agricultural sector eventually suffocates under the weight of economic distortions associated with a lack of property rights in longstanding Path B or Path C cases. The case studies at the end of this chapter demonstrate in greater detail how this transpires.

Figure 5.1c examines urban policy bias in the Path A and Path B/C groups. From the start of land redistribution with property rights (Path A) or land redistribution without property rights (Paths B/C), public policy and decision-making is more heavily biased in favor of urban areas over rural areas in the Path B/C cases. These countries are more likely to privilege urban citizens over rural ones when it comes to providing basic public services such as education and clean water, hiring employees into the bureaucracy, or respecting civil liberties. Rural dwellers are effectively second-class citizens under regimes that preside over a property rights gap in the countryside. By contrast, there is relative parity between rural and urban groups in the Path A cases after land redistribution begins. The fortunes of rural inhabitants relative to urban ones generally improves in both the Path A and Path B/C groups over time. But parity is never reached in the Path B/C cases and urban bias remains substantial for many decades under a property rights gap.

The initial gap in urban policy bias between the Path A countries and the Path B/C countries and the maintenance of this gap does, however, raise an alternative explanation for the Figure 5.1c findings: that perhaps urban bias is not reinforced by a property rights gap but is instead driven by the same underlying conditions that generate a property rights gap to begin with. This alternative cannot be entirely rejected. Nor is it entirely inconsistent with the theory. An authoritarian regime whose ruling coalition excludes large landowners may simultaneously drive a property rights gap and adopt urban policy bias. Nonetheless, in a fully specified regression with urban policy bias as the dependent variable, the key cumulative titling gap variable from Chapter 4 is a robust and substantively important predictor even after introducing other Chapter 4 variables that capture important determinants of a property rights gap: regime type, the exclusion of large landowners from the ruling coalition, and an interaction between these variables. This suggests that urban policy bias is not merely epiphenomenal. A property rights gap hobbles the rural sector and makes it easier for a regime to tilt its policies in favor of urban inhabitants without having to face backlash from the countryside.

Figure 5.1d indicates that property rights gaps are associated with higher levels of income inequality. The Path B and Path C countries that generate a property rights gap through land reform have systematically higher and more persistent inequality relative to the Path A group. This is consistent with the theory. A property rights gap stunts savings and investment among land reform beneficiaries and keeps them in the countryside. This drives economic divergence between the countryside and cities.

There are several caveats to Figure 5.1d, however. First, the inequality data used in this figure are only available starting in 1979 and all of the Path A countries had already been engaged in land redistribution for at least a decade and a half by this time. A comparison of inequality in the short-term aftermath of the initiation of land redistribution therefore cannot be made for the two groups. Furthermore, because Argentina began and ended land redistribution much before 1979, and Colombia and Uruguay started land redistribution roughly 60 years prior to when data on inequality are available for them, the Figure 5.1d comparison case for Path A is only Costa Rica. A regression framework is therefore again a helpful addition for this analysis because it generates inferences not only on the basis of whether a property rights gap exists but also on the basis of its extent. The results support Figure 5.1d: a larger property rights gap is associated with greater income inequality.[6]

---

[6] Like for the Figure 5.1C, the cumulative titling gap remains a robust and substantively important predictor even after introducing regime type, the exclusion of large landowners from the ruling coalition, and an interaction between these variables, which could drive the difference in inequality between the Path A and Path B/C groups as captured by the initial intercept shift between the lines in Figure 5.1D.

Figure 5.1e investigates economic development in the Path A and Path B/C groups. These two groups of countries started with nearly identical levels of income per capita at the time land redistribution with property rights (Path A) or land redistribution without property rights (Paths B/C) began. In the subsequent fifteen years, however, these two groups diverge. The Path A countries grew substantially quicker than their Path B/C counterparts. This suggests that the economic distortions associated with a lack of property rights in the countryside outweigh the economic benefits of a reduction in the political and economic power of large landowners and a more equal distribution of landholdings.

The gap in development between the Path A group and Path B/C group then closes for a period after fifteen years. This is mainly driven, however, by somewhat anomalous circumstances in two Path A countries. Uruguay began land redistribution around the start of the period of analysis in 1920 and then got slammed by the Great Depression in the mid-1930s. Argentina grew rapidly while redistributing land but then drops from the sample fifteen years after entering because it halted land redistribution. Stripping these cases out of the Path A group yields a Path A trend line in income per capita that continues to grow beyond 15 years from the initiation of land redistribution. Because the countries in the combined Path B and C group vary a lot temporally in when they began land reform without granting property rights and include many post – Great Depression cases, they are not subject to the same issue as Uruguay regarding entering the Great Depression.

Roughly thirty years after the initiation of land redistribution with property rights (Path A) or land redistribution without property rights (Paths B/C), economic development again diverges between the two groups in Figure 5.1e. The divergence is again substantial and, this time, it is permanent. Countries that live under a many-decades-long property gap, such as Bolivia, Cuba, the Dominican Republic, or Mexico, begin to face significant economic headwinds compared with countries that grant property rights to the beneficiaries of land reform from the beginning, such as Colombia or Uruguay.[7] This divergence is perhaps all the more striking because many of the same countries that generated large and longstanding property rights gaps adopted muscular import-substitution industrialization programs that stoked significant economic growth while property rights gaps still prevailed. Classic examples are Bolivia and Mexico. Path B countries that close the property rights gap after a shorter period of time, such as Panama, by contrast, were better positioned to recover from the economic drag of a sluggish rural sector.

---

[7] A separate analysis that breaks the property rights gap into its constituent components – land redistribution and the extension of property rights over redistributed land – demonstrates that while land redistribution without property rights has no positive discernible impact on economic development over time, and perhaps a negative impact, the effect turns positive once there is a property rights reform granting full property rights to former land reform beneficiaries.

5.2 POLITICAL CONSEQUENCES OF THE PROPERTY RIGHTS GAP

There is abundant reason to suspect the property rights gap also has political consequences in light of its broad social and economic consequences. Authoritarian rulers that generate property rights gaps have political goals in mind alongside broader social and demographic engineering. The political consequences can linger for long periods under a persistent property rights gap even after its architects are no longer in office.

The first consequence of a large property rights gap that swamps the countryside is the evisceration and stagnation of rural political power. The theory in Chapter 3 argues that the redistribution of land without attendant property rights aids in creating a politically pliable, dispersed support base. Land reform recipients that lack property rights are more likely to remain working in the rural sector where they are geographically dispersed. Their lack of property rights stunts agricultural productivity and dynamism and creates reliance on the state for subsidies, credits, inputs, and dispute resolution. Governments presiding over a property rights gap therefore typically create a panoply of agencies to address these rural problems. They coercively wield the threat of withdrawal of support if beneficiaries engage in resistance, recalcitrance, or autonomous organization that could threaten the incumbent regime's power.

The dispersed nature of land reform recipients that are reliant on the state enables an incumbent regime to position itself as the hub of a hub-and-spoke system of aid to individual peasant families or small-scale peasant groups. Regimes that force land reform beneficiaries to interact with them individually on an annual basis can more easily manipulate beneficiaries and pressure them one by one into supporting the status quo rather than forming broad-based political movements for change.[8]

This limits the capacity of rural groups to formulate, obtain, and exercise political power. And it positions urban constituencies to exercise greater political voice. Unlike rural dwellers, it is harder to divide and conquer urban dwellers given their geographical concentration, which lowers the cost of collective action. This gives urban inhabitants greater de facto power. And when urban leaders capture de jure power against the backdrop of a large property rights gap, there is an off-the-shelf playbook that enables them to further entrench urban political power at the expense of the countryside.

Property without rights and the coercive leverage it generates for the state are also the roots of clientelism in the countryside. Vote buying, turnout buying,

---

[8] This suggests a corollary: that a property rights gap should undermine the formation of organized rural rebellion. I find empirical support for this hypothesis using data on the incidence of guerrilla warfare from Banks' CNTS Data Archive and a similar analysis strategy to that detailed for the other outcomes. Guerrilla warfare was overwhelmingly rooted in rural areas in Latin America during the period of study, as exemplified by the FARC's insurgency in Colombia and Shining Path's insurgency in Peru.

and machine politics thrive when political parties can gain individualized knowledge about voters and when voters are poor and relatively uneducated (Stokes et al. 2013). Distributing contingent and reversible benefits to individuals in exchange for their votes becomes relatively more attractive for parties under these circumstances than developing programmatic policy platforms.

Dispersed land reform recipients that lack property rights and face difficulties in getting the inputs they need to thrive are a clientelistic party's dream come true. This is even more so the case given that a property rights gap is associated with stagnant rural populations that are geographically fixed to a plot of land. This reduces the cost of gaining knowledge about voters and interacting with them (Albertus 2013). An electorate that is susceptible to clientelistic appeals presents political parties with overwhelming incentives to use their resources in a particularistic fashion to tilt voters in their favor. A single dominant political party that runs the state and presides over sham elections can even draw on government aid to funnel selectively to voters in an effort to tilt the electoral playing field to their advantage.

Assessing the Political Consequences of the Property Rights Gap

In order to assess the political consequences of the property rights gap systematically, I follow the same analysis strategy that was used earlier in the chapter to assess the social and economic consequences of the property rights gap. I therefore compare political consequences in the Path B and Path C countries from the time they opened up a property rights gap against the political consequences in the baseline Path A countries from the time these countries began conducting land reform while granting beneficiaries property rights. The result is the comparative evolution of political outcomes after the same number of years since the beginning of reform in each of the two groups. As with the social and economic consequences of property rights gaps examined previously, because the driving phenomenon of interest is the property rights gap, Path B cases drop from the analysis after they begin closing the property rights gap and Path A cases drop out when no land redistribution has occurred for five consecutive years.

Data and Measures for Outcomes

The analysis examines two different social and economic consequences of the property rights gap. The first outcome is the balance between rural and urban political power. This variable is taken from the V-Dem database. Data are available from the beginning of the time period. It captures the extent to which political power is distributed according to urban–rural location. The unscaled version varies from 0, in which people living in urban areas have a near monopoly on political power, to 5, in which people living in rural areas have much more political power than their urban counterparts. V-Dem then converts the ordinal scale to interval using a Bayesian item response theory measurement model. Higher values therefore indicate that rural populations are vested with greater relative political power.

The second outcome captures clientelism through the prevalence of one particularly common and virulent manifestation: vote buying. This variable is taken from the V-Dem database with available data starting at the beginning of the period. It captures the extent of the distribution of money or in-kind gifts to individuals and small groups in order to influence their decision of whom to vote for or their decision of whether to vote at all. The unscaled version varies from 0, in which there is systematic, widespread, and almost nationwide vote buying or turnout buying by almost all parties and candidates, to 4, in which there is no evidence of vote buying or turnout buying. V-Dem then converts the ordinal scale to interval using a Bayesian item response theory measurement model. I flip the scale so that higher values indicate more prevalent vote buying.

Analysis Results
Figure 5.2 displays the results for how the property rights gap differentially impacts political outcomes that succeed land reform with property rights in Path A countries and land reform without property rights in Path B or C countries. As was similarly noted in the discussion of the social and economic consequences of property rights gaps, the differences depicted in Figure 5.2 also hold in a regression framework that uses the cumulative titling gap from Chapter 4 as the key independent variable and that takes into account time trends, country fixed effects, and important time-varying factors that could affect the political outcomes and be correlated to the presence and size of a property rights gap.[9] The regression results are in Appendix B.

Figure 5.2a examines the balance between rural and urban political power in the Path A and Path B/C groups. Political power is concentrated more heavily among urban groups in the Path B/C cases from the outset of either land redistribution with property rights (Path A) or land redistribution without property rights (Paths B/C). This is anticipated by the theory: rural groups are typically politically disadvantaged under a property rights gap. Contrast this with the Path A cases in which rural political power is greater from the time land redistribution begins. Between five and ten years after the initiation of land redistribution with property rights in the Path A cases, rural political power increases. Given how this variable is coded and scaled in V-Dem, the range from 0.5 to 1 among the Path A cases corresponds roughly to a situation in which political power is either balanced between rural and urban areas or urban areas have somewhat more political power but not significantly more.

---

[9] Results are also similar when controlling for the key factors from Chapter 4 that drive the generation of property rights gaps to begin with. This suggests that these outcomes are not simply epiphenomenal.

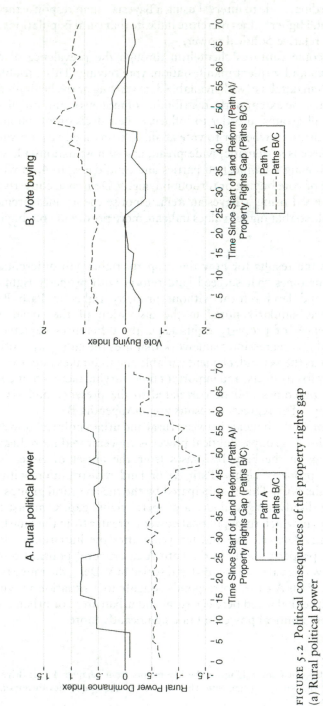

FIGURE 5.2 Political consequences of the property rights gap
(a) Rural political power
(b) Vote buying

The rural–urban power balance remains stable in favor of urban areas in the Path B/C cases for the first 40 years after the generation of a property rights gap. The range from −0.5 to −1 corresponds to a circumstance in which urban groups have much more political power than rural groups. Rural power erodes even further after this time to the point at which urban groups have a dominant hold on power before it increases to a degree. Parity in political power is never even close in the Path B/C cases. Urban predominance is unchallenged for decades under a property rights gap.

Figure 5.2b indicates that a property rights gap is linked to greater prevalence of vote buying and turnout buying. The Path B and C countries that generate a property rights gap through land reform are characterized by more pervasive clientelistic links between political parties and voters relative to the Path A group. The marketplace for votes in these contexts erodes the expressive and ideological value of voting in favor of its instrumental benefits. The incidence of vote buying in the Path B and Path C cases grows as the property rights gap endures.

The results in Figure 5.2 together paint the picture of a disempowered and politically manipulable, if not quiescent, countryside. The property rights gap drives rural inhabitants that lack property rights into lives of quiet desperation. It is a daunting challenge under these circumstances to effectively encourage politicians or parties to faithfully represent and act on their interests. As Chapter 4 indicates in the context of land titling, it often takes democracy along with a rare electoral victory in favor of the countryside, or a push from outside in a moment of crisis, to encourage politicians to act on rural demands.

5.3 ILLUSTRATIVE CONSEQUENCES OF THE PROPERTY RIGHTS GAP IN PATH A, PATH B, AND PATH C CASES

I next turn to a series of three case studies on the consequences of the property rights gap in order to illustrate more concretely the substantive importance of the analyses. Each case follows a distinct canonical property rights gap path. I begin with a Path A country, Costa Rica, in order to demonstrate the consequences of land redistribution that takes place while granting land reform beneficiaries property rights over the land that they receive. I then outline a Path B country, Mexico, which demonstrates the pernicious consequences of a large property rights gap and the divergence that begins to occur when the property rights gap is closed. Lastly, I detail a Path C country, Cuba, which generated a large and enduring property rights gap that has unleashed a host of ongoing economic, social, and political pathologies.

Each case first provides a brief overview of the nature of land reform and property rights that set that country on Path A, Path B, or Path C. I then trace the outcomes highlighted earlier in this chapter in the following groupings: (i) agricultural production and broader economic development; (ii) the rural–

urban divide, including changes in agricultural labor, urban policy bias, and rural–urban political power; (iii) inequality; and (iv) clientelism.

Path A: The Path to Prosperity in Costa Rica

Costa Rica followed canonical property rights gap Path A and never opened up a property rights gap in the countryside. This is in spite of the fact that the country has had an active program of land redistribution since the early 1960s (see Figure 2.4). Land reform beneficiaries have always received land titles and registration with their land grants.

Pressure for land reform in Costa Rica grew following the economic dislocations of the Great Depression and WWII. The government began distributing state-owned lands in frontier zones but this was insufficient to relieve demographic pressure. A more ambitious land reform proposal that aimed at redistributing private property and establishing a social function to land was debated in the 1950s but it was scuttled in the legislature due to opposition by large landowners. The legislature finally passed a land reform in 1961. The law had a heavy emphasis on protecting private property and included a provision requiring prior full compensation for expropriated land (Seligson 1980, 126). Land redistribution therefore proceeded slowly but methodically. And it ran in parallel to a substantial program that centered on titling peasant claims over public lands.

The government began land redistribution by acquiring inexpensive land in remote areas and creating peasant settlements. But mounting infrastructural costs, continued land conflicts in developed areas, and other limitations shifted the focus. The government embarked upon a new style of agrarian reform known as the Río Cañas model by the late 1960s. Four principles guided their expanded agrarian reform efforts: (i) settlements should be located in developed regions; (ii) new projects should be formed on already established farms; (iii) projects should be demonstrably economically viable; and (iv) peasants should select themselves for the projects (Seligson 1980, 133–134). Two types of projects were developed using these guidelines: an individual parcel program and "self-run communal enterprises." The government granted land reform beneficiaries titles to the plots they received. It left the provision of credit to private banks.[10]

The government engaged in a limited number of expropriations of large estates through the 1970s in areas of rural unrest and distributed them to beneficiaries – often to land squatters. This strategy met the most pressing demands for land from the landless. But it lacked a coherent agrarian development vision.

---

[10] As part of the broader land reform program, the government also titled public lands to colonizers and occupants who had long been settled there and helped to resolve disputes where there were conflicting claims (Seligson 1980).

Land reform policy shifted to integrated rural development beginning in the 1980s. Costa Rica's reorganized land reform agency dropped reactive land expropriations in favor of the negotiated, targeted purchase and distribution of private land for the formation of rural settlements in small farms. The government increased credit provision to land beneficiaries, took on physical and social infrastructure projects, and stimulated production markets (Picado and Silva 2002, 132–133). The land reform agency also began collaborating more closely with other state institutions to support land reform.

Roughly 6 percent of all cultivable land in Costa Rica had been redistributed to land reform beneficiaries with property rights by 2010. Nearly 15 percent of the landless population received land through land redistribution focusing just on the 1960s and 1970s (Seligson 1984, 34).

Agricultural Production and Economic Development

Land reform beneficiaries quickly began to excel relative to other workers in small-scale agriculture. Production was concentrated in annual crops such as rice and beans, though a significant number of beneficiaries also grew bananas and coffee for export (Seligson 1984, 36). Reform beneficiaries outperformed national average yields for nonmechanized crops like grains and beans (Seligson 1984, 37). Beneficiary income increased relative to the national minimum wage (Seligson 1980, 137).[11] The country's gross national product grew at rates between 5 percent and 7 percent from 1960 to 1980, bolstered by increases in exports of key agricultural products like coffee, sugar, and bananas (Fields 1988, 1494–1497). While production of these crops initially remained dominated by large landowners, the less-mechanized banana production became a staple for land reform beneficiaries. Bananas for export became the single largest value crop on reform settlements by the mid-1970s notwithstanding the continued presence of foreign companies in banana production like the United Fruit Company (Seligson 1984, 36).[12] The government successfully negotiated greater participation of small, independent banana producers in multinational operations under the supervision and coordination of the Costa Rican National Banana Association (Ellis 1983, 348). And as the share of small farms has increased and the share of large farms has decreased throughout the duration of Costa Rica's land reform, the production of

[11] Coffee and sugar production was already highly mechanized in Costa Rica by this time and most beneficiaries did not have access to updated machinery. Production of these crops was dominated by large landholders and beneficiary farms underperformed national yield averages.

[12] This was a time of major changes in the role of foreign companies in the banana sector throughout Central America. Costa Rica, Guatemala, Honduras, Panama, and Colombia formed a banana cartel (UPEB) in 1974 and went into open war with multinational fruit companies by renegotiating land and tax concessions, worker regulations, banana prices, and export taxes (see, e.g., Bucheli 2008). Meanwhile, the United Fruit Company was forced to shed some operations due to antitrust litigation in the United States. And its CEO committed suicide in 1975 during an unfolding corruption scandal that involved bribing the Honduran president to reduce UPEB's export tax.

coffee, bananas, and sugar produced by small farmers has increased considerably.[13]

Agricultural productivity increased along with the progression of land reform. Data from the Food and Agriculture Organization indicate that average yields per capita from key crops like cereal grains, beans, bananas, coffee, and sugar were greater in 2009–2013 than their 1961–1965 averages, while average production in tons per capita has increased for cereal grains, bananas, sugar, and coffee. The total land area under production has increased for all of these crops except grains.

Costa Rica's economy has grown rapidly since the initiation of land reform. Costa Rica had the ninth highest level of income per capita in Central and South America in 1965 ($372) according to the World Bank's World Development Indicators and it was below the regional average. It had the fourth highest income per capita in this region at just over $12,000 by 2018.

The Rural–Urban Divide
The rural sector has transformed dramatically against the backdrop of Costa Rica's growing economy. National census data indicate that the share of economically active Costa Ricans in the agricultural sector decreased from 50 percent in 1963 to 13 percent in 2011. But rural Costa Ricans have not been left behind. To the contrary, the state has increased its focus on closing the country's urban/rural welfare differences since the start of land reform in the 1960s. Various administrations – especially those of the Partido Liberación Nacional (PLN), which governed from 1962–1966, 1970–1978, and 1982–1990 – built clinics in rural areas and sent health workers there (Morgan 1990, 211), adopted redistributive social programs, expanded social security, and invested in infrastructure such as highways to link rural and urban areas (Colburn 1993, 71–72; Rottenberg 1993, 140).

Census data indicate that 96 percent of rural Costa Ricans were literate in 2011. This was close to the urban literacy rate and a significant jump over the 80 percent rural literacy rate in 1963. The percentage of rural Costa Ricans that had not completed primary school dropped from 85 percent to 27 percent over the same period. Meanwhile, census data indicate that the percentage of rural citizens with social security has reached near parity with urban dwellers at 85 percent. And as of 2000, 99.5 percent of households in large cities and 92.2 percent in villages were connected to water and connectivity to electricity was 99.7 percent and 93.3 percent, respectively (Locher 2000, 117). Furthermore, according to World Bank data, the proportion of state employees drawn from rural areas is proportional to rural population size, suggesting equal access to state jobs.

---

[13] The 2014 agricultural census indicates that 70 percent of coffee, 60 percent of bananas, and 41 percent of sugarcane is produced on farms under five hectares.

Rural Costa Ricans have long exercised their political power. Longstanding democracy in the country along with mandatory voting means that rural populations have historically had a voice in politics. And their influence has increased since land reform began (Booth 2007, 336). The PLN itself was founded by José Figueres Ferrer, who worked on a farm before rising to the presidency.[14] Figueres served three times as president, including once in the 1970s after the land reform began. Between 1970 and 1982, 14 new peasant organizations registered with the Ministry of Labor and Social Security; between 1983 and 1990, 126 such organizations were founded (Edelman 1999, 255–256). Peasant groups regularly engaged in public protests and other nonviolent collective action to advance their goals in the decades following the start of land reform (Anderson 1990, 91–92). The state was generally responsive to their demands (Seligson 1980, 119–121). Furthermore, four of the six heads of state during the first 25 years after the reform began hailed from cities other than the capital of San José and three came from smaller rural areas.

Inequality
Costa Rica has seen an increase in smallholding in the rural sector and a reduction in poverty and urban–rural inequality since implementing its land reform program. Agricultural census data indicate that between 1963 at the outset of land reform and 2014, the percentage of farms under 5 hectares in size increased from 36 percent to 55 percent while the percentage of farms larger than 50 hectares dropped from 15 percent to 9 percent of farms.

Land reform beneficiaries earned twice the income of landless farmers by the 1970s and income growth among reform beneficiaries outpaced minimum wage increases in the early 1970s (Seligson 1980, 90; 137). A total of 49 percent of all rural income accrued to the top 10 percent of earners in 1961; this declined to 36 percent of all rural income by 1979 (CEPAL 1986, 24). Poverty climbed during an economic recession in the early 1980s and the state targeted most rural relief at the agricultural export sector (Rodriguez and Smith 1994, 382). But rural poverty and inequality resumed their decline after the crisis: the share of agricultural workers below the poverty line decreased from around 31 percent in 1981 to 14 percent in 1989 and the share of poverty concentrated in rural areas dropped (Morley 1995, 61).

Some indicators of social stratification have increased as the country has shifted toward open market policies and encouraged the rise of industries like tourism. Nonetheless, income inequality in the country as a whole remains lower now than before the land reform.

Clientelism
The granting of property rights with land in Costa Rica has limited the ability of political parties to manipulate land reform beneficiaries politically. Recall that

---

[14] Figueres was also educated in the United States.

land reform beneficiaries earned twice what the landless earned a decade after the reform began. This limited the need for direct state support among land reform beneficiaries. Furthermore, because private banks recognize the land titles that beneficiaries received, rural workers typically relied on inputs and credits from the private sector rather than the state (Seligson 1980, 92). The state began providing credit directly to land beneficiaries through the Caja Agraria as it shifted to a model of integrated rural development in the 1980s. But pushed by simultaneous state retrenchment due to economic crisis and the shift toward neoliberalism, as well as the high costs of these projects, the government sought external loans and international financing for many projects (Picado and Silva 2002, 120).

There is consequently little evidence that parties used the reform to forge clientelistic links with beneficiaries. The reform unfolded slowly and the pace of expropriations, land distribution, and titling was determined by the state's financial ability rather than political party quid pro quos with voters (Seligson 1979, 163).

If anything, evidence suggests a more independent and politically active set of land beneficiaries. Survey data from 1976 on beneficiaries and nonbeneficiaries, for instance, demonstrate higher rates of voting among land beneficiaries as well as participation in political meetings and rallies (Seligson 1984, 40).[15] At the same time, beneficiaries worked for political parties and contributed money to candidates and parties at lower rates than nonbeneficiaries. And they were much more likely to ask the land reform agency for assistance with a problem than government bureaucrats, elected officials, or figures from a political party (Seligson 1984, 41).[16]

Path B: The Path to Delayed Development in Mexico

Mexico followed canonical property rights gap Path B by first generating and then closing an enormous property rights gap. Land redistribution began in Mexico following the Mexican Revolution as large landowners were knocked back on their heels. Over the span of 70 years, the PRI expropriated and redistributed to peasants over 50 million hectares of private land. This amounted to more than a quarter of all of Mexico's land area. The state also recognized indigenous land claims over millions of hectares of additional lands.

Land reform beneficiaries in Mexico, however, faced major property rights limitations. Land was granted communally as *ejidos* to entire villages. Peasants acquired the right to use and work the land individually or collectively but faced

---

[15] This is in spite of the fact that turnout in Costa Rica is generally higher among more educated and wealthier citizens.

[16] A total of 43.3 percent of survey respondents who were land beneficiaries had asked the land reform agency for help on a problem whereas these figures were 8.5 percent for a government office, 10 percent for a municipal executive, and 8.1 percent for a political party member (Seligson 1984, 41).

a host of restrictions to property rights. Neither villages nor individual peasants could alienate their land or leverage it as collateral to access commercial loans. Peasants could neither lease plots nor were they permitted to leave their plots idle for more than two consecutive years. Moreover, they did not receive formal land titles.

The government legislated an end to land redistribution in the early 1990s. On the back of a major debt crisis followed by a currency crisis, and with NAFTA looming, it shifted gears and pursued land formalization through a program called PROCEDE as part of a series of structural reforms initiated by IMF and World Bank intervention. Land reform beneficiaries received formal property registration, plot delineation, and land titles within the *ejidos* they lived on. The government also dropped a host of property rights restrictions within *ejidos* such as the prohibition on leasing land. The property rights gap in Mexico's land reform sector closed with this property rights reform.

Mexico is therefore anticipated to have experienced many of the negative outcomes of a large property rights gap followed by an improvement in outcomes after it closed its property rights gap.

Agricultural Production and Economic Development

Mexico's land reform generated fleeting economic growth as peasants who had strong incentives for maximizing immediate production received land. But the absence of property rights generated inefficiencies that stunted long-term growth in the country's agricultural sector and in the overall economy throughout the twentieth century. This is despite the robust overall growth from the 1940s through the 1970s that became known as the Mexican economic miracle.

The Mexican government dominated the provision of agricultural credit and inputs given the lack of property rights. Decreasing state investment in *ejidos* over time, combined with efforts to restrict farmers from interacting with private credit or land markets, compounded peasant dependence on the government and production inefficiency (Albertus et al. 2016, 156). Land became overexploited within *ejidos* as rural populations grew. This drove down yields. Private farm productivity came to far outperform that in *ejidos* (Gordillo et al. 1998, 158; Albertus et al. 2016, 156). Lamartine Yates (1981, 134) calculated that by 1970 crop output per hectare was around 40 percent higher in small private farms than in the established *ejido* sector. *Ejido* grain yields were 52 percent of the national average and *ejido* fruit yields were 63 percent of the national average by 1992 (Marsh and Runsten 1996, 172). Inefficiency in agriculture spilled over into broader economic transformation: land reform was associated with slower state-level overall economic growth where it was implemented most intensely (Albertus et al. 2016).

Production indicators for Mexico's key agricultural products have generally improved since the country implemented PROCEDE. Data from the Food and Agriculture Organization indicate that average yields per agricultural worker from 2015 to 2017 for corn, beans, wheat, sugarcane, and cereal grains – the bulk of Mexico's top agricultural products by planted area – were higher than the 1989–1991 averages on the eve of PROCEDE. The vast majority of this production, including 90 percent of corn, 92 percent of beans, 73 percent of wheat, and 90 percent of sugarcane, comes from small and medium producers.[17] While there are few empirical analyses that directly examine how titling through PROCEDE per se affected yields in the *ejido* sector, some evidence from corn production suggests that titling was productivity-enhancing (Acosta Peña 2008).[18]

Overall economic growth has been robust since the early 1990s – albeit not without some serious hiccups. This has transformed the lives of the poor. Just over 14 percent of the rural population lived below the World Bank's international poverty line of $1.90 per day in 2014, down from around 28 percent at the equivalent marker in the early 1990s (Villagómez Ornelas 2019, 2).

The Rural–Urban Divide
Mexico's property rights gap paved the way for the generation and entrenchment of a deep rural–urban divide in public policy and political power. Between marginal profits in agriculture and a lack of land tenure security, many land beneficiary families generally could not afford for younger generations to leave the farm. This stunted migration into urban areas where most opportunities for upward mobility could be found (Gordillo et al. 1998). The share of economically active Mexicans in the agricultural sector barely declined in the first three decades following the end of the revolution, dropping only from 71 percent in 1920 to 66 percent in 1950. Almost everyone employed in agriculture had parents employed in agriculture, as opposed to greater inter-generational occupational mobility in urban areas (Felix 1977, 113). Even by 1990, nearly 30 percent of the population worked in agriculture despite the fact that the share of agriculture as a percentage of the country's GDP had declined to only 7 percent.

Policy bias toward Mexico's largest cities grew. The Mexican government became progressively more committed to industrialization beginning in the 1940s. The state privileged urban infrastructure, provided heavy subsidies to businesses in industry, and protected nascent urban industries from import competition while simultaneously scaling back investment in the countryside (Eckstein 1982, 71). The social safety net, like many countries in Latin America, developed to cover urban and formal sector workers to a much greater degree

---

[17] Large producers are defined as those for whom production value exceeds one million pesos annually.
[18] PROCEDE is also associated with shifting landholding patterns as claimants to *ejido* lands increased (de Ita 2006) along with out-migration (de Janvry et al. 2015), complicating analyses of changes in productivity.

than rural and informal sector workers. For instance, while social security, pensions, minimum wages, and unemployment insurance were extended to state employees and blue-collar workers in more urban-centered jobs in industry such as manufacturing, many peasants did not benefit from social security, medical insurance, or other social welfare programs (Stavenhagen 1966, 482).

Healthcare policy is illustrative. President Cárdenas targeted healthcare improvements to rural areas for a brief period after the revolution. Cárdenas encouraged medical student trainees to conduct social service in rural areas and supported public health programs in *ejidos* (Eckstein 1982, 85). But this shifted dramatically in the 1940s as the property rights gap grew. Healthcare in Mexico became targeted heavily at urban areas. By 1970, 54 percent of all doctors worked in the four largest cities, which in turn counted 18 percent of the population (Eckstein 1982, 84). The rural poor, by contrast, lacked access to medical facilities and coverage.[19] The Ministry of Public Health and Public Assistance was confined largely to cities, serving an estimated 4 percent of the rural population (Eckstein 1982, 84).

State investment in education similarly drifted toward urban centers. Outcomes reflected this focus. Notwithstanding an important rural education and literacy campaign in the 1930s, by 1970 only 26 percent of rural primary schools went beyond the first four grades and only 9 percent of all rural pupils completed the four grades. Meanwhile, investment in higher education increased disproportionately and benefited the upper income strata of urban Mexicans (Felix 1977, 113–114).

The shift toward urban policy bias in Mexico mirrored patterns in the social origins of recruitment into the country's political elite. As the Mexican Revolution faded into the distance and the property rights gap grew, ossifying poverty traps in the countryside, the PRI began to draw its leadership more heavily from cities. A total of 38 percent of office-holding political elites and 42 percent of the echelon of political elites holding upper-level offices hailed from a state capital or city in the period 1917–1940 (Smith 1979, 75). These figures climbed to 46 percent and 60 percent in the period 1946–1971, respectively.[20] Smith (1979, 76) writes that "the military campaigns of the Revolution mobilized the rural population, made it an active participant in politics, and elevated numerous sons of rural and small-town families to positions of national prominence. When things later quieted down, the big-city types took over again." Ironically, whereas political support for the PRI was highest in rural areas, driven by its legendary and well-oiled clientelistic party machine, its leadership and policymakers came from the cities.

[19] Even in the cities, institutional coverage of health care was concentrated among major private business and the state sector.

[20] Cities are defined as settlements with more than 20,000 inhabitants as of 1921. The percentage of the population living in cities shifted from 17 percent in 1930 to 24 percent in 1960.

Several important rural–urban dynamics have shifted since the implementation of PROCEDE beginning in the 1990s even though the urban–rural divide remains significant. Rural mobility has increased substantially with the introduction of secure property rights. This has enabled rural inhabitants to migrate to gain education or better work opportunities. De Janvry et al. (2015), for instance, find that being a PROCEDE beneficiary increased the probability of having a family member migrate to urban areas or the United States. Members of *ejidos* with yields below national averages became far more likely to migrate, especially relative to uncertified and more productive farms. Rural migration, while difficult, can be a route to upward mobility and has in turn generated an increase in remittances to the families of migrants from rural areas (Esquivel 2011; Taylor et al. 2008).

Rural education has also been substantially revised. In addition to constitutional changes recognizing cultural and linguistic diversity, a major law federalizing basic education has enabled more tailor-made local solutions to education shortfalls such as community-based education (Corvalán 2006, 56). Greater attention to and investment in education in rural areas has paid off. According to census data, in towns with fewer than 2,500 residents, 61.8 percent of the population over 15 had not completed primary school in 1990; this dropped to 37.7 percent in 2010. Illiteracy among residents of towns smaller than 2,500 people was 15.7 percent as of 2010 relative to 25.4 percent in 1990.

Inequality

Land access improved substantially through Mexico's longstanding land reform. The breakup of many of the country's largest estates drove down land inequality. The landholding Gini dropped from an incredible 0.96 in 1930 (Eckstein 1982, 53) to 0.62 by 1960 (IFAD 2001, 118). The leveling of wealth through the revolution and radical policy shifts in the 1910s–1930s also drove down economic inequality in the subsequent several decades (Felix 1977).

But economic inequality between urban and rural areas grew as agricultural productivity in the land reform sector stagnated and demographic stasis set in. The country's Gini index increased by 16 percent between the 1950s and 1960s on the back of policy shifts and polarized returns to growth, returning the country to a level of economic inequality last witnessed on the eve of the Mexican Revolution (Felix 1977, 112).[21] Rural inequality and poverty eclipsed that in urban areas. By the 1960s there was a yawning income disparity between the industrializing north and agricultural south and central regions. Residents in Mexico City, Guadalajara, and Monterrey comprised 16 percent of Mexico's population in 1963 but earned one-third of national income while small farmers that comprised 45 percent of the country's population earned just one-fourth of national income (Felix 1977, 112).

---

[21] Felix (1977, 112) estimates a Gini index of 0.61 at the end of Mexico's Porfiriato period in 1910.

Inequality simultaneously increased within the rural sector. Credit availability to private farmers was much greater than to *ejidos* and this gap widened over time. While the amount of credit accessed by private farms increased eight-fold between 1950 and 1970, credit to *ejidos* showed little to no growth in that time (Sanderson 1984, 112–113). Declining access to credit meant most *ejidos* were unable to afford new farming technologies as they became available (Gordillo 1998, 158). This caused productivity to stagnate and increased the economic gap between the private and land reform sectors in the countryside.

Economic inequality has improved to a degree since the start of PROCEDE. Mexico's overall Gini coefficient declined from 0.503 in 1994 to 0.434 in 2016 according to the World Bank's World Development Indicators. Inequality in rural areas has similarly declined, driven by progressive social programs such as Procampo and Progresa (which was first rolled out in rural areas) as well as remittances from abroad (Esquivel 2011). This is an important finding given that PROCEDE induced migration out of *ejidos* (de Janvry et al. 2015, 167). Meanwhile, a 2001 World Bank study estimated that PROCEDE increased off-farm income for *ejido* families by over 1,000 pesos annually as landowners became able to lease their land if they opted to work in other sectors (Deininger and Bresciani 2001, 24–25).

Clientelism
The lack of property rights among land reform beneficiaries in Mexico suppressed small private markets for credit, seeds, and farming tools. Larger banks were reluctant to offer credit to farmers without a title. This ensured a baseline of peasant dependence on the state for the basic resources needed to survive. *Ejidos* needed to toe the line politically to receive these resources from the PRI. Local agrarian agencies were liable to deny workers access to state subsidies if they did not support the party (Albertus et al. 2016, 156). Internal social pressure encouraged compliance: the communal nature of land ownership and the fact that resources were granted to communities as a whole created incentives for individuals to encourage their neighbors to support the PRI. And the hub-and-spoke links between the state and individual *ejidos* created a crucial role for intermediaries to mediate between *ejidos* and the government; these intermediaries often became political bosses with tight links to the PRI (Gordillo et al. 1998).

That the lack of property rights inhibited mobility enhanced the PRI's political leverage over land reform beneficiaries. The inability to sell or lease land tied *ejido* members to the farm where the PRI could gain greater knowledge about them through repeated interactions. Albertus et al. (2016) find that land reform translated directly into electoral support for the PRI and that this support was enduring.

The PRI began to lose its vicelike grip on land reform beneficiaries when it began granting them property rights. De Janvry et al. (2014) demonstrate that support for the PRI eroded among land title recipients under the PROCEDE program. These recipients shifted their support toward the pro-market PAN party, which was ideologically to the right of the PRI and its chief competitor. PAN support among title recipients increased in each election cycle measured over the 15 years following the introduction of PROCEDE (de Janvry et al. 2014, 222).

Path C: The Path to Underdevelopment in Cuba

Cuba followed canonical property rights gap Path C. Fidel Castro's government began confiscating property from the former Batista regime and opposition groups beginning in 1959 through the Law for the Recovery of Misappropriated Property. This was a signature policy of the Cuban Revolution. It was followed by two major agrarian reform laws in 1959 and 1963 that set increasingly strict landholding ceilings and expropriated enormous swathes of private land. Meanwhile, the state nationalized major United States – owned sugarcane holdings and purchased small and medium-sized plots from the private sector. Purchases from the private sector continued for decades after the revolution. Land expropriations and nationalizations alone came to exceed 7 million hectares of land.

Most land reform beneficiaries did not receive property rights over land. Others received insecure and incomplete property rights. The government converted many large estates into various stripes of state-owned and state-run cooperatives that employed rural workers essentially as wage earners (Álvarez 2004, 2). And the private plots that some land beneficiaries received were not divisible and could only be sold to the state or transferred by inheritance (Thomas 1971). This effectively dismantled private property rights in the land reform sector. Castro announced in 1974 that the government would encourage land socialization with the intent of collective production for the remaining private farmers that owned 1.5 million hectares of land (Álvarez 2004, 6). The number of independent small private farmers decreased with the creation of the resulting cooperatives. By 1993 the private sector only controlled 9 percent of agricultural land (Álvarez 2004, 7).

The Cuban government opened up an enormous property rights gap in the countryside through its land reform that eventually came to swallow nearly the entire agricultural sector and more than the country's share of quality, easily cultivable land (see Figure 2.6). That property rights gap continues today.

Agricultural Production and Economic Development

Cuba's land reform sparked an immediate spike in economic and agricultural production as underutilized land was put into production. But these increases lasted only a few years (Zimbalist and Eckstein 1987, 7). Over a quarter of government investments went to the agricultural sector in the first 25 years after the reform (Rodriguez 1987, 29) despite the fact that the share of agriculture as a percentage of the country's GDP decreased from 18 percent to 13 percent between 1961 and 1981 (Ghai et al. 1988, 121). Total agricultural production showed little acceleration from prerevolutionary growth over this period and agricultural imports dwarfed exports. Meanwhile, though exact records vary, the number of workers in Cuba's agricultural sector increased from about 550,000 in the years before the revolution to about 750,000 by 1980 (Ghai et al. 1988, 6; 103). Agricultural productivity therefore declined on a per capita basis for many key crops like sugar (by 8 percent), beans (by 93 percent), tobacco (by 19 percent), and tubers (by 76 percent) in spite of typically longer harvest seasons; meanwhile, citrus and rice exhibited productivity gains (by 90 percent and 20 percent, respectively) (Forster 1981, 7).

The United States embargo against Cuba slowly chipped away at its economy and forced it to generate other trading partnerships. One of the most lucrative was its partnership with the Soviet Union. The Soviets purchased Cuba's majority export, sugar, at up to double the open market rate (MacEwan 1981, 190). The Cuban government consequently forced many farms to convert to sugarcane production. The result was a reliance on most food imports and a volatile agricultural economy dependent almost solely on sugarcane yields (Palma et al. 2015, 79). Nearly half of land under cultivation was devoted to sugarcane production by 1990 (Ziegler and Vanderbush 2015, 148). Sugarcane workers' wages were tied to national yields, and in times of low output, workers often tried to switch jobs locally or move to urban areas, which in turn created a labor shortage and exacerbated production crises (MacEwan 1981, 54). Others were content with having a guaranteed salary but lacked incentives to maximize their individual output due to the government's wage standardization (MacEwan 1981, 145).

After the Soviet Union collapsed, these economic vulnerabilities twinned with tightening US sanctions drove the country into a major economic crisis. The Cuban economy contracted by more than a third from 1989 to 1993, imports plummeted by 75 percent, exports dropped by 79 percent, and average caloric intake diminished by 30 percent (Ziegler and Vanderbush 2015, 148). The government responded by loosening state controls on crop production and allowing peasants to form their own cooperatives. This effectively let out slack in property rights restrictions. The economy staged an impressive recovery, but many of the fundamentals regarding sugarcane export reliance and the importing of most food remained the same. The Cuban economy continues to suffocate under state control and an absence of property rights.

The Rural–Urban Divide

The rural–urban divide in Cuba in terms of policy and political power has been unusual within Latin America and anomalous to a degree from the perspective of theoretical expectations. The departure, however, is driven largely by the government's communist ideology and the particular nature of the Cuban Revolution (Colburn 1993).

Consider healthcare, education, and social security. The government expanded and reorganized its healthcare system in the 1960s in an effort to generate universal and free healthcare access that included the countryside. It disproportionately invested in rural areas in the decade after the revolution to counteract previous urban bias in care (Eckstein 1982, 86). The government required medical students to spend two years in rural service before graduating (Colburn 1993, 69). Lifespans quickly improved and preventable deaths such as high infant mortality plummeted (Ghai et al. 1988, 123). In terms of education, the government implemented a massive and expensive literacy program shortly after the revolution that built a swathe of new schools, tripled the number of educators nationwide (Rodriguez 1987, 31), and brought volunteers – mostly urban students – to live and teach in rural communities. The result was a virtual elimination of illiteracy (Bowles 1971, 488). Social security was extended widely to nearly all Cubans (Colburn 1993, 69).

While these policies have had an enormous impact, some elements remain or have become more uneven over time along the urban–rural divide. For instance, there is still a marked difference in the degree of educational attainment between urban and rural students. Rural students are significantly less likely to continue beyond primary school than urban students (MacEwan 1981, 89–90). As of 2017, whereas 70 percent of the country's primary schools are located in rural areas, 89 percent of secondary schools are in urban areas (ONE 2018, 10).

Furthermore, other government policies and practices serve to entrench government control over rural areas and the favoritism or cordoning off of urban spaces. For instance, the Cuban government implemented restrictions on rural movement to Havana for the first time in 1997. And the piecemeal introduction of restricted markets to address problems like food shortages has had clear urban–rural distributional consequences. Market vendors located closer to Havana quickly gained a clear advantage over their more peripheral counterparts. State estimates in 1980 suggested peasant farmers selling in Havana markets earned up to 40,000 pesos annually compared with an average yearly state salary of 1,500 pesos for agricultural workers (Deere 1992, 831–832). With this windfall, some private farmers began bribing state farms for their government-allocated inputs and resources, creating further production and income disparity in the sector (Deere 1992, 832). The country briefly shut down these markets due to rural protests but then re-established and expanded them as part of a loosening of economic controls after the collapse of the Soviet Union.

Inequality

The Cuban government invested heavily in reducing inequality and made dramatic progress in doing so initially. The country's Gini coefficient of income inequality plummeted from 0.47 to 0.26 in the first twenty years after the Cuban Revolution and large landholding elites largely disappeared (Ghai et al. 1988, 23; 123).

Eventually, however, the property rights gap made inequality increasingly difficult to contain. For instance, the government began allowing peasants to sell goods on a restricted marketplace as it became progressively more difficult to control all food distribution without generating shortages or other undesirable economic distortions. Private farmers dropped staple goods like sugar, rice, and beans and began producing either goods not available in state ration stores (such as pork and plantains) or expensive fruits like papaya (Deere 1992, 831–834). Because the government dictated which crops state farmers could grow, private producers – who were relatively few in number – had an exclusive ability to take advantage of this opening. This generated economic and social stratification given relatively low state salaries and high prices for quality market goods.

Broader market expansions and the economic shock that came with the collapse of the Soviet Union and loss of aid and trading revenue have further exacerbated inequality, in part by forcing the country to quickly attempt to counter the economic distortions of its enormous property rights gap. Social, racial, and economic inequality are now rising and social services are becoming more anemic (see Hansing 2017).

Clientelism

By reorienting the agricultural sector toward cooperatives and state farms and rendering small farmers subject to strict oversight, the Cuban government constructed a dense web of relationships with individual farmers while positioning itself centrally as the indispensable purveyor of the necessities of rural life. This all-encompassing web cannot be escaped. It inexorably traps rural inhabitants in clientelistic links to the government.

There was a proliferation of independent peasant organizations at the time of the Cuban Revolution. The Castro government consolidated them all into the National Association of Small Peasants (ANAP). The National Bank financed credit to small farmers that was administered through ANAP (MacEwan 1981, 58). The association surveyed credit applicants for political loyalty before approving any support (Domínguez 1978, 450). Cooperative members received favorable credit rates (Rodriguez 1987, 29). The state also offered free inputs and technical aid for private farmers that joined ANAP and exempted small farmers from tax (Rodriguez 1987, 29). Even private farmers eventually could not afford to produce without state support and came to rely on the state for credit and supplies (Ghai et al. 1988, 83–84).

Peasant dependency and hierarchical state control eases the coercive and informational costs of governing and provides levers for the state to forestall and stanch autonomous rural collective action. Counterbalancing the enticements of rural engagement with the state, ANAP leaders were required to participate in state-sponsored civil institutions like civil defense brigades and members were expected to enroll in political education courses where they studied the state's revolutionary ideals (Domínguez 1978, 456–458). And ANAP could wield the stick: it would confiscate land or eliminate subsidies from individual workers that dissented against the state and its system (Domínguez 1978, 450).

5.4 CONCLUSION

Property rights shape the opportunities and limitations of rural life. They also have wide-ranging consequences for economic, political, and social life writ large. Property rights gaps can impact whether a country follows a path to prosperity, a path to delayed development, or a path to underdevelopment.

Redistributive land reform has the potential to deliver gains to agricultural productivity and even broader economic growth. But a lack of property rights for land reform beneficiaries can sap their economic dynamism. Land reform that generates a property rights gap threatens to squander its economic potential by stymieing investment, hobbling land markets, and distorting labor markets. That the distribution of land typically comes without the extension of property rights to beneficiaries helps to explain why land reform is so often viewed as a failure in the policy world despite the fact that land inequality is seen as counterproductive to growth.

That land redistribution often does not deliver development is not an oversight or blunder. It is the cost of doing business for the authoritarian regimes that typically enact major land reform. And the political benefits are more than sufficient recompense: creating a property rights gap keeps most rural dwellers in the countryside where they are more easily tracked and manipulated and pose less of a political threat than if they flooded into cities. The myriad problems that a property rights gap creates for rural individuals serve as the very hooks that a deft incumbent regime can use for clientelistic ends. Meanwhile, political power under a property rights gap progressively tilts in favor of urban areas over rural ones. The result is that a government that presides over a property rights gap can tighten the noose on the countryside, extracting stability and even political support at the very same time as the prospects for success and mobility among rural populations are being strangled. All of this tends to fuel rural–urban inequality over time as the countryside languishes.

6

Opening and Closing a Property Rights Gap in Peru

Chapters 6 and 7 take a complementary approach to the previous two chapters. Chapters 4 and 5 provide panoramic empirical tests of the causes and consequences of property rights gaps at the country-year level. Chapters 6 and 7 instead examine in detail the property rights gap and its constituent local-level components in a single country: Peru.

This chapter begins by outlining the origins of Peru's massive property rights gap that began in the 1960s and endured into the 2000s. The timing and circumstances of the opening and closing of this property rights gap, leading the country along canonical property rights gap Path B, illustrate the theoretical predictions in Chapter 3 well.

But the principal aims of these chapters are to more carefully examine the theory's causal mechanisms and to test its observable implications. I do so using primary and secondary documents, interviews, and a wealth of original subnational data on the scope of Peru's land reform, subsequent property rights, and a host of social, demographic, and economic variables that I largely constructed through fieldwork and archival work.

These chapters demonstrate the internal validity of the theory and its utility for understanding spatial and temporal variation in localized property rights gaps and their consequences within countries. Local property rights gaps in Peru that were generated in the 1970s as part of the national property rights gap shaped local social and economic outcomes in a manner consistent with what Chapter 5 anticipates. They drove a slower shift out of working in agriculture, lower agricultural productivity and educational attainment, and higher rates of inequality and poverty. The relatively long duration of the property rights gap also helps to develop further observable implications of the theory.

6.1 CASE SELECTION FOR SUBNATIONAL ANALYSIS

Several reasons support the decision to examine Peru in greater detail. First, the key macro-level factors that the theory links to the opening and the closing of a property rights gap varied substantially over time in Peru since the early twentieth century. Peru cycled between democracy and dictatorship over the last century. The political composition of ruling elites and their coalitional links to landowners and peasants varied as well. Landowners at times had a strong presence in democratic legislatures and were at other times nearly absent. In addition, the country was buffeted by economic crises that forced it into structural adjustment programs for which it had to ask for assistance from international lenders. This variation enables a careful tracing of the causal mechanisms that link these factors to the creation or elimination of a property rights gap. In this way, this chapter contributes internal validity to the theory and the empirical tests in Chapter 4.

Second, both land redistribution and the extension of property rights to former land reform beneficiaries in Peru have been the subject of considerable scholarly attention. A series of important arguments have been advanced to explain the timing and structure of these policies. Applying the theoretical framework developed in this book nonetheless contributes to existing scholarship in an original manner. This demonstrates the theory's utility in making sense of important cases and illuminating the mechanisms at work.

Third, Peru's military regime documented internal decision-making within the Ministry of Agriculture regarding the structure of landholding among land reform beneficiaries. These documents enable a granular study of the logic of land distribution and property rights as well as insights to perceived advantages and risks of withholding property rights from land reform beneficiaries.

Finally, Peru's military regime meticulously recorded each and every land expropriation and subsequent distribution to peasant beneficiaries. I assembled a research team to gather comprehensive original data on the scope and intensity of Peru's reform and paired it with land registration data and with subsequent social and economic outcome data that link back to Chapter 5: the share of the population working in agriculture, agricultural productivity, urban bias as measured by rural educational attainment, inequality, and income per capita. The case of Peru therefore presents one of the first opportunities to test hypotheses about the development consequences of land reform and property rights at a very local level over the course of decades despite the fact that scholars across numerous disciplines have long conjectured about these policies. Furthermore, the nature of how Peru's land reform was implemented – through agrarian zones that were delimited well before the reform – enables a clean identification strategy for empirical analysis. I explain this last point in detail in Chapter 7.

6.2   THE GENERATION OF A PROPERTY RIGHTS GAP IN PERU

Table 6.1 lists the key variables that this book's theory links to the generation, retention, and closing of a property rights gap for each government of Peru between 1939 and 2011. The table includes the regime type under which each government ruled, whether or not there was a coalition split between ruling

TABLE 6.1 *Factors impacting the property rights gap in Peru, 1939–2011*

President	Years in office	Regime type	Elite split	Landowner power in legislature	Pressure for closing property rights gap during structural adjustment	Property rights gap outcome
Manuel Prado	1939–45	Civilian Dictatorship	Low	High	N/A	None
José Bustamante	1945–48	Democracy	High	High	N/A	None
Manuel Odría	1948–56	Military Dictatorship	Low	N/A	N/A	None
Manuel Prado	1956–62	Democracy	Low	High	N/A	None
Ricardo Pérez Godoy	1962–63	Military Dictatorship	Limited	N/A	N/A	Limited redistribution without property rights in Cusco region
Nicolás Lindley López	1963	Military Dictatorship	Low	N/A	N/A	None
Fernando Belaúnde	1963–68	Democracy	High	High	N/A	1964 Agrarian Reform Law passed but weakened by Congress; 380,000 hectares from 1964–68 granted mainly to individuals with title linked to repayment

(*continued*)

TABLE 6.1 (*continued*)

President	Years in office	Regime type	Elite split	Landowner power in legislature	Pressure for closing property rights gap during structural adjustment	Property rights gap outcome
Juan Velasco Alvarado	1968–75	Military Dictatorship	High	N/A	N/A	Large PR gap formed: 1969 land reform Decree Law 17716; 5.8 million hectares redistributed without property rights from 1968–75
Francisco Morales Bermúdez	1975–80	Military Dictatorship	High	N/A	N/A	Large PR gap grows: Continuation of Decree 17716; 2.7 million hectares redistributed without property rights from 1975–80
Fernando Belaúnde	1980–85	Democracy	Low	Low	N/A	Large PR gap remains: small trailing land redistribution under previous laws; PR strengthened via laws to enable breakup of agrarian collectives to individuals

Alan García	1985–90	Democracy	Low	Low	N/A	Large PR gap remains: continued breakup of agrarian collectives but no formal property rights program
Alberto Fujimori	1990–2000	Democracy (1990–1991)/ Dictatorship (1992–2000)	Low	Low	High	PR gap shrinks: laws and programs aimed at individual land titling (e.g., 1992 Special Land Titling Project [PETT])
Alejandro Toledo	2001–06	Democracy	High	High	N/A	PR gap shrinks: individual land titling via PETT continues
Alan García	2006–11	Democracy	Low	High	N/A	PR gap shrinks: individual land titling via PETT/COFOPRI continues

Note: In some years there was not an operative legislature. The only period of major structural economic adjustment occurred under Fujimori. President García refused to undertake major reforms.

Sources: Albertus (2015); Ballantyne et al. (2000); Carter and Alvarez (1989); Cleaves and Scurrah (1980); COFOPRI (2008); Gilbert (1977); Lastarria-Cornhiel (1989); Mayer (2009); McClintock (1981).

political elites and landed elites, the relative power of large landowners in the legislature (if there was an effective legislature with autonomous powers), and the degree of international pressure for closing a property rights gap in the context of structural economic adjustment. The final column of the table indicates the outcome in terms of the property rights gap. Table 6.1 guides the discussion that follows.

Peru's economy until the 1960s largely revolved around land. According to census calculations, 50 percent of the economically active population in 1961 worked in agriculture. Demonstrating stark inequalities, however, the 1961 agricultural census documented that the largest 1 percent of landowners held 80 percent of private land whereas 83 percent of farmers held properties of 5 hectares or less, representing only 6 percent of private land. Land tenure relations varied widely but were archaic in many regions. This was especially the case in the semifeudal haciendas of the highland sierras. Most indigenous peasants in these haciendas farmed small plots for family consumption on the owner's land in exchange for labor on the hacienda. These peasants were not free to move and the owner could rotate or retract land at his discretion.

A wide range of political entrepreneurs long appealed to peasants by promising redistributive land reform. The first major political party to do so was the American Popular Revolutionary Alliance (APRA). But reform was stymied until the 1960s. The military largely protected the wealth and power of the preexisting landowning elite due to factors such as the recruitment of elites into the military's upper ranks (Lowenthal 1974, 121). Furthermore, large landowners organized politically under episodes of democracy to directly capture a large portion of seats in the legislature. This was facilitated by a press favorable to (and owned by) elites, literacy restrictions on voting, coercion of rural voters, elites' disproportionate financial resources, and a host of other factors. The result was that large landowners entirely blocked land redistribution in the early to mid-twentieth century in spite of repeated flip-flopping between dictatorship and democracy.

The position of landowners became more precarious in the early to mid-1960s. Peasant organizers successfully staged a series of large-scale strikes and land invasions in the southern highlands. A series of short-lived military regimes in 1962–1963 sought to undercut the most serious flashpoints and expropriated several large estates in the La Convención and Lares valleys in Cusco for distribution to peasants (Masterson 1991, 187). But the policy was ad hoc and went no further.

The return to democracy in 1963 brought Fernando Belaúnde to power. Belaúnde campaigned on a platform that prominently incorporated land reform. This garnered him considerable popular support and even generated a new wave of land invasions in the Andes in anticipation of reform. But Belaúnde's initial political coalition was heterogeneous and included both pro-reform ministers and a substantial number of ministers from landed families.

Although landowners lost a foothold over time, they kept a chokehold on the legislature. A land reform law did squeak through Congress in 1964. It envisioned distributing land to individuals, cooperatives, and communities, depending on location and prior land tenure relations. But landholding interests added so many modifications that the law as originally proposed ended up riddled with holes like swiss cheese. Even a smooth expropriation required 51 steps and at least 22 months to implement (Cleaves and Scurrah 1980, 41). Landowners had effectively used their position in the legislature to strangle reform.

Belaúnde did manage to redistribute just shy of 400,000 hectares of land to peasants (Matos Mar and Mejía 1980, 103). He did so mainly in conflictive areas of the southern highlands. The government only expropriated two coastal haciendas, one in Casma (Ancash department) and one in Huaral (Lima department). It split up and distributed most of this land to individual peasant families that were working on traditional haciendas, though it also granted some collectively (Matos Mar and Mejía 1980, 103). Individual land reform beneficiaries received their land with a limited but important encumbrance: they would not be granted full title until they had repaid the value of the land over twenty years. They would lose the land if they did not meet this requirement (Matos Mar and Mejía 1980, 99–101).[1] As it would happen, a new land reform would occur first.

A series of scandals and crises bedeviled the later years of Belaúnde's term in office. The military again stepped in amid the public turmoil to seize power in an October 1968 coup. Consistent with the theory laid out in Chapter 3, military rule in Peru under General Velasco set the stage for redistributing land but withholding property rights from beneficiaries. Velasco's ruling officers hailed from the middle class and did not include landed elites (see Albertus 2015, 200–204). Velasco instead saw landed elites as a rival to the military's authority and autonomy. This generated strong incentives to crush landed elites through land redistribution. And there was little to restrain the military's actions after it shuttered all independent institutions that could check its power.

General Velasco embarked on a radical experiment to fundamentally reshape Peruvian society. This was a monumental undertaking. Decree Law 17716 in 1969 set strict landholding ceilings at 150 hectares or lower (depending on location) and expropriated land, capital assets, and animals on properties larger than the stipulated threshold. It typically redistributed expropriated land as cooperatives to former enterprise or hacienda workers that had labored on the property. It also distributed land to adjacent indigenous communities living on

---

[1] The government paid expropriated landowners mainly in government bonds that were never honored. In one interview I conducted in Lima on January 26, 2018, a politician whose family was expropriated by Belaúnde indicated that the family is still seeking compensation from the government for their land.

marginal lands in some cases. The regime later lowered landholding ceilings even further.

The military did not grant land reform beneficiaries property rights over their land. It retained co-ownership of cooperatives until the mortgage on the land was paid and it obligated cooperatives to repay the value of the land to the government over a 20-year period, along with any debt that the cooperative took on in order to finance inputs, mechanization, and other investment. Ownership was never given over to cooperatives during military rule.[2] The regime also prohibited land sales, leasing, and the use of assets as collateral for loans. This was true even for the small number of private households that were granted individual plots under the reform.

Law 17716 drastically altered land tenure relationships and property ownership. It was implemented most rigorously from 1969 to 1976. Land reform tapered precipitously after this due to the rise to power of General Morales Bermúdez and a severe late-1970s economic crisis. The military had expropriated and redistributed roughly half of all private agricultural land by the end of its rule in 1980.

Withholding Property Rights from Land Reform Beneficiaries

In prior work, I examined the logic and patterns of Peru's land redistribution program (Albertus 2015, Ch. 6). But what explains why the military regime withheld property rights from beneficiaries? After all, the structure of property rights under the military's reform differed radically from those under its democratic predecessor, which had mainly doled out expropriated lands to individual families.

Myopia and Ideology

Two logics detailed in Chapter 3 undoubtedly contributed to the ways in which land was redistributed and property rights delineated in Peru: myopia (and in particular competing regime goals) and ideology.[3] Consider first the economic goals of the regime that competed with granting land reform beneficiaries formal and alienable property rights. Scholarship on the military regime's inner functioning indicates that the government viewed retaining economies of scale in production and agricultural output to meet urban food consumption demand as critical (Cleaves and Scurrah 1980). Contemporaneously documented internal Ministry of Agriculture discussions support this

---

[2] See McClintock (1981, Ch. 2) for a detailed discussion of the structure and management of cooperatives.

[3] State capacity also played a role in how property rights operated in practice. Unlike the alternative argument in Chapter 3, however, limitations to state capacity did not prevent the provision of secure and complete property rights. After all, this was not the regime's goal. Rather, weak state capacity undermined control in cooperatives to a degree. For instance, some cooperatives subverted rules regarding the hiring and firing of managers (McClintock 1981).

assessment (Ministerio de Agricultura 1971b). The immediate breakup of large estates and the granting of properties to peasant proprietors could have risked a shift toward subsistence agriculture and a short-term spike in the price of food. And in areas of high land pressure, excessive land fractionalization could have posed a threat to rural livelihoods and economic dislocation associated with migration to cities.

Organizing land in cooperatives of beneficiaries provided the regime with the ability to amalgamate expropriated haciendas along with smallholders and indigenous communities and vertically integrate them into regional economic centers and national economic goals (García 1970, 392). Rationalized and more centralized planning could then harness these cooperatives for improved economic growth. The government's retention of joint title over land and prohibition on alienation by cooperatives ensured a further backstop against challenges to scale in production.

The regime settled on two principal and novel types of cooperatives: *Cooperativas Agrarias de Producción* (agrarian production cooperatives, or CAPs) and *Sociedades Agrícolas de Interés Social* (agrarian social interest societies, or SAISs). A CAP was composed of permanent laborers jointly responsible for managing a single estate. A SAIS, by contrast, was an association composed of permanent laborers from a number of neighboring estates as well as local communities that did not share in the land, labor, or capital of the estates but could participate in their management and receive a share in their profits (Mayer 2009; McClintock 1981). Incorporating adjacent communities had the benefit of broadening the scope of the land reform. SAISs often incorporated indigenous communities who had been previously dispossessed of their land by the growth of haciendas prior to the land reform. Many, though not all, of the most modernized and capitalized enterprises, particularly on the coast, became CAPs. The government formed a number of SAISs from livestock haciendas in the highlands. However, it created CAPs and SAISs throughout the country.

A second motive for creating state-led cooperatives was ideological in nature and ran through ideas surrounding the necessity for social change in the countryside. This motive took time to cohere and was somewhat fluid. Important scholarship indicates that the regime sought to build social solidarity and elevate peasant attitudes of themselves and their role in society through cooperatives (Cant 2012; McClintock 1981; Seligmann 1995). While the regime was explicitly anticommunist (McClintock 1981, 52–54), and top figures had diverse and shifting views (Pease García 1977), the core coalition surrounding General Velasco (known as the Earthquake Group) was composed of radical high-level colonels. Like Velasco himself, who was born into a sprawling working-class family in Piura, these colonels hailed from Peru's provinces, born to largely impoverished families (Kruijt 1994, 46). Rodríguez Figueroa and Gallegos had humble Cuzco roots. Fernández Maldonado was born in a small town in remote Moquegua. Hoyos was from Cajamarca and initially joined the Army as a volunteer soldier.

One particularly influential international example that the regime drew from for policy design and implementation was Yugoslavia (Cant 2012, 33). Under the leadership of Josip Broz Tito, Yugoslavia was seen as having used an emphasis on class and economic organization (including agricultural collectives and cooperatives) to successfully forge national solidarity where ethnic divisions and elite domination rooted in a foreign imperial past had long predominated.

The Peruvian government rolled out a powerful series of widely disseminated posters and other propaganda to portray the agrarian reform as the collective fulfillment of longstanding rural struggles, led by popular heroes such as Túpac Amaru II, to topple colonial-era vestiges and oppressive elites and return Peru to the spirit of its independent and powerful Incan past (Cant 2012, 22). Figure 6.1 displays two posters typical of the time. The poster on the left reads, "190 years later, Tupac Amaru is winning the war." The poster on the right, in celebration of Peasants' Day, reads, "We are free, the revolution is giving us the land."

The government sought to raise peasant class consciousness through the structure of its reforms. The focus was on social and class solidarity over

FIGURE 6.1 Posters celebrating land reform in Peru
Source: Posters were printed by the Office for Dissemination of the Agrarian Reform. The image on the left is taken from Cant (2012, 21). The image on the right is taken from Cant (2012, 29).

individual or ethnic rights and on cooperative ownership over individual interests. The regime created a popular mobilization organization (SINAMOS) to promote social solidarity and, among other tasks, sent its agents into cooperatives to train managers, promote collective work effort, and aid in administration while seeking to undermine centrifugal forces and community leaders with an independent streak. For instance, in an interview I conducted in Lima on February 6, 2018, a former SINAMOS operative who worked in Ancash in the early 1970s told me that he viewed his job as "to mobilize consciousness for social ends" and to "politicize" the peasantry.

Social Control
There was a third abiding motive that dovetailed with the first two: social control. The military regime was not nefarious – to the contrary, it had ambitious development goals – but it was rigidly hierarchical and unaccountable. It sought not only to inculcate peasants with a specific set of values and beliefs but also to stamp out political and social organization that occurred outside the auspices of official channels to the extent possible. Asserting control over the countryside was far easier if, rather than create millions of independent peasant smallholders, the regime could cultivate a small number of clear local agrarian leaders that they could interface with and influence to meet the regime's goals tied to agricultural production, the retention of rural populations in the countryside, social peace, and active peasant support (Matos Mar and Mejía 1980; Mayer 2009; McClintock 1981). This militated toward forcing beneficiaries into aggregate production units.

The logic of control also underpinned creating hooks into communities that the regime could use to influence crucial peasant behaviors tied to production decisions, forestalling communist and other agitators, and recruiting support into government-run programs and organizations that were oriented toward channeling peasant support for the regime (such as SINAMOS). As Hunefeldt (1997, 116) describes it, "the state appointed managers for the cooperatives who, in turn, sought to expand their internal power and legitimacy by enlarging their bureaucratic clientele within the cooperative ... [P]roduction decisions were subordinated to political maneuvering."[4]

All of this was easier if land reform beneficiaries did not have property rights or individual ownership over the land that they received. This rendered them less autonomous and more susceptible to government demands. Many peasants opposed this arrangement and tried to push back. Lastarria-Cornhiel (1989, 142) writes that, "There was pressure from the beneficiary families from the beginning for more individual production and less collective land." Similarly, the noted economist and scholar of the reform José María Caballero, writing at

---

[4] More precisely, cooperatives had an Administrative Council that was responsible for policy formulation in the cooperative. This council would select three candidates for the director position and the Ministry of Agriculture would select one of these.

the end of military rule, concluded that, "In most instances cooperative members did not want – and still do not want – the cooperative (although they normally prefer it to the hacienda); instead, they definitely favor land distribution" (Caballero 1981, 45). One peasant skeptically mused at the outset of land reform, "We don't know whether we will have a new life or just a new patron, the government which has expropriated the hacienda to form the cooperative" (quoted in Gall 1971, 287).

Production itself remained on individual plots in many highland areas despite the fact that land and profits belonged to cooperatives. Many cooperatives more generally tried to subvert or evade government initiatives. Kay (1985, 164) concludes that, "In the absence of genuine mass participation, the collective co-operative model had to be imposed from above and was perceived as a constraint by the very people it was supposed to benefit." Indeed, that the government retained land ownership and outsized influence, and even required debt payments on land, angered peasants (McClintock 1981, 293–294).

The government ignored peasant preferences and pressed forward with the goal of organizing large cooperative production units that could not be subdivided, which turned out to be harder than it had initially anticipated (Lastarria-Cornhiel 1989, 142). The government also pushed beneficiaries into the National Agrarian Confederation (CNA). The CNA was a peak agricultural-sector organization that established corporatist control over peasant actions and doled out critical credits, loans, and subsidies that peasants could not acquire from the private sector given their lack of property rights. The government used the state-run Agrarian Bank, the Agricultural Development Bank, and the CNA together to provide compliant and active peasant groups with the bulk of credit, inputs, and investment (McClintock 1981, 42). The Agrarian Bank increased credits substantially in the first phase of military rule, winning peasant support and compliance with cooperative rules and production guidelines (McClintock 1981, 289). By contrast, loans to medium- and small-sized farms decreased.

Peasant land reform beneficiaries that opposed the government's interventions or joined rival organizations were asking for trouble. Mayer (2009, 6) writes that, "Civilian opposition was not treated kindly. Organized unions affiliated with left-wing parties [the regime's biggest political threat] were divided by the creation of parallel Velasco organizations, demobilizing them with rough tactics." The military regime sent bureaucrats into the cooperatives to directly intervene in their management. It also deployed agents from SINAMOS to agitate for and monitor peasant groups. In addition, it used the Agrarian Bank to threaten the withdrawal of loans for cooperatives that failed to comply with stipulations such as hiring a director (McClintock 1981, 302). The regime consequently knew which peasants were supportive and which opposed to the regime, joining rival groups such as the independent Peasant Confederation of Peru (CCP).

Many cooperatives encountered economic problems by the mid-late 1970s and strained under the weight of centrifugal forces. While wages were generally rather high in cooperatives, and appreciated by members, they were not embedded within a comprehensive and predictable compensation strategy and therefore did not serve as strong an incentive to collaborative work achievement as they otherwise could have. This is in part because income distribution was perceived as unfair in many (though not all) cooperatives: "the correlation between hard work and high pay was far from perfect," alienating workers (McClintock 1981, 226). At cooperatives with higher wages and profits, members worked longer hours daily for the cooperative, whereas where wages were lower and losses outweighed profits, members worked less for the cooperative and devoted more time to private economic activities. Work quotas were often pegged to quantity rather than quality. This encouraged cooperative members to complete their required work as fast as possible in order to allocate the remainder of their time to alternative money-making activities. Furthermore, corruption within management boards and promotions based on social or political reasons rather than skill and experience also served as a disincentive to collaborative work achievement (McClintock 1981, 225; 230).

The state exerted even more direct control over cooperatives in an attempt to address these issues. Changes in wages and work conditions had to be directly approved by the Ministry of Agriculture. And rather than influencing the elected leaders of cooperatives, the state replaced some of them directly with government functionaries (for instance, in the sugar cooperatives on the northern coast).

These changes did not infuse the cooperatives with more economic dynamism. Agricultural production grew at a tepid 1.8 percent from 1970 to 1976, which was less than population growth and only one-third of GDP growth during the period (Kay 1985, 161).[5] It flat-lined in 1977 and turned negative in 1978, compounded by drought. Price controls and subsidies oriented toward urban food consumption further chipped away at the productivity of domestic agriculture. Yet the land reform did serve the goal of generating male employment in agriculture, tripling the rate of growth vis-à-vis the previous decade (Kay 1985, 161). In short, the developmental legacy was retaining peasants in rural areas despite economic stagnation in agriculture.

Social Control in the Valle del Santa

The military government's drive to control and manipulate peasants by redistributing land to them but withholding property rights – at the risk of pushback and broader economic distortions – is evident in numerous cases of land adjudication across the country. Here I consider the case of Valle del Santa.

---

[5] It is worth noting, however, that some cooperatives suffered less from free-riding problems, and some cooperatives were responsive to government efforts in 1975–1976 to increase incentives for collaborative work achievement (see McClintock 1981, 234–239).

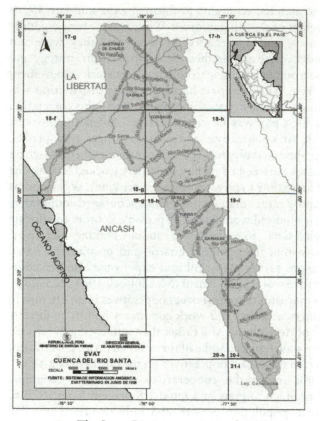

FIGURE 6.2 The Santa River system in northern Peru

Internal Ministry of Agriculture documents clearly lay out the tradeoffs in withholding property rights in this region despite the top-down drive to do so.

The Valle del Santa is a valley spanning the Santa River that is one of the largest hydrographic features of Ancash department in northern coastal Peru. Part of the Santa Valley also extends into southern La Libertad department. Figure 6.2 is a map of the Santa River system.

The Ministry of Agriculture first expropriated a series of 23 large properties in the lower Santa Valley that comprised 15,432 hectares of land in the coastal districts of Santa and Chimbote in the department of Ancash and part of the district of Virú in the department of La Libertad.[6] It then sought to adjudicate these properties to 2,356 peasant families comprising nearly 12,000 individuals. The properties had high-quality land and were mainly dedicated to producing corn, rice, and cotton as well as raising cattle. In December of 1971, the Ministry of Agriculture circulated an internal study, generated by

---

[6] This discussion and the details and quotes herein draw from Ministerio de Agricultura (1971a).

Agrarian Zone 3 officials, to link together a number of these properties into a large production settlement known as a Project of Integrated Rural Settlement (PIAR). PIARs served as important amalgamated units of cooperatives across Peru during military rule.

The Valle del Santa PIAR was initially to be composed, in turn, of seven distinct cooperatives that were ostensibly to operate "autonomously" of one another. The Ministry of Agriculture intended to organize these cooperatives into both CAPs and SAISs. The actions of these cooperatives were to be coordinated through a central cooperative body that would provide complementary services to the cooperatives, help to coordinate joint production plans and dedicated resources to those ends, and regulate compensation within the individual cooperatives by receiving the profits of the cooperatives and then returning them after engaging in activities such as setting minimum and maximum salaries for workers.

The government would ultimately place bureaucrats and technical personnel within these cooperatives to monitor them and aid their operation. In addition, it would play a critical role in the central cooperative body, which would come to be the main conduit of technical assistance, marketing, loans and credits, indispensable inputs, research associated with agricultural production, and compensation rules that guided profit-sharing across constituent cooperative units and families within those units. Figure 6.3 indicates the structure of the Santa Valley PIAR.

The Ministry of Agriculture's plan faced peasant pushback in the Santa Valley. Some peasant families advocated for the adjudication of land in individual plots. In response to a series of economic, social, and production studies and plans, the Agrarian Zone 3 officials recommended increasing the number of cooperatives in the PIAR to nine and adjudicating the lands of one property, Tangay, which comprised 1,757 hectares of land, to 113 families in individual plots. These families, however, would be "provided only the necessary services" from the central cooperative body (Ministerio de Agricultura 1971a, 3). This relegated them to second-class citizens within the PIAR. Furthermore, for other families to be integrated into the PIAR and provided with state supports, they had to give up the plots they had previously farmed within the ex-haciendas they worked on: "Those who persist in maintaining their individual position will be relocated" to other areas of the valley – areas with "available land" – which was typically so because it was of lower quality and less productive (Ministerio de Agricultura 1971a, 5).

Most peasants quickly understood their precarious position and got in line with respect to their cooperatives and the central cooperative body. Take for instance peasants who came to comprise the cooperative Tambo Real within the Santa PIAR. At the time of the formation of the cooperative there was strong social organization through youth organizations, worker associations, clubs of mothers, and others who "at the outset opposed the process of agrarian reform but that is no longer the case..." (Ministerio de Agricultura 1971a, 12). A better-off group of peasant renters at the time of the land reform also

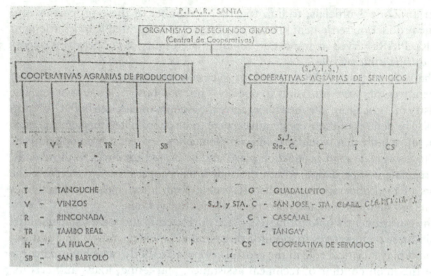

FIGURE 6.3 Organization of PIAR Santa
Source: Ministerio de Agricultura (1971a, 27).

sought to "manipulate information that was distributed about the process of agrarian reform" to other peasants throughout the valley, and "constituted a threat to the execution of the process of transforming the agrarian structure" (Ministerio de Agricultura 1971a, 11). Officials sought to isolate this group and unite other peasants against them as "a common antagonist."

The Agrarian Zone 3 officials also provided an overview of what they viewed as the advantages and disadvantages of the various cooperative forms of organization in Santa (Ministerio de Agricultura 1971a, 4–22). They began with "advantages to social order," noting that the plan would promote internal leaders and equity, and that it would provide a floor for peasant well-being. Recall that peasants could not alienate their land or shares within cooperatives, so ensuring at least a minimum living standard would give them incentives to remain engaged rather than abandon them entirely and migrate to cities. And the generation of internal leaders would enable the regime to connect to natural conduits of peasant influence within the cooperative. Officials also indicated economic advantages to the cooperative structure: economies of scale, production and consumption complementarities, ease in targeting investments and credits, permanent rural employment for cooperative members (including members that remained landless but worked for cooperatives), and the ability to absorb population growth internally within cooperatives.

Officials also noted the disadvantages, or "more accurately, the 'risks'" of their plan. The first was that without the proper training and buy-in of peasants into the cooperative structure – which was hardly a foregone conclusion – the cooperatives could founder economically. This could in turn generate social disorder within the cooperative more broadly. These concerns ultimately called for ever deeper state intervention in cooperatives to ensure peasant coordination in production and squelch dissenting views over how cooperatives should operate. Tied to this point, the Ministry of Agriculture indicated that it would have to play a direct advisory role in cooperatives at least in their initial phase. The risk here was in an eventual hand-off of greater authority and management to peasants themselves, which would have to be "carefully planned" and "gradual" in nature to avoid economic and social disruption. Another risk was the possibility of "group egoism" among the cooperatives that comprised the PIAR. One proposal was to use the central cooperative body to ensure that none of the cooperatives became too powerful or productive relative to the others.

6.3 CLOSING THE PROPERTY RIGHTS GAP AFTER THE END OF LAND REFORM

The episode of military rule in Peru from 1968 to 1980, known as the *Docenio*, was one of Latin America's longer episodes of military rule in the twentieth century. Unlike many others, Peru's military government engaged in very little outright repression and faced no significant rural uprisings. It came to be known as a *dictablanda*, or a "soft dictatorship," as opposed to the much more typical *dictadura*, or "hard dictatorship," that presided in countries such as Argentina, Chile, or Guatemala.

Peru's economy foundered in the late 1970s and popular strikes and marches snowballed. The military convoked a constituent assembly in response and called elections to return Peru to democracy in 1980. Peru's president prior to the military coup, Fernando Belaúnde, was reelected as president in 1980. Governments over the next several decades considerably strengthened the property rights of land reform beneficiaries, closing the property rights gap along the lines of canonical property rights gap Path B.

The conditions under which this occurred are largely consistent with the theory laid out in Chapter 3. Nevertheless, there was one additional background factor outlined in Chapter 3 that played a particularly important role as well: ideology.[7] The 1980s and 1990s in Latin America was an era of transition to both democracy and free markets, especially after the demise of the Soviet Union and the rise of the Washington Consensus. Peru was strongly

---

[7] Myopia (especially competing state goals) and state capacity had less of a role in closing Peru's property rights gap, though the former helps to shed light on its slow initiation under democracy due to the need to fight the Shining Path insurgency in the countryside in the 1980s and the latter helps makes sense of unevenness in closing the property rights gap across Peru's territory, and especially within more autonomous indigenous communities.

influenced by these trends, even if at times it ran counter to certain aspects of them – such as a turn to authoritarianism rather than democracy in the 1990s.

Ideology

The international environment and ideas surrounding property rights had shifted by the 1980s. Major international financial institutions, particularly the IMF and the World Bank, began more vigorously promoting economic orthodoxy as a cornerstone of development. These institutions favored not only economic and financial liberalization but also privatization and individual property rights. Latin America took this shift on the chin as the debt crisis of the early 1980s and subsequent currency and financial crises discredited prevailing import substitution industrialization development thinking and statist economic policies more broadly.

Peru was not immune to these influences. It suffered high inflation and economic crises in the late 1970s and early 1980s. Many blamed the military's nationalist and social ideas of economic organization for distorting investment and production incentives. These ideas were manifested in a proliferation of state enterprises with monopoly privileges, worker participation in company management and shareholding, and a raft of limitations to property rights and barriers to private business.[8] A brutal El Niño year further eroded the economy in 1982–1983. President Belaúnde was forced to borrow from the IMF and made tepid but ineffectual efforts at liberalization. His successor, Alan García, instead pursued heterodox economic policies that pushed Peru into hyperinflation and severe economic contraction. The drumbeat of foreign pressure for structural reform grew louder, especially since Peru was receiving development loans from the World Bank under the first several years of García's presidency and its foreign debt was ballooning.

Structural reform also found prominent proponents within Peru. Most notable was the economist Hernando de Soto. De Soto's influential book *The Other Path* pointed to how the state's poor property rights provision and enforcement gave rise to its enormous informal sector and systematically deprived citizens of the structures and institutions that they needed in order to thrive economically. The implication was that social and political instability, and the root causes of Peru's simmering Civil War that were linked to underdevelopment, could not be overcome in the absence of major property rights reforms.

These ideas were at the fore when Peru took its most significant steps toward closing the property rights gap in the 1990s under President Alberto Fujimori. They "reflected the thinking of those like Hernando de Soto, who saw the unlocking of private assets as key to development. It also reflected the views of

---

[8] The military regime itself began dialing back some of its most radical reforms under General Morales in the late 1970s. Morales changed the industries law, deemphasized social property, devaluated the *sol*, and entered negotiations with the IMF to stabilize the economy.

the World Bank, which supported similar schemes in neighboring countries like Bolivia's Ley INRA" (Crabtree 2002, 141–142). Peru became a poster child for property rights in certain ways and even contributed to international development trends focusing on property rights. As Glavin et al. (2013, 129–130) write, "land rights … have become a key element within the neoliberal agenda for market-led development, not least due to the influence of the Peruvian economist Hernando de Soto within international institutions and national governments."

Regime Type and International Pressure

While the broader international environment and the role of ideas contributed to Peru closing its property rights gap after the military retrenched from power in 1980, this is only a part of the story. The theory in Chapter 3 sheds important light on the domestic political logics that operated in this particular global environment. It helps to make sense of why the property rights gap closed when and how it did, and how the closure was linked to Peru's dramatically shifting political sands even as many ideological influences remained relatively stable.

The first step to closing the property rights gap came in response to popular pressure under democracy. The second step occurred as Peru turned back to dictatorship and faced enormous pressure by international lenders during a structural economic adjustment program to shore up property rights in exchange for desperately needed economic assistance. The property rights gap then continued to close after Peru returned to democracy.

Property Rights Strengthen under Democracy from 1980–1990
Popular pressure to break up the cooperatives and strengthen individual property rights was formidable by the time Belaúnde returned to the presidency in 1980.[9] This pressure translated into policy given that large landowners had been drastically weakened politically. Legislation in 1980 and 1981, especially Law 2 and Law 85, facilitated the fragmentation and transfer of many of cooperative farms to their members. Cooperatives could petition to change their status: "Thus, a legal opportunity was created to channel pressures toward parcelization." Many cooperatives seized this opportunity. Some dissolved amid internal conflicts over profit-sharing and labor.[10] Others dissolved because members simply wanted to work the land in family units.

---

[9] This pressure was not uniform, however. Privatization of the former cooperatives faced opposition both from the weakened losers of the 1969 agrarian reform and from part of Peru's radical left (Crabtree 2002, 139), then represented by the *Izquierda Unida*.

[10] One former cooperative administrator from Cañete, for instance, indicated that conflict and stealing within the cooperative provided pressure to split it up in 1980. Furthermore, the cooperative had consistently underpaid its debt to the Agrarian Bank. Interview by the author, Lima, Peru, January 29, 2018.

Comprehensive data on the contemporaneous extent and pace of parcelization do not exist because there was no explicit government program or agency that aided in parcelization and there was no agricultural census while it was occurring. Partial estimates from surveys, however, suggest that approximately three-fourths of coastal production cooperatives dissolved by 1986 (Carter and Alvarez 1989, 156).

The new democratic regime in the 1980s, in the meantime, struggled with economic crises, an unstable party system, and the rise of guerrilla war in the countryside driven largely by the rebel group Shining Path. State agencies consequently foundered in providing further support and property formalization to land reform beneficiaries. The insurgency in particular made the very notion of land titling controversial given serious limitations to state control in rural areas. Many land reform beneficiaries therefore became small-scale farmers operating without land titles in the wake of the breakup of cooperatives (Carter and Alvarez 1989). Transfers of cooperative lands to individual members did not include a formal property title in a majority of instances but merely an informal document provided by the former cooperative (Fort 2008, 4). Transfers were undocumented altogether in some instances. Moreover, by establishing a minimum size for formal plots, the agrarian reform had relegated more than 700,000 smallholders to informal status (Giugale and Cibils 2007, 558).

The election of Alan García in 1985 at first threatened the parcelization process. García initially supported associative enterprises in the rural sector (Hunefeldt 1997, 114). After all, in many ways they were a politically convenient equilibrium to encounter from the perspective of any government seeking rural cooperation, legibility, and control. But popular pressure caused a quick about-face and the García government shifted its focus to continued privatization of the cooperatives. Meanwhile, long-term pressure for titling from smallholder peasant associations that had formed in the late 1970s and 1980s was building.[11] The National Smallholder's Association (ANAPA), for instance, explicitly aimed to obtain titles for former cooperative workers that had inherited land when their cooperatives were privatized. In coordination with the National Agrarian Organization (ONA) and, later, the Peruvian Peasant Confederation (CCP), ANAPA used strikes and mass meetings to achieve its aims (Moreno 1994, 58).

The actual effect of smallholder associations such as ANAPA on titling was mixed. Hunefeldt (2014) argues that ANAPA was crucial for a shift in policy under García and specifically a shift in support from cooperative farms to privatization. Hunefeldt (2014, 243) writes that this shift "probably was the first time in Peruvian history that organized sectors of rural workers directly imposed their will on a government." But at the same time, Crabtree (2002,

---

[11] See Crabtree (2002, 152) and Moreno (1994) for further information on these associations and their aims.

138) argues that the Shining Path insurgency in rural areas greatly weakened smallholder associations' influence. The centralization of authority under President Fujimori, who was elected in 1990, weakened it further (Crabtree 2002, 151–154).

Runaway inflation and the spread of Shining Path under García without doubt sapped government attention away from rural development and property rights reforms.[12] García's government creaked under Peru's growing debt burden and was isolated from international financial markets when he limited debt service payments to no more than 10 percent of export earnings (Pop-Eleches 2008, 118). Foreign reserves dwindled and inflation soared in the late 1980s. Yet García rejected the implementation of free market structural adjustment reforms and consequently could not turn to the IMF or other international lenders for support. While property rights had been strengthened for land beneficiaries through the parcelization process, beneficiaries still lacked formal land titles. Only roughly 10 percent of all land parcels in Peru were formally registered by 1990 (Fort 2008, 4).

Closing the Property Rights Gap: Dictatorship Responds to External Pressure in the 1990s

Peru elected Alberto Fujimori president in free and fair elections in 1990. Fujimori inherited rampant inflation, a large debt overhang, and a metastasizing domestic insurgency that was rapidly growing in part due to its connections with a major coca boom in the Upper Huallaga Valley. Fujimori abandoned the heterodox economic policies he advocated during his campaign shortly after his inauguration in favor of orthodox neoliberal policies that "followed IMF prescriptions to the letter" (Crabtree 2002, 139). In a series of policies that came to be known collectively as "Fujishock," Fujimori raised consumer prices, liberalized the economy to trade, privatized industries, and lowered interest rates. Agricultural imports, dominated by cereals, dairy, and oils, doubled within five years of implementing these policies.[13] Fujimori managed to pass Legislative Decree 653 in 1991 for the rural sector. This further relaxed restrictions on the transfer of cooperative land by permitting its subdivision as well as land sales, transfers, rentals, and mortgaging.

Fujimori's rapid and dramatic change of course on overall economic policy resulted directly from a series of meetings between Fujimori and IMF and Japanese officials prior to his inauguration (Stokes 1997, 2002; Crabtree 2002). At the meetings, it was communicated to Fujimori that if he avoided

---

[12] The cooperative structure and the government's ties to it also made it easier for the military to interface with rural inhabitants to operate its counterinsurgency campaign (Albertus 2020), making property rights reform somewhat less attractive.

[13] This is from 1992–1997 (see Food and Agriculture Organization 2000b). Exports (predominantly sugar, fishmeal, cotton, and coffee) also doubled, but since they comprised only half the value of imports, net imports doubled in value.

immediate, painful economic adjustment, Peru could not count on international financial institutions for the critical support he needed to stabilize the country under his leadership (Stokes 1997, 217).

The IMF support for Peru in Fujimori's first two years in office, however, was not financial. Peru was not eligible for a formal IMF program until 1993 because it was still in arrears from the García administration (Pop-Eleches 2008, 274). Nonetheless, the carrot of IMF support was there. Facing legislative opposition to his economic policies, as well as his efforts to wholeheartedly unleash the military on the insurgency, Fujimori shuttered Peru's Congress and concentrated power in the executive. The IMF merely batted an eye at Fujimori's anti-democratic moves. Fujimori had otherwise normalized relations with international financial institutions by the end of 1992 and had paved the way for additional external aid – which Peru still desperately needed. When the IMF began crafting conditions for entering into a new program, Fujimori eagerly signed on the dotted line.

Fujimori initiated a large-scale land titling program known as the Special Land Titling and Cadaster Project (PETT) at the behest of the IMF and Inter-American Development Bank (IDB) as part of its broader liberalizing economic reforms. PETT was approved in 1992 and began operating in 1993. It was run out of the Ministry of Agriculture with the objective of formalizing rural land rights across the country, including mapping property boundaries, creating a land cadaster, and distributing and registering titles centrally.

Pressure from international financial institutions, especially the IMF and IDB, on this major reform to secure property rights was decisive (Crabtree 2002, 141–142; Glavin et al. 2013).[14] But unlike the military generals that governed Peru during the 1970s, Fujimori also had to consider domestic pressures. To fully cancel elections was off the table while receiving critical foreign assistance. Instead it held unfair elections that failed to meet democratic standards. So while Fujimori had a decided advantage over the political opposition, he still had to secure enough domestic support to build a winning coalition in the run-up to elections in 1995. These electoral considerations went hand-in-hand with international pressure to help drive property rights reforms in this case.

Subsequent land legislation under Fujimori built from these first steps and was similarly heavily influenced by external pressure. For instance, the Land Law of 1995 stipulated that beneficiaries of Peru's land reform would receive formal title to their land. The law reflected influence from the World Bank, which was simultaneously supporting related legislation in countries such as Mexico and Bolivia.

Peru's property rights gap shrank considerably under Fujimori through these property rights reforms (see Figure 2.6).

---

[14] However, the IDB did not begin supporting the program with loans until 1996.

The Property Rights Gap Continues to Close under Democracy in the 2000s
The property rights gap in Peru declined still further under Fujimori's democratically elected successors once Fujimori himself was forced to resign in the face of overwhelming evidence of abuse of power and corruption. Presidents Toledo (2001–2006) and García (2006–2011) continued granting formal property rights to rural land reform beneficiaries and other rural inhabitants due to the popularity of the land titling program.[15] PETT had distributed formal land titles over approximately 1.9 million rural plots by 2007. It issued more than 1 million titles between 1996 and 2002. PETT and follow-up registration efforts titled roughly 45 percent of rural plots (Bandeira et al. 2010). Implementation was uneven between the highlands and the coast: 70 percent of land in coastal areas received titles whereas only 28 percent of land in the highlands received titles over this period. Communal demands drove a substantial portion of land in Peru's highlands to be titled as communal properties (Bandeira et al. 2010).

The Inter-American Development Bank ramped up its financial and technical support of PETT's titling efforts after Peru's return to democracy. It granted new loans to PETT in 2002 and 2006. PETT merged with the agency Comisión de Formalización de la Propiedad Informal (COFOPRI) in 2007, which engages in both urban and rural titling. COFOPRI continues rural titling in Peru today.

6.4 CONCLUSION

The analysis of Peru in this chapter verifies many of the insights from previous chapters while also deepening several aspects of the theory. It provides a granular picture of factors driving the property rights gap in a particular case by conducting process tracing of the conditions under which Peru opened and closed its property rights gap.

The enormous property rights gap that Peru's military regime generated between 1969 and 1980 occurred under centralized authoritarian rule in which large landowners were entirely excluded from the governing coalition. Viewing these landowners as rivals, the military systematically attacked and expropriated them and then redistributed their land to peasants. But they also withheld property rights from land reform beneficiaries. The ruling military regime forced beneficiaries into cooperatives and prohibited the partitioning, sale, leasing, or mortgaging of land. There was little peasants could do about it.

---

[15] As under presidents Belaúnde and García, property rights reforms were not uncontroversial during Fujimori's tenure. Fujimori's land titling program "exposed numerous longstanding disputes over land rights" (Crabtree 2002, 147). For example, in the department of Puno, land titling exacerbated conflict between the winners and losers of the military's land reform given that some of the losers had returned to forcibly occupy the lands initially distributed to land reform beneficiaries. However, these disputes were not sufficiently disruptive to block land titling efforts from moving full speed ahead.

Subsequent democratic regimes were more responsive to peasant demands and allowed the breakup of cooperatives as well as land sales. These policy shifts strengthened property rights security. But more complete property rights did not arrive until after a democratically elected leader, Alberto Fujimori, shut down congress and centralized power in the face of a major economic crisis and a metastasizing rural insurgency. As Fujimori embarked on a radical structural economic adjustment program for Peru with the help of the IMF and the World Bank, he acceded to external pressure to extend more complete property rights to the Peruvian countryside. The granting of formal property rights to former land reform beneficiaries ramped up throughout his tenure. A series of democratic leaders that took office after Fujimori was run out then continued and strengthened the property rights reform programs given their popularity.

7

The Long-Term Consequences of Peru's Property Rights Gap

Peru has advanced in leaps and bounds in closing its property rights gap in the last several decades. Nonetheless, the majority of land reform beneficiaries lived under the shadow of a property rights gap for two or three decades, and in some cases longer. How did the property rights gap shape social and economic life in Peru over the long term?

To answer this question, I conducted fieldwork and built a research team to gather comprehensive original data on the extent of Peru's land reform. I then paired that data with land registration data and a host of data on the same social and economic outcomes in Peru that Chapter 5 examines, albeit at a much more fine-grained level than in Chapter 5. I also digitized reams of data from Peru's censuses prior to and at the outset of the land reform, constructed data on road penetration and land quality from historical maps and satellite data, and linked these data to Peru's land reform-era administrative divisions to examine how localized property rights gaps impacted local social and economic development over the long run. These localized property rights gaps are conceptually similar to the broader country-level property rights gaps examined in previous chapters. They capture the cumulative amount of land that was redistributed to land beneficiaries in a locale up until a given period without attendant property rights.

This approach ensures a close match with the theory. This chapter also has the added benefit that vis-à-vis Chapter 5, it uses an entirely different research design and level of analysis more suited to causal identification: a geographic regression discontinuity design using Peru's districts, its smallest administrative unit, as the unit of analysis.

I find evidence consistent with the prediction that countries such as Peru that follow canonical property rights Path B should experience delayed development. Larger property rights gaps at the local level in Peru are subsequently linked to a higher share of the population working in agriculture, lower agricultural

227

productivity, lower levels of educational attainment that indicate urban policy bias, greater inequality, and higher poverty rates reflective of lower income per capita. The findings are not driven by land reform being targeted at areas that were already poorer or more rural, selective sorting of individuals in the wake of land reform, or by generating greater conflict during Peru's civil war that raged in the 1980s and 1990s.

The long duration of Peru's property rights gap also provides fertile terrain for developing further extensions to the theory. Herculean efforts to close the property rights gap from the mid-1990s to the present generated partial convergence in the pernicious consequences of the property rights gap in Peru. This reflects the delayed development associated with property rights gap Path B. But some consequences, especially delays in urbanization and persistent poverty, are still apparent today. This suggests limitations to later capturing the potential economic and social gains of redistributing property if property rights are withheld for long periods of time.

Where property rights gaps fester for decades in a pattern akin to canonical property rights gap Path C, intervening factors can make reversing their negative consequences difficult even if the property rights gap is eventually closed or mostly closed, tracing Path B. Land concentration can return and then be cemented in by land titling programs, rural social realities can become entrenched and difficult to change, and economic activity can be rerouted in path-dependent ways that make it difficult to subsequently create economic dynamism in deprived rural areas without major and costly state interventions. Peru's experience with a long-lasting property rights gap illustrates some of the dynamics that can pull Path B trajectories of delayed development toward Path C trajectories of stubborn underdevelopment.

7.1 MAKING USE OF PERU'S AGRARIAN REFORM ZONES FOR CAUSAL IDENTIFICATION

One empirical challenge in examining the effects of the property rights gap on subsequent development outcomes in Peru is that land reform was not assigned randomly. There could be underlying reasons that led some areas to be targeted with more land redistribution than others, thereby opening up a larger property rights gap. And these factors could be correlated to later development trajectories.

I make use of a unique design feature of Peru's land reform in order to examine the net effects of Peru's property rights gap on later development outcomes. The reform was conducted from the start through twelve regionally based agrarian reform zones that covered the country. These zones did not generally map onto the borders of Peru's twenty-four departments or other major administrative borders. A thirteenth agrarian reform zone was created in 1974.

Peru's government conceived and delimited agrarian reform zones for entirely different purposes well before General Velasco's land reform. Beginning in WWII when the United States was concerned with disruptions to food availability, it began funding regional agricultural development in Peru as a way to promote production and agricultural exports. This relationship was originally crafted as a five-year partnership. But it was renewed and grew in the wake of the war. Peru's Agrarian Research and Promotion Service (SIPA) built from this early program with technical support from the Organization for American States and the United States Agency for International Development (USAID) and formally created agrarian zones in 1960 to promote agricultural development and differentiation.

SIPA supported agricultural development and extension through research, experimentation, technical assistance (such as introducing new crops), and promotion (such as market development). It took a regional approach to development to "incentivize the zonal diversification of agricultural production in order to maximize producer profits" and create regional economies of scale and expertise (SIPA 1967, 2). SIPA delineated twelve "Agrarian Zones" on the basis of "ecological conditions, social conditions, transportation routes, and access to markets" (SIPA 1967, 10). All but one transcended department borders. This was in part to integrate far-flung mountainous and jungle departments with regional market hubs or coastal ports and in part to take advantage of regional complementarities (SIPA 1967).

In practice, SIPA conducted minimal study of the peripheral areas of these zones where zonal boundaries were drawn. This is partly because officials were working with very fragmented and limited information about many rural parts of the country. Zonal boundaries were drawn just *before* the 1961 census. This was Peru's first agricultural census. Population information was also outdated. The previous population census was in 1940 and only garnered an 87 percent response rate. SIPA officials therefore centered zones around economic hubs in distinct ecological zones within the country and stitched them together to try to integrate outlying areas into markets and to boost production there (SIPA 1967). Early maps in the years leading up to delineating zones had differing and somewhat meandering boundaries that demonstrated fluid outlying boundary areas. These early maps did not feature detailed topographic features that are critical to Peru's unique geography. Zonal boundaries typically cut directly through departments and provinces.[1]

General Velasco's government grafted land reform implementation on top of existing Agrarian Zones and their operational offices a decade later for several reasons. First, creating an entirely new administrative structure would have threatened the reform's rapid rollout, which was key in eliminating the most powerful landowners before they could organize resistance (Albertus 2015,

---

[1] This is not to say that Peru's government was unaware of its geography. But knowledge linking this geography to agricultural production and well-being was very limited.

Ch. 7). Second, the small number of zones had development and planning advantages: zones would encompass swathes of expropriated haciendas along with smallholders and indigenous communities that could be reorganized into large cooperatives and vertically integrated into regional economic centers and national economic goals, thereby ameliorating excessive land fractionalization in regions with high land pressure (García 1970, 392). Finally, the mandate for top-down control and the need for careful selection of regional managers militated toward a small number of zones (Cleaves and Scurrah 1980).

When agrarian reform was routed through Agrarian Zones, it became operationally rooted in region-specific land reform offices for zonal reform implementation. These offices were centered in the highest priority areas for land reform. They often operated out of department capitals where they interfaced with local bureaucracies that aided implementation because of the rapid way in which the reform was rolled out.

The utilization of Agrarian Reform Zones generated uneven land reform implementation in practice. Some areas received much more attention from the Ministry of Agriculture than other areas even when both areas were adjacent and had similar landholding structures. Several contemporary accounts document a discontinuous shift in land reform "treatment" probability for districts within a given agrarian zone that were inside versus outside the core department where the agrarian zone (and regional land reform office) was centered. Districts in the zonal core were more likely to experience land reform than districts "trapped" in the zonal periphery. Echevarría (1978, 151), for instance, points out that "peripheral areas or provinces, other than the central department where the corresponding agrarian zone is located ... receive little attention because of lack of resources."

Why was this the case? Department-level bureaucracies had more expertise and information about their own departments rather than neighboring departments. For instance, land records and registries were often held locally by departments. It was also harder for zonal land reform officials to thoroughly conduct land reform in "peripheral" parts of an agrarian reform zone that contained districts outside the core department because that required coordination with distant, and in some cases hard to reach, department-level bureaucracies that had the most intimate knowledge of their own territories. And there were limitations to resources for land reform officials and imperatives to move quickly.[2] The result was that that districts in "peripheral" areas of a land reform zone received less land reform than "core" areas.

Internal Ministry of Agriculture documents indicate that bureaucrats raised concerns about the inadequacies of the Agrarian Reform Zone geography for the purposes of an even spread of land reform across the country. Officials at the National Center for Training and Research for the Agrarian Reform

---

[2] Information on zonal budgets and the location of major zonal personnel indicate both limited resources and a bias toward "core" Agrarian Reform Zone departments.

(CENCIRA), which headed the Zonal Committee on Training that did the planning for land reform implementation within agrarian zones, convoked a conference of directors of the Agrarian Reform Zones at the outset of the land reform to hear their concerns. The directors reported that their personnel and resources at the time were insufficient to do a thorough job with land reform. And they made clear that they did not have the resources to train administrators in far-flung peripheral areas of their zones that were directly involved in doing land reform (Ministerio de Agricultura 1971b).

Officials acknowledged their concerns about unevenness in agrarian reform implementation but treated them as a necessary and practical limitation. The early Director of Promotion and Diffusion of Agrarian Reform, Efraín Ruíz Caro, delivered the government's position in a speech to zonal directors at the conference: "[A]lthough the Agrarian Reform is not progressing at the same speed in all departments, this reflects the necessity to consolidate, for example, the application of the Law ... For human and technical reasons, as well, it is necessary to observe an order of priority."

To reiterate, districts in the department where the regional agrarian reform office was located within a given Agrarian Reform Zone became the "core" part of the zone. Districts in other departments inside the zone that were not the host of the zone's central office were effectively deemed peripheral.

Figure 7.1 displays two maps that show agrarian reform zone boundaries, core and peripheral zonal areas, and department boundaries. Figure 7.1 shows the final agrarian reform zone boundaries and numeric identifiers after Zone 13 split from Zone 10 in 1974. This was the only major zonal change during the reform.

The discrepancy between Peru's political-administrative divisions and its agrarian reform zones presents an opportunity to examine how the property rights gap impacted later development outcomes while avoiding common sources of bias due to confounders. Within a given agrarian reform zone, the assignment of districts to a zonal core or periphery in areas close to the core/periphery geographic boundary can be viewed as quasi-random. Later I demonstrate that districts located close to these borders are statistically indistinguishable from their counterparts on the other side of the border.

But might there be compound treatment effects along the department borders that constitute core/periphery boundaries within agrarian reform zones? Identification in this case requires invoking the compound treatment irrelevance assumption (see Keele and Titiunik 2015, 133–136): the assumption that the only feature of districts that affects the outcome is the treatment of interest (land reform) as opposed to other potential treatments that may vary along the core/periphery boundary. I will return to this further ahead. But it bears emphasizing here that Peru is a unitary rather than federal country and had a high degree of centralization before and throughout this period. Departments had common institutions and served as administrative units of the central government (Arce 2014, 140n3).

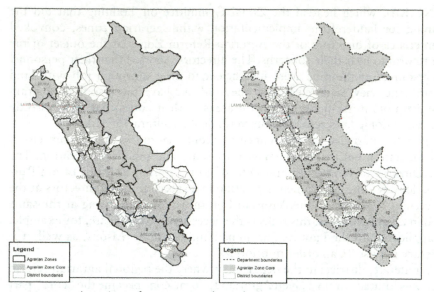

FIGURE 7.1 Agrarian reform zones and zonal cores in Peru
Notes: Bolded solid lines indicate agrarian reform zone boundaries (left subfigure).
Dotted lines indicate department boundaries (right subfigure). Departments are
labeled. Shaded areas of the map cover districts in a zonal core and the white areas
cover districts in a zonal periphery.

Departments do matter, however, for implementing central government
policy initiatives. There are department-level bureaucracies with local
expertise and information suited to local policy implementation. For a typical
agrarian zone spanning multiple departments, this implies that the federal zonal
Ministry of Agriculture bureaucrats collaborated with and more effectively
coordinated activities with the administrative apparatus of the core
departments where they were located to a greater degree than with
neighboring peripheral departments. Peripheral areas within agrarian reform
zones were therefore not administrative peripheries overall in Peru. They were
only peripheral in the context of the agrarian reform zone geography used for
land reform implementation. I confirm this empirically later in the chapter.

7.2   DATA

To test the effects of property rights gaps on later development outcomes,
I analyze data on the distance of districts to the nearest geographic boundary
between an Agrarian Reform Zone's core and periphery, land reform from
1969 to 1980 when the military redistributed land while withholding
property rights, subsequent rates of holding a land title, and development
outcomes tied to the property rights gap. The unit of analysis is the district.

These are very small administrative units: the median district had a population of 3,267 people circa the 1972 population census. I generate a dataset of all of Peru's roughly 1,675 districts from the mid-1970s. I minimize the extent to which changing political geography impacts the results by aggregating variable values to district boundaries from the time land reform began. I also create several composite units of districts where large expropriated properties spanned district boundaries. This yields 1,571 districts.

Agrarian Reform Zones and Land Reform without Property Rights

A district's exposure to land reform treatment – and therefore a property rights gap – is determined by whether it is located in the core department of an agrarian reform zone or in a peripheral area. I accessed district-level maps that Peru's Ministry of Agriculture used for land reform implementation in order to construct Agrarian Reform Zone boundaries and to determine whether districts were located in the core or periphery of an agrarian reform zone. I scanned these maps and geo-referenced them to current maps. I then used ArcGIS software to map demarcation lines. The resulting dataset contains information on which agrarian reform zone a district is located within, whether a district is in a zonal core or periphery, and the distance between a district's centroid and nearest agrarian reform zone core/periphery boundary.

In practice, although the likelihood of a district receiving land reform shifted discontinuously when moving from outside to inside an agrarian reform zone's core, the probability of reform did not shift from zero to one. Some peripheral districts received land reform and some core districts did not. In the context of a regression discontinuity research design, this scenario calls for specifying a variable for potential land reform treatment to capture the land reform "take-up" effect.

I constructed an original dataset that registers all land expropriations from 1969 to 1980 in order to capture land reform "take-up." This dataset documents nearly 21,000 expropriations covering slightly more than 10 million hectares of land in active private use, abandoned or long-fallowed private land, and agriculturally unproductive (often public) land (*eriazos*). In collaboration with a Peruvian research team, these expropriations were identified in a comprehensive search through publications of the official government daily, *El Peruano*. By law, *El Peruano* published all supreme decrees, supreme resolutions, and ministerial resolutions that expropriated individual properties. These decrees and resolutions contain detailed information regarding the property owner, district location, the amount of land expropriated, and information regarding whether associated fixed or mobile assets were expropriated.

The land reform variable I construct captures the percentage of a district's land redistributed via the main land reform legislation from 1969 to 1980. This variable includes land in active private use (74.6 percent of land distributed) and abandoned or long-fallowed private land (12.2 percent of land distributed). Remaining lands were agriculturally unproductive and typically public (13.2 percent of land distributed) and were covered by different legislation than private lands. They should not therefore impact development outcomes the same way. I test this explicitly later.

Figure 7.2 depicts the geographical distribution of land reform. Land expropriations are spread across Peru's twenty-four departments. The areas most affected were northern coastal departments such as Ancash, La Libertad, and Piura, and the southern highlands of Apurímac, Cusco, Huancavelica, Pasco, and Puno. Land reform also varied substantially across districts within these departments. And it was significant in other departments such as Arequipa, Ayacucho, Huánuco, Junín, and Lambayeque. Less reform occurred in lowland eastern jungle and southern coastal departments.

In the core districts of agrarian reform zones included in the analyses later in the chapter, the mean percentage of land redistributed represents 41.4 percent of privately held, noncommunal land. The government expropriated more than half of privately held agricultural land in 38 percent of core districts. Redistribution averages 52.9 percent of privately held agricultural land for core districts within 50 km of the core/periphery boundary.

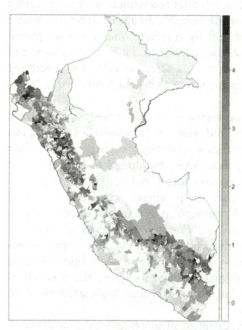

FIGURE 7.2 Geographical distribution of land reform in Peru, 1969–1980
Note: Figure displays the log percentage land area expropriated by district from 1969–1980.

Peripheral districts of agrarian reform zones included in the analyses, by contrast, experienced less land reform. But nearly three-quarters of them still experienced some land reform and 57 percent had at least 5 percent of their privately held agricultural land redistributed. Redistribution averages 37.8 percent of privately held agricultural land for peripheral districts within 50 km of the core/periphery boundary.

This discussion and the research design strategy inform the nature of the counterfactual to intensive land reform treatment without property rights in Peru. Land reform without property rights cannot be compared to land reform with complete property rights: there were no large estates that were redistributed to land reform beneficiaries with complete property rights. Constructing such a counterfactual within a given country at a specific point in time is difficult because governments rarely redistribute land to some individuals with property rights and to others without property rights simultaneously for the reasons elaborated in Chapter 3.

The counterfactual is also not a complete absence of land reform in which the hacienda economy persists and then potentially modernizes. Rather, the control group consists of districts in which a larger share of middle-sized landowners, and perhaps a few landowners with properties even somewhat bigger than this group, escaped the reach of the land reform law either because their properties were slightly smaller than landholding ceilings or because the bureaucratic process of land reform moved slowly enough locally such that land reform halted before they were expropriated.[3] Some middle-sized landowners even received expropriation exemption certificates (*certificados de inafectación*) in 1973 – similar to the *certificados de inafectabilidad* in Mexico mentioned in Chapter 3 – that protected them from future expropriation against a backdrop of shrinking landholding ceilings. These landowners, who maintained their land and property rights, would be better positioned in the post-reform era to invest in mechanization and capital improvements to their land or to diversify their investments into other economic sectors. And they could better afford to send their children to school and even to institutions of higher education in Lima or large regional cities.

Land Titles

The first set of dependent variables captures the property rights gap several decades after land reform. In particular, I examine whether the incidence of holding a land title varies by exposure to land reform. Data on land titles are from Peru's two post–land reform agricultural censuses of 1994 and 2012. These censuses collected data on whether individual plots were held with a land title. Land titles at this time in Peru were a key property rights indicator. Titles impacted whether individuals could defend their property

[3] See, for instance, Matos Mar and Mejía (1980, 166–68) for more discussion of this group.

against counterclaims, how easily they could sell, lease, or subdivide land, and whether they could use it as collateral to obtain loans. I consequently calculate variables capturing the proportion of plots in a district with land titles for both 1994 and 2012.

These are the best available data on property rights in Peru during this period. The two censuses also have the advantage that they capture property rights essentially at the two bookends of property rights reform in Peru: at the outset of the major land formalization and titling efforts initiated by PETT and again when it had made enormous progress in closing the property rights gap to bring Peru closer in line with a property rights gap Path B trajectory. Empirically verifying the localized existence of a large property rights gap, rooted in as-if random land reform exposure around agrarian zone core/periphery boundaries, followed by the closing of this gap provides ideal conditions for generating high-quality estimates of how the property rights gap impacted a host of development outcomes.

The census data are well suited to the analysis but they are not perfect. First, the 1994 census was conducted shortly *after* the beginning of land titling in Peru through PETT in 1993. This would bias *against* finding a property rights gap across core/periphery agrarian reform zone boundaries to the extent that PETT began titling areas with rampant informality. However, the dates line up closely. The subsequent 2012 agricultural census took place when the property rights gap was closed to a very substantial degree after the flurry of granting property rights in the 1990s and 2000s. The gap in data between 1994 and 2012 do not enable an examination of precisely when a property rights gap may have closed across core/periphery agrarian reform zone boundaries. Second, these censuses did not ask about whether an individual is a beneficiary of the military's land reform program. This again adds some noisiness to the data by lumping peasants unaffected by the land reform with peasants that received land through the reform. However, given the broad extent of the Peruvian military's land reform program and the massive property rights gap it systematically left in its wake as cooperatives broke up, the data should be able to pick up the hypothesized effects.

Development Outcomes

A second set of dependent variables captures a host of development outcomes that are linked theoretically to the property rights gap. These are the same social and economic outcomes that Chapter 5 examines. There is therefore a tight coupling between the theory and empirics at both an aggregate country level and at the localized subnational level.

If indeed a property rights gap persisted for a long period of time after the military's land reform in Peru – which the data on land titling from 1994 and 2012 should reveal – then this rights gap should have had important consequences. It should have led to a slower economic transformation away from agriculture, lower agricultural productivity, lower levels of educational attainment that indicate urban policy bias, and higher rates of inequality and poverty. I gathered data to test all of these theoretical implications. As with the data on land titling, I examine development data from both the eve of major property rights transformation and from the twilight of the property rights gap once land formalization had widely taken root. I draw on data from censuses, household surveys, and satellite imagery.

In contrast to data on social and economic outcomes of the property rights gap in Peru, there are no localized data available that enable credible tests of the political outcomes that Chapter 5 highlights: the balance of rural versus urban political power and the prevalence of clientelism and vote buying. There are two principal reasons for this. The first is that the military was deeply skeptical of political parties. It did not leave a strong party presence when it retreated to the barracks and returned Peru to democracy in 1980. Electoral volatility and unstable parties – many of which did not have the resources or longstanding presence to build clientelistic voter ties – filled in the gap. The second reason is that growth of the Shining Path insurgency in the countryside in the 1980s and early 1990s drove state retrenchment. Both of these dynamics thwarted data generation and complicate the creation of accurate and theoretically well-motivated measures. The analyses consequently focus on social and economic over political outcomes.

The first set of variables capture development outcomes in the early to mid-1990s. These data are based on Peru's 1993 population census. A first variable is the percentage of the economically active population that works in agriculture. If a property rights gap encourages land reform beneficiaries that lack rights to remain on their land to protect and farm it, then agricultural labor should be more prevalent where there was a greater extent of land reform under the military. This variable is from Peru's 1993 population census.

A second variable is agricultural productivity. A property rights gap should limit agricultural productivity by making it difficult for land reform beneficiaries that lack rights to use their land as collateral to access loans for expensive farm inputs, transition to more efficient mechanized farming equipment, and invest in long-term improvements in their land and in infrastructure. Of course, productivity can also be influenced by access to markets, local infrastructure, growing conditions across Peru's diverse topography, and the scale of production.

The earliest available district-level data on agricultural production are from the Ministry of Agriculture from 1997. Data on the planted land area, production, yields, and prices of all major crops are collected monthly by personnel from the regional dependencies of the Ministry of Agriculture according to a structured procedure with the support of regional agrarian statistical authorities.[4] These personnel then report the data to the statistical offices within regional directorates, who in turn report the data to the Office of Economic and Statistical Studies within the national-level Ministry of

---

[4] The specific methodological guidelines are available from the Ministry of Agriculture as "Lineamientos Metodológicos – Estadística Agraria."

Agriculture. I measure productivity as gross production value in current soles per agricultural worker.[5]

The remaining variables that are measured in the early 1990s are from Peru's 1993 population census. A third variable captures urban bias. A property rights gap should disadvantage rural dwellers from being able to access the same opportunities and services that urban dwellers enjoy, and the state should not remedy this disparity. One critical opportunity is education. A property rights gap should encourage individuals to drop out of school earlier to work in agriculture and make families less likely to be able to afford their children attending school rather than contributing to the family's income. It should therefore be associated with higher percentage of households whose head is illiterate. I utilize population data on the reading and writing capacity of household heads in the agricultural sector to construct this variable.

A fourth variable captures inequality. As rural workers with property rights make productivity-enhancing investments and urban workers gain more marketable and remunerative skills that facilitate upward mobility, individuals that face a property rights gap stagnate. Data on income inequality are not available for Peru in the early 1990s. I therefore generate an inequality measure as the ratio of households that have three or more basic unmet needs relative to households that have one or zero basic unmet needs. Census enumerators track five inadequacies in basic household needs: inadequate housing (such as dirt floors or major structural deficiencies), overcrowded housing, a lack of access to clean running water and sewerage, having a young child that does not attend school, and high economic dependency as indicated by a household head without a primary school education and either all family members unemployed or four or more household members actively working.[6] The use of both urban and rural dwellers to construct this measure helps to capture the urban–rural divide that can drive net inequality as Chapter 5 outlines.

A fifth variable is poverty. This variable proxies for income per capita and should be higher where income per capita is lower. Insecure property rights over land can generate underinvestment, obstruct rural land markets, and create economic distortions in the allocation of labor. This can fuel poverty and stagnation together with a lack of access to basic services that would otherwise facilitate upward mobility. I measure poverty as the share of the agricultural population that has more than one basic unmet need. Basic needs are defined in the same way as for the inequality measure.[7]

---

[5] I use data on agricultural population from the most proximate census in 1993. Results are similar if agricultural population is estimated for 1997 via interpolation between the 1993 and 2007 censuses.

[6] I also tested a different measure of labor inequality that yielded similar results. The measure was calculated as the share of temporary and part-time workers in agriculture relative to the share of agricultural laborers that report sufficient income. Data on both variables are from the 1994 agricultural census.

[7] Results are similar with a higher threshold as well such as more than two basic unmet needs.

The second set of variables on development outcomes come from the late 2000s and 2010s. If indeed the property rights gap had been largely closed by this period, then it is conceivable that a history of more intensive land reform in an area should no longer drive negative development outcomes. On the other hand, it could take time for areas that long faced a property rights gap to catch up to areas that did not. And intervening dynamics that cause land reform areas to have persistent negative development outcomes through another channel could have cropped up during the time of a large property rights gap. For instance, land transactions between the 1990s and 2000s could undo the effects of closing a property rights gap. An analysis of the longer-term consequences of land reform without property rights under the military on development outcomes in the 2000s and 2010s can help to shed further light on this possibility.

I start by constructing a set of measures that are directly comparable to those from the earlier period. I turn to Peru's 2007 population census to build variables for the percentage of the economically active population that works in agriculture, educational attainment, inequality, and poverty. This was the next population census that followed Peru's 1993 population census and the only other one up until the writing of this book for which data are available. The variable for agricultural productivity is built from 2007 production data from the Ministry of Agriculture divided by the number of agricultural workers from the 2007 population census.

Starting in the late 2000s, however, new and higher-quality measures of certain key development outcomes – in particular income per capita – had become available for the first time in Peru. I consequently examine a set of additional measures of economic well-being that were not available in the 1990s. The first proxies for economic well-being with a more fine-grained measure of poverty than those available from the 1993 and 2007 censuses alone (the censuses did not directly collect data on household income or expenditures). The earliest set of especially high-quality estimates of localized poverty in Peru are from the National Statistics Institute's 2009 Map of Poverty. These estimates use census data paired with household survey data on information such as spending and profession following the methodology proposed by Elbers et al. (2003).[8] I use a standard metric of poverty from the 2009 poverty map, the poverty gap index, which captures the depth of poverty by estimating how far on average the poor are from the poverty line.[9] This measure varies between 0 and 1, with higher levels indicating greater poverty.

---

[8] For a discussion of improvements in poverty measures in Peru in the years leading up to 2009, see the discussion on pp. 13–14 of the National Statistics Agency's publication on the 2013 Map of Poverty: www.inei.gob.pe/media/MenuRecursivo/publicaciones_digitales/Est/Lib1261/Libro.pdf.

[9] Results are similar using a poverty severity index, which captures the average of the squares of the poverty gaps relative to the poverty line and therefore takes higher values when there is greater inequality among the poor.

I also separately examine data on nighttime satellite luminosity from 2015. Nighttime luminosity is now widely used as a proxy for socioeconomic development because it is highly correlated with income per capita and economic output (Chen and Nordhaus 2011). Data are from the Defense Meteorological Satellite Program's Operational Linescan System (DMSP). DMPS registers satellite images that enable the estimation of artificial luminosity with the precision of one square kilometer. From this information a village-level measure of luminosity was created, which was then averaged across villages to calculate a district-level measure.

Covariates

I also gathered data on covariates relevant to the property rights gap and development. Data on these covariates serve two functions: to aid in assessing balance prior to treatment across districts on either side of the agrarian reform zone core/periphery boundary and to control for any residual imbalance attributed to differences between these groups of districts that could confound the findings. After all, the development outcomes that I focus on could have been impacted by a host of other factors besides land reform. But this should not pose inferential concerns for this particular analysis if the identification assumption behind the regression discontinuity design holds and all relevant factors aside from land reform treatment vary smoothly at the agrarian zone core/periphery boundary.

The first set of covariates capture dynamics tied to population size and state capacity. I use district population size from the 1961 population census. Population size may impact several dependent variables such as the share of the labor force in agriculture. Larger populations can also increase the efficiency of providing schooling or policy interventions to address poverty. A second covariate is road density. I calculate this variable as the number of meters of roads and established paths per square kilometer. Greater road penetration can enhance development outcomes by enabling the state to extend its control. Road network data are calculated via GIS software by overlaying a map of Peru's districts on a 1973 Peruvian map of road networks and established paths across the country produced jointly by the national Touring and Automobile Club and the Banco de Crédito del Perú.

I use the number of state employees per district calculated from the 1961 census in order to measure state administrative capacity. State employees are individuals who worked for a government entity or agency and received a salary or commission for that work. Examples include members of the Civil Guard (the main police force dedicated to maintaining public order), members of the Republican Guard (engaged in border control, guarding government buildings, and prison custody), and the Investigative Police. I log the state personnel variable to normalize its distribution.

I gathered data on a second set of covariates that capture important geographic features of Peru's rough terrain. The projection of state power can vary by terrain. Land use and agricultural production can also vary with terrain. I calculate measures of district elevation and average terrain slope. These variables are calculated on the basis of satellite data from the US Geological Surveys's National Elevation Dataset. Values are calculated by overlaying a map of Peruvian districts on 30 arc-second (1 km) resolution elevation and slope data and calculating district-level means.

The dataset also includes several variables for district land characteristics. The first is district area from the National Statistics Institute. Larger districts present greater land area for potential expropriation. The second is the percentage of cultivable land. Higher land quality raises the value of property and therefore incentives to formalize it. Land quality can also proxy for a more productive agricultural region, which can positively impact development. This variable is calculated from the FAO's Global Agro-Ecological Zones database using 5 arc-minute grid cells averaged within districts. A third land-related variable is the number of hectares of land under private ownership from the 1972 agricultural census, adjusted for pre-1972 land expropriations.[10] This variable captures the potential stock of private land available for redistribution.

A final set of covariates captures historical indigeneity and patterns of contestation between indigenous groups and large landowners. Indigenous groups in Peru have different patterns of landholding than mestizos and have long pushed against the appropriation of their land and labor by colonizers and postcolonial elites. This could shape patterns of land expropriation, subsequent demands for and actual land titling, and other development trends.

I use three variables to capture these considerations. The first is a 1961 census measure of the percentage of the population whose mother tongue was a native language such as Quechuan or Aymaran rather than Spanish. This captures the presence of indigenous Peruvians who have long been relatively neglected in development efforts by the Peruvian state. Furthermore, indigenous groups have pushed for collective rather than individual property rights at a higher rate than mestizos, which was not initially PETT's focus when it began land titling.[11] The second variable is whether a district is located in the colonial-era *mita* catchment zone. This geographic region within the highlands was under a forced mining labor regimen during Spanish rule. Dell (2010) shows that the *mita* zone had long-run negative development effects in Peru. Data are constructed from Dell (2010). The third variable measures conflictive social movements prior to the late 1960s. This helps address whether the property rights gap was opened wider in areas with a greater propensity for conflict and

---

[10] There are not similar district-level data on landholding in previous censuses in Peru.

[11] The somewhat different nature of the demand for property rights among indigenous groups in part dates back to traditional customary authority over land, which was disrupted during Spanish colonial rule.

where rural dwellers had been historically repressed by large landowners. I construct prior conflictive social movements from Kammann (1982), who details rural social movements, their causes, and participants dating from Peru's independence from Spain until the late 1960s. Most conflictive movements in this source occurred between the 1920s and 1960s.

Table 7.1 displays summary statistics for the main variables, covariates, and additional variables that arise later in the analysis. Some are scaled for ease of presentation in the results that follow.

TABLE 7.1 *Descriptive statistics for regression discontinuity analyses*

Variable	Mean	Std. Dev.	Min.	Max.	N
Distance to agrarian zone core (km.)	27.74	112.07	−987.89	775.23	1571
Land reform (share of district area)	0.13	0.23	0	1	1571
Population (thds.)	6.58	13.65	0.05	291.89	1571
Road density (tens of meters per sq. km.)	4.94	7.3	0	103.61	1571
State personnel (log)	2.68	1.46	0	8.37	1571
Elevation (thds. of meters)	2.69	1.45	0	5.12	1571
Slope (degrees)	5.66	3.67	0	19.53	1571
District area (hds. of sq. km.)	8.17	27.48	0.02	516.69	1571
Cultivable land (percent area)	7.02	9.20	0	90	1571
Private land area (tens of thds. of ha.)	1.22	7.12	0	268.05	1571
Indigenous population	0.49	0.42	0	1	1570
Mita zone	0.33	0.47	0	1	1571
Prior social movements (tens)	1.48	7.52	0	130	1571
Economically active population in agriculture, 1961	0.74	0.21	0	0.98	1549
Literacy rate, 1961	0.51	0.22	0	1	1567
Poverty (*chozas*), 1961	0.17	0.18	0	0.99	1317
Poverty (dirt floors), 1961	0.86	0.22	0	1	1310
Inequality (hacienda power), 1961	0.02	0.09	0	0.93	1568
Plots with title, 1994	0.4	0.28	0	1	1555
Economically active population in agriculture, 1993	0.69	0.23	0	0.98	1566
Agricultural productivity, 1997 (tens of thds. of soles per ag. worker)	0.55	2.2	0	61.13	1528
Literacy rate, 1993	0.8	0.12	0.25	1	1568
Inequality, 1993	0.32	0.68	0	14	1570
Poverty, 1993	0.41	0.18	0	0.99	1568

(continued)

TABLE 7.1 (*continued*)

Variable	Mean	Std. Dev.	Min.	Max.	N
Reform of uncultivable lands (share of district area)	0.01	0.03	0	0.73	1571
Distance to placebo agrarian zone boundary (km.)	−533.52	392.57	−1429.46	95.21	1571
Plots with title, 2012	0.27	0.23	0	1	1554
Plots with registered title, 2012	0.2	0.21	0	1	1554
Economically active population in agriculture, 2007	0.6	0.24	0.01	0.97	1565
Agricultural productivity, 2007 (tens of thds. of soles per ag. worker)	0.6	0.68	0	9.22	1534
Literacy rate, 2007	0.86	0.08	0.45	1	1568
Inequality, 2007	0.07	0.16	0	4.24	1569
Poverty, 2007	0.23	0.14	0	0.89	1568
Poverty Gap Index, 2009	0.17	0.11	0	0.62	1570
Nighttime luminosity, 2015	0.11	0.46	0	6.5	1560
Land inequality (Gini), 2012	0.79	0.17	0.05	1	1556
Agricultural land inequality (Gini), 2012	0.64	0.17	0	1	1556
Agricultural land inequality excluding communities (Gini), 2012	0.62	0.16	0	1	1556
Immigrants (percent of population, 1993)	12.14	9.22	0.51	79.98	1533
Total conflict events, 1980–2000	782	37.87	0	661	1571

7.3 RESEARCH DESIGN

The empirical analyses utilize a regression discontinuity (RD) design. Units with a score above a given cutoff in an RD design receive treatment whereas those below the cutoff do not. These two groups of units can be compared to study the causal effect of treatment on some outcome provided that units just above the cutoff and just below the cutoff are not abruptly different.

The unit of analysis in the present context is the district. A district's exposure to the treatment of land reform without property rights during military rule is determined by whether it is located in the core department of an agrarian reform zone. Land reform treatment consequently depends on the distance of a district to an agrarian reform zone core/periphery boundary (the score). The cutoff is normalized to zero: districts with negative scores located outside a zonal core do not receive land reform whereas districts inside a zonal core with a positive score do. Provided these two groups of districts are not otherwise abruptly different, an RD design enables an examination of the (local) average effect at the cutoff of exposure to the property rights gap on subsequent outcomes of interest.

The discontinuity I examine is fuzzy rather than sharp. The likelihood of a district receiving land reform during military rule shifted discontinuously, but not from zero to one, when moving from outside to inside an agrarian reform zone core/periphery boundary. The fuzzy RD parameter can be interpreted as a local average treatment effect at the cutoff for "compliers" (see, for example, Cattaneo et al. 2018).

This fuzzy parameter is estimated as the ratio of two sharp RD effects: the effect of treatment assignment on the outcome (or intention-to-treat effect) and the effect of treatment received on the outcome (or take-up effect) using two-stage least-squares methods. The estimand is as follows:

$$\tau_{FRD} = \frac{\lim\limits_{x \downarrow 0} \mathrm{E}(Y_i | X_i = x) - \lim\limits_{x \uparrow 0} \mathrm{E}(Y_i | X_i = x)}{\lim\limits_{x \downarrow 0} \mathrm{E}(D_i | X_i = x) - \lim\limits_{x \uparrow 0} \mathrm{E}(D_i | X_i = x)} , \tag{1}$$

where τ_{FRD} identifies the effect of exposure to land reform without property rights on a given outcome variable of interest; Y_i is the measure of the outcome of interest in each district i; D_i is a variable for potential land reform treatment; and X_i is the distance from each district's centroid to the agrarian reform zonal core/periphery boundary.

I use nonparametric local polynomial methods to fit two separate regression functions, one above and one below the cutoff. The estimated RD effect is then calculated as the difference between the two separate regression intercepts. In particular, and following common practice, I utilize local linear regression to estimate the following:

$$Y_i = \alpha + \tau_{\hat{FRD}} C_i + \beta_1 Z_i + \beta_2 X_i + \beta_3 C_i \cdot X_i + \varepsilon , \tag{2}$$

where C_i is an indicator for land reform treatment exposure and is coded as "1" when a district is within an agrarian reform zone core; X_i is located within a bandwidth b of the agrarian reform zonal core boundary; and Z_i is a vector of covariates. I estimate the first-stage treatment equation for τ_{FRD} using D_i as an instrument, measured as the percentage of a district's land area that is affected by the military's land reform, while including other exogenous covariates as is now standard practice.[12]

---

[12] Although D_i is continuous rather than binary in this case, τ_{FRD} will still converge to the ratio of limits in Equation 1. See, for instance, Dong et al. (2018) for a discussion of identification for RD designs with a continuous treatment. The local causal effect under continuous treatment is interpreted as a weighted average of district treatment effects among districts that would change treatment intensity when shifting across the zonal core/periphery boundary. Results are similar when D_i is binary and equal to one when over half a district's land is reformed.

The local linear regressions I estimate follow Cattaneo et al. (2018) by employing weights calculated by applying a triangular kernel function to the distance between each unit's score and the cutoff. This requires choosing a bandwidth for implementation. I draw on methods developed by Calonico, Cattaneo, and Titiunuk (2014) to choose an optimal bandwidth that minimizes mean squared error (MSE), while employing robust confidence intervals that account for the asymptotic bias ignored by conventional inference in the context of MSE minimization. Observations outside the bandwidth receive zero weight. I cluster standard errors by agrarian zone since land reform, land titling, and development may exhibit cluster dependence within agrarian reform zones.

For theoretical consistency and clean empirical identification, the analysis restricts the sample to agrarian reform zones where (i) the major land reform legislation applied; (ii) reform zone boundaries did not change; and (iii) there was both a core and peripheral area. The first criterion eliminates Zones 8 and 9. The military's 1969 Decree Law 17716 did not cover these sparsely populated Amazon jungle zones. Land reform in these zones mainly focused on colonizing public lands. This did not create a property rights gap as conceptualized in this book (see Chapter 2). The second criterion eliminates the initial Agrarian Zone 10, which the government later split into two zones (Zones 10 and 13). The status of some districts as core or peripheral in this zone shifted over time. The third criterion eliminates Zone 12 (Puno). Puno was the only agrarian reform zone whose boundaries aligned entirely with its department boundaries. It therefore had no within-zone peripheral districts. Beyond these considerations, I also restrict the analyses to rural districts with populations less than 100,000 in 1961. This drops major urban areas such as Arequipa, Callao, Chiclayo, Lima, Trujillo, and several others where development is overwhelmingly driven by factors other than land and property rights over land.

7.4 INVESTIGATING ESTIMATION AND IDENTIFICATION ASSUMPTIONS

This section takes three important steps that aid in assessing the main results further ahead. First, I provide evidence that there were no systematic differences in development across the RD boundaries prior to land reform and the rise of a property rights gap. Second, I present results from covariate balance tests that validate the identification assumption. Third, I discuss issues tied to potential compound treatments along the core/periphery boundary.

Pre-Land Reform Differences in Social and Economic Life

Before examining the effects of a property rights gap on relevant development outcomes, it is important to evaluate whether there were systematic differences in development in core versus peripheral areas of agrarian reform zones prior to land reform. It is conceivable, for instance, that areas that experienced more land reform and a larger property rights gap also ranked lower on the social and economic dimensions examined as outcomes in the post–land reform period. The land reform may have even improved welfare but to a degree insufficient for convergence with areas that experienced less land reform.

Several pieces of evidence cast doubt on this possibility. First, the literature on Peru's land reform refutes the notion that it was targeted at the least developed areas. It was squarely aimed at the largest landowners (Albertus 2015; McClintock 1983). Many of these landowners resided in more affluent parts of the country such as the northern coast. While these landowners employed a poor and abused sector of the population, this population generally did not comprise society's poorest and most marginalized individuals. "Middle-class" peasants became the land reform's biggest beneficiaries (McClintock 1981). The land reform impacted the poorest peasants, often among marginalized indigenous groups, to a lesser extent.

Second, social and economic data on well-being prior to the land reform suggest that differences between the core and peripheral areas of agrarian reform zones were negligible. Consider first measures for the share of the economically active population working in agriculture and educational attainment as measured by adult literacy. I gathered district-level data on these variables, which are comparable to the later measures from the 1990s and 2000s, from the 1961 census.

Figure 7.3 presents balance tests indicating that there was no discernible difference in the economically active population working in agriculture and in adult literacy in districts spanning the core/periphery boundary prior to the land reform. A full table of the results displayed in Figure 7.3 and the results displayed in the other figures that follow in this chapter, including treatment and control sample sizes, bandwidths, and estimated differences, can be found in Appendix C at the end of the book.

Poverty data directly comparable to that used in the 1990s and 2000s are unfortunately not available prior to the land reform given differences in census questions and methodology. Nonetheless, it is possible to construct proxies for poverty from the pre-reform era. The arguably best proxies rely on information on the quality of housing. This information is available from the 1961 census. Poor families, and especially those that farm, are much more likely to live in houses built of temporary materials such as wood covered with branches, straw, and mud as opposed to cement or other permanent materials. I consequently gathered district-level data from the 1961 census on the share of families living in dwellings built of temporary materials (*chozas*) as a first proxy for poverty. In a second and related proxy, I gathered data on the share of households with dirt floors as opposed to improved floors that consist of materials like wood or concrete. Figure 7.3 indicates that there was no discernible difference in poverty across the core/periphery boundary prior to the land reform using these measures.

District-level data on agricultural productivity and inequality prior to the land reform are not available. However, like poverty, it is possible to construct

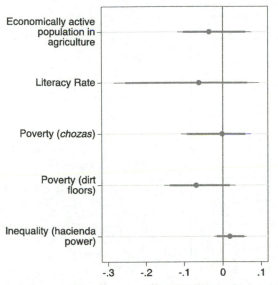

FIGURE 7.3 Development characteristics prior to a property rights gap
Note: Running variable is distance from agrarian reform zonal core boundary. Point estimates indicate average treatment effect at cutoff using local linear regression with a triangular kernel and MSE-optimal bandwidth. Thick lines indicate 95 percent robust confidence intervals. Thin lines indicate 90 percent robust confidence intervals.

a proxy for inequality. I turn to data from the 1961 Directorio de Centros Poblados to do so. This source comprises an exhaustive list of all 80,000 cities, towns, informal settlements, small villages, *fundos*, and haciendas in each district of Peru circa 1961 as well as the population living in each of the enumerated settlements. I constructed a measure of the percentage of a district's rural population that lived on large haciendas with at least 500 inhabitants using these data. This helps to capture hacienda power over the local labor poor and therefore the extent of rural dependence on particularly powerful large landowners. Figure 7.3 again indicates no distinguishable difference across the core/periphery boundary prior to the land reform using this measure.

All of these tests together suggest that districts along the core/periphery boundary were similar on these dimensions prior to the generation of a property rights gap during the land reform period. To the extent that these districts later differ after the rise of a property rights gap, evidence would point to the land reform era as marking the point of divergence.

Covariate Balance Tests

The RD approach taken here assumes that all relevant factors other than treatment vary smoothly at the agrarian reform zonal core boundary. This identification assumption is required for districts located just outside a zonal

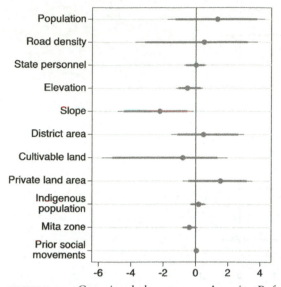

FIGURE 7.4 Covariate balance across Agrarian Reform Zone core boundary
Note: Running variable is distance from agrarian reform zonal core boundary. Point estimates indicate average treatment effect at cutoff using local linear regression with a triangular kernel and MSE-optimal bandwidth. Thick lines indicate 95 percent robust confidence intervals. Thin lines indicate 90 percent robust confidence intervals.

core to be appropriate counterfactuals for districts located just inside a zonal core. I run balance tests on the following district characteristics in order to assess this assumption: population size, road density, state personnel, elevation, slope, district area, percentage of cultivable land area, privately held land area, the proportion of the population that is indigenous, whether or not a district is located in the mita catchment zone, and prior social movements. These tests use local linear estimation with an MSE-optimal bandwidth and robust confidence intervals.[13]

Figure 7.4 presents the results for these covariates. There is no evidence of imbalance for any covariates except slope. Balance is therefore similar to what one would expect if the treatment had been randomly assigned. The fact that the covariates vary smoothly around the cutoff supports the RD continuity assumptions that are key for a valid RD design.

Compound Treatment Irrelevance

Any additional threats to inference in this case would have to occur along agrarian reform zone core/periphery boundaries and not be linked to the factors directly examined in Figure 7.4. Given that the core/periphery

---

[13] I also tested whether the density of distance from the zonal core was continuous at the cutoff. This hypothesis could not be rejected at conventional levels of statistical significance.

boundary within an agrarian reform zone always traces department boundaries, the chief concern would be compound treatment effects that (i) run along department borders; (ii) could affect long-term social and economic development outcomes separately from the property rights gap; (iii) are not examined in Figure 7.4.

Compound treatments are common in geographic RD designs and require invoking the compound treatment irrelevance assumption for identification purposes (see Keele and Titiunik 2015). This assumption cannot be directly tested. But context and additional evidence can help to assess the appropriateness of the irrelevance assumption in any given case.

Several important pieces of evidence suggest that compound treatments along the RD boundary are not driving the results in this particular case. First, consider that Peru is a unitary state. With the exception of a brief period from 1990 to early 1992, and beginning again in the 2000s, citizens in Peru did not locally elect department governors. The central government instead appointed governors. Governors therefore did not have different policy platforms, mandates, and institutions that they could shape according to local concerns but rather operated at the behest of the central government.[14] Departments were policy-takers with common institutions and operated as administrative units of the central government. Peru also conducted taxation and spending at the national level. Velasco's land reform reflects this centralization: it was designed and implemented from Lima by a unified and hierarchical military command without garnering regional input (Cleaves and Scurrah 1980).

Furthermore, judicial and police jurisdictions that trace departmental boundaries and that could have theoretically been important for development via property rights protection, contract enforcement, and impacting transaction costs were largely unimportant during the period of analysis. The judiciary was centralized and lacked independence and the police were eclipsed at least until 2000 by the more centralized, largely autonomous military that was charged with conducting counterinsurgency during Peru's civil war. The police largely patrolled urban areas far from the hinterlands.

The historiography on the delineation of Peru's departmental borders supports the lack of early and longstanding departmental border discontinuities or consequential jurisdictions that could drive the findings (see Albertus 2020). Departments were long based on population centers rather than territoriality that tightly incorporated hinterlands. Consequently, as Figure 7.4 indicates, districts around department borders do not exhibit discontinuous jumps in state capacity, land suitability, or land use patterns that could impact development. Furthermore, Figure 7.3 demonstrates that development characteristics were similar in districts across core/periphery boundaries *prior to* the property rights gap when other "irrelevant" treatments would have been operative.

---

[14] Even from 1990–1992, transfers to regions were withheld, undermining governors.

7.5 THE PROPERTY RIGHTS GAP AND DEVELOPMENT OUTCOMES

The results in Figures 7.3–7.4 and the discussion of compound treatments lend credibility to the research design and establish parity in relevant social and economic factors prior to the rise of a property rights gap in Peru. The next question is, what were the effects of the property rights gap? This section first provides the main RD results from the dawn of the closing of Peru's property rights gap. Second, it presents a set of placebo tests. Third, it examines RD results from the late 2000s and 2010s when the property rights gap was largely closed. Finally, it explores why closing the property rights gap might not have immediately eliminated development disparities.

The Effect of Land Reform on the Property Rights Gap and Development Outcomes in the Early 1990s

Figure 7.5 presents the main RD results for the early 1990s at the outset of Peru's efforts to close the property rights gap. The analyses first estimate the effect of land reform exposure on the incidence of holding a land title. They then estimate the effect of land reform on other social and economic outcomes.

The results take into account the geographical nature of the discontinuity. Assuming that the average treatment effect is constant along the boundaries separating agrarian reform zone cores and peripheries would ignore the two-dimensional nature of the design by collapsing distance from the cut point into a single dimension (Keele and Titiunik 2015). Such an approach, for instance, would assume that a district in one agrarian reform zone can be compared with a district in a different agrarian reform zone.

I address the geographic nature of analysis in three complementary ways. First, following Dell (2010), I estimate a polynomial function that controls for smooth functions of geographic location. I model this using a second-order polynomial in latitude and longitude. Second, I introduce controls for latitude and longitude coordinates of the nearest point along the zonal border cutoff. Third, following Dell (2010), I modify the regression model expressed in Equation 2 to include boundary segment fixed effects. These segments correspond to the boundaries separating each agrarian reform zone core from its periphery.

The first row of Figure 7.5 reports the baseline results for land reform exposure on rates of holding a land title in 1994. The first-stage results in the right-hand-side box of Figure 7.5 show that the effect of treatment assignment on actual treatment status is statistically significant and in the expected direction. A district that is located just inside an agrarian reform zonal core, has 7.4 percent more of its land area subjected to land reform on average than when it is just outside an agrarian reform zonal core.

The first row treatment effect results indicate that when a district is barely inside an agrarian reform zonal core, the rate of holding a land title is lower than when it is barely outside a zonal core. This effect is also statistically significant.

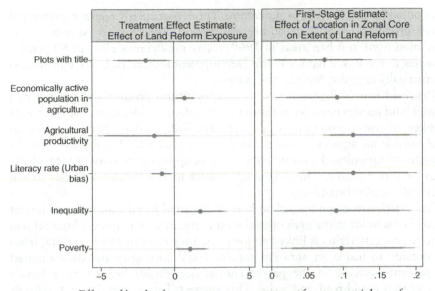

FIGURE 7.5 Effect of land reform on outcomes on eve of property rights reform
Note: Running variable is distance from agrarian reform zonal core boundary. Point estimates indicate average treatment effect at cutoff using local linear regression with a triangular kernel and MSE-optimal bandwidth. Thick lines indicate 95 percent robust confidence intervals. Thin lines indicate 90 percent robust confidence intervals.

The interpretation of the magnitude of the causal effect is more complicated than in a typical sharp RD setup given continuous treatment. But given that moving from just outside to just inside an agrarian reform zonal core increases land reform by an estimated 7.4 percent of land area, the impact of a similar move on the rate of holding a land title is an estimated 14.2 percent decrease. Recall that single large landholdings were typically redistributed among many peasants.

These findings demonstrate that the property rights gap that Peru's military created over land that it redistributed continued to redound negatively on property rights by the early 1990s. This is not surprising from the perspective of the discussion earlier in the chapter. But it provides an important empirical underpinning to the estimates of the effects of land reform without property rights on other social and economic outcomes.

The remaining rows of Figure 7.5 turn to these outcomes. The second row examines how land reform exposure impacted the share of the economically active population working in agriculture by 1993. As anticipated, greater intensity of land reform without property rights is associated with higher rates of employment in agriculture. Districts impacted by land reform to a greater degree remained more rural two decades later. Moving from just outside to just inside an agrarian reform zonal core yields an estimated 6.6 percent increase in the share of the economically active population that works in agriculture. This is particularly relevant given rapid overall urbanization in Peru during this period. Whereas 56 percent of the population lived in urban areas in 1969, today the figure is close to 80 percent according to the World Bank's World Development Indicators. Land reform areas systematically lagged in this transformation.

The third row of Figure 7.5 turns to agricultural productivity per worker. Greater land reform intensity without the attendant provision of property rights is linked to lower agricultural productivity. Shifting from barely outside to barely inside an agrarian reform zonal core yields a 0.15 point drop in the measure of agricultural productivity. This is approximately one-third of the mean of this variable. The first-stage results in this model are also strong statistically and substantively.

The fourth row examines urban bias as captured by educational attainment among households in the agricultural sector. Again as anticipated, land reform without property rights is linked to lower literacy rates in 1993. Shifting from just outside to inside an agrarian reform zonal core generates an estimated 9.3 percent decrease in the percentage of households headed by a family member that could read and write. This suggests lower attendance in schools and higher dropout rates in areas of greater land reform, placing rural individuals in these areas at a disadvantage compared to their urban counterparts regarding opportunities for upward mobility vis-à-vis rural individuals in areas that experienced less land reform.

The fifth and sixth rows of Figure 7.5 investigate inequality and poverty, respectively. Both are higher in areas of greater exposure to the military's land reform. Poverty, for instance, increases by an estimated 11.2 percent when moving from just outside to inside an agrarian reform zonal core.

In short, Figure 7.5 establishes that the military regime's granting of property without rights in the 1970s left a legacy of incomplete property rights and also distorted the social and economic landscape of rural areas by the 1990s. Land reform stunted urbanization, productivity, and educational attainment while contributing to higher rates of inequality and poverty.

Placebo Tests

I next conduct a set of placebo tests in order to demonstrate that the research design is not simply uncovering a false positive or reflecting an anomaly of the data structure.

I first conduct tests to ensure that the RD is unable to uncover the effects of land reform on rates of holding a land title at a location other than the true agrarian reform zone core/periphery boundary line (see Imbens and Lemieux 2008). I create "placebo" cutoffs at 5 kilometer intervals of either side of the true boundary line and rerun the model from the first row of Figure 7.5 using these alternative cutoffs. The first six rows of Figure 7.6 display the results. None of the alternative placebo borders return statistically significant second-

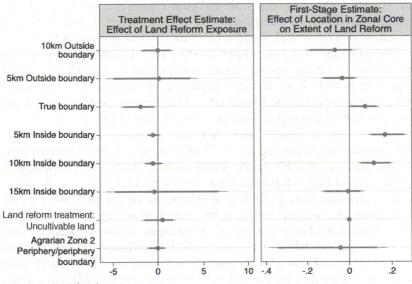

FIGURE 7.6 Placebo tests
Note: Running variable is distance from agrarian reform zonal core boundary in rows 3 and 7 and distance to the placebo boundary indicated for rows 1–2 and 4–6. In last row, running variable is distance from Agrarian Zone 2 periphery/periphery boundary between Cajamarca and Amazonas/La Libertad. Point estimates indicate average treatment effect at cutoff using local linear regression with a triangular kernel and MSE-optimal bandwidth. Thick lines indicate 95 percent robust confidence intervals. Thin lines indicate 90 percent robust confidence intervals. The point estimates and confidence intervals in the last three rows of Figure 7.6 are scaled.

stage results.[15] The first- and second-stage results drop off quickly using placebo boundaries that incorporate districts outside of the core areas of agrarian reform zones. The first-stage results drop off more slowly using placebo boundaries inside the core areas of agrarian reform zones. This suggests that, albeit with some real limits, land reform exposure increased somewhat within core zones as one moves farther inside the core/periphery boundary. But this effect breaks down for placebo boundaries within more than 10 kilometers inside the true boundary.

I also conduct a separate placebo test that exploits the fact that Peru's land reform treated uncultivable lands (*eriazos*) differently than cultivable lands for the purposes of distribution. The law classified uncultivable land as land not cultivated or occupied due to a lack or excess of water. Much of it was relatively undesirable, arid land that the government sought to incorporate into the

---

[15] The point estimates and confidence intervals for the models in the last three rows of Figure 7.6 are scaled for presentational reasons. See Appendix C for the complete results.

agricultural sector through large-scale irrigation works. Most was held by municipalities, state-owned enterprises, and other government bodies. Due to being smaller in extent and readily identifiable and transferable by the government, this land was not subject to the same discontinuity in reform intensity across agrarian reform zonal core/periphery boundaries. Land reform on uncultivable lands did not displace large landowners, nor did it center on properties farmed by residential serflike tenants. It therefore did not generate a property rights gap as conceptualized in this book.

The seventh row of Figure 7.6 shows that agrarian reform zone core/periphery boundaries did not impact the likelihood of a district receiving land reform affecting uncultivable lands. Furthermore, there is no association between this type of land reform and rates of holding a land title.

As a final placebo test, I examine whether, as anticipated, there is no discernible difference in land reform across agrarian reform zone periphery/periphery boundaries. There are several boundaries within agrarian reform zones where a "peripheral" department from the perspective of land reform implementation borders another peripheral department. The longest such boundary is in Agrarian Zone 2 where the eastern border of Cajamarca abuts the western boundary of Amazonas and the province of Bolívar in La Libertad (see Figure 7.1). As row eight of Figure 7.6 demonstrates, treating the Cajamarca side of the border as a placebo agrarian reform zone core reveals no discontinuity in land reform intensity or in rates of holding a land title.

Taken together, these placebo tests support the RD design and its ability to exploit exogenous variation in examining how local property rights gaps in Peru impacted subsequent development outcomes.

The Effect of Land Reform on the Property Rights Gap and Development Outcomes by the 2000s

Figure 7.7 next presents a set of RD results from the late 2000s and 2010s when Peru had largely closed the property rights gap. The analyses first estimate the effect of land reform exposure on the incidence of holding a land title by the time of Peru's 2012 agricultural census. They then estimate the effect of land reform on other development outcomes as in Figure 7.5.

The row one results indicate that although the location of a district as inside versus outside the core of an agrarian reform zone impacted the extent of exposure to land reform, the incidence of holding a land title by the time of the 2012 agricultural census is statistically indistinguishable across this boundary. In other words, the military's granting of land to beneficiaries without property rights had no discernible impact on holding a land title by 2012. The property rights gap by this period had largely closed. Row two confirms these results using the incidence of holding a land title that was inscribed in a public land registry. These findings conform to the discussion in the previous chapter on the closing of the property rights gap from the mid-1990s through the 2000s.

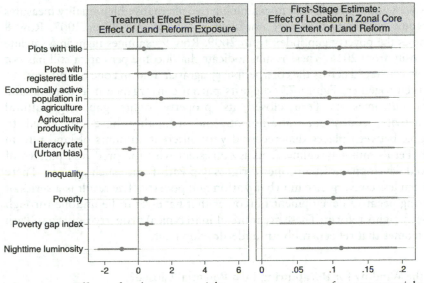

FIGURE 7.7 Effects of early property rights gap on outcomes after property rights gap largely closed

Note: Running variable is distance from agrarian reform zonal core boundary. Point estimates indicate average treatment effect at cutoff using local linear regression with a triangular kernel and MSE-optimal bandwidth. Thick lines indicate 95 percent robust confidence intervals. Thin lines indicate 90 percent robust confidence intervals.

Did the removal of the property rights gap around former core/periphery agrarian reform zone boundaries by 2012, however, generate convergence in development outcomes along these boundaries? The results in the remaining rows of Figure 7.7 indicate partial but incomplete convergence.

Rows 3 through 7 of Figure 7.7 analyze the same development outcomes as in two through six of Figure 7.5 but with data from 2007. The measures are also directly comparable to the development outcome measures in Figure 7.5. The share of the economically active population working in agriculture remained higher in districts with greater exposure to the military regime's land reform and illiteracy remained lower. The magnitude of the coefficient on illiteracy drops by almost half, however, suggesting some convergence. Inequality was higher in areas of greater land reform intensity, although the p-value on this coefficient is just short of conventional statistical significance and its magnitude drops over five-fold vis-à-vis 1993, indicating convergence on this outcome as well. Convergence is much more complete for agricultural productivity across the core/periphery agrarian reform zone divide. And poverty is no longer measurably higher in core agrarian reform zone areas either. The poverty result, however, could in part be due to broader countrywide improvements in meeting basic unmet needs, which is what the poverty measure in Row 7 hinges on.

Rows 8 and 9 instead turn to examining two alternative high-quality measures of income per capita that were not available in either 1993 or 2007. Row 8 examines the poverty gap index from 2009. Row 9 examines nighttime satellite luminosity from 2015. These results indicate that income per capita still has not entirely converged across the core/periphery agrarian reform zone boundaries.

Taken together, Figure 7.7 suggests partial convergence in economic and social outcomes as Peru closed its property rights gap. Agricultural productivity, educational attainment, and inequality have converged to a degree between places that received very different amounts of land reform under Peru's military regime. This is consistent with the predicted pattern of delayed development in a property rights gap Path B case such as Peru. There has been less convergence in urbanization and poverty. The result is a series of lingering negative development outcomes that have yet to be undone through property rights reform. These are more akin to typical property rights gap Path C outcomes that reflect stubborn underdevelopment.

Has the Window for Recapturing Lost Potential Closed?

The findings in Figure 7.7 beg an important question: can the negative developmental effects of a property rights gap always be reversed over time? Can the extension of more complete property rights to former land reform beneficiaries through land formalization and titling programs recapture the development potential of land reform, or can other factors arise that prevent "catch-up" in development?

Chapter 5 suggests that extending property rights over land previously granted without property rights can yield beneficial effects. However, Peru's experience demonstrates that early choices in land reform program design can have long-term consequences, not all of which are easily reversed. It is possible that it will simply take more time for Peru's elimination of the property rights gap to catalyze greater urbanization, equality, and increased income per capita. But other evidence suggests that Peru's land titling effort came too late to fully capture the potential economic gains of a more egalitarian distribution of land. Convergence in development outcomes due to closing the property rights gap may have been frozen in place by countervailing dynamics.

Landholding inequality in zones of intense land reform had unsurprisingly declined substantially vis-à-vis prior to the land reform after Peru's land reform cooperatives broke up in the 1980s and 1990s. Data on landholding inequality patterns from the 1994 census indicate that landholding inequality in rural districts was significantly lower in core regions of agrarian reform zones relative to peripheral regions. But landholding inequality patterns in areas of intense land reform had changed significantly by the time of the 2012 agricultural census.

Figure 7.8 presents a series of RD regression results structured similarly to those in previous figures. The figure demonstrates using data from 2012 that land

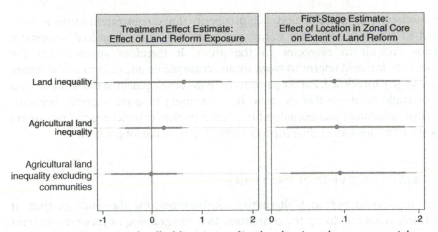

FIGURE 7.8 Return to landholding inequality by the time the property rights gap is closed
Note: Running variable is distance from agrarian reform zonal core boundary. Point estimates indicate average treatment effect at cutoff using local linear regression with a triangular kernel and MSE-optimal bandwidth. Thick lines indicate 95 percent robust confidence intervals. Thin lines indicate 90 percent robust confidence intervals.

inequality in areas of greater land reform intensity was statistically indistinguishable from that in areas of lower land reform intensity by this time. The results hold for overall landholding inequality (Row 1), inequality in the distribution of exclusively agricultural land (Row 2), and whether or not indigenous communities are included in the calculation of the landholding Gini given that communities tend to have joint land ownership over larger areas (Row 3).

Although district-level data do not exist because of initial land informality in the wake of the military's land reform and incomplete property registers, convergence in landholding inequality in Peru was likely driven by land sales and transfers between the early 1990s and 2000s. This period witnessed rapid economic growth in Peru, the entrance of mining companies at a broad scale, and a newfound ability to alienate land. For example, one agronomist who managed two cotton enterprises in the Valley of Cañete that the Velasco government expropriated and who then came to work in a technical capacity for the subsequently formed cooperative told me in an interview that, in recent years, new investors and some former landowners from the area had purchased plots that land reform beneficiaries received when the cooperative broke up.[16] There were also economic shocks such as the 1998 El Niño and contagion economic effects of the Asian financial crisis that could have encouraged distressed smallholders to sell their land.

Consequently, relatively equal but poor rural areas with widespread land informality following the military's land reform became more unequal decades

---

[16] Interview by the author, Lima, Peru, January 29, 2018.

later, with poverty mixed in alongside prosperity. Land registration seems to have helped to cement in this new status quo such that residual underdevelopment remains difficult to overcome in the areas. It therefore appears that the opportunity for land reform to work as an economic engine in Peru in the future is now largely foreclosed. Earlier patterns of underdevelopment in the wake of land reform could reinforce this dynamic by continuing to drive ongoing behavior linked to investment and accumulation, again further entrenching the remaining negative consequences of the property rights gap over the longer term.

7.6 ALTERNATIVE EXPLANATIONS

There are several potential alternative explanations for the findings that, if confirmed, would undercut the contention that the granting of property without rights per se had negative long-term development consequences in Peru. This section explores the main alternatives: that there were selective population shifts around the core/periphery boundary after land reform that impacted development, and that land reform catalyzed greater violence during Peru's internal conflict.[17] I discuss the logic of each of these alternative explanations and the results from empirical analyses that test them. The full results are in Appendix C.

Selective Sorting

One alternative explanation for the findings is that there was selective population sorting around the core/periphery boundary. Perhaps because the land reform was so effective at eliminating large landowners, peasants relocated in large numbers after the fall of the military regime to land reform areas where they could enjoy greater autonomy and farm without competing against larger producers. This may have strained local resources and led to worse development outcomes over time.

I examined data on the percentage of residents in a district that had recently immigrated there in the last five years in order to test this alternative. Data are from the 1993 population census. I find no evidence in favor of this explanation. If

---

[17] I also tested whether the military's land reform undermined the provision of public goods that peasants relied on to meet their basic necessities. For instance, Dell (2010) argues that large landholding in Peru was historically associated with stronger incentives for investing in public goods and the political connections necessary to extract benefits from the state. The elimination of large landowners locally would, by extension, lead to a decline in the provision of public goods and potentially worse development outcomes as a consequence. The theory is not entirely inconsistent with this, though it suggests that a decline of public goods following land reform is driven more by urban bias rather than a lack of large landowners with encompassing interests and should therefore impact public goods that have a strong rural/urban dimension such as education (see the results in Figures 7.5 and 7.7). There is little evidence that greater land reform is linked to poorer public goods provision for goods that have less of a clear-cut rural/urban political dimension such as access to improved water sources and sanitation or road density.

anything, immigration into areas of greater land reform intensity was lower. This is consistent with the fact that because the land reform did not grant title to individuals over their property, individuals faced complications in alienating their land and rural land markets were sluggish, which encouraged beneficiaries to remain on their land and made it difficult for outsiders to legally enter land reform communities.

Conflict Intensity during Peru's Civil War

A second alternative explanation for the findings is that perhaps land reform stoked greater conflict during Peru's civil war. This could have indirectly generated negative development outcomes for reasons unrelated to property rights. The tail end of land reform in Peru coincided with the onset of major civil conflict. An estimated nearly 70,000 people were killed in Peru's internal conflict from 1980 to 2000. Many more suffered from torture, imprisonment, rape, and displacement. The violence began with the guerrilla group Shining Path seeking to bring down Peru's central government with a Maoist-style insurgency and to construct a form of agrarian communism rooted in indigenous peasant communities.

One factor long hypothesized to have impacted the spread of Peru's internal conflict is the 1970s-era land reform given its wide geographic scope and transformational economic and political consequences. Numerous scholars argue that the land reform held the potential to deflate peasant support for guerrillas by improving economic and social conditions and reducing grievances over inequalities and insufficient government support (Mason 1998; McClintock 1984; Seligmann 1995). However, many of these same authors argue that land reform implementation undercut its potential for reasons tied to raising peasant expectations but not meeting them (Seligmann 1995) or generating intercommunal tensions between reform beneficiaries that received direct land access and neighboring communities that did not (Berg 1992; McClintock 1984; Palmer 1986). The state's indiscriminate counterinsurgency violence may have also undercut the potential inoculating effects of land reform on conflict (Mason 1998).

I analyzed data from Peru's Truth and Reconciliation Commission (CVR) to test this alternative explanation. The CVR was a well-funded organization run by reputable commissioners. It collected evidence and testimonies of human rights abuses through various regional centers following Peru's conflict. Documented human rights abuses include murders, forced disappearances, extrajudicial killings, illegal detentions, kidnappings, forced recruitment, torture, rape, and woundings. This information was centralized and crosschecked for consistency, veracity, and duplicates with the help of top academics and young professionals. The CVR gathered testimonies for several years and ultimately published several detailed conflict databases in 2004. These databases are widely viewed as the most comprehensive accounts of Peru's internal conflict.

The findings undermine this alternative explanation. Greater land reform intensity is actually associated with *fewer* total conflict events perpetrated by guerrilla groups, self-defense groups, paramilitaries, or civilian or other groups. These events consist of one or more acts of violence within a clearly established geographical location and specific date and with a clear sequence of events and protagonists. In related work, I find that land reform dampened conflict by facilitating counterinsurgency and intelligence gathering by the state, building local organizational capacity such as *rondas campesinas* that was later used to deter violence, undercutting the Marxist left, which was a chief political rival to Shining Path, and increasing the opportunity costs to supporting armed groups (Albertus 2020).

7.7 CONCLUSION

This chapter uses a series of regression discontinuity analyses to examine the effects of local property rights gaps on long-term development outcomes. That it reaches a similar set of conclusions to those in Chapter 5 while taking such a different methodological approach helps to add confidence to the theory this book develops.

I find that the decades-long property rights gap in Peru had important long-term social and economic consequences. Areas of more intense land reform implementation in the 1970s had lower rates of land title holding by the early 1990s, just before Peru started a major land titling program. This property rights gap is tied to a higher proportion of the labor force working in agriculture, lower agricultural productivity and educational attainment, and higher rates of inequality and poverty.

There was partial, albeit incomplete, convergence in these outcomes by the late 2000s after Peru closed its property rights gap significantly along the lines of a property rights gap Path B trajectory. Agricultural productivity converged and educational attainment and inequality converged to a degree. There was less convergence in urbanization and poverty.

Further analyses suggest extensions to several aspects of the theory in order to understand incomplete development convergence upon the closing of a property rights gap. Partial convergence in this case is likely due to land reconcentration that occurred coterminously with major land formalization, cementing in landholding inequality. At the same time, given the duration of the rural property rights gap, economic activity may have been rerouted in path-dependent ways that are now difficult to overturn. This again cements in winners and losers of the property rights gap. These findings suggest limitations to recapturing the potential economic and social gains of redistributing property if property rights are withheld for long time periods.

8

Property Rights Gaps around the World

Property rights gaps have been a feature of rural life in many countries around the world over the last century. Over one and a half billion people, and perhaps as many as two billion, have spent the better part of their lives cultivating land that they receive from a government through a land reform program but that lacks property rights. Extended families in some cases have farmed property without rights for generations. Many of them continue to do so today.

This chapter tells this story from several different angles. It first provides a sense of the scope of this story as well as how the book's theory makes sense of it. I introduce an original and complete account of the main features of property rights over land that governments have granted or withheld through all major cases of redistributive land reform that have occurred across the globe since 1900. This encompasses whether land is held individually versus collectively or by the state, whether land ownership is formalized, whether the land that beneficiaries receive is defensible against counterclaims, and whether there are significant restrictions to alienability. I also present information on how long property rights gaps endure following each case of major land reform and the extent to which governments support their rural sectors in other ways such as providing investment in inputs and credit support.

Of the forty-four major land redistribution programs around the world since 1900, thirty-seven have been followed by at least a partial property rights gap. The theory proves very useful in understanding the opening and closing of property rights gaps around the world. The few cases of major land reform in which no property rights gap was generated – reflecting canonical property rights gap Path A – either occurred under democracy (as in the interwar Baltic states) or in dictatorships just after WWII where the United States played an important advisory role (Japan, South Korea, and Taiwan).

261

Nearly all of the thirty-seven cases in which countries generated a property rights gap following major land reform did so under dictatorship when the coalition of ruling political elites excluded landed elites. Governments in twenty-five of the thirty-seven cases then followed canonical property rights gap Path B and closed the property rights gap fully or at least partially. Closing the property rights gap occurred under radically different circumstances. Democracies closed nearly two-thirds of the property rights gaps. Typically this occurred in response to popular pressure. Peasant demands were successful in a substantial number of these cases in part because they won positions in ruling coalitions and because any remaining large landowners were too weak to capture legislative posts that would empower them to successfully oppose the extension of property rights to land reform beneficiaries. In the remaining cases, ruling regimes – both democratic and autocratic – closed the property rights gap in response to external pressure from international lenders during programs of structural economic adjustment.

A remaining set of countries have followed canonical property rights gap Path C and therefore have never closed their property rights gap. These are overwhelmingly dictatorships such as Cuba and China that have not been forced into capitulation by international lenders during times of economic vulnerability.

This chapter also examines property rights gaps in depth in two countries outside of Latin America: Portugal and China. These cases contribute to the external validity of the statistical results and demonstrate the utility of the theory in shedding light on puzzling elements of well-studied cases that are typically explained through competing arguments. They also suggest extensions to the theory as well as its predictive power.

Many casual observers might find the generation of a property rights gap in late twentieth-century Europe somewhat surprising. But this is exactly what occurred under a tumultuous episode of military-dominated rule in Portugal in the mid-1970s just before dictatorship in Western Europe was snuffed out.

China is interesting in part for an altogether different reason: it generated the largest property rights gap in modern history just after WWII. This had enormous human consequences in ensuing decades and today it serves to maintain China as the world's most rural country for its level of economic development. China began a decades-long series of radical reforms to other aspects of property rights security over both rural and urban land in the late 1970s despite retaining key elements of its rural property rights gap. These reforms infused new dynamism in the countryside and were fundamental to China's economic miracle in recent decades. This twisting path to the present vividly illustrates how the opportunities and livelihoods for hundreds of millions of Chinese citizens continue to be defined by the world's largest property rights gap.

8.1   THE NATURE OF PROPERTY RIGHTS GAPS AROUND THE WORLD
SINCE 1900

Previous chapters in this book demonstrate that property rights gaps have been regular features of land redistribution programs in Latin America. Governments that redistribute land from large landowners to peasants typically withhold property rights from peasant beneficiaries. But is this tendency specific to Latin America, or is it a more general feature of redistributive land reform programs?

Table 8.1 demonstrates that this trend is broadly generalizable. The table lists all major land reform programs since 1900 in which redistribution was a cornerstone of reform. This is the possibility set where a potential property rights gap could be opened.

The table also examines critical features of the property rights held by land reform beneficiaries. This enables distinguishing where the cases fit within the three broad categories of canonical property rights gaps outlined earlier in the book. The first is the set of Path A countries that never opened up a property rights gap despite conducting major land redistribution. The second category consists of Path B countries that opened a property rights gap and then later closed that property rights gap. The third category includes Path C countries that opened a property rights gap and have not closed it, at least up until the present day.

I define major land reform as the redistribution of at least 10 percent of a country's cultivable land over a continuous period with at least one year having over 1 percent of cultivable land expropriated.[1] This criterion enables capturing the largest and most consequential property rights gaps. Major reforms of this nature have the greatest capacity to significantly reorder the countryside. The theory should get most of these particularly important cases right if it is to be generalizable.

Concentrating on major land reforms, of course, leaves aside minor reforms that were either small relative to country size or did not center on land redistribution.[2] Numerous cases from Latin America demonstrate earlier in this book that even small property rights gaps can have a significant impact

---

[1] This definition follows Albertus (2015). That land redistribution has to reach 10 percent of cultivable land over a continuous period by this definition means that Colombia and Uruguay are not included in the sample. Both of these Path A cases exceeded this amount of land redistribution over the period but had pauses in their land reform programs at various times such that no continuous sequence of reform exceeded the threshold.

[2] In keeping with the discussion and justification in Chapter 2, this definition therefore also excludes land reforms that are characterized mainly by the colonization of state-owned land (such as land reforms in Colombia or the Philippines), land tenancy reforms that do not directly involve land transfers (such as Sri Lanka's 1958 Paddy Lands Bill), land titling programs that do not involve land transfers or involve only state-owned lands (such as much of the titling of Australia's Aboriginal communities), and nationalizations of land under customary land tenure structures (such as Zambia in 1975). For a broader accounting of and treatment of these alternative reforms, see Albertus (2015, Ch. 8), Lipton (2009), and Bhattacharya et al. (2019).

TABLE 8.1 *Major land reform programs and resultant beneficiary property rights worldwide, 1900–2010*

Country	Years of land reform	Collective/ state ownership	Land ownership formalization	Defensibility of ownership	Restrictions on sales/ rentals	Input/ credit support	Duration of property rights gap	Details of land redistribution
				Path A cases				
Czechoslovakia	1918–37	No	Strong	Strong	No	Significant	N/A	Czech-led reform, German discrimination
Estonia	1917–26	No	Strong	Strong	Yes	Significant	N/A	Baltic-German, church, state lands seized
Latvia	1920–37	No	Strong	Strong	No	Significant	N/A	Mainly targeted Baltic Germans
Lithuania	1920–30	No	Strong	Strong	No	Significant	N/A	Mainly targeted nobles' land from Russia
Japan	1946–49	No	Strong	Strong	Yes	High	N/A	Under post-WWII US occupation
South Korea	1948–58	No	Strong	Strong	Yes	High	N/A	Japanese lands and large holdings
Taiwan	1949–55	No	Strong	Strong	Yes	High	N/A	KMT after Chinese Civil War

Afghanistan	1979–83	No	No	Weak	Yes	Low	Until present; started to close in 2000s	Amidst Soviet invasion
Albania	1945–67	Yes	No	Weak	Yes	Significant	Largely closed in 1990s	Aftermath of WWII
Bolivia	1953–85	No	Weak	Weak	Yes	Low	Until 2000s	MNR reform after 1952 revolution
Bulgaria	1920–23	No	Weak	Weak	No	Low	Largely closed in 1990s	Stamboliski; private and village lands
Bulgaria	1945–58	Yes	No	Weak	Yes	Significant	Largely closed in 1990s	Aftermath of WWII
Chile	1967–73	Yes	No	Weak	Yes	Significant	Until approximately end of 1970s	Frei and Allende; Pinochet reversed some
East Germany	1945–60	Yes	No	Weak	Yes	Low	Until 1990s	Aftermath of WWII
El Salvador	1980–85	Yes	No	Weak	Yes	Significant	Largely closed in 1990s and 2000s	Most under military junta
Greece	1918–25	No	No	Weak	Yes	Low	Closed in late 1920s and 1930s	Venizelos; absentee, large lands to refugees
Guatemala	1953–54	No	No	Weak	Yes	Significant	Partly closed in 1950s with reversal; closed further beginning in 2000s	Under Arbenz; military reversed some

(continued)

TABLE 8.1 (continued)

Country	Years of land reform	Collective/ state ownership	Land ownership formalization	Defensibility of ownership	Restrictions on sales/ rentals	Input/ credit support	Duration of property rights gap	Details of land redistribution
Hungary	1945–62	Yes	No	Weak	Yes	Significant	Until 1990s	Communists, independent smallholders
Mexico	1917–92	Yes	No	Weak	Yes	Low	Until 2000s	Targeted large owners: most under PRI
Mongolia	1929–32	Yes	No	Weak	Yes	Low	Until present; initial steps to close in 1990s and 2000s	Targeted nobility and Buddhist church
Nicaragua	1979–89	Yes	No	Weak	Yes	Low	Until present; largely closed by 2010s	Sandinistas following 1979 revolution
North Vietnam	1954–56	Yes	No	Weak	Yes	Low	Began to close in 1990s and 2000s	Lao Dong Party, transfers and rent refunds
Panama	1968–83	Yes	No	Weak	Yes	High	Until 2010s	Military rule under Torrijos
Peru	1964–90	Yes	No	Weak	Yes	Low	Until present; largely closed by late 2000s	Most under military rule 1968–80

Country	Years							
Poland	1944–48	No	No	Weak	Yes	Significant	Until 1990s	Aftermath of WWII
Portugal	1975–76	No	No	Weak	Yes	Low	Until the 1980s	Carnation Revolution under military
Romania	1921–37	No	No	Weak	No	Low	Until 1990s	King Ferdinand after territorial expansion
Romania	1944–48	Yes	No	Weak	Yes	Low	Until 1990s	Aftermath of WWII, communist pressure
South Vietnam	1956–73	No	Strong	Weak	Yes	Significant	Defensibility strengthened in 1990s and 2000s	Ordinance 57 and US-backed land-to-tiller
Soviet Union	1917–27	Yes	No	Weak	Yes	Low	Partly closed in 1990s	Soviet Decree on Land and 1922 Code
Sri Lanka	1972–90	Yes	Weak	Weak	Yes	Significant	Until present; began to close in 2000s and 2010s	1972 law following 1958 Paddy Lands Bill
Tanzania	1963–76	Yes	No	Weak	Yes	Low	Until present; initial steps to close in late 2000s and 2010s	Nationalization followed by villagization

(*continued*)

TABLE 8.1 (*continued*)

Country	Years of land reform	Collective/ state ownership	Land ownership formalization	Defensibility of ownership	Restrictions on sales/ rentals	Input/ credit support	Duration of property rights gap	Details of land redistribution
				Path C cases				
Brazil	1964– present	No	No (prior to late 1980s)	Weak	Yes	Low	Until present; new land distributed not facing PR gap	1964 Land Act; continued by INCRA
China	1949–52	Yes	No	Weak	Yes	Low	Until present	Communist Party following Civil War
Cuba	1959–63	Yes	No	Weak	Yes	Low	Until present	Castro reform following Cuban Revolution
Dominican Republic	1934–85	No	No	Weak	Yes	Low	Until present	Trujillo, military, democratic regimes
Egypt	1952–78	No	Weak	Weak	Yes	Significant	Until present	Following Free Officers coup
Ethiopia	1975–88	Yes	No	Weak	Yes	Low	Until present	Derg reforms
Iran	1962–71	No	Weak	Weak	Yes	Significant	Until present	White Revolution under the Shah

North Korea	1946–47	Yes	No	Weak	Yes	Low	Until present	Aftermath of WWII
Venezuela	2005–present	Yes	Weak	Weak	Yes	Significant	Until present	Under Chávez and 2005 Land Law
Yugoslavia	1921–30	No	Weak	Weak	No	Low	Until country's dissolution	Mainly targeted Germans and Hungarians
Yugoslavia	1945–54	No	No	Weak	Yes	Low	Until country's dissolution	Aftermath of WWII under Communists
Zimbabwe	1992–2016	No	No	Weak	Yes	Low	Until present	White lands targeted by Mugabe

Notes: Major land reform is defined as expropriation and redistribution of at least 10 percent of cultivable land over a continuous period with at least one year having over 1 percent of cultivable land expropriated. Cultivable land area are from the FAO. Data are from Albertus (2015). Collective ownership indicates substantial collective, communal, or state operation and ownership of land transferred via reform (at least 30 percent) for at least a decade. Land formalization indicates the identification of rights holders and the legal recognition of rights and uses together with options for their demarcation and registration. Formalization is considered "weak" when formalization leaves out a significant portion of land beneficiaries, when not all rights are legally recognized, or when there are significant deficiencies in demarcation or registration of titles. Defensibility of ownership indicates the ability of those who hold legally recognized land rights to effectively call on the state for the consistent enforcement of those rights. Restrictions on sales/rentals indicate legal restrictions on the timing of sales/rentals or the use of land to be sold or rented. Agricultural input and credit support is coded "low" when access to support is heavily restricted to certain parts of the farming population or support is uniformly insufficient relative to demand; "significant" when access faces restrictions for a minority of farmers and support is sufficient relative to demand for some farmers; and "high" when access to support is broad and support is sufficient relative to demand for nearly all farmers.

Sources: Afghanistan: Pryor 1992, United States Agency for International Development 2018; Albania: Chan-Halbrendt 2013; Bolivia: Binswanger-Mkhize et al. 2009, Bottazzi and Rist 2012, El-Ghonemy 1992, Thiesenhusen 1995; Brazil: Alston 1999, Binswanger and Deininger 1997; Bulgaria 1920–23: Jörgensen 2006; Bulgaria 1916–58: Meurs et al. 1999; Chile: Kay 2002; China: Binswanger and Deininger 1997, Wong 1973, Lin 1990; Cuba: Powelson and Stock 1990; Czechoslovakia: Kotáko 1948, Macek 1922, Mathias and Pollard 1989, Šíma 2000; Dominican Republic: Gil 1999, Thiesenhusen 1995, Stanfield 1989; East Germany: Turner 1987; Egypt: Powelson and Stock 1990; El Salvador: Kay 1998, McElhinny 2006; Estonia: Jörgensen 2006; Ethiopia: Crewett and Korf 2008; Greece: Kontogiorgi 2006; Guatemala: Binswanger and Deininger 1997, Thiesenhusen 1995; Hungary: Pryor 1992, Kapstein 2017, Platt et al 1970, Powelson and Stock 1990; Japan: Galor et al. 2009, Studwell 2013; Latvia: Švábc 1929, Plakans and Wetherell 1966, Eglitis 2002; Lithuania: Bennich-Björkmanand and Aarelaid 2012, Valciukiene et al 2015, Wegren et al. 1998; Mexico: Albertus et al. 2016; Mongolia: Myadar 2009, Pryor 1992; Nicaragua: Broegaard 2009, de Laiglesia 2003, Enriquez 1991, Enriquez 1997, Kay 1998, Thiesenhusen 1995; North Korea: Lee 1963; North Vietnam: Kirk and Tuan 2009; Panama: Priestley 1986, United States Agency for International Development 2014; Peru: Matos Mar and Mejía 1980, McClintock 1981, Thiesenhusen 1989; Poland: Caski and Lerman 2002, Polish Academy of Sciences Institute of Geography 1956, Pryor 1992, Roney 2000, Swinnen 1999, Yakowicz 1979; Portugal: Bermeo 1986; Romania: Mathias and Pollard 1989, OECD 2000, Cartwright 2001; South Korea: Binswanger and Deininger 1997, Galor et al. 2009, Kapstein 2017; South Vietnam: Robinson 2003; Soviet Union: Atkinson 1983, Lipton 2009; Sri Lanka: Price et al 1999, Samaraweera 1982, Singh 1989, World Bank 2017; Taiwan: Binswanger-Mkhize et al. 2009; Tanzania: Binswanger-Mkhize et al. 2009, Powelson and Stock 1990, Scott 1998; Venezuela: Albertus 2015; Yugoslavia: Brashich 1954, Dovring 1970, Mathias and Pollard 1989; Zimbabwe: Binswanger-Mkhize et al. 2009. See online appendix for bibliography of sources.

on the people who live under them. This is particularly true if they drag on for decades at a time. Nonetheless, the bulk of minor land reforms do not cluster close to the 10 percent redistribution threshold constituting major reform. Most fall far short of that threshold.

The property rights features outlined in Table 8.1 are those detailed at length in Chapter 2: whether land is held individually versus collectively or by the state, whether land ownership is formalized, whether the land that beneficiaries receive is defensible against counterclaims, and whether there are restrictions to selling or renting land, which are the most significant restrictions on alienability. To provide a broad comparative picture that is both theoretically informative but also parsimonious, I use categorical variable codings that aim to highlight whether a substantial portion of land reform beneficiaries hold or are deprived of these property rights. These variables together illuminate whether several complementary aspects of a property rights gap operated among land beneficiaries. They therefore aid in assessing whether the status quo among a significant portion of land reform beneficiaries was one of having property without rights.

I code collective or state ownership in the affirmative when there is substantial collective, communal, or state operation and ownership of land transferred via reform (at least 30 percent) for at least a decade. Few land reforms that fulfill these criteria are borderline cases. Where land is collectivized or owned by the state in the wake of reform, it is often at a sweeping scale that encompasses nearly all land reform beneficiaries, as in many Eastern European countries or China after WWII, in Latin American countries such as Cuba, Mexico, or Peru, or in South and Southeast Asia. Other countries either do not pursue this route at all (such as South Korea or Greece) or collective and state ownership play a negligible role in land reform (such as Bolivia).

Land formalization indicates the identification of rights holders and the legal recognition of rights and uses together with options for their demarcation and registration. I classify land formalization as strong if land beneficiaries receive specific, formal, and registered rights. Land formalization is absent if land reform beneficiaries do not receive land titles, if land titles do not indicate property delimitations, or if land titles are not linked in any way to a property registry or land cadaster. Formalization is considered "weak" under the following intermediate circumstances: (i) land titling occurs but formalization leaves out a significant portion of land beneficiaries, such as beneficiaries from a specific region of the country, ethnic group, or demographic group; (ii) land titling occurs but not all rights are legally recognized; (iii) land titling occurs but there are significant deficiencies in demarcation or registration of titles such as failing to convert temporary land certificates into registered titles if holders are required to meet certain criteria during a specified period of time and compliance does not yield a title.

Defensibility of ownership indicates an ability for those who hold legally recognized land rights to effectively call on the state for the consistent enforcement of those rights. Defensibility is weak where land reform beneficiaries do not hold legally recognized rights at all. Adjudication and enforcement in these cases will be arbitrary and inconsistent. But there may be steep barriers to enforcement even where land rights are legally recognized. For instance, land titles may not be linked to a land registry, land registries may be incomplete or partially overlapping and conflicting, or registries may not be linked to a land cadaster. Defending a legitimate land beneficiary claim is not as easy or predictable in these circumstances. Defensibility can also be hampered by years-long delays in litigation due to a lack of land courts or a systematic bias against land reform beneficiaries. Strong defensibility for land reform beneficiaries is rare. It is typically only present where land claims are formalized and registered in an orderly (and often centralized) way and a system of land courts or judges exists to adjudicate land claims and protect land reform beneficiaries.

Restrictions on selling or renting land indicate legal restrictions on the timing of selling or renting land or the use of land to be sold or rented. For instance, land reform beneficiaries may be prohibited from selling their land for a period of time after receiving it or until they have repaid the government for the value of the land. These are fairly common restrictions. Another example is that land reform beneficiaries may only be allowed to sell their land to purchasers who will retain its use for agricultural purposes. In still other cases, land use is restricted to the original land reform beneficiary and beneficiaries are prohibited from renting out their land to other users.

These features of property rights should be examined in concert rather than individually in order to understand the nature of property rights as a whole in a given case. For instance, land can be held collectively but also be formalized and defensible – although this was rarely the case as land reform was historically practiced. As another example, land may be held individually, formalized, and linked to a property registry, but there may be restrictions to sales, such as a ten-year prohibition on sales after receiving land. This certainly limits property rights but does not do so permanently and is unlikely to have long-term consequences for economic decision-making.

Table 8.1 also indicates the level of governmental support for agricultural inputs and credits. This support can impact the long-term developmental consequences of land reform along with property rights over land. I classify agricultural input and credit support as "low" when access to support is heavily restricted to small parts of the farming population or support is uniformly insufficient relative to demand. Governments in these cases often do not subsidize credit for land reform beneficiaries, do not prioritize investments in improving rural infrastructure, and do not provide research and extension services. Or they may do so at a very limited scale that in practice fails to impact the livelihoods of most land reform beneficiaries. They may even hobble land reform beneficiaries by overvaluing exchange rates to favor domestic industry and shunting rural investment and support to large landowners. I classify agricultural input and credit support as "significant" when access to support faces restrictions for only a minority of farmers and support is sufficient relative to demand for some significant portion of farmers.

In these cases, the government may invest heavily in infrastructure such as irrigation in some important areas but not others; it may generously subsidize credit only to land reform beneficiaries growing certain crops or working the land in certain ways; or it may create agencies to provide subsidized inputs for many but not all land reform beneficiaries. I classify agricultural input and credit support as "high" when access to support is broad and support is sufficient relative to demand for nearly all farmers. These are cases in which the government invests heavily in providing generous services, inputs, and supports to land beneficiaries across the board.

Finally, Table 8.1 indicates how long a property rights gap over distributed land endured and provides brief details on the historical context in which land reform occurred.

The first and the most important point that Table 8.1 conveys is that property rights gaps in the context of land redistribution programs are the norm rather than the exception. All but seven of the forty-four major land redistribution programs around the world since 1900 – which easily impacted more than 1.5 billion people in nearly every region of the world – are Path B or Path C cases that generated at least a partial property rights gap. The seven Path A cases that constitute exceptions include Czechoslovakia, Estonia, Latvia, and Lithuania in the interwar period as well as Japan, South Korea, and Taiwan shortly after WWII. The overwhelming majority of major land reforms have delivered land to beneficiaries without rights.

Some countries have generated property rights gaps by nationalizing land and granting land reform beneficiaries mere usufruct rights over property. Zimbabwe and Ethiopia are illustrative examples. Other countries generated property rights gaps by forcing peasant beneficiaries into collectives and prohibiting any form of land alienation. Many Eastern European countries did this after WWII, as did Portugal in the mid-1970s and Mexico over the course of most of the twentieth century. Still other countries generated property rights gaps by failing to formalize land ownership or provide beneficiaries with defensibility of their property. Governments in these cases often fail to distribute land titles, distribute provisional titles that are never formalized, or distribute titles that are not linked to any other administrative systems such as a property register or land cadaster. One example of this is Venezuela beginning in 2005.

Most governments that generate a property rights gap do not flood the countryside with agricultural support in the form of credits and inputs. Agricultural support is typically spotty or minimal – just enough to enable rural dwellers to eke out an existence but not enough to enable them to thrive, accumulate wealth, and enjoy upward economic and social mobility as well as greater autonomy and independence. This is hardly surprising from the perspective of the theory in Chapter 3. Governments typically generate property rights gaps to gain coercive leverage over their rural subjects and bed down threats by maintaining dispersed and passive rural populations that can serve as a political counterweight to cities.

Governments are much more likely to provide robust financial support to rural areas when they are invested in the independence of the countryside and in rural development as a pillar in economic transformation writ large. This typically obviates a property rights gap as well. The nascent developmental states in Japan, South Korea, and Taiwan are perhaps the most prominent exemplars. These countries conducted land reforms characterized by land-to-the-tiller programs that created independent small farmers largely out of former renters while providing generous agricultural inputs and credits. They put in place limited restrictions on land sales and rentals only to prevent the reconstitution of large holdings. These programs share key similarities with several interwar land reforms in Europe, particularly in the Baltic states. Land reform with property rights and robust support for rural development in these three Asian cases had important support from the United States. But it was also powerfully motivated by anti-communism and the threat of instability if reform did not placate peasants. Its success was underpinned by growing and focused state power.

Property rights gaps that are generated in the context of redistributive land reform are rarely closed quickly. To the contrary, Table 8.1 indicates that whether a country traces Path B or Path C following land reform, most property rights gaps fester for years or even decades. Most countries that have generated property rights gaps retain them for at least a generation. Many Eastern European countries, for instance, created property rights gaps in the wake of WWII and did not close them until the fall of the Berlin Wall. Countries in South and Southeast Asia that generated large property rights gaps such as Sri Lanka and Vietnam similarly retained those gaps for long periods, as did most countries in Latin America. And in the Path C cases, such as China and Cuba, property rights gaps forged generations ago continue to persist in the present day.

To be sure, property rights gaps were relatively short-lived in several cases. Examples include Greece in the 1920s–1930s and Portugal in the 1970s–1980s. But these are exceptions rather than the rule.

8.2 CONDITIONS LINKED TO OPENING AND CLOSING PROPERTY RIGHTS GAPS AROUND THE WORLD SINCE 1900

Table 8.1 indicates that a large majority of the cases of major land reform around the world since 1900 have been followed by yawning and persistent property rights gaps in rural areas. This is consistent with theoretical predictions as well as with trends in land reform and property rights gaps in Latin America. But what are the political conditions under which property rights gaps around the globe have opened and closed? Do they conform to the theoretical expectations that this book lays out?

Table 8.2 investigates these questions systematically. This table first indicates, drawing from Table 8.1, whether property rights over redistributed land are granted or withheld in the context of major land reform. It then codes the two key theoretical determinants of the generation of a property rights gap from the time in which a country was conducting major land redistribution:

regime type and the presence of a coalitional split between ruling political elites and landed elites. Recall from Chapter 3 that authoritarian regimes that are ruled by nonlanded elites are the governments most likely to redistribute property without rights.

Regime type is coded mainly using the Polity IV index as in Chapter 4. I code a regime as democratic if it has a Polity score above 5 and as authoritarian if a regime has a Polity score of 5 or less. I also refer to the dichotomous regime data from Boix, Miller, and Rosato (2013) because there is disagreement as to the nature of some borderline regimes. I label a regime as a hybrid between democratic and authoritarian where the Polity index and the Boix, Miller, and Rosato data sources diverge in coding a particular regime. I follow the same coding rules laid out in Chapter 4 to code a coalitional split between ruling political elites and landed elites.

Table 8.2 next indicates the years during which a given country acted to close a property rights gap, if present.

Finally, Table 8.2 codes the main factors that the theory links to closing property rights gaps or not opening them up to begin with: regime type, the power of large landowners in the legislature, whether peasants are incorporated into or allied with the ruling governing coalition, and the presence of external pressure in the context of structural economic adjustment. The theory in Chapter 3 indicates that property rights gaps are most likely to close under democracy. Closing a property rights gap is particularly propitious when landed elites have a weak presence in the legislature such that they cannot block the extension of property rights to land beneficiaries even if it may threaten their interests for some reason, and when peasants are incorporated into or allied with the ruling governing coalition. Property rights gaps may also close under both democracies and dictatorships in the face of external pressure when countries are forced into structural economic adjustment programs.

I code landowner power in the legislature as "high" when landowning interests can both block and formulate policy. This occurs when landowners are a powerful bloc within one or several political parties that form a legislative majority. I code landowner legislative power as "significant" if landowners can block most policies that contravene their interests but not necessarily formulate and pass policy themselves. This is typically the case when landowners are a legislative minority but still hold enough seats to veto policies antithetical to their interests. Relatedly, landowners may have a minority position within a divided party or coalition that has a legislative majority. I code landowner power in the legislature as "low" when landowners can neither block nor formulate policy through the legislature. For instance, they may have no representation in the legislature at all, a legislature may not exist, or landowners only hold a small minority of seats that is insufficient even to veto policy proposals.

I code peasant incorporation into the ruling governing coalition using the same coding rules detailed in Chapter 4. Finally, I code external pressure in the context of structural economic adjustment building from the measure used in Chapter 4. I first examine whether a country has implemented major structural reforms to financial sector liberalization in the previous five years following Abiad et al. (2010). I then examine whether lenders in the context of structural reform exert pressure to make assistance contingent on property rights reforms that close the property rights gap. I turn to country-specific secondary sources on the scope of structural adjustment and the role of external pressure for episodes that occurred prior to the start of the Abiad et al. (2010) data.

Table 8.2 displays the same three broad categories of cases as in Table 8.1: those that follow Path A, those that follow Path B, and those that follow Path C.

Consider first the Path A countries that never generated a property rights gap. These cases should be rare according to the theory that this book advances. On the one hand, authoritarian regimes that have the institutional capacity and political incentives to redistribute land should also want to withhold property rights from land beneficiaries. On the other hand, democratic regimes that have incentives to grant property rights to land beneficiaries are often too institutionally constrained to be able to successfully redistribute land at a significant scale.

Table 8.2 bears out these tensions. Only seven countries over the last century have managed to redistribute a substantial amount of land without generating a property rights gap. Four did so in the interwar period: Czechoslovakia, Estonia, Latvia, and Lithuania. Three more countries redistributed land without generating a property rights gap shortly after WWII: Japan, South Korea, and Taiwan.

The theory speaks to one side of each of these sets of cases. The provision of property rights under democracy in the interwar European cases is unsurprising per the theory. But the scale of initial redistribution itself is unanticipated. For the post–WWII Asian cases, by contrast, redistribution itself is unsurprising given the authoritarian nature of rule and the new political impotence of large landowners. It is instead the provision of property rights that is more puzzling. To be sure, foreign pressure by the United States did play a role in these latter cases in a way consistent with the theory, but that is not the full story.

To better understand the Path A cases in their entirety requires looking beyond the theory to some of the alternative explanations for property rights gaps or the lack thereof. The Path A group demonstrates the important roles of two factors highlighted in previous chapters that can impact both large-scale land reform and property rights: ideology and state capacity. Land reform in all of the Path A cases occurred just after war. In each case it had an anti-communist streak. Incumbent governments in the Path A cases sought to root out foreign landowners and large domestic landowners that stoked rural resentment, sowed the seeds of rural labor militancy, and served as rival powers to incumbents. They then trained state resources on supporting rural development, providing property rights protections to land beneficiaries, and stemming land reconcentration.

TABLE 8.2 *Factors linked to the creation and closing of property rights gaps worldwide, 1900–2010*

Country	Years of land reform	Property rights over distributed land	Conditions of opening property rights gap		Conditions of closing property rights gap or not opening property rights gap				
			Regime type	Ruling coalition split with landed elite	Years closing property rights gap	Regime type	Landowner power in legislature	Peasants in governing coalition	External pressure in structural adjustment
					Path A cases				
Czechoslovakia	1918–37	Granted			None opened	Democracy	Low	Yes	No
Estonia	1917–26	Granted			None opened	Democracy	Low	Yes	No
Latvia	1920–37	Granted			None opened	Democracy	Low	Yes	No
Lithuania	1920–30	Granted			None opened	Democracy/authoritarian	Low	Yes	No
Japan	1946–49	Granted			None opened	Foreign occupied	Low: foreign influence dominated	No	Yes
South Korea	1948–58	Granted			None opened	Foreign occupied/authoritarian	No legislature	No	No
Taiwan	1949–55	Granted			None opened	Authoritarian	No legislature	No	No

(*continued*)

Path B cases

Country	Years of land reform	Property rights over distributed land	Regime type	Ruling coalition split with landed elite	Years closing property rights gap	Regime type	Landowner power in legislature	Peasants in governing coalition	External pressure in structural adjustment
Afghanistan	1979–83	Withheld	Foreign occupied	Yes	2000s–present	Foreign occupied/hybrid	Low: foreign influence dominated	No	No
Albania	1945–67	Withheld	Authoritarian	Yes	Largely closed in 1990s	Hybrid/democracy	Low	Yes	Yes
Bolivia	1953–85	Withheld	Authoritarian	Yes	1990s–2000s	Democracy	Significant	Not until 2006	Yes
Bulgaria	1920–23	Limited	Authoritarian	Yes	Largely closed in 1990s	Democracy	Low	Intermittently	Yes
Bulgaria	1946–58	Withheld	Authoritarian	Yes	Largely closed in 1990s	Democracy	Low	Intermittently	Yes
Chile	1967–63	Withheld	Democracy	Yes	Largely closed in mid-late 1970s	Authoritarian	No legislature	No	Yes
East Germany	1945–60	Withheld	Authoritarian	Yes	1990s as part of Germany	Democracy	Low	No	Yes
El Salvador	1980–85	Withheld	Authoritarian	Yes	Largely closed in 1990s and 2000s	Democracy	High	No	Yes
Greece	1918–25	Withheld	Authoritarian	Yes	Late 1920s–1930s	Democracy	Low	No	No

Guatemala	1953–54	Withheld	Hybrid	Yes	Partly closed in 1950s with reversal; closed further beginning in 2000s	Authoritarian	No legislature in mid-1950s; high in 2000s	Not until 2008	Yes in 2000s
Hungary	1945–62	Withheld	Authoritarian	Yes	1990s	Democracy	Low	Yes	Yes
Mexico	1917–92	Withheld	Authoritarian	Yes	1993–2000s	Authoritarian	Significant	Yes until 2000	Yes
Mongolia	1929–32	Withheld	Authoritarian	Yes	1990s–present	Democracy	Low	Yes	Yes
Nicaragua	1979–89	Withheld	Authoritarian	Yes	Mid-1980s; 1990s–present	Democracy	Low	Yes until 1989; yes starting in 2007	No
North Vietnam	1954–56	Withheld until mid-late 1980s	Authoritarian	Yes	1990s–present	Authoritarian	Low	No	Yes
Panama	1968–83	Withheld	Authoritarian	Yes	2000s–2010s	Democracy	Low	No	No
Peru	1964–90	Withheld	Authoritarian	Yes	1990s–present	Authoritarian	Low	No	Yes
Poland	1944–48	Withheld	Authoritarian	Yes	1990s	Democracy	Low	Yes	Yes
Portugal	1975–76	Withheld	Authoritarian	Yes	Late 1970s–1980s	Democracy	Significant	Yes until 1978	Yes in mid-1980s
Romania	1921–37	Withheld	Authoritarian	Yes	1990s	Democracy	Low	Yes	Yes

(continued)

Country	Years of land reform	Property rights over distributed land	Regime type	Ruling coalition split with landed elite	Years closing property rights gap	Regime type	Landowner power in legislature	Peasants in governing coalition	External pressure in structural adjustment
Romania	1944–48	Withheld	Authoritarian	Yes	1990s	Democracy	Low	Yes	Yes
South Vietnam	1956–73	Limited	Foreign occupied	Yes	1990s–2000s as part of Vietnam	Authoritarian	Low	No	Yes
Soviet Union	1917–27	Withheld	Authoritarian	Yes	Partly closed in 1990s in Russia	Hybrid	Low	No	Yes
Sri Lanka	1972–90	Withheld	Democracy/hybrid	Yes	2000s present	Hybrid/democracy	Low	Yes	No
Tanzania	1963–76	Withheld	Authoritarian	Yes	Late 2000s–present	Authoritarian	Low	No	No^
Path C cases									
Brazil	1964–present	Withheld until 1980s	Authoritarian	Yes	Not closed; new land distributed has PR				
China	1949–52	Withheld	Authoritarian	Yes	Not closed				
Cuba	1959–63	Withheld	Authoritarian	Yes	Not closed				
Dominican Republic	1934–85	Withheld	Authoritarian/democracy	Yes	Not closed				
Egypt	1952–78	Limited	Authoritarian	Yes	Not closed				
Ethiopia	1975–88	Withheld	Authoritarian	Yes	Not closed				

Iran	1962–?	Limited	Authoritarian	Yes	Not closed
North Korea	1946–47	Withheld	Authoritarian	Yes	Not closed
Venezuela	2005–present	Limited	Hybrid/authoritarian	Yes	Not closed
Yugoslovia	1921–30	Limited	Authoritarian	Yes	Not closed
Yugoslovia	1945–54	Withheld	Authoritarian	Yes	Not closed
Zimbabwe	1992–2016	Withheld	Authoritarian	Yes	Not closed

Notes: See Table 8.1 for further details on property rights over distributed land. Regime type is coded using Polity IV index and Boix, Miller, and Rosato (2013). Where these sources diverge, and in particular if a regime either has a Polity score above 5 but is coded as a dictatorship by Boix, Miller, and Rosato, or if a regime has a Polity score below 6 but is coded as a democracy by Boix, Miller, and Rosato, I code a regime as a hybrid between democratic and authoritarian. Ruling coalition split with landed elite is from Albertus (2015). Landowner power in the legislature is considered "high" when landowning interests can block and formulate policy, "significant" when they can block most policies that contravene their interests but not necessarily formulate and pass policy, and "low" when they can neither block nor formulate policy or have no representation.

^ There was external assistance in this case, and even a degree of pressure given Tanzania's history of international donor relations. But it did not occur during a structural adjustment program, which had come previously.

Sources: Afghanistan: United States Agency for International Development 2018, United States Department of State 2015; Albania: Swinnen 1999, Teqja et al. 2000, The World Bank Group 2013; Bolivia: Bottazzi and Rist 2012, Klein 2011; Brazil: Albertus et al. 2018, Ondetti 2008; Bulgaria: Jörgensen 2006, Meurs et al. 1999, Muers and Begg 2005; Chile: Albertus and Menaldo 2018, Kay 2002, Thiesenhusen 1995; China: Wong 1973; Cuba: Thomas 1971, Valdés Paz 1997; Czechoslovakia: Cornwall 1997, Kotátko 1948, Macek 1992, Mathias and Pollard 1989, Thompson 1993; Domincan Republic: Gil 1999, Thiesenhusen 1995, Turits 2003; East Germany: Anderson and Zelle 1995, Beckmann and Hagedorn 1997, Bogaerts et al. 2002, Ho and Spoor 2006, Jeffress 1991, Laschewski 2014, Southern 1993; Egypt: Albertus 2015, Powelson and Stock 1990; El Salvador: Clichevsky 2003, Mason 1986, McElhinny 1986, Robinson 2003; Estonia: Jorgensen 2006, Vaskela 1996; Ethiopia: Crewett and Korf 2008; Greece: Kontogiorgi 2006, Mavrogordatos 1983, Mouzelis 1976, Ploumidis 2012, Seferiades 1999; Guatemala: Ameringer 1992, Granovskv-Larson 2010, Wittman and Salvidar-Tanaka 2006; Hungary: Csaki and Lerman 2003, Gehmacher et al. 1999, Hanley et al. 2002; Iran: Tai 1974, Hooglund 2012, Powelson and Stock 1990; Japan: Galor et al. 2009, Kapstein 2017, Kawagoe 1999; Latvia: Eglitis 2002, Plakans and Wetherell 1996, Švābc 1929; Lithuania: Bennich-Björkmanand Aarelaid 2012, Wegren et al. 1998; Mexico: Albertus 2015, Albertus et al. 2016, de Ita 2006; Mongolia: Ginsburg 1995, Mcarn 2004, Munkherdene 2018, Mvadar 2009, Pryor 1992; Nicaragua: Broegaard 2009, de Laiglesia 2003, Enriquez 1997, Kay 1998, Thiesenhusen 1995; North Korea: Lee 1963; North Vietnam: Akram-Lodhi and Haroon 2004, Kirk and Tuan 2009, Ravallion and Van de Walle 2008; Panama: Peeler 1998, Priestley 1986, United States Agency for International Development 2014; Peru: Albertus 2015, Crabtree 2002; Poland: Csaki and Lerman 2002, Gorlach and Mooney 2005, Yakowicz 1979; Portugal: Bermeo 1986, de Almeida 2016; Romania: Cartwright 2001, Gehmacher 1999, Mathias and Pollard 1989, Vaskela 1996; South Korea: Galor et al. 2009, Kapstein 2017, Mitchell 1949; South Vietnam: Kapstein 2017; Soviet Union: Atkinson 1983, Leonard 2011, Wegren 2003; Sri Lanka: Devotta 2016, Samaraweera 1982, Singh 1989, Udayakantha 2017, World Bank 2017; Taiwan: Albertus 2015; Tanzania: Nord 2009, Pederson 2010, Schreiber 2017, Scott 1998, World Bank 2019; Venezuela: Albertus 2015; Zimbabwe: Albertus 2015, Pazvakavambwa and Hungwe 2009. See online appendix for bibliography of sources.

The interwar European cases provide rare examples of democratic countries managing large-scale land redistribution. Governments expropriated ethnic minority out-groups in these cases, such as the Baltic Germans in Estonia and Latvia. These out-groups abruptly and completely lost their political power at the end of WWI and were swept out by newly empowered peasant majorities and an emergent nationalism that transcended social class and that eschewed communism.

The post–WWII Asian cases are interesting for a different reason. Land redistribution in these cases did not occur under democracy but governments nonetheless granted land reform beneficiaries strong property rights. In each of these cases, the United States played an important role not only in supporting land reform but also in supporting the form that it would take: granting land to individual families rather than collectives or the state and also providing families with property rights (Kapstein 2017, Ch. 4). After all, family farming was a fundamental pillar of the American founding. This is a point that President Truman noted in a 1950 speech supporting land reform in Asia.

However, in contrast to most historiography, the United States did not impose land reform on Japan, South Korea, and Taiwan. Instead, as Kapstein (2017, 98) writes and demonstrates, "more often it encouraged and sought to influence the reforms that local governments were already elaborating." Leaders in these countries were firmly politically split from the landlord class that had long dominated the countryside and were already laying the early institutional and policy groundwork for state developmentalism. After all, political and economic challenges associated with systemic vulnerabilities were acute. Of paramount concern were the linked threats of foreign attack from North Korea and China and domestic instability via rural discontentment and communist infiltration of the countryside (Doner et al. 2005). This was especially the case in South Korea and Taiwan. Governments began to quickly build expert-based and coherent bureaucracies that could collaborate with organized private actors to spur national economic transformation (Doner et al. 2005, 341). This began with rural development and import substitution. These dynamics helped speed these governments along the path to prosperity that the nature of their Path A land reforms had set them on.

In other words, international pressure in these cases mainly took the form of a meeting of the minds in which the United States sought out and worked with like-minded domestic officials and bureaucrats in crafting and implementing land reform. Furthermore, in all of these cases, the United States sought to curtail Japanese imperial power and forestall communist appeals to the broader population.

Land reform in Japan began under the occupation of the United States military. The interim Japanese government at first independently drafted a land reform bill in October 1945 to devolve land to the tiller (Kapstein 2017, 104). The US issued its land reform mandate in December of that year. Seeking to bring a close to the feudal era and rewire the political basis of Japanese power, the US occupation authority under the direct oversight of General MacArthur worked in concert with domestic actors to implement a final, sweeping land reform that incorporated granting property rights to smallholders.

The American-led post–WWII military government in South Korea also put into motion a land-to-the-tiller reform in 1948 in an effort to eliminate large Japanese landholdings on the Korean peninsula and undercut popular support for communism. The South Korean government vigorously continued this reform in 1950 and maintained it even during the Korean War. It granted private property rights to recipients from the beginning to provide a safeguard against the threat of rural communist infiltration from North Korea and ensure that the new status quo would become quickly engrained even if the Americans left.

Taiwan, like South Korea, had a post–WWII landlord class with close Japanese ties given the island's history of Japanese colonialism. The incoming Kuomintang party (KMT) forces from mainland China saw these landlords as a rival threat to their power and quickly sought to destroy them through land reform. The United States aided their land reform efforts, in part through the Joint Commission on Rural Reconstruction (JCRR). This assistance differed from that of the United States occupying forces in Japan and South Korea during the major structural overhaul of their postwar economies. Nonetheless, it played an important role in land reform. The JCRR helped to reorganize farmers' associations, which were important in mediating landlord–tenant disputes, setting rents, and surveying local land ownership among other land reform implementation functions. The JCRR also conducted cadastral surveys and provided agricultural credit. Behind the nature of aid to Taiwan was the desire to help it rapidly industrialize as a way to withstand the palpable geopolitical threats from neighboring communist China. As in South Korea, Taiwan granted private property rights to land reform recipients.

Next consider the Path B cases in Table 8.2. This is the category of countries that generated a property rights gap in the context of land redistribution and then later closed – or at least partially closed – that property rights gap. This represents nearly 60 percent (25 out of 44) of the cases of major land reform over the last century.

Almost all of the countries that fall into this category generated a property rights gap under the conditions anticipated by the theory. Take Portugal as an example. A military coup toppled the longtime Salazar/Caetano Estado Novo in April 1974 in what became known as the Carnation Revolution. Incoming officers replaced national and local political elites and passed radical legislation in 1975 aimed at "liquidating fascism and landowners" in "a general attack to private property" (Almeida 2007, 64). They quickly seized more than a million hectares of land in favor of workers and expelled traditional landowners. Military rule during the Carnation Revolution was short-lived and unstable. But this does not explain why property rights were withheld from land reform beneficiaries. Secure property rights were never on the table. The military instead sought to destroy existing property relations and create workers' cooperatives on distributed land (Bermeo 1986, 73). The plan to create cooperatives faced some internal resistance within the armed forces and even the workers' unions but it was enacted anyway (Bermeo 1986, 65–67). I return to this case later in this chapter.

There are several exceptional cases in the Path B category in which property rights gaps were not opened by authoritarian regimes whose ruling political elites were split from landed elites. Most notable are Chile, Guatemala, and Sri Lanka. These are the only cases of democratic or semidemocratic countries generating large property rights gaps through land redistribution. They all hold several circumstances in common that Chapter 4 ties to land redistribution. The first is that each of these countries engaged in their most intense phases of land reform under leaders of the hard ideological left. The second is that their leaders each faced relatively low institutional constraints to their rule. Regimes with weak checks and balances that at times treaded a fine line between democracy and dictatorship generated these property rights gaps. In two of these cases, Chile and Guatemala, reactionary coups toppled incumbent regimes, rolled back land reforms, and restored property rights. In the case of Sri Lanka, later governments responded to popular pressure for property rights and began to close the property rights gap of their own accord. After all, there was considerable demand for individual rather than collective farms from the beginning (Gooneratne and Samad 1979, 281).

There are two other countries that did not generate a property rights gap under dictatorship per se in the presence of a coalitional split between ruling political elites and landed elites. However, the circumstances approximated these due to foreign occupation. The first country in this camp is Afghanistan. The Soviet Union occupied Afghanistan in the late 1970s and implemented a redistributive land reform program in anything but democratic fashion. The Soviet Union also withheld property rights from land beneficiaries in Afghanistan as it did back at home. The second country in this camp is South Vietnam. The United States implemented a major land-to-the-tiller program in South Vietnam as concerns grew about contagion effects from the land reform in North Vietnam. In contrast to the Soviets in Afghanistan, the United States sought to extend property rights to land beneficiaries as well through land titling and related efforts (Kapstein 2017, Ch. 5). Although a significant property rights gap was not generated, the defensibility of land claims for beneficiaries was weak given the insurgency that raged in the countryside.

The countries in the Path B category eventually closed – or made significant progress in closing – the property rights gaps that they had previously created. The governments closing property rights gaps were almost always different from the ones that generated them. Furthermore, and consistent with the theory, the governments that closed existing property rights gaps were frequently democratic in nature. A total of seventeen out of the twenty-five cases of major land reform in this category closed property rights under democracy.

The modal route to closing a property rights gap under democracy operates through responsiveness to popular pressure. Greece is an illustrative example. A series of prime ministers expropriated large estates belonging to the Ottomans and the monarchy after WWI at a time when the franchise was heavily restricted and the military had substantial influence in politics. The government did not title or grant secure property rights to the private land that was redistributed in the early to mid-1920s, however, in part because of refugee flows and an enormous number of irregular land transactions. The Greek government prioritized land redistribution over property rights and retained formal ownership of the land it had expropriated. Prevailing property rights quickly changed after a transition to democracy in 1926. Land tenure insecurity alongside an economic crisis radicalized the demands of peasants for property titles and secure possession rights. The Greek parliament responded by passing a law in 1929 that secured the possession rights of land reform beneficiaries and issued provisional title deeds until plots were surveyed and beneficiaries repaid their debts to the state (Kontogiorgi 2006, 139–140).

Peasants actually won positions within the ruling coalition or forged close alliances to the ruling political elite in some cases where democracies closed property rights gaps. In other cases, any large landowners that survived land redistribution were too politically weakened to oppose the extension of property rights to land reform beneficiaries. Popular demands for property rights in these cases were either impossible to ignore, impossible to block, or both. Many Eastern European countries emerging from communism after the fall of the Berlin Wall are illustrative. In countries such as Albania, Bulgaria, Hungary, or Romania, peasants received land after WWII but were later forced into collectives. But rural interests were later incorporated into the protest movements that ultimately toppled communism and came to govern in its wake. Democratic governments in these countries quickly privatized collectives and secured the property rights of their members.

Efforts to close a property rights gap under democracy can be supercharged, and even catalyzed, by external pressure from international lenders during programs of structural economic adjustment where countries are asking for other forms of assistance. Pressure from the IMF and World Bank for privatization and securing property rights in Eastern European countries in the 1990s piled on top of domestic demands. The same was true in Bolivia in the 1990s. In other cases, such as El Salvador in the 1990s or Portugal in the 1980s, external pressure played more of a catalytic role given that domestic demand for property rights had either not coalesced or faced some degree of opposition.

This dynamic is not unique to democracy. In seven cases of major land reform, authoritarian regimes or semi-democracies closed large property rights gaps under pressure from foreign lenders in exchange for much-needed assistance to resolve economic crises. Mexico, Peru, and Russia all faced this pressure in the 1990s for disparate reasons. Vietnam faced similar pressure in the wake of the Asian Financial Crisis. Incumbent regimes in each case chose to extend greater property rights to former land reform beneficiaries and outlive the crisis with a weakened grip on the rural sector rather than try to go it alone in a spiraling crisis. In Mexico, this choice may have been one of the factors contributing to the demise of the PRI's iron grip (which had long been strongest in the countryside) and a transition to democracy.

External pressure to close a property rights gap does not always transpire in the context of structural economic adjustment programs. It can also come more directly through foreign aid, as in Tanzania, or through foreign threats. Moreover, in one case in this category – Afghanistan – a longstanding property rights gap began to be closed under direct foreign occupation. The United States sought to undo the property rights gap in Afghanistan that the Soviet Union had created there decades earlier. This case has perhaps the closest parallels to cases such as Japan and South Korea where large-scale land reforms never yielded property rights gaps in part because of the influence of the United States as an occupier.

The third and final category of countries in Table 8.2 are Path C cases. These are countries that generated a property rights gap by redistributing land but withholding property rights from beneficiaries and that have not closed this gap. The countries in this category are Brazil, China, Cuba, the Dominican Republic, Egypt, Ethiopia, Iran, North Korea, Venezuela, Yugoslavia, and Zimbabwe. It is a mostly unsurprising bunch from the perspective of the theory. All of these countries remain solidly authoritarian with the exception of Brazil, which transitioned to democracy in the mid-1980s, the Dominican Republic, which transitioned to democracy in the late 1970s, and Yugoslavia, which dissolved as a country in 1992. Authoritarian regimes spearheaded land redistribution in each of these countries when landed elites were marginalized and isolated from the ruling political elite. Ruling political elites seized the opportunity to attack and destroy their rivals while generating coercive leverage over land beneficiaries by granting them property without property rights. This served them well politically and in most cases continues to do so.

The two partial outliers in this group from the perspective of the theory are Brazil and the Dominican Republic. Chapter 4 outlines why the property rights gap in these countries persisted in spite of the introduction of democracy. Important in both cases, and consistent with the theory, was remaining landed elite power in the legislature that could benefit from an ongoing property rights gap as well as relatively intermittent engagement with the international lenders that more effectively pressured other countries in Latin America for property rights reforms amid economic crises in the 1980s and 1990s.

8.3 CASE STUDIES

The overall trends in Tables 8.1 and 8.2 suggest that this book's theory regarding the creation and closing of property rights gaps has empirical purchase in regions far different from Latin America. This section looks at two cases of property rights gaps outside of Latin America in greater detail: Portugal starting in the mid-1970s and China in the wake of its civil war.

Applying the theory to these cases casts new light on traditional accounts and helps to demonstrate the utility of the theory. These cases also demonstrate potential extensions and limits to the theory.

The case of Portugal helps to illustrate the utility of the theory even in a case classically viewed through the lens of ideology, partisan polarization, and elite capture. Land redistribution and the formation of worker cooperatives on collectively held nationalized land in mid-1970s Portugal is often painted as the natural consequence of a communist-directed attempt at a people power revolution (Barreto 1987). The subsequent breakup of cooperatives is typically depicted as an elite-led counter-revolution – or at least one driven by northern capitalists – that reversed the revolution (Cardoso 1977; Lucena 1977). While Portugal's experience does illustrate the power of ideology, it also demonstrates the value of political regimes, coalitions, popular demands, and external pressure in understanding the generation, maintenance, and ultimate demise of a large property rights gap in a context very different from that in Latin America. Applying the theory to this case also complicates the traditional narrative by shedding light on debates over social control and property rights among members of distinct political groupings.

Finally, the Portuguese case indicates the importance of cross currents within popular demands for greater property rights under democracy. Democracies not only respond to the demands of land reform beneficiaries. Geographical, occupational, and even within-class splits among small landowners and peasants can at times generate conflicting demands for property rights and even property. In some cases, land reform beneficiaries will lose out or win merely partial victories. This insight provides additional nuance to the theory regarding the link between democracy and property rights.

Like Portugal, the case of China demonstrates the value and limitations of understanding the distribution of property and property rights through the lens of ideology. The China case also sheds light on the role of state capacity in making decisions over property rights. The Chinese Communist Party (CCP) initially set to redistributing land to individuals along with land titles and other property rights after it won the Chinese Civil War. However, internal debate and deficiencies in land registries slowed this outcome. The regime ultimately reversed course and collectivized land in the face of considerable peasant resistance.

China steadfastly retained its rural property rights gap from the 1950s through the 1970s. This came at an enormous human cost: the Great Famine, in which tens of millions of Chinese starved to death.[3] Sobered by this appalling catastrophe and seeking a new path after Mao's death, the Communist Party began experimenting with a series of carefully orchestrated changes to both rural and urban property

---

[3] The property rights gap was hardly the only cause of the famine. It was also driven by career incentives and political radicalism associated with officials in pursuit of political advancement (Kung and Chen 2011).

rights. These reforms breathed life into the agricultural sector and eventually served as a critical underpinning of China's spectacular growth since the 1990s. But core elements of the property rights gap still remain in place. Across these changes, China's property rights gap has played a crucial role in regime maintenance, slowing urbanization, easing the regime's control of its citizenry, and ensuring that land is available as a social safety net of last resort.

Portugal: Property and Rights from the Estado Novo to Joining the European Economic Community

The Portuguese countryside south of the Tagus River, which bisects the country, was governed primarily under the *latifondo* system in the early to mid-twentieth century in a similar fashion to southern Spain and southern Italy. Middle and upper-class landowners (mostly absentee) owned the *latifundia* in the south. Landless peasants who lived in adjacent agro-towns worked these lands (Graham and Wheeler 1983, 344). This contrasted with northern Portugal, where land ownership was dominated by *minifundia*, small low-yield parcels of land that small-scale farmers owned and worked primarily for subsistence. Table 8.3 illustrates the contrast between the distribution of landholdings in the south, principally within the Alentejo region in the table, and other regions of Portugal.

The *latifundia* were chronically underdeveloped. Only 42 percent of *latifundia* plots were irrigated by 1966 and they had stagnant yields drastically lower than the rest of Europe's from the mid-1950s to the early 1970s (Mailer 1977, 156; King 1978, 118). Many landholdings were not used for farming and the choice of less labor-intensive crops such as cork and eucalyptus trees meant widespread unemployment and poverty in the countryside as most peasants could not find work between November and March (Mailer 1977, 156).[4] The ruling Salazar government attempted to mechanize agriculture via subsidies and price tariffs. This had the effect of decreasing employment by distorting the labor/capital ratio rather than increasing employment through complementarity (Fernandes 1973, 24; 28). Land redistribution during this period was nonetheless off the table. *Latifundarios* were among the most important allies of the solidly authoritarian Salazar regime (Bermeo 1986, 15). Although large landowners had lost ground to ascendant industrialists and bankers by the end of the Salazar regime, "their alliance [with Salazar] persisted, and they could depend on the repressive forces to protect their interests" (Chilcote 2012, 112).

---

[4] Inefficiently low levels of farm employment and the resulting precarious economic situation for peasants was largely a holdover from feudalism, with absentee landowning families eschewing productive farm activity for leisure-sector purposes such as hunting and the production of luxury goods such as cork (King 1978, 118; Mailer 1977, 156). Almeida (2016, 188) emphasizes the paltry incentives for investment, thanks to high levels of landholding concentration.

TABLE 8.3 *Distribution of landholdings in Portugal prior to land reform*

Districts	Landholdings thousands	(%)	hectares	(%)	Active population thousands	(%)	Land per active person hectares	Average size of land-holdings hectares
				Northwest				
Viana	43.8		67.0		60.7		1.1	1.5
Braga	61.1		135.7		68.4		2.0	2.2
Porto	62.2		120.7		48.4		2.5	1.9
Aveiro	68.9		132.4		47.8		2.8	1.9
Viseu	81.4		213.7		834		2.5	2.6
Coimbra	70.4		146.9		53.9		2.7	2.1
Northwest total	387.8	48.0	816.5	16.4	364.6	40.5	2.2	2.1
				West				
Leiria	60.5		149.2		52.0		2.5	2.9
Lisboa	41.6		150.7		46.8		3.6	3.2
Santarém	55.5		352.9		63.9		6.4	5.5
West total	157.6	19.6	652.9	13.0	162.8	18.0	4.0	4.1
				Northeast				
Vila-Real	43.6		164.9		54.0		3.8	3.0
Bragança	31.5		314.7		39.3		10.0	8.0
Guarda	43.7		259.6		41.2		5.9	6.0
Co. Branco	44.3		409.0		43.2		9.2	9.5
Northeast total	163.1	20.1	1,150.6	23.2	177.7	19.5	6.4	7.0
				Alentejo				
Portalegre	16.2		469.9		43.7		10.6	29.0
Evora	11.4		572.0		35.9		15.3	50.1
Beja	20.8		753.9		50.0		15.0	36.2
Setúbal	17.3		293.9		32.9		8.9	16.9
Alentejo total	65.7	8.1	2,089.7	42.0	162.7	18.0	12.9	31.6
				Algarve				
Faro	34.3	4.2	276.1	5.4	37.7	4.0	8.3	8.0
TOTAL 18 districts	808.5	100.0	4,983.1	100.0	895.3	100.0	5.5	6.2

Source: Cabral (1978, 435).

The regime unsurprisingly consistently sided with landowners over peasants during wage disputes given the alliance between the ruling regime and large landowners. When peasants went on strike in 1953 in the Alentejo region, for example, the National Republican Guard (GNR) responded by gunning down more than one hundred peasants and executing strike leaders in an extrajudicial fashion (Mailer 1977, 157). Social agencies were similarly brutal and extractive. They demanded rents from agricultural workers but provided little in the way of medical services or food. These conditions conspired to radicalize peasants in southern Portugal, particularly in the Alentejo, where the Communist Party of Portugal (PCP) often outvoted even the Socialists despite the fact that the Socialists held much more national-level prominence. Under the Estado Novo regime, however, votes counted for very little.

Land Reform Restructures the Countryside

Land redistribution in Portugal after the fall of the Estado Novo regime occurred along the lines anticipated by this book's theory. Portugal was fighting a series of metastasizing and increasingly costly colonial wars in the 1960s as it struggled to retain control over possessions such as Angola, Guinea-Bissau, and Mozambique. Military conscription from the metropole became longer and more onerous, causing mass emigration. A group of junior officers mounted a coup that toppled the regime in April 1974. This group of officers, which became known as the Movement of the Armed Forces (MFA), was immediately supported by a broad swathe of civilians.

Portugal cycled through a series of short-lived military and civilian governments after the MFA seized power and cut Portugal's overseas colonies loose. Military officers effectively controlled these governments whereas large landowners found themselves sidelined from power for the first time in decades. The circumstances were ripe for land reform, which came down like a sledgehammer in 1975 and continued into mid-1976 as the regime sought to destroy large landowners. The MFA set its sights on the south of the country where landholding inequality was highest. It rapidly seized nearly half of all privately owned land by setting low landholding ceilings while expelling large landowners. It also nationalized land that was irrigated through public systems. This ultimately amounted to approximately one million hectares of land (King 1978; Rutledge 1977).

The land reform dovetailed with burgeoning worker occupations of large estates in early 1975. The government ratified some of these occupations, expelled workers in others, and expropriated additional land that had never been occupied. It also pushed back against land occupations by declaring them illegal. The government viewed them as "damaging to the agrarian reform and therefore reactionary" (Bermeo 1986, 68–9).[5]

---

[5] This did not stop extralegal land occupations, which continued throughout much of the south (Bermeo 1986, 72–3).

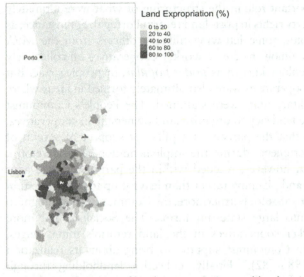

Land Expropriation (%)
0 to 20
20 to 40
40 to 60
60 to 80
80 to 100

Porto •

Lisbon •

FIGURE 8.1 Intensity of land expropriation and land nationalization in Portugal
Source: Author, based on Drain (1982).

Figure 8.1 displays a map of the percentage of land area expropriated or nationalized through the land reform at the parish level, which is Portugal's lowest level administrative division. The land reform data are based on Drain (1982). I verified these figures by accessing expropriation-level data from the archives at the Ministry of Agriculture in Lisbon. The map displays expropriation intensity calculated by dividing the extent of expropriation by parish land area. It is based on reconstructed administrative divisions that prevailed in Portugal at the time of the land reform.

Property without Rights under Military Rule

The brief series of military and civilian governments in Portugal focused mainly on destroying existing property relations and running out large landowners rather than securing property rights for land reform beneficiaries. However, various governments did dedicate energy to restructuring property rights. Worker-owned cooperatives (known as UCPs) emerged as the dominant form of organization on collectively occupied lands. The government helped to establish more than 500 new production units averaging nearly 2,000 hectares each (Barreto 1987, 232). These cooperatives typically joined several large farms together. This actually generated greater land concentration while also enhancing direct land access for laborers (Barros 1980, 86). Most cooperative enterprises were run by an elected board of directors and a fiscal council that served as the executive and legislative bodies, respectively. All workers had a single vote, owned one share in the cooperative, and were required to attend general assemblies that held elections and made long-term production decisions by vote. The government retained legal ownership of the land.

Ideology played an important role in the structuring of what were ultimately insecure and unstable property rights in post–land reform Portugal. For instance, as Bermeo (1986, 63–69) notes, some left-wing military officers from the MFA worked with local farmers' unions to create worker cooperatives on collectively occupied land under an ideology known as *poder popular*, or people's rule. But Bermeo underscores that cooperatives were also ultimately formed in areas where neutral and right-wing military units were stationed. The People's Communist Party initially supported the tendency to organize land ownership in cooperatives. This was important given that the party was a pillar of support of several of Portugal's provisional governments during the implementation of land reform. The idea of *poder popular*, however, receded within the party over time as it sought to centralize power and planning rather than leave it up to disparate rural organizations (Bermeo 1986, 68–69). Furthermore, the Communists had sought to turn expropriated lands into large state-run farms. The Socialists had more vigorously advocated worker cooperatives in the land reform's initial stages, though workers brought in Communist support to bring about its realization (Ferreira and Marshall 1986, 82).[6] Finally, collective landholding through cooperatives held a degree of popular appeal as well from workers' associations that sought to quickly exploit the land that they had occupied or otherwise received.

But there was hardly ideological or social consensus on cooperatives as the chief form of property rights despite the fact that the government ultimately imposed them on land reform beneficiaries across the board. There was internal resistance within the MFA to the establishment of cooperatives. On the eve of land reform, even some radical generals such as General Vasco Gançalves opposed them, arguing at an MFA assembly on January 4, 1975: "Are rural workers already sold on the idea of cooperatives? Are small farmers? . . . We run grave risks politicizing ourselves so rapidly" (quoted in Bermeo 1986, 52). Consistent with this, some workers' unions in areas of extreme land inequality supported the project of agrarian reform but not as achieved through land occupation and the creation of cooperative production structures (Bermeo 1986, 65–67). Other workers preferred smaller cooperative units that would allow for greater participation in management and production control (Barros 1980, 86). Finally, when Portugal transitioned to democracy in 1976 and the Socialists won power, they immediately set to work weakening cooperatives and setting the stage for their ultimate demise. Popular pressure encouraged their efforts to do so.

Nonetheless, and especially after April 1975 elections for a Constituent Assembly, leading military members of the government actively sought to redistribute land through worker occupations and the formation of cooperatives. For instance, the MFA held "Sessions of Enlightenment" in

---

[6] Bermeo (1986, 57) argues that the Communists were much weaker in practice than they have often been made out to be: "To view the occupations as products of the PCP's orchestration is to overestimate the party's unity and power."

some towns that helped to form workers' commissions and village councils that would shortly thereafter organize collective land seizures (Bermeo 1986, 66). But as a new wave of occupations began to challenge state power, the fourth provisional government sought to exert even more centralized control over the process of land expropriation and distribution and sought, with mixed effects, to end occupations (Bermeo 1986, 68–71).

Chilcote (2012, 111) underscores the tension between ideology and imperatives of control among leading military figures and leftist allies, as well as popular push-back:

The path to socialism confronted issues of struggle on the left: centralized command versus local participatory democracy, authoritarianism versus pluralism, discipline versus spontaneity. The MFA's consolidation of power conflicted with pressures to open up the system, and its effort to transform itself into a political movement was unacceptable to the emerging popular forces.

Closing the Property Rights Gap under Democracy

The Socialist Party won 35 percent of the national vote in the April 1976 legislative elections that paved the way to democracy in Portugal, soundly beating the 14 percent vote share of the Communists. The newly founded Confederation of Portuguese Farmers (CAP) quickly pushed the new government to change agrarian property rights. The CAP formed as a broad-based national farmers' association that united farmworkers, peasants, and larger landowners alike. It sought to loosen the government's grip over cooperatives through tools such as loans and credits, which many workers had come to view as tools of manipulation and control. It also aimed to win more benefits for the small farm sector and to limit what some viewed as the excesses of the agrarian reform (Bermeo 1986, 178–197). CAP speeches and publications in 1975 and 1976 declared fights "against dictatorship" and the "total collectivization of land." The CAP was largely responsible for running out the Socialists' 1976 Minister of Agriculture, Lopes Cardoso, who was seen as too connected to the policies of the dictatorship.

The Socialists dramatically changed course on agrarian reform in late 1976 and immediately set to dismantling cooperatives and parceling the land among private individuals along with complete property rights. This suggests that a lack of property rights granted to land reform beneficiaries in Portugal was not simply a mechanical result of leftist ideology or popular demand for cooperatives. Those factors gained influence due to the particular nature of the series of authoritarian regimes that held power and that had the capacity to impose top-down imperatives on society.

The Socialist-led government of Mário Soares appointed António Barreto as Minister of Agriculture to replace Lopes Cardoso. Barreto introduced the concept of the "autonomous farmer" and increased credit restrictions to cooperatives while forcing them to repay debts, attempting to force them into insolvency as many were deeply in debt or underproductive (Almeida 2007, 64; Almeida 2016, 193–194). Barreto himself later wrote: "For an entire year the military and their civilian allies wrote the laws and applied them with none other than revolutionary legitimacy. This was one of the sources for despotism. . . . The revolution failed upon elections, as they do most of the time" (Barreto 1987, 334–335).

Efforts to devolve cooperative landholdings into individual ownership ramped up in 1978 as the Social Democrats took power. The Social Democrats passed the Sà Carniero laws in 1979 and 1981 that seized land from cooperatives and distributed them to farmers who applied through a state-system process to farm the lands privately (Almeida 2007, 67). Applicants had to demonstrate that agriculture was their main source of income. Some of these seizures became violent, particularly when cooperatives were forced to return land to the state to pay off mounting debts and when their workers did not have new plots lined up.

But many small sharecroppers and tenant farmers supported the new laws over the maintenance of cooperatives (Almeida 2016). Many cooperatives were disbanded over the next decade and their collective landholdings distributed to private, individual farmers. Portions of the cooperatives in numerous cases were "reserved" for return to former landowners according to an elaborate points system based on land use, land quality, location, and taxes. This earned the particular ire of die-hard cooperative supporters in the south, particularly those affiliated with the Communists, who tarred Barreto's initiatives as counter-revolutionary. But the trend marched on. The number of employees working collectively held land dropped from 59,000 in 1977 to 26,000 in 1979, and by 1984 the number of collective farms had dropped to 330 (Raven 1988, 42).

External Pressure and the Final Push for Extending Property Rights
The popular demands for more complete and secure rights by some rural groups was not the only driving factor behind Portugal's extension of property rights to land reform beneficiaries. There was also external pressure at work. Portugal applied to join the European Economic Community (EEC) in 1977. Its economy at the time was faltering and the country entered into a loan agreement with the IMF. In seeking to draw Portugal closer to convergence with other Western European economies, the IMF pushed it to diminish government spending and the role of the state in the economy. This was one important factor that encouraged the government to withdraw generous financial support from cooperatives, especially the "emergency credits" that covered gaps between salary payouts and harvest profits (Almeida 2016, 193).

Portugal's final integration into the European Economic Community in 1986 and a drought during the summer of 1987 pressured the Social Democratic–run government into passing a further set of laws harmonizing their agricultural policies with that of fellow EEC members. The government passed a multifaceted law in 1988 "to correct the excesses of the revolutionary period; . . . to create a climate of social stability and peace; to provide for the survival of the private sector; to reconsider the Agrarian Reform in order to

accord with the principles of the European Economic Community..."
(Almeida 2016, 195). This dovetailed with a ten-year effort by the EEC to
invest in Portuguese agriculture and bring it in line with that of other EEC
members in terms of production, infrastructure, and marketing. These
initiatives together with the late 1970s laws effectively buried what little
remained of cooperative farms.

China: Causes and Consequences of the World's Largest Property Rights Gap

China's route to a property rights gap unsurprisingly differs in the particulars
from Portugal's path, though the background conditions and the brute force
nature of reform share numerous affinities. These cases diverge wildly, however,
in their consequences. This is largely due to the differences in the nature and
duration of the property rights gaps in the two countries.

China's vast expanse and topographical diversity generated geographic
variation in landholding concentration and land tenure relations across the
country by the early twentieth century despite the fact that private ownership
predominated. Although land concentration and tenancy were common
throughout China, they were more prevalent in the south than in the north (Sun
1936; Tang 1924, 241). Tenancy overall in China was approximately 20 percent in
1937 (National Land Commission 1937, 34). Meanwhile, the largest 3–4 percent
of landowners in northern China possessed 20–30 percent of the total arable land
while a similar group of landowners in the south owned 30–50 percent of the land
(Sun 1936). These figures indicate that China's rural sector was comparatively less
unequal than that of nearby Taiwan and South Korea at the time. Taiwan's pre–
land reform tenancy rate was 43 percent (Galor et al. 2009, 164). Landlords in
South Korea in the 1930s formed 2.7 percent of farm households yet owned
64 percent of the arable land (Cho 1964, 21).

Tawney (1932, 37) hypothesizes that the difference in tenancy rates between
northern and southern China was mainly driven by differences in soil
productivity. Relatively lower soil yields in the north made tenancy less
profitable and land a less attractive investment. The more fertile land in
southern China made investments in land more profitable by comparison.
This encouraged higher rates of land concentration and tenancy in the south
of the country. These patterns also dovetailed with the broad difference between
rice production in the south and wheat production in the north.

Land reform at the national level was not on the agenda in the early twentieth
century in China despite the fact that landholding inequality and peasant
poverty stirred resentment in the countryside. The ruling KMT allied itself
with landlords and business leaders where possible. It sought to centralize its
power starting in the 1920s by crushing a communist insurgency in the north,
fighting off Japanese incursions in coastal areas, and resisting regional power-
grabs.

Land Reform: From a Trickle to a Torrent
The KMT never successfully imposed ordered throughout the country.
Communist rebels formed a politically autonomous military in the north that
fought the KMT tooth and nail from the time Chiang Kai-shek rose to lead the
KMT in 1927. The rebel forces viewed large landowners as their enemies and
did not draw from them for social and economic support. To the contrary, the
rebels experimented with land reform in their bases in north and northeast
China in order to eliminate landowners and cultivate direct peasant support (see
Wong 1973, Ch. 1–2). The nascent CCP proposed land reform laws as early as
1928. But land reforms prior to 1942 were often short-lived and their effects
hobbled by party infighting (Wong 1973, 12).

Large-scale civil war then broke out in the aftermath of WWII as the Japanese
were forced out of China and Taiwan. The Chinese Nationalists under the KMT
sought to stamp out the Communist insurgency in mainland China. But
infighting between the KMT party organization and the bureaucracy,
military, and Youth Corps weakened the Nationalists. The Nationalists'
inability to control their local branches and party members compounded this
problem (Myers 2009, 189).

The Communists' efforts at land reform ramped up as they gained strength.
They proposed their first broad attempt at land redistribution in the 1946
"May 4th Directive." The 1947 Outline Land Law later formalized this
proposal. Land belonging to the Japanese, collaborators, and local landlords
was to be confiscated or donated and redistributed among peasants.[7] The CCP
carried out this land reform from 1946–1948 in north and northeast China (the
"Old Liberated Areas").[8]

Withering Communist attacks on the mainland forced the KMT to retreat to
Taiwan by 1949. The CCP seized the state and conducted a frontal assault on
landed interests. It vigorously conducted land reform from the time it legislated
the Agrarian Reform Law on June 30, 1950 to the spring of 1953.[9] This land
reform law mainly affected the "New Liberated Areas" that the KMT
previously controlled and that therefore did not experience land redistribution
during the Civil War (Zhang and Zhao 1985, 315).[10] Figure 8.2 is a map
showing the timing of land reform throughout different parts of the country.

The 1950 law did not legislate a landholding ceiling. It instead stipulated,
"the land, draft animals, farm implements, and surplus grain of the landlords

---

[7] As Johnson (1962, 19) notes, however, the CCP abandoned its most radical ideas for land reform
during the war itself.

[8] A famous novel about land reform in this period was written by Ding Ling, who herself took part
in land reform in a village in Chahar in 1947: *Taiyang zhao zai Sanganhe shang* (The Sun Shines
on the Sangan River).

[9] Translation of the 1950 Agrarian Reform Law can be found in Selden (1979).

[10] The 1950–1953 land reform also excluded areas occupied by minorities, which held significant
territory in the provinces of Xinjiang, Tibet, Qinghai, Guizhou, Gansu, Yunan, Guangxi,
Guangdong (Zhang and Zhao 1985, 314; Barnette 1953, 188).

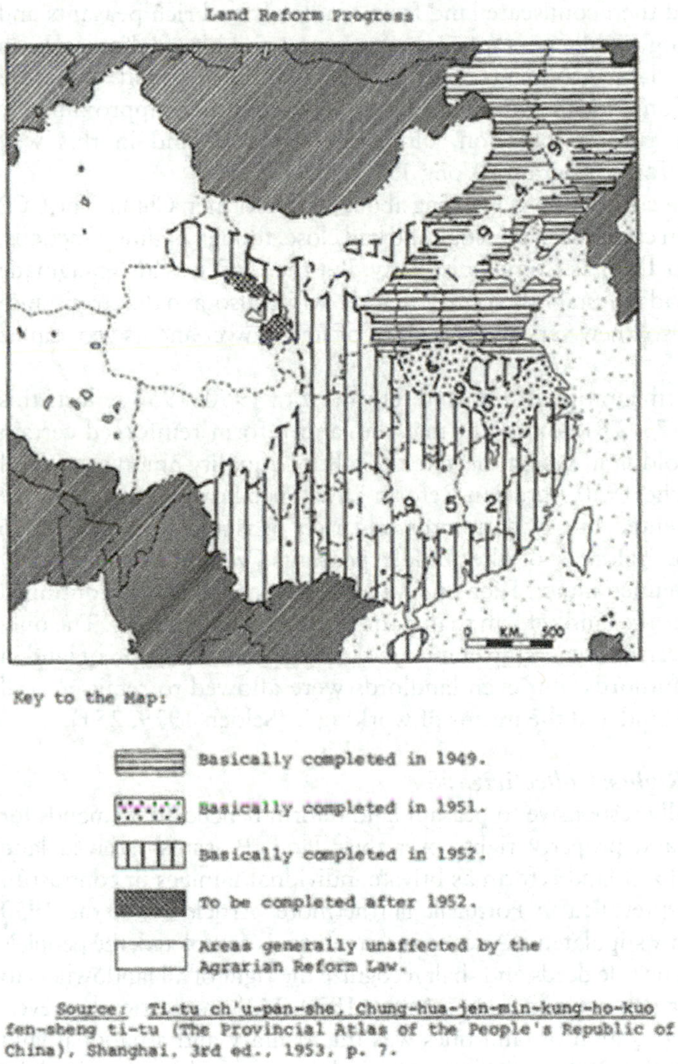

Land Reform Progress

Key to the Map:

▤	Basically completed in 1949.
⬚	Basically completed in 1951.
⬚	Basically completed in 1952.
▨	To be completed after 1952.
☐	Areas generally unaffected by the Agrarian Reform Law.

Source: Ti-tu ch'u-pan-she, Chung-hua-jen-min-kung-ho-kuo fen-sheng ti-tu (The Provincial Atlas of the People's Republic of China), Shanghai, 3rd ed., 1953, p. 7.

FIGURE 8.2 Areas affected by China's 1950 land reform by year
Source: Wong (1973, 130).

shall be confiscated, but their other properties shall not be confiscated." The central government passed down land reform implementation to regional governments and in turn to the *xian* (county) level. The government set up Land Reform Committees that CCP party members headed in order to lead and direct land reform while Peasants' Associations at the village level were responsible for the actual confiscation and redistribution of land. Party cadres mobilized peasants and set the land reform in motion. Local Peasants'

Associations would then confiscate land from landlords and rich peasants and redistribute it among middle peasants, poor peasants, and hired laborers. Each of these formal class groupings had official definitions and therefore consequences.[11] Some 430 million peasants, constituting approximately 88 percent of the rural population, ultimately received land in this way through the land reform program (Wong 1973, 129–130).

Ideology played a critical role in bringing about land reform in China. The CCP trained its activists in communist ideology and had close, though at times fractious, links with the Soviet Union's Communist Party. But the CCP was also pragmatic and knew that it had to establish control quickly while also avoiding resistance where possible. It also knew very well the limits of state power and its geographic unevenness.

The actual implementation of the land reform from 1950–1953 reflects this tension. Wong (1973, 78) points out that the land reform reinforced certain inequalities in the old land system despite the talk of equality among the rural proletariat and in the 1950 Agrarian Reform Law. Specifically, only excessive portions of land rented out by landlords and rich peasants were subject to redistribution. The holdings of the middle peasants, which were generally above average, remained intact. Rich and middle peasants therefore continued to be better off after the land reform than poor peasants and laborers. The only part of the old pattern of ownership eliminated was the concentration of land in the hands of the landlords. But even landlords were allowed to retain a local average holding of land and the means of working it (Selden 1979, 251).

Property without Rights: Collectivization

The CCP was initially responsive to peasant land reform beneficiary demands for direct land access and property rights over their land. Peasants received land through the 1950–1953 land reform as private individual families in contrast to the collectives that prevailed in Portugal. Furthermore, Article 30 of the 1950 Agrarian Reform Law stipulated, "After agrarian reform is completed, the people's government shall issue title deeds and shall recognize the right of all landowners to manage, buy, sell, or rent out land freely" (Selden 1979, 243). In practice, however, the issuance and registration of land titles was fragmentary and a national land cadaster nonexistent (Ho 2005, 60). This state weakness seriously undermined the defensibility of new peasant landholdings – a point that the CCP would seize on just a few years later as it sought to collectivize land.

Private landholding in China did not last long. There was a turn to collectivization by the mid-1950s. Wu Chueh-nung, China's Vice Minister of

---

[11] Local activists, together with party cadres, conducted a peasants' conference with local villagers to determine everyone's formal class status prior to redistributing land. The classification of rural class status among landlords, rich peasants, middle peasants, and poor peasants can be found in Selden (1979, 218–225). For a broader discussion of the origins and assignment of these class labels, see Kraus (1981) and Waldner and Hu (2009).

Agriculture, characterized collectivization in two steps: (i) the reorganization of agricultural production through mutual-aid teams and agricultural producers' cooperatives; and (ii) the collectivization of agriculture nationwide on the pattern of collective farming in the Soviet Union (Barnette 1953, 190).

Experiments with various forms of cooperatives began even before the completion of the 1950–1953 land reform. The CCP carried out two campaigns prior to the completion of land reform. The first set up "mutual-aid teams," in which four or five households pooled their labor, farm tools, and draft animals for harvest seasons. The second set up "elementary cooperatives," in which 20–30 households combined their labor and farm implements in a unified scheme but individuals retained ownership of the land and implements (Lin 1990, 1231). These efforts went farthest in northeast China in the early 1950s (Barnette 1953, 199).[12] Similar to the 1950–1953 reform, party cadres and village political workers set out to mobilize local peasant activists and set up model cooperatives in order to start a snowball effect of converting the countryside to cooperatives (Barnette 1953, 194). Although membership in the mutual-aid teams and cooperatives was technically voluntary, resistant peasants were summoned to meetings and made to stay there for days or even weeks if necessary until they "voluntarily" agreed to join (Becker 1998, 51).

Some influential CCP figures simultaneously began pushing for the formation of "advanced cooperatives" in which all means of production – including land – would be collectivized. The example of the Soviet Union collectivizing agriculture, investing in development, and propelling itself to superpower status within a generation was a powerful motivating factor (Pryor 1992, 52). Mao Zedong was one of collectivization's most important advocates. Liu Shaoqi was one of the prominent leaders who instead advocated proceeding slowly on collectivization (Unger 1985, 590). Mao argued that collectivization would generate group enthusiasm and therefore greater productivity than the sum of individuals composing it, that it would raise socialist consciousness, and that it would fundamentally improve the living standards of the peasantry. He also made the case that collectivization would tightly adhere peasants to the Communist Party (Pryor 1992, 52–55). These logics took pride of place over economies of scale in agriculture or propitious social conditions that made China ripe for collectivization.

Collectivization also won adherents among officials who had a hard time reckoning how individual peasant landholders could flourish where land registration was spotty and the state weak. This could set the stage for atomization and independence from the national socialist project. It could

---

[12] More generally, Yang (1996) argues that because wet-rice cultivation was not subject to economies of scale, collective agriculture was more suited to provinces in northern China dominated by the cultivation of wheat. Rice cultivation was later associated with greater economic reform propensity.

also render peasants subject to influence, abuse, and even dispossession by middle or rich peasants.

Proponents of collectivization within the CCP won the debate in the summer of 1955. The government ordered peasants into collectives in groups of 100–300 households (Lin 1990, 1231).[13] In practice, this often occurred by converting cooperatives into collectives and grouping them together.

Peasants lost their individual land claims in the collectivization process. Remuneration in a collective was based solely on labor contribution and took the form of work points. The income of a household depended on the number of work points earned by the family members and on the average value of a work point (Lin 1990, 1231).

A new policy issued by the CCP in 1958 amalgamated all collectives into even larger communes. The average commune was composed of some 5,000 households, 10,000 workers, and 10,000 acres (Lin 1990, 1234). The government carried out the collectivization effort on a national scale that targeted the entire rural population (Selden 1979, 342). While only 500 collective farms were organized at the end of 1955, a total of 753,000 collective farms had been established by the end of 1957 (Lin 1990, 1232). More than 99 percent of the rural households in China were organized in collectives by the end of 1958. Remuneration in communes was mainly based on subsistence needs and only partly on labor contribution (Lin 1990, 1234).

Land ownership over the communes themselves was initially somewhat ambiguous. The CCP wavered from 1959–1962 between whether production brigades or production teams would be the owners of land (Ho 2001, 405). The Eighth National Party Congress ultimately decided that production team would be the primary accounting unit and would own the land.

Economic and Social Consequences of China's Property Rights Gap

China had created the largest property rights gap in modern human history by the mid-late 1950s. This property rights gap remained frozen in place for a full two decades without significant changes. In this respect it differed substantially from Portugal's property rights gap of the mid-1970s, which was quickly snuffed out after Portugal's rapid transition to democracy. As anticipated by this book's theory and the empirical results in Chapter 5, China's property rights gap would come to define economic and social life in China in many ways. Some aspects of it generated devastating human impacts.

The first major consequence of China's property rights gap was its impact on agricultural production and ultimately the Great Famine. Agricultural production in China initially grew in the wake of land reform. Official statistics indicate a 58 percent increase in gross output value of agriculture from 1949–1954 (Wong 1973, 245), though this also coincided with a period

---

[13] Documents pertaining to the CCP's directives on the collectivization movement can be found in Selden (1979, 331–350).

of high population growth. Collectivization similarly started off with impressive success: agricultural output increased continuously from 1952 to 1958. But early economic growth was quickly replaced by drastic economic failure. Grain output dropped 15 percent in 1959 and reached only about 70 percent of the 1958 level in 1960 and 1961.

The result was the Great Famine: a disastrous three-year period that resulted in an estimated 30 million excess deaths and 33 million lost or postponed births in 1958–1961 (Ashton et al. 1984). Lin (1990, 1229) summarizes previous explanations for collectivization's economic failure: (i) three successive years of bad weather; (ii) bad policies and mismanagement in the collectives and at the national level during the Great Leap Forward campaign (which introduced misguided policies such as the Great Sparrow Campaign, which sought to eradicate sparrows that ate crop seeds but backfired in an explosion of crop-eating insects that lost their natural predators and devastated crops); and (iii) incentive problems due to the unwieldy size of collectives. Lin (1990) hypothesizes a fourth cause of the Great Famine that effectively invokes the property rights gap: the CCP's policy to deprive rural households of the right to withdraw from collectives, which eroded work incentives and contributed to free-riding problems. Walker (1966, 427) further hypothesizes that collectivization generated stagnation in agriculture by severely curtailing private investment.

Recent literature similarly attributes the economic failure of collectivization to problems tied to the withholding of property rights. Collectivization undermined peasant incentives to work due to the deprivation of private property rights and restrictions on labor mobility (Sun et al. 2017). Difficulties in labor supervision and egalitarianism in labor remuneration also eroded work incentive (Li 2018). Failures in central planning aggravated agricultural production problems still further by diverting agricultural resources to industry and contributing to malnutrition among peasants, which lowered productivity (Yang 2008).

To be sure, the property rights gap was not the only cause of the Great Famine. Career incentives and the political radicalism of officials pursuing political advancement – who at times were misreporting agricultural production – also drove decision-making patterns that exacerbated problems with economic output and amplified human suffering and death (Kung and Chen 2011). But the panoply of problems unleashed by the lack of property rights undoubtedly helped to set the stage for major malfunctions in agriculture.

A second outcome of China's property rights gap was stagnation in education. The devastating economic results of the collectivization movement put a strain on government budgets and significantly limited the scope and amount of public investment in education. Public expenditure on education declined from 12 *yuan* per student in 1952–1955 to 8 *yuan* in 1956 and the share of education in the public budget similarly declined in the late 1950s (Perkins and Yusuf 1984, 174). Collectivization enabled the Chinese government to address this financial pressure by transferring the responsibility of rural education directly to communes. It took this step in 1958. Lu Dingyi, the Head of the Central Propaganda Department in 1960, actually sought to limit secondary school education, arguing that if it were made universal it would draw too much manpower away from production (quoted in Price 1975, 35).[14]

A third consequence of China's property rights gap was the rise of an enormous disparity in living standards between cities and the countryside. The collectivization of rural resources enabled the CCP to divert some of these resources to kick-starting industrialization (Yang 2008). The government relocated some 16.4 million peasants to cities in 1958 to support the expansion of industry and construction (Li and Yang 2005, 845). This was roughly twice the size of the existing industrial labor force. It simultaneously mobilized investment funds to plough into industrialization. Capital investment was concentrated in heavy industries.[15] In addition, the CCP created an "iron rice bowl" of lifetime employment, housing, and a host of social services for urban workers that rural dwellers did not have access to (Wallace 2014, 72).

A fourth result of the property rights gap in China was exceptionally slow rural–urban transformation. Only 18 percent of China's population lived in urban areas in 1978. This figure was the same 15 years prior. The country has rapidly urbanized since then, but even so, it only became majority urban in 2011. China today is one of the most rural countries on earth for its level of per capita income. This is in part due to the property rights gap in China during collectivization along with associated national policies restricting internal migration. Collectivization meant that individuals could not alienate land and therefore would have to start over if they moved to urban areas. There was also strict state control over internal rural–urban migration through the *hukou* system of household registration in order to stabilize collective membership and food production and ensure that cities would not be overwhelmed by migrants that might pose a threat to stability (Wallace 2014, 72). Labor registration tied most rural dwellers to the farm (Powelson and Stock 1990, 372).

This long contributed to surplus labor and lower living standards in the countryside. It also fueled illegal out-migration. Some rural dwellers decided to try to illegally immigrate to cities or abroad rather than fester in rural areas where land pressure was growing. Those that ended up in cities in China have

---

[14] Basic education was later prioritized starting in the late 1960s during the Cultural Revolution and primary education became a single-track five-year system across rural and urban areas (Fu 2005, 3). Although rural–urban inequality in education later reemerged, China made important strides in improving literacy (for more discussion see Rozman and Bernstein 1981 and Peterson 1997).

[15] Most urban residents worked in state-owned enterprises. Work incentives in these enterprises were similarly distorted as in rural collectives, though not in the same ways given differences in enterprise structures and state control (Walder 1986).

helped to fuel an informal urban sector that is deprived of state services and access to social programs. While Deng Xiaoping relaxed some policies surrounding rural–urban migration in the late 1970s, setting the stage for greater rural out-migration, internal migration remains a source of tension and inequality within the country. Rural migrants to urban areas have long been treated like second-class citizens and face systematic labor discrimination (Wallace 2014, 73). Moreover, many return periodically to rural areas to protect their land access (Zhao 1999).

Rural and Urban Property Rights Reforms Catalyze an Economic Miracle

China's agricultural sector continued to stagnate in the decade prior to Mao Zedong's death. But China's new leadership sought to revitalize the sector after Mao died in the late 1970s and some of his closest supporters were arrested. As at the outset of collectivization, a debate arose within the party over diagnosing the failure in agriculture, but there was broad agreement that changes had to be made to breathe new life into the countryside (Unger 1985, 590). In a first tepid step, part of the leadership encouraged agricultural production teams to decentralize production among smaller labor groupings to generate a tighter coupling between individual work contribution, collective output, and payment from harvests. The results were mixed. Those politically affiliated with Deng Xiaoping believed that the lingering problems reflected a deeper malaise: that too radical a form of socialism had been imposed on a backward countryside in the 1950s (Unger 1985, 590).

The next reform move was much bolder and entailed dismantling the communes and decollectivizing agricultural production. Several reformist party secretaries, Wan Li and Zhao Ziyang of Anhui and Sichuan provinces, with the support of Deng Xiaoping began experimenting with giving individual families the responsibility for cultivating particular plots of land. Family cultivation occurred in some cases under the supervision of its local team (*bao chan dao hu*). In other cases, families faced the simple stipulation that they help meet the team's crop-quota deliveries to the state (*da bao gan*).

Deng's opponents in the party viewed his reform proposals as "ideologically retrograde," which Deng's faction rebutted with a call to abandon dogmas and "seek truth from facts" (Unger 1985, 591). Deng's star rose as his experiments began to bear fruit. Wan Li and Zhao Ziyang were promoted. Provincial and county officials took note and began prodding villages into breaking up collective farms in favor of peasant smallholding. The government then broadly introduced the contract system known as the Household Responsibility System in 1979 through which farmers obtained land use rights and profit rights within collectives and were allowed to keep what they produced beyond government quotas.

The government honed an institutional arrangement that separated land use rights from land ownership rights in rural collectively owned lands in the decades that followed. Rural land remained collectively owned but was contracted to individual rural households on progressively extended terms. The government gave farmers the rights to use, profit from, and transfer their contracted land during the contract period. It set land contracts at 15 years in 1984 in order to stabilize expectations over future land use and encourage investment and production. The government then extended land contract terms to 30 years in 1994. By 2008, it announced that land contract terms would remain the same indefinitely (Shouying 2019). The 2003 Rural Land Contract Law further protected land rights for farmers and was reaffirmed in the 2007 Property Law.

Important rural property rights restrictions remain despite these reforms. Land became owned by the farmers' collective of the administrative village through the 1999 Revised Land Administration Law (Ho 2001, 405–6). This meant that peasants still could not alienate their land or leverage it for loans. Rural land in China today remains owned by collectives.

Nonetheless, the practical consequence of rural reforms initiated since the late 1970s was an evolution toward greater rural property rights security. As a result, and consistent with the theory, some of the negative economic and social consequences of the property rights gap in China reversed. Agricultural production grew rapidly from 1979–1984. It outpaced other sectors of the economy and generated large surpluses. The breakneck pace continued from 1984–1994. Total agricultural output grew by 13.3 percent annually during this period and per capita output also rapidly advanced (Huang 1998, 76–78). Outsized agricultural performance in the 1980s contributed to shrinking rural–urban inequality.[16] Urbanization simultaneously increased and picked up steam in the 1990s with China's shift toward a more industrial economy.[17]

In contrast to these developments, urban/rural policy bias was more mixed. Rural areas, for instance, received increased agricultural subsidies and state-led efforts at industrialization. On the other hand, educational outcomes were more strongly determined by state policies other than property rights. Education in the late 1970s reverted from a more egalitarian (though poor-quality) system imposed during the Cultural Revolution to a two-track system in which the state funded urban education to meet the demands of industrialization while local governments often struggled to fund rural education (Fu 2005). This fueled a growing urban–rural educational divide when coupled with other policies such as the *hukou* registration system (Hao et al. 2014).

Ironically, one critical remaining feature of the property rights gap in China – the collective ownership of rural land with the state as a steward – is responsible

---

[16] This was also driven by the rise of rural township and village enterprises, which employed surplus rural labor in nonagricultural rural construction (Shouying 2019).

[17] The share of the population living in urban areas grew 7 percent in the 1980s, 9 percent in the 1990s, and 13 percent in the 2000s according to the World Development Indicators.

in part for China's massive economic boom since the 1990s. The secret: local governments seize rural lands, rezone them as urban, and make them cheaply available to investors and developers who promise to stoke economic growth and fill local coffers with tax revenue that can be used to further expand. This boom, however, has centered on urban over rural areas and furthered the central government's core political and economic goals, indicating the enduring political value of its rural property rights gap. Even so, that this dynamic has not suffocated the countryside highlights how a capable state under the right conditions can compensate for a lack of property rights that will otherwise choke off development.

To understand this dramatic and transformational shift in China's development trajectory requires unpacking a series of political reforms that began in the 1980s. President Deng Xiaoping initiated a series of decentralizing reforms in the 1980s that gave local governments more discretion over economic policy. Local revenue became more closely tied to local policy and the health of the local economy such as township and village enterprises.[18] Furthermore, and propelled by the success of separating use rights from ownership in rural land, the central government extended this reform to urban lands.

Urban land in China today remains state-owned. But urban land use could not even be transferred, leased, or mortgaged prior to the 1980s. The government held a monopoly on land use and would allocate it for free to individuals or entities for unlimited time periods. The 1987 constitution lifted many restrictions on land use and allowed local governments to sell land use rights to users for specified periods of time. Users, in turn, could profit from and transfer their use rights. Subsequent reforms allowed users to mortgage use rights. Local governments began selling state-owned land use rights through tenders, auctions, and bidding processes. This generated a flood of resources for local development. What emerged in China was therefore a dual-track property rights regime with a strict divide between rural and urban lands.

China's reforms to urban land rights fueled a boom in land markets, real estate development, and business investment as local governments transferred urban land use rights to users in exchange for fees. Land use efficiency increased and investment grew as users gained greater property rights (Rithmire 2015). However, China in the 1980s remained an overwhelmingly rural country. Local governments quickly ran up against limits to the urban land under their control just as economic growth and urban development began to take off. Cities were

---

[18] A number of authors attribute the mid-1980s economic boom in China to reforms that granted townships and villages the right to retain much of the profits from township and village enterprises locally (e.g., Oi 1999; Oi and Walder 1999). This generated incentives for local officials to set up and support the growth of these enterprises, which in turn were used to fund local officials' salaries and local public goods.

encircled by less dynamic rural lands. That set the stage for a slow motion but metastasizing land grab.[19]

The kingpin that presides over China's rural/urban divide is the state. The enduring lack of individual property ownership places the state as the ultimate arbiter of land allocation between rural and urban areas. Its chief tool is as consequential as it is seemingly mundane: zoning.

Local governments have the authority to rezone rural land and convert it to urban land. Upon doing so, they can turn around and sell land use rights for industrial, commercial, residential, infrastructural, or other purposes. Driven by increasing demographic pressure and revenue incentives, such as the 1994 fiscal and tax reforms that strengthened the fiscal capacity of the central government at the expense of local governments and the subsequent elimination of the agricultural tax in 2006, local governments since the 1990s have increasingly gobbled up rural lands and converted them to urban land. Nearly five million hectares of rural land were expropriated and converted to state land for urban use from 1996 to 2010 (Shouying 2019). The figure was 540,000 hectares in 2012 alone, an all-time record. Placing land at the center of local government finance and influencing its conversion rate has enabled the central government to use land for critical macroeconomic management, particularly stimulating growth and managing business cycles (Rithmire 2017).[20]

The one-way trend in favor of urbanization in China has meant that urban property rights over land are distinctly more secure than rural property rights over land. Local governments can quickly nullify rural land rights. This occurs not just in urban peripheries where rural lands are most at risk, but also in the middle of the countryside if a local government decides to build a new population center, new infrastructure for cities in the region, an industrial park, or some other endeavor.

Local governments often paid little to the rural agricultural collectives that formally owned rural land when the trend to convert rural land into urban land began in force.[21] After all, local governments that could acquire rural land cheaply and turn around to lease it to urban developers could pocket the difference.[22] This began to spark vigorous resistance in the countryside.

---

[19] As Rithmire (2015) demonstrates, land liberalization has also faced setbacks, as in the wake of the real estate bubble in the early 1990s. Furthermore, locales have taken differing strategies in the pursuit of economic growth and stability, which has impacted local land arrangements.

[20] Contrary to some accounts, Rithmire (2017) argues that the utility of land institutions for macroeconomic management led the CCP to intentionally reorganize local government fiscal and financial institutions around land in the mid-1990s.

[21] The Land Administration Law only required local officials to compensate farmers for the agricultural value of their land rather than the often much higher market value.

[22] A 2011 survey of almost 1,800 villages estimated that of those villagers who lost their land, they were compensated at about 2.5 percent of the value received by local governments when the latter turned around and leased the land for commercial or industrial purposes (Landesa 2012).

Estimates suggest that more than 50 million farmers in China had lost their land through expropriation by 2010 (Li 2011). Of the roughly 200,000 "mass incidents" of collective protest in this year, more than 65 percent were driven by rural farmers angry at losing their land on what they viewed as unfair terms (Landesa 2012). The result has been a spike in negotiations with rural villages and their inhabitants who lose their property to land conversions as well as an associated increase in compensation (Wang et al. 2017).

Even so, this arrangement has been immensely profitable to local governments and generated a frenzy in industrialization, real estate development, and urban population growth. This has in turn fueled local government land revenue growth, which has been used to enhance public services and infrastructure, promote still greater investment, and fund even more land conversion. Some entrepreneurial local governments have even borrowed against converted lands that act as collateral to finance large-scale developments (Shouying 2019).[23]

That remaining limitations to rural property rights in China have played a central role in its economic miracle in recent decades indicates that a property rights gap itself does not necessarily doom a country as a whole to underdevelopment. But the discussion also indicates strong rural–urban distributional implications of China's growth strategy that are consistent with the theory given the second-fiddle nature of rural land rights since the 1990s. Economic development has tilted heavily toward urban coastal areas in this period and rural–urban inequality has grown starkly. Land institutions have complemented fiscal and financial institutions in benefiting local governments, the central government, public sector firms, powerful real estate developers, and urban dwellers while imposing costs on rural actors like peasants that are forced to cede ground (Rithmire 2017).

Political Consequences of China's Property Rights Gap

China's rural property rights gap generated a host of negative economic and social outcomes, especially from the 1950s to the 1970s. But these were counterbalanced by one particularly valuable final consequence: political control. The CCP has long maintained a large and dispersed rural population with tight links to Communist Party officials and activists through land ownership, land use, and agricultural production. Party ties to and oversight over rural communities remained strong even after decollectivization and continue to the present day.

In concert with other official policies, the regime's control over rural populations through the property rights gap has facilitated the ability of the

---

[23] Despite the evident successes of this model, its risks and limitations in terms of land use, over-leveraging by local governments, and rural unrest have driven the government to examine more sustainable alternatives to rural–urban integration. Deininger et al. (2019) analyze one large government experiment in alternative property rights reforms carried out in Chengdu in 2008.

regime to implement what it views as stabilizing policies even if they are unpopular. For instance, rural control enabled the regime to impose the One Child Policy in 1980 despite the fact that it was bad for rural families who wanted more labor to aid in production (Greenhalgh 2008).

The rural property rights gap has also enabled the CCP to stem some of the most significant challenges to its rule. Perhaps most importantly, the CCP has used rural dwellers as a counterbalance against urban centers. Cities in China serve as an economic engine but are also the biggest liability for regime stability due to their heightened possibility of instability and collective action (Wallace 2014).

This is not to say that there are not also rural threats to stability. Most notably, the greater economic and social dynamism in the countryside in recent decades that followed from greater rural property rights came with an increase in rural autonomy and even protest, as anticipated by the theory. "Mass incidents" of collective unrest increased in a fairly secular and incredibly steep manner throughout the 1990s and 2000s by roughly twentyfold, driven by rural inhabitants' organization against government encroachments on rural lands and land rights (Göbel and Ong 2012).[24] By 2005, one veteran China expert wrote that, "the Beijing leadership is in danger of losing control of vast tracts of the countryside" in response to snowballing land-related protests.

This conclusion was overstated despite the continued rise in unrest. Increased rural autonomy and well-being has not translated into either complete independence from the government or a loss of government control. Rural dwellers continue to rely on the government for favorable policies and inputs because they do not own and cannot alienate their land. The government's tools of political monitoring, in turn, have become ever more sophisticated in an effort to identify, deflate, and stifle dissent in a targeted manner. Furthermore, the central government has effectively driven a wedge between itself and local governments when it comes to political trust and confidence. While individuals may lose faith in local officials, that often does not translate into grievances against the central government (Cui et al. 2015).

The result is that the enormous rural property rights gap, along with other policy tools such as the *hukou* system that moderate internal migration, has lent the CCP valuable control over population flows and collective action. The reliance of rural dwellers on the CCP for continued land access and production, as well as their lack of an exit option, encourages them to limit their claim-making to local and specific issues rather than broad systemic ones.

If the CCP were to grant peasant families complete property rights, they would risk the much more dangerous possibility of peasants alienating their land and moving to cities en masse to try to catch up with their urban

---

[24] Göbel and Ong (2012, 18) estimate the figure at 8,700 mass incidents in 1993, approximately 87,000 by 2005, and nearly 200,000 by 2010.

counterparts. This could spark one of the largest mass migrations in human history and would strain state resources and control in unpredictable and risky ways that could bring down the regime.

Zhu Rongji, China's Vice Premier, made essentially this point in 1994, several years after the Tiananmen Square protests and as debates raged over selling urban residency rights through revisions to the *hukou* system: "[P]easants will all wish to go to the big cities and make lots of money. How can this be tolerated? ... Today, we still need to...make peasants stay in the rural areas" (quoted in Wallace 2014, 101).

8.4 CONCLUSION

This chapter provides an overview of all major cases in which governments could have generated a property rights gap through redistributive land reform around the world since 1900. It codes the main features of property rights over redistributed land in each of these cases. And it examines, through the framework of the book's theory, the conditions under which governments formed and subsequently closed these property rights gaps.

The principal finding that emerges is that the determinants of opening and closing property rights gaps in countries around the globe largely mirror those found to be decisive in the context of Latin America. The authoritarian governments that typically redistribute land, motivated by coalitional splits with landed elites, almost always press their advantage over society by withholding property rights from land reform beneficiaries. Closing the property rights gap tends to occur under democracy, especially if peasants are integrated into the ruling coalition and large landowners are not strong enough, interested enough, or institutionally positioned to block it. Property rights gaps also close under both democracy and dictatorship when governments that preside over a gap are forced by international lenders to undergo structural economic adjustment in exchange for a lifeline out of a major crisis.

Through case studies of Portugal and China, this chapter also demonstrates the utility of the theory in explaining the timing and features of specific property rights gaps that are often viewed through the lens of ideology or state capacity. These cases additionally illustrate ways in which the theory can work in a complementary fashion with alternative explanations and be extended in fruitful new directions.

9

Conclusion

Ownership and rights over land have shifted radically around the world over the last century. Feudalism, colonialism, land appropriation, and unfettered frontier settlement over the course of several centuries generated highly unequal land access and ownership in many countries by the 1800s. As states developed and political systems became more centralized, some governments attacked this issue head-on by splitting up large landholdings and redistributing land to individuals or communities.

Governments that embarked on major projects to reorder the countryside typically did not transfer the rights and privileges that large landowners enjoyed over their land to the new beneficiaries that received that land. Beneficiaries typically received land with highly incomplete property rights or no property rights at all. Governments replaced systems of unequal private land ownership that were dominated by a small number of large landowners with systems in which armies of rural dwellers labored on nationally owned land under usufruct, received property communally with imposed limitations on their ability to manage, gain benefits from, and transfer land, received property as individuals without receiving land titles, or received land titles that faced restrictive encumbrances or that were not respected.

In short, land beneficiaries are often forced to wander in a sort of property rights purgatory. Sometimes this lasts for generations. Property rights informality blooms under these scenarios. Today billions of people are still living with the consequences. This book systematically identifies the use of property despite lacking attendant rights over that property and seeks to explain the origins and consequences of these "property rights gaps."

Political regimes are fundamental to generating a property rights gap through the distribution of property without rights. This is in part because it is politically difficult to redistribute property to begin with. The plural nature of democratic institutions affords opponents of redistributive land reform – who are often quite powerful – a multiplicity of avenues to block major change. Authoritarian regimes do not have to abide by institutional strictures in the same way. They have the political capacity to crush rivals that oppose them and deprive opponents of recourse to a third party that has the institutional authority and resources to protect their interests.

Not all authoritarian regimes seek to crush large landowners. Some are allied to landowners or even count landowners within their inner circles. But large landowners can also be rivals to some authoritarian regimes. Their outsized economic power and dominant position in the countryside can pose a threat to incumbent leaders. Landowners can use their powers to try to oust an incumbent regime or to raise the costs of ruling. Authoritarian regimes that perceive this threat and that do not rely on the political support of landowners to rule will try to neutralize them. Land redistribution is a particularly potent tool because it strips large landowners of their single most important resource. Subsequently distributing that land to a large number of peasants for whom land access becomes foundational to their livelihood is attractive because it makes redistribution very logistically difficult to reverse.

Land redistribution can be wildly politically popular among land recipients. Granting land access to the landless or precarious tenant farmers that face abusive and arbitrary landlords can give them a quick economic bump and improve their social status. But when a government upends the property rights of large landowners and embarks on reordering the countryside, there is frequently a lag before new property rights are established. Some governments choose for ideological reasons to limit new property rights, others favor alternative priorities to reestablishing property rights, and still others struggle with the administrative burden. But it does not take long for any government to recognize the golden opportunity of ruling over a countryside whose inhabitants are largely devoid of property rights.

Rural dwellers that receive land access through the government but that lack property rights face basic obstacles to flourishing that force them to repeatedly turn to the government for help. This is the basic currency for exerting social control over the countryside through dependency and tactics of divide and conquer. Any government would salivate at the chance of having such leverage over a large portion of the population – whether this is intentional to begin with or not. Governments that preside over a property rights gap therefore typically retain or even widen it unless they are forced otherwise.

Persistent property rights gaps have a host of perverse development consequences that can drive long-run underdevelopment. They generate a reliance on agriculture over a demographic shift to cities and urban economies, stunt agricultural productivity, and inhibit broader economic growth. Property rights gaps drive a wedge between cities and the countryside. This facilitates public policymaking that systematically favors urban dwellers and that results in a yawning gap of urban–rural inequality over time. And property rights gaps often stymie individual political expression, facilitating clientelism as longstanding social hierarchies between landowners and peasants evaporate and new political actors – frequently those tied to the incumbent government – seek to quickly fill that gap. For the typical government that presides over a property rights gap, the political advantages of a property rights gap are more than sufficient recompense for its economic and social costs.

Not all property rights gaps last forever. While some persist to the present day, many longstanding property rights gaps in the countryside have closed fully or in part as former land reform beneficiaries are extended more secure property rights.

Property rights gaps are most likely to close under democracy. Democracies are often hamstrung when it comes to the large-scale redistribution of assets within society. But they can more effectively translate popular demands into policy when the nature of these demands does not transgress the interests of powerful minorities. Democracies are more likely to grant property rights than redistribute property, whereas dictatorships are more likely to redistribute property than grant property rights.

Democracies are especially likely to close a property rights gap when peasants are incorporated into the ruling coalition and are therefore in a position to directly push for greater property rights protection. But this does not itself guarantee success. If the remnants of landed elites are threatened by rights extension and can organize through democratic institutions to block stronger property rights, as has occurred historically through legislatures, then a property rights gap can persist.

Democracies that face popular pressure to close a property rights gap are not the only ones that close these gaps. There is an alternative route to closing a property rights gap that does not rely directly on political regime type: foreign pressure. All countries at times face the slings and arrows of financial panics, currency imbalances, debt servicing, or major economic recessions. Sufficiently severe crises of this sort can force a country to seek help from international financial institutions. Since WWII, these international institutions have typically demanded economic and political reforms as a condition for receiving lending support. Privatization and greater property rights security can be part of these reforms, thereby closing a rural property rights gap.

This book provides systematic and wide-ranging evidence in favor of these claims. I first draw from key insights in the property rights literature to create a set of measures of property rights over property. I then gathered data through fieldwork and archival work across Latin America on the scope of land redistribution and on the nature of property rights over that land in order to build a common dataset on the generation, maintenance, and closing – or the absence – of property rights gaps. This dataset spans every country in the region from 1920–2010. It represents the most comprehensive dataset ever gathered on rural property rights, and, critically, it enables comparisons across countries over time. This has never been done before. From this dataset emerges the first complete picture of property rights gaps in Latin America – or in any other region.

I use these data to develop a typology of three main property rights gap trajectories. Countries may never generate a property rights gap, may generate a gap and then close it, or may generate a gap and never close it. I then demonstrate using a wide set of empirical tools that this book's theory helps to explain which of these trajectories any given country may follow. I garner evidence from large-scale statistical analyses of Latin American countries over time, case studies, regression discontinuity analyses using subnational data from Peru, and broad cross-country comparisons. That all of this wide-ranging evidence supports the theory is a powerful testament to its explanatory power.

9.1 REINTERPRETING LONG-TERM POLITICAL AND ECONOMIC DEVELOPMENT IN LATIN AMERICA

This book's theory on the origins and closing of property rights gaps speaks in novel ways to the influential debate regarding long-term trajectories of economic and political development in Latin America. Engerman and Sokoloff (2002), for instance, prominently argue that initial geographic conditions in the New World colonies led to different labor and land tenure relations that influenced the long-term structure of institutions as well as inequality. These authors highlight three distinct types of New World colonies. The first encompasses those colonies with climates and soils that were well suited for the production of sugar and other highly valued crops characterized by extensive scale economies associated with the use of slaves (such as Brazil and Cuba). This created a large, poor, disenfranchised segment of population. The second category includes colonies with a substantial native population that survived European contact and in which land and native labor was possessed by a few colonizers, leading to large-scale estates and mining characterized by tribute (such as Mexico and Peru). The third category spans colonies with populations of European descent that had similar levels of human capital where land was abundant and capital requirements were low. Native populations in this third group were comparatively small and climates and soils were suited to wheat and other grains amenable to small-scale farming rather than slave labor (such as Argentina and Uruguay).

In contrast to this third category, colonies based on large-scale extraction became characterized soon after initial settlement by extreme inequality in wealth, human capital, and political influence. These colonies tended to adopt institutions that were significantly less progressive and more extractive and were less likely to fund local public investments and services. These patterns became self-reinforcing, persisting well into the twentieth century and even up to the present day (Engerman and Sokoloff 2002, 84).

Acemoglu, Johnson, and Robinson (2002) concur with Engerman and Sokoloff about a "reversal of fortune" in economic conditions whereby formerly wealthy regions at the time of colonization later became relatively poor and poorer regions became wealthy. However, they point to patterns of European settlement as the root of this reversal. Where Europeans settled due to a lower disease burden and sparser native populations (such as Argentina and Uruguay), they set up good institutions for themselves that then persisted. By contrast, colonizers set up extractive institutions in initially wealthier, more populated areas such as Peru and Mexico. Institutional persistence, under their account, is driven by political inequality rather than economic inequality as Engerman and Sokoloff suggest.

This book offers two important correctives to these influential accounts. First, these authors overlook the fact that in many Latin American countries in the post-colonial era, exclusive, authoritarian political institutions and ossified economic structures carried the seeds of their own demise. Rulers that rose to power from former out-groups either via social revolutions or via military coups faced few checks on their rule and conducted broad, effective attacks directly on long-entrenched landed elites. This paved the way for wide variation in both land redistribution and in property rights reforms beginning in the twentieth century. This variation existed even among countries with similar factor endowments and initial disease burdens.

Second, large-scale land redistribution did in fact substantially reduce landholding inequality in the countryside. It also severed longstanding patron–client relations. This ended persistence in economic institutions. However, these reforms did not significantly reduce income inequality since land reform beneficiaries were not given the property rights protections they needed to thrive. To the contrary, regimes deliberately withheld property rights and instead enmeshed beneficiaries in relations of dependence on the state.

But when democracy arrived – as it did throughout nearly the entire region – popular demands for property rights spurred policy reforms and many countries closed the property rights gap. This set the stage for more productive agricultural sectors and egalitarian rural social relations. Economic growth consequently accelerated. But some countries never reaped these gains. This was particularly the case in countries where the property rights gap endured for a long period and economic crises and a retreat by the state from the countryside enabled land reconcentration to proceed prior to solidifying property rights.

9.2   LIMITATIONS TO THE PROPERTY RIGHTS PARADIGM AND A NEW RIGHTS AGENDA IN LAND

This book demonstrates that opening a property rights gap in the countryside has detrimental effects on long-term development. But property rights are not necessarily a silver bullet for development in and of themselves. This is true both for the land reform sector and for rural land more generally.

Rural areas can be productive for years or, in exceptional cases, even several decades without entirely secure or well-defined property rights. China since the 1980s and Mexico in the 1930s–1940s are two prominent examples. Rural development advances in some cases because government support in rural areas compensates for a lack of property rights. In other cases, it advances due in part to a progressive strengthening of property rights despite residual incompleteness. These policy countercurrents can, however, stall or run their course, placing a ceiling on rural development. Separately, in certain contexts – especially settings where customary land tenure prevails – formal property rights have little discernible impact on rural investment, land markets, and productivity (Brasselle, Gaspart, and Platteau 2002; Deininger and Feder 2009; Sikor 2006).[1]

At the same time, naively applying a one-size-fits-all model of property rights, as exemplified by international advocacy of individual neoliberal-style property rights from the 1980s–2000s, can actually backfire and generate obstacles to development. Adopting this stripe of property rights without the proper safeguards and sensitivity to context can lead to the dispossession and displacement of relatively poor rural dwellers by more powerful actors, especially when there are lucrative investment opportunities through rural land acquisition or during times of economic crisis. This can end up flooding cities with rural migrants. It can drive huge informal settlements in urban peripheries and attendant problems with service provision and urban poverty. And it can generate conflict.

Resisting property rights reforms or initiatives to strengthen property rights is not the answer. This book and a wealth of other research show that insecure property rights have consequential negative effects in most contexts. Furthermore, land titling programs and investment in rural land are proceeding apace around the world. Governments that ignore this reality risk disadvantaging their rural inhabitants that lack property rights.

A more productive path forward is to provide more nuanced and context-specific property rights rather than one-size-fits-all rights to those that lack them. Depending on the place, this might entail securing communal property rights, layering multidimensional rights, or providing individual or family-based rights that take into consideration gender inequities in landholding.

How can this be done in practice? The new Voluntary Guidelines on the Responsible Governance of Tenure of Land, Fisheries, and Forests, produced by the Food and Agriculture Organization of the United Nations and supported by other international lenders such as the World Bank, is a good start. The guidelines urge governments, agencies, and advocates to respect, record, and strengthen "legitimate" land tenure rights in the pursuit of strengthening food

---

[1] See Chapters 2 and 3 for further discussion.

security, protecting the environment, and reducing poverty and hunger. Where these rights are not formally recorded, this will require convoking meetings, consulting property registries and other state records, and visiting rural areas directly to see where claims are uncontested and to provide low-cost ways to safeguard and strengthen the practiced rights that exist. And it will require a dispute resolution mechanism where claims are contested. These guidelines represent the first international document on agreed principles for land tenure governance. The Group of 20 nations, the UN General Assembly, and many other groups have endorsed them.[2]

However, the theory that this book advances suggests that encouraging governments to strengthen property rights themselves will yield quite uneven uptake. Dictatorships left to their own devices rarely have strong incentives to secure the property rights of rural dwellers that lack them. And large landowners may be able to block reforms that strengthen property rights across the board in some democracies as well.

This leaves a role for the international community. International institutions such as the World Bank have promoted a very specific property rights paradigm in recent decades rooted in neoliberal economic thought. Their most determined pressure and greatest success has come during times of vulnerability for countries in the throes of economic crisis. To the extent that some governments or powerful landowners oppose strengthening rural property rights in order to maintain rural social control, it would be foolhardy for international institutions to forego their ability to take advantage of crises to pressure for reform. But they should not privilege expedience in reform over the now-standard guidance that communities and individuals affected by reforms to their tenure rights should have a hand in shaping how property rights are identified, recorded, and strengthened from the start. Furthermore, international lenders and other international agencies should expand and make more attractive – perhaps through heavy subsidies – the large series of parallel programs used to assist countries that voluntarily want to reform their systems of property rights, typically through land formalization programs.

One vital consideration moving forward should be to ensure that strengthening property rights over rural land actually generates beneficial effects for rights holders. Being sensitive to securing complex or overlapping rights as they are currently practiced is fundamental for respecting the demands and integrity of communities. However, where land rights are highly variable or intricately overlapping, creating a rainbow of rights can also yield an implicit rights hierarchy. Some rights may be easier to record, recognize, or transfer than others. Investors, buyers, and business counterparts may consider this in their decision-making, in turn affecting the opportunities that communities have for

---

[2] The Guidelines have also helped to encourage international support of the United Nations and World Bank's Principles for Responsible Agricultural Investment, which calls on investors in agriculture and food systems to respect land tenure rights.

development. Navigating these tensions and rationalizing more complex property rights systems is going to be one of the biggest challenges for governments, international actors, communities, and individuals in the coming decades.

9.3 PROPERTY RIGHTS AND THE RISE OF MARKETS

This book focuses mainly on rural populations and agriculture in the land reform sector. But the broadest contours of the theory are generalizable. All developing countries confront challenges and opportunities with the creation of markets and the management of property rights in those markets. The theory can help to shed light on property rights in other economic sectors aside from rural land. And its implications can extend to participants that do not first receive their endowments through state-led redistribution. The remainder of this chapter illustrates the utility of applying the theoretical framework to several of these alternative contexts.

States are often central actors in generating new markets or enabling the rise of new markets in areas far removed from rural land. States can set rules and policies that incentivize certain activities, create the infrastructure for new markets, and even intervene directly to create or support market players.

Of course, markets can also arise as the byproduct of benign neglect or structural economic change. Unregulated portions of the economy can leave actors that operate in those sectors free to develop linkages within the domestic economy or with foreign countries. And economic shifts, such as urbanization and industrialization, can create new classes of actors such as capitalists that can capture market share.

An incumbent government with sufficient capacity can choose whether to provide property rights to participants in these new markets. If an incumbent chooses not to provide secure property rights within a new market, a subsequent government may choose to extend property rights within it. Furthermore, a subsequent government can revise existing property rights in a market to strengthen them, weaken them, or to favor a new group while disfavoring another.

This generates an evolution of property rights over time that is analogous to the property rights gap over land that this book focuses on. For instance, a government that presides over the discovery of subsurface mineral or oil wealth may not create a legal regime that delineates and enforces property rights for market participants involved in natural resource extraction. A government that presides over the growth of urban squatter settlements at the peripheries of major cities may not title occupants or inscribe them in property registries or a land cadaster. A government that oversees a boom in technology may not create a patent office to verify and enforce intellectual property over technological innovations. Later governments can close these

TABLE 9.1 *The evolution of property rights in new markets*

	Government B		
	Strengthen property rights in new market	Shift who has property rights in new market	Weaken property rights in new market
Government A Provide broad property rights in new market	Updating of strong, broad property rights (Path A)	Erosion toward selective property rights (Path C)	Broad erosion to weak property rights (Path C)
Provide selective property rights in new market	Property rights in market become more even (Path B)	Rotation of winners and losers in property rights (Path C)	Former winners join losers in property rights (Path C)
Withhold property rights in new market	Evolution toward strong property rights (Path B)	Evolution toward selective property rights (Path C)	Equilibrium of poor property rights (Path C)

Note: Government A and Government B rule sequentially over a new market.

property rights gaps, open gaps that did not exist, or reconfigure winners and losers.

Table 9.1 captures these broad dynamics of property rights in new markets. Consider a sequence of two governments that rule consecutively over a new market. The first government, Government A, can broadly provide complete property rights to participants in that new market, provide selective property rights (either widely providing only partial rights among participants or providing complete rights targeted at only a specific segment of participants), or withhold property rights from market participants. The second government that takes power after Government A, Government B, can make a similar set of choices.

Distinct trajectories of property rights result when considering the sequential actions of both Government A and Government B. No property rights gap is created when both governments broadly provide and uphold property rights in the new market. This is analogous to the property rights gap Path A that this book outlines. When Government A opens up a property rights gap that Government B closes, the result is analogous to the property rights gap Path B that this book outlines. When Government A opens up a property gap that Government B upholds, the consequence is analogous to the property rights gap Path C that this book outlines. The same path is followed if Government A does not open a property gap but Government B opens one.

There are also related property rights gap paths that are linked to the selective provision of property rights. For instance, Government A may provide property rights to some participants in a new market but not others. Government B may then shift who has property rights. For instance, it may simply substitute winners for losers, granting property rights to those that lacked them and stripping property rights from those that enjoyed them. This rotation generates a Path C trajectory for former property rights winners from the first period who become losers in the second period. It simultaneously generates a Path B trajectory for former property rights losers from the first period who become winners and receive property rights in the second period.

This book's theory about the generation, maintenance, and closing of property rights gaps over rural land provides insights into how to understand the evolution of property rights within new markets as Table 9.1 displays. In particular, it points to how the nature and composition of a country's political institutions as well as coalitional dynamics and foreign pressure can shape broad trajectories in property rights gaps. Of course, these are hardly the only factors that impact property rights in new markets. They can also be shaped by exogenous factors such as transaction costs or the nature of externalities associated with extraction or by myriad other endogenous factors.

Authoritarian regimes that do not comprise the balance of actors of a particular sector of the economy have incentives to provide weak property rights in that sector to generate coercive leverage over the firms and actors that operate in it. By contrast, authoritarian regimes that incorporate the balance of a given sector have incentives to provide selective property rights only to connected elites within the sector over other unconnected participants in those markets. The regime retains coercive leverage over the weaker actors by splitting the sector in this way and can even use them to set an example for connected actors lest they run afoul of the regime. Weak actors have little recourse. The result is effectively a stripe of crony capitalism.

Now consider democratic regimes. Democracies that comprise the balance of actors in a particular market sector will act to provide property rights to that sector unless there is a strong minority interest with the incentives and capacity to oppose those property rights. Even democratic regimes that do not comprise the balance of actors in a particular sector of the economy may still be forced to provide property rights to that sector through representation and accountability mechanisms like those that Chapter 3 details. An organized sector can successfully win property rights protections even if it sits on the sidelines of government provided that a powerful minority interest is not organized against rights extension.

Selective or weak property rights may prevail, however, if a sector is neither incorporated into the ruling coalition nor organized. Actors within the sector that would prefer selective property rights can attempt to lobby or organize for such an arrangement over broad property rights since it may give them a competitive advantage. Or selected firms may simply resort to pulling personal favors from government officials. In the absence of successful efforts along these lines, the sector may face weak property rights across the board. After all, a democratic government, like an authoritarian one, may favor some sectors over others depending on the nature of political competition. For instance, if an incumbent's constituency centers on the urban poor, the government may strengthen property rights for urban squatters without strengthening rural property rights. This is particularly likely to occur if rural interests that are excluded from the winning coalition are unorganized and therefore cannot effectively force the government to heed its demands, and when they are unlikely to be electorally important for the foreseeable future.

Foreign pressure can also strengthen property rights separately from these regime and coalitional determinants of the nature of property rights.[3] Regimes and coalitions can help to steer the character of new property rights in a particular direction. But the nature and degree of outside pressure can override this when a regime is in dire need of foreign assistance or cooperation.

Table 9.2 summarizes these predictions.

This theoretical framework illuminates several broader puzzles about states and markets in new ways, such as why governments would unilaterally erode property rights in certain markets and why governments would ever extend property rights to what seem to be relatively weak social actors.

Take the first puzzle: why governments would unilaterally erode property rights. After all, eroding property rights can stymie investment, generate uncertainty, foment grievances, and risk short-circuiting economic growth. One key reason why a government would go down this road, which builds from this book's theory, is due to the quest for social and political control. Regimes can gain powerful coercive leverage over actors in important economic sectors if these actors have insecure property rights. Why is that the case? Like with incomplete property rights in land, incomplete property rights in other areas – such as intellectual property, banking, urban housing, or subsoil rights – render market participants vulnerable. These actors can be abused, stolen from, and taken advantage of, all without predictable legal recourse. This vulnerability makes these actors seek assistance in order to continue to operate as they would like. A regime can then position itself and the state apparatus as the provider of that assistance. This relationship generates a dependence on the regime for operating successfully in markets. That, in turn, gives the regime coercive leverage over market participants, lest it withdraw support and render market participants subject to the litany of obstacles to doing business.

---

[3] Although I consider here the case when foreign pressure is supportive of property rights protections, as it has been in recent decades, it is also possible for foreign pressure to support the erosion of property rights. One example is Soviet pressure for land collectivization in Eastern Europe after WWII.

TABLE 9.2 *Political regimes, coalitions, foreign pressure, and property rights*

	Sectoral balance in coalition	Sectoral balance out of coalition
Dictatorship	Selective property rights in sector to connected actors/firms ("crony capitalism")	Weak property rights across sector
Democracy	Strong property rights in sector	Sector broadly organized: strong property rights in sector
		Sector divided: selective or weak property rights in sector
Foreign pressure for stronger property rights	Strong property rights in sector	Strong property rights in sector

Next consider the second puzzle: why governments would extend property rights to relatively weak social actors that do not have substantial collective action capacity and are not well connected politically. One reason is that these social actors might be important for an incumbent party's political fortunes. This is of course more likely to be true under democracy. Imagine that an incumbent party that inherits a large property rights gap must face competitive elections in the near future and the weak social actors in question are a critical slice of the electorate that could swing either in their favor or against them. If this constituency is demanding greater property rights, then the incumbent party may be compelled to respond to these demands by granting more complete or secure property rights.

A separate reason is that an incumbent government may face a substantial economic crisis that it cannot manage on its own. The best hope to stem the crisis and survive politically may be to turn to international assistance. But the government may have to forfeit autonomy over certain policy decisions if they seek assistance. For instance, foreign actors may demand greater property rights security in a certain sector of the economy. The goal of these foreign actors could be to mitigate the likelihood of the crisis repeating itself, or it could stem from ideological or developmental motivations, or it could derive from self-interest if the demand for property rights security is twinned with a demand to open the sector to foreign participation. Regardless, weaker social actors that operate in that sector can quickly be bestowed more complete property rights.

The theoretical framework also speaks to the phenomena of crony capitalism and developmentalism. Crony capitalism is a system in which individuals who have close ties to political incumbents that are charged with designing and enforcing policies receive selective favors of substantial economic value (Haber 2002). Table 9.2 identifies the political conditions that are most propitious for crony capitalism to develop and the macro factors that impact when this equilibrium is likely to change – in particular, a transition to more broad-based and accountable democratic governance or through foreign pressure.

The framework outlined here is also consistent to an extent with authors who argue that democracy is not necessary for development (for example, Haggard 1990; Kohli 2004). Provided there is a tight coalitional alliance between ruling political elite under authoritarianism and a dynamic group of economic actors, those economic actors can potentially flourish. The argument does suggest, however, that economic development will be patterned. Authoritarian regimes tend to selectively extend property rights – if they extend them at all – only to politically connected actors or firms in a sector. Other actors will struggle and likely fail. Entire economic sectors or groups that are not politically connected will get the short end of the stick. If the government selectively favors a tranche of capitalists, for instance, their workers are more likely to be repressed and delivered unfavorable public policies. Nonetheless, this can set the stage for focused, deliberate, and sometimes highly effective economic development. Chapter 8 discusses several canonical cases such as South Korea and Taiwan.

Illustrative Examples of Shifting Property Rights

This section provides a brief but illustrative overview of how property rights have arisen and in some cases shifted in a diverse set of markets in a way that is consistent with the theoretical framework that is summarized in Figure 9.2. In doing so, it demonstrates how the theory can aid in understanding broad trends in the evolution of property rights. I focus on three cases: subsoil property rights over oil in Mexico, subsoil property rights over mineral deposits in the United States, and property rights in the banking sector in Venezuela. Together these cases have traversed nearly all of the circumstances covered by Figure 9.2.

Several of the cases also help to cast doubt on the alternative explanation that property rights gaps are merely a function of state capacity rather than willingness. Take the cases of subsoil mining rights in the United States and property rights in the banking industry in Venezuela. As the discussion will indicate, no property rights gap arose in mining in the mid-1800s in the United States despite the fact that it was vastly less developed and had much weaker state capacity – especially on the western frontier – at the time prospectors discovered subsoil minerals compared to Venezuela in the 2000s when it began weakening property rights in the banking sector. Indeed, Venezuela had already established secure property rights in its banking sector prior to weakening those rights. Political regimes and coalitions are much better predictors of property rights in these cases than state capacity.

The cases also cast doubt on ideology as a sufficient explanation. Property rights over subsoil oil extraction in Mexico and in the banking sector in Venezuela have shifted under the very same leaders. At the same time, property rights in subsoil mining in the United States were remarkably stable in the decades following mineral discoveries despite significant changes in the ideology of western state governors and elected officials in the federal government. The same is true of stable property rights in the banking sector in Venezuela from the 1960s to the 1980s despite important ideological shifts in government.

Subsoil Resource Rights in Mexico in the Late Nineteenth to Early Twentieth Century

Subsoil rights to natural resources belonged to Mexico as a nation prior to its independence from Spain. This ensured that the ruling Spanish crown – an authoritarian colonial presence *par excellence* – could lay claim to valuable mined resources such as silver and gold. Local colonial authorities engaged in mining had to share revenues with Spain and could be sacked or recalled if the crown viewed them as too threatening, autonomous, untrustworthy, or slothful. This presented powerful incentives for compliance with imperial authorities.

The longstanding legal precedent over subsoil rights in Mexico shifted under the rule of longtime dictator Porfirio Díaz with the Mining Law of 1884.[4] The law stipulated that subsoil mineral rights belonged to the surface landowner.[5] Díaz later extended the law in 1892 to stipulate that landowners could freely exploit oil in the subsoil without special government concessions. The government passed a law further clarifying property rights as the "exclusive property" of the surface landowners in 1909.

Why did Díaz, a personalist authoritarian leader, make this shift toward more secure subsoil property rights? High energy costs in the early to mid-nineteenth century had been a major bottleneck to economic development in independent Mexico. The government had to import costly coal and oil to meet the growing demand of railroads, mining interests, manufacturing, and electrical power (Meyer 1972). Powerful and politically connected economic elites in these sectors wanted Díaz to lower their energy costs in an effort to expand business and to make it more profitable. Subsoil resource property rights could have been extended selectively to this group of connected elites. But they did not themselves have the knowledge and expertise for discovery and

---

[4] The Mining Law was in fact enacted under President Manuel González (1880–1884), a trusted ally of Díaz's who served an interregnum period during the Porfiriato before Díaz amended the constitution to enable indefinite reelection. Díaz was nonetheless seen as the power behind the throne.

[5] As Haber et al. (2003, 240–241) point out, however, this was not fee simple ownership. Surface owners had exclusive rights over subsoil water and oil but the government could reallocate other mining claims if miners did not work them.

extraction at the time. So when Díaz created a forum for miners to shape policy (the Sociedad Mexicana de Minería) in 1883 that was composed of private mining interests and government functionaries, it quickly began drafting federalized reforms to subsoil property rights.

Meanwhile, there was a blossoming oil industry across the northern border in the United States that had the capital to expand operations.[6] Other international players such as Royal Dutch/Shell were also interested in entering new markets. Díaz's initial moves to strengthen subsoil property rights piqued the interest of several wealthy foreign oil companies and prospectors, who began pushing for even stronger property rights protections for investments in Mexico as well as tax concessions (Haber et al. 2003). One example was the California oil baron Edward Doheny. Doheny was introduced to Mexican government officials by the US ambassador and would serve as a conduit for US policy over the protection of subsoil property rights for American firms operating in Mexico in the late 1800s and early 1900s.

Díaz responded by further strengthening subsoil property rights. Foreign oil companies swooped in like a hawk. They bought up hundreds of thousands acres of land in Mexico and acquired leases to exploit the subsoil rights of even more land. One example was Doheny's powerful Mexican Petroleum Company. The company came to hold some 1.5 million acres of Mexican land. Another was the British firm El Águila. El Águila leased nearly one million acres of land in Mexico for oil extraction (Hall 1995, 18).

Mexico's new subsoil property rights legislation was broad-based and fairly strong. But the Díaz regime was personalist and uninstitutionalized. Rights enforcement concerns were reasonable. Major firms therefore sought to further ensure the protection of their property rights and investments. Firms turned to the muscular political backing of their home countries. They also resorted to what Haber et. al (2003) call "vertical political integration," a mechanism for generating credible commitments in environments with weak or partial institutions. El Águila, for instance, incorporated in Mexico and then distributed stock to prominent members of the political elite affiliated with Díaz, who in turn sat on the company's board (Haber et. al 2003, 197). In other words, cronyism was a valuable extra insurance policy against property rights violations.

The early twentieth century Mexican Revolution upended the property rights regime that Porfirio Díaz had established over the subsurface. The Revolution ran out Díaz's closest allies and upended Mexico's relationships with foreign business interests. Three main political factions jockeyed for authority in the resulting political vacuum. The first faction consisted of small farmers from central Mexico represented by Emiliano Zapata. These peasants had lost their land during the Porfiriato. Meanwhile, the development of mining, railroads, and manufacturing

---

[6] The same was true of mining companies in the United States that had expertise in extraction and smelting that was scarce in Mexico (Haber et al. 2003, 238–240).

under Díaz generated a fledgling labor movement that was severely repressed during the Porfiriato. Pancho Villa represented this faction politically. Finally, because Díaz had favored an elite group of industrialists and bankers, a contingent of merchants, mine owners, and ranchers from Mexico's northern states opposed the monopoly rights granted to Mexico City's new powerbrokers. Álvaro Obregón represented this third faction.

Venustiano Carranza forged a new constitution in 1917 in an attempt to cohere these factions. One key element of the constitution was Article 27. Article 27 declared all land, water, and subsoil resources to be vested in the nation, which in turn had the authority to transfer title to private parties. This had the potential to deal a fatal blow to the property rights that foreign oil interests and domestic and foreign mining firms had come to enjoy under Díaz.[7] The United States and Great Britain vigorously opposed its application. Both countries had politically powerful nationals with major firms that would be affected. They also had concerns about the flow of resources needed to conduct WWI (Hall 1995).

A series of legal memoranda produced by the government in the next several years indicate that it was willing to compromise on the application of Article 27 while preserving the ability to take a harder stance in the future (Hall 1995, 140–145). In fits and starts, Mexico at first sought to partially apply Article 27 of the 1917 constitution. It sought to tax oil production through royalties, require applications for government concessions to legally drill, and for a brief period even physically sought to prevent drilling by foreign companies (Hall 1995, 19–20). But it did so in vain under withering pressure from the American government and foreign oil and mining companies.

Residual domestic instability and the need to consolidate a stable political coalition to underpin the new government exacerbated Mexico's inability to apply the law. The country cycled through a series of leaders in the wake of the revolution that alienated one or more of the key factions from the revolution and consequently failed to consolidate power. The first leader to find firm footing was Plutarco Calles. Calles first rose to power in 1924 and, in 1929, founded what became the hegemonic PRI by inviting influential generals, regional elites, nascent industrialists, and labor bosses to join his new political party. Each of these groups brought along a vast network of political supporters with them. Calles remained the power behind the presidency until Lázaro Cárdenas came into power and sidelined Calles and his allies.

As Mexican politics stabilized and foreign resource extraction firms retained their precarious position at the sidelines of the halls of power, successive governments stepped up efforts to restrict the property rights of foreign firms in order to bring them to heel. This coincided with a broader turn to domestic political and economic reliance via import substitution industrialization and

---

[7] Domestic mining firms also recognized the potential to benefit at the expense of foreign mining firms if they could enter into or tightly ally with the new post-revolution ruling coalition.

a newfound Mexican nationalism. Calles attempted to put a sunset clause on existing oil concessions in 1925. Oil companies appealed the move and the Supreme Court ruled it unconstitutional in 1927. Cárdenas pushed harder, and the legislature enacted an expropriation law in 1936 that legalized the expropriation of land or property for purposes of national importance. This eroded subsoil property rights across the board. And it set the stage for a final, electrifying act: Cárdenas wholesale expropriated the oil industry in 1938. The PRI subsequently used nationalized oil production to support its political and economic goals.

Subsoil Mining Rights in the United States

The evolution of property rights over subsoil natural resources in Mexico contrasts starkly with property rights to mineral resources in the United States. Unlike in Mexico, valuable subsoil mineral resources in the United States were discovered on the western frontier in the context of democracy. Early mining interests quickly became economically and politically important. This generated strong property rights in a manner consistent with the theory.[8]

Consider the case of subsoil mining rights in Nevada, where legal change evolved along similar lines to – and formed precedent for – mining law change in other parts of the west (Libecap 1978). Very early mining in Nevada in the early to mid-1850s, prior to statehood, occurred under informal and unwritten ownership agreements. This changed radically with the discovery of the Comstock Lode in 1859. The Comstock Lode was a mammoth vein of mainly silver ore–bearing quartz. The value of mining output jumped with the discovery from around \$67,000 annually to \$2.5 million annually by 1861 and the local population mushroomed (Libecap 1978, 343).

Prospectors quickly established a formal mining camp government called Gold Hill. The district wrote rules regarding the establishment and protection of private claims, such as the recording requirements for locating a claim, the size of individual allotments, procedures for marking boundaries, and requirements necessary to maintain ownership.[9] It also appointed a permanent claim recorder and ad hoc miners' court. This form of governance spread to other nearby mining areas as well in rapid order as further discoveries were made.

As mining on the Comstock became more capital-intensive and larger scale, pressure built for establishing a territorial government that could provide judicial authority and legally enforce property rights. Nevada officially became a territory in March 1861. The first address of the president of Nevada's upper legislative chamber underscored both the importance of

---

[8] The way in which strong subsoil property rights in the United States arose parallels property rights in other early frontier markets. Organized interests in the nascent lumber industry in Wisconsin, for instance, quickly won strong private property rights over access to timber within forests (Hurst 1964).

[9] The following description draws heavily from Libecap (1978, 343–347).

property rights to miners and the responsiveness of the government to their demands:

We are called upon to make laws of a peculiar character ... [T]he principal resources of this territory exist in its marvelously rich mines, which for their proper development and advancement require judicious thought and enactments by which titles to them can be secured and permanency given to that class of property.[10]

This declaration was followed by action: the new legislature quickly set up a judicial system and delineated how courts could be used to protect private mining claims. The courts upheld mining camp rules regarding dividing deposit veins in sections whose boundaries extended vertically from surface end lines. It also upheld the de facto practice of allowing miners to follow their section of a vein wherever it ran underground, provided that it did not intersect the vein of another potentially competing mining claim. This became a cornerstone of American mining law and gave the courts a central role in adjudicating the often tricky question of whether mines with competing claims accessed distinctly separate veins.

Subsoil property rights in Nevada faced one final and potentially existential threat: the federal government. Both Congress and the executive considered taxing mining operations and even selling off mining lands in order to help pay off debt from the Civil War. These options were on the table in part because of Nevada's status as a territory and the fact that its nascent subsoil property rights regime was not yet formally recognized at the federal level. In terms of the theory, whereas mining interests had become closely integrated into Nevada's territorial government, they did not have a strong position within the political coalition that ruled at the federal level.

Mining interests rallied to the cause. They lobbied successfully first for Nevada statehood, which the federal government granted in 1864. They then worked to refine and strengthen existing mining rights within the state legislature. In turn, Nevada's state legislature lobbied on behalf of organized mining interests against federal proposals to abrogate local property rights. From its stronger position as a state, and drawing strength from mining interests in other western states and territories, it successfully vouchsafed local property rights. Mining rights in Nevada were largely settled by 1868. Indeed, there were no major conflicts over claims despite a continued rise in the value of mining output. And, with a mining sector galvanized to organize in the pursuit of complete and well-protected property rights, the legal framework for subsoil mining rights became federal law.

Mining interests remained well organized even as the Comstock Lode declined and the Nevada economy diversified beyond mining. Property rights in the sector remained well defined and strongly protected as mining groups

---

[10] Quoted in Libecap (1978, 345).

shifted in and out of governing political coalitions at the state level and as broader mining interests shifted in and out of coalitions at the national level.

Property Rights in the Banking Sector in Venezuela

Property rights in the banking sector in Venezuela in recent decades illustrate a different and more volatile trajectory than property rights over subsoil resources in either Mexico or the United States. They have also evolved in a different way than property rights over the main asset examined in this book – rural land. Venezuela's slide into dictatorship under Presidents Chávez and Maduro greatly weakened property rights for a wide range of property owners that previously enjoyed relatively well-defined and secure rights. In line with the theory, economic actors in sectors of the economy that were not tightly integrated into or allied with the Chávez/Maduro coalition, such as large landowners in the agricultural sector, have faced a steep erosion of their property rights across the board.

In other sectors such as banking, however, privileged insiders have selectively retained their property rights and profited handsomely – at least while their sometimes tenuous political connections lasted.[11] The result was the rise of a new set of crony capitalists known as the "*boliburguesía*," a select group of Venezuelan businesspeople derided as a neo-bourgeoisie whose profits derive from their political connections to Chávez's Bolivarian Revolution.

Venezuela was a precocious democracy in Latin America. It transitioned to democracy in 1959 and was stable for decades. A major economic crisis in the 1990s wreaked havoc on the party system and economy and paved the way for the 1998 election of the political outsider Hugo Chávez. Nearly all of Chávez's closest advisors were political outsiders and a number of them were co-conspirators from Chávez's ill-fated 1992 coup attempt that landed him in jail. Chávez began systematically dismantling Venezuela's checks and balances upon reaching the presidency.[12] He forged a new constitution that abolished Venezuela's upper legislative branch and strengthened the executive. He packed the judiciary with partisan allies through a 2004 law and did the same with the electoral commission. Chávez then won a referendum to eliminate presidential term limits in 2009. Meanwhile, he used state resources as a cudgel to batter his opponents and tilt the electoral field in his favor.

Chávez's newfound political coalition excluded large landowners in agribusiness and ranching. The government consequently moved quickly to erode property rights in rural land across the board in an effort to marshal rural social control and ensure a cheap food supply. One major plank in this effort was the revised Law of Land and Agrarian Development that came into force in 2005. The law succeeded in rewriting the definition of property rights

---

[11] See Ellner (2020) on the vacillating nature of these connections.

[12] See Albertus (2015, Ch. 7) for more details on the erosion of Venezuela's democracy.

underpinning titles, relegating over 90 percent of landowners to informal or insecure status overnight (Albertus 2015).

Banking was a different story. Chávez let technocrats run the Central Bank at the outset of his presidency and continued business as usual with respect to servicing foreign debt and encouraging foreign investment. The banking sector was a critical source of funding for Chávez's Bolivarian Revolution and kept the economy humming despite increasingly unorthodox monetary and exchange rate policies. This made Chávez reticent to kill the golden goose. After all, the banking sector had only recently been put back in order after major disruptions in the 1990s.

From Venezuela's return to democracy in 1959 through the 1980s, Venezuela's major economic interests, including banks, leveraged personal connections to politicians of the two main political parties that ruled the country (Coppedge 2000). The relatively loose coalitional foundations and pragmatic streak of these parties encouraged business leaders to avoid siding clearly with a single party and instead hedge their political bets. Banks during this period competed, colluded, and divided market share, but they organized together in favor of strong property rights and nearly always had a foot in the door of government.

Banks lost their traditional position for the first time under the Pérez government in the late 1980s to early 1990s. Pérez built an economic cabinet of radically pro-market technocrats and crafted an IMF-supported neoliberal shock therapy program with almost no business input (Coppedge 2000, 127–128). The program relaxed regulation and bank supervision and ultimately drove a banking crisis and massive bank bailouts.[13] Organization within the banking sector collapsed as banks started to fail during the crisis (Henry 2003, 111–112). Rafael Caldera's more independent administration that began in 1994 largely politically excluded the sector (Coppedge 2000, 135). The government nationalized a number of banks and closed other banks. It seized half of the industry while at the same time providing insider and fraudulent loans to select firms that had personal political connections (Henry 2003, 112–113). In other words, property rights during the mid-1990s became selective rather than broad-based as they had been in the first several decades of Venezuelan democracy.

The government reestablished stronger and more broad-based property rights as it overhauled the banking sector under IMF supervision. It strengthened financial regulation and liberalized the sector. Foreign banks entered and competed against domestic banks with strong property rights protections. This was the environment that Chávez stepped into after his election in 1998.

A turning point in Chávez's initially hands-off relationship with the banking industry came with a 2002 coup that briefly displaced Chávez from office and

---

[13] For further details, see for instance Henry (2003, 111–115).

a general strike in 2002–2003 by the opposition that sought to force a new presidential election. Many prominent business figures, particularly those tied to the main business federation, Fedecámaras, actively supported attempts to remove Chávez. Much to their detriment, Chávez first weathered the storm and then set out selectively punishing these challengers with a vengeance.

A key weapon that Chávez deployed was a selective erosion of private property rights. The Chávez government cut businesspeople that fell from favor off from benefits such as preferential dollars, contracts, and state credit (Ellner 2020, 171–172). The government selectively harassed business enemies, levied arbitrary and politically motivated investigations into their dealings, revoked their licenses, and even expropriated them.

The *boliburguesía* arose in their place. Politically connected bankers became a key part of the *boliburguesía* while unconnected ones lost key benefits, faced unduly harsh and costly oversight and government litigation, and were ultimately expropriated. The period 2004–2008 was a golden era for the politically connected. There was a boom in business mergers and acquisitions with a raft of state and private assets transferred to private actors with close government connections (Corrales and Penfold-Becerra 2011, 66).

For instance, Arné Chacón, the brother of the minister of science and technology and a friend of Chávez's from the time of Chávez's failed 1992 coup attempt, at first became a government tax official and then amassed a fortune by acquiring banks and insurance companies. In a 2005 interview, he reported that despite being broke, he acquired a 49 percent stake in one bank in return for business he would draw to it: "It's perfectly normal that, since I'm close to the government, they would deposit more money in my bank" (Corrales and Penfold-Becerra 2011, 178fn24).

The banking sector as a whole went on a tear in ensuing years with the rotation in winners and losers. An oil boom propelled the economy through most of the 2000s. Outsized government spending further fueled expansion. Currency controls stoked consumer spending by keeping much of the tidal wave of cash trapped in the country. Interest rates dipped below inflation rates, further goosing the loan industry. Bank profits soared. Profits just in 2006 increased by 33 percent and the banking and insurance industries' contribution to GDP rose 37 percent.[14] Banks raked in commissions as intermediaries through bond sales by the state-owned oil company Petróleos de Venezuela. They also profited from other government schemes. For instance, the Venezuelan government bought risky Argentine bonds to support its leftist government. Banks in turn snapped up these bonds at the official exchange rate and then sold them in dollars and profited by buying local currency at a higher rate on the black market.[15]

---

[14] See Jens Erik Gould, "Boom Times for Banks in Venezuela," *New York Times*, June 15, 2007.
[15] Jens Erik Gould, "Boom Times for Banks in Venezuela," *New York Times*, June 15, 2007.

These profits outweighed a growing number of requirements that banks had to meet to satisfy government regulations. The government required banks to dedicate 32 percent of their loans to particular spheres of the economy including agriculture, microcredit, and housing. And the central bank increased cash reserve requirements for banks in an attempt to stem inflation.

The lights at the party began flickering in 2009. Some of those who had won selective property rights came under the harsh glare of the government as the price of oil dipped and government revenue began to decline, causing balance of payments pressure amid a frozen exchange rate. Inflation spiked, as did the black market exchange rate for dollars, exacerbating a fiscal crisis. The economy began to shrink. Meanwhile, several government cronies managed to illicitly use deposits in several smaller banks to finance more acquisitions.

Chávez had snuffed out any remnants of democracy in Venezuela by this time. The *boliburguesía* had nowhere to turn if they ran afoul of the government. The deposit scandal was just such a moment. Chávez turned against several former allies in late 2009 with the support of their rivals within the dominant ruling party. The government arrested Arné Chacón and several other bankers, including a billionaire named Ricardo Fernández. Fernández had obtained a monopoly contract to sell food to Mercal, a chain of state-controlled supermarkets. His banks had received mountains of government deposits and loans from state banks (Corrales and Penfold-Becerra 2011, 178fn24). The government seized seven banks in rapid succession.

Chávez used the occasion to remind the banking industry of its vulnerability to having its property rights rewritten. He publicly threatening the industry: "I warn the country's private bankers: I'll take away any bank from anyone who slips up." Chávez even mooted nationalizing the sector as a whole.

In the ensuing years, the Chávez and then the Maduro ruling coalition tightened to a smaller group of trusted military generals, party insiders, and selected civilians. The Venezuelan government continued to provide selective property rights to politically favored bankers while punishing those that failed to toe the government line. However, consistent with the theory, the favored group became smaller and even their property rights weakened. The government seized the mid-sized bank Banco Federal in June 2010, citing liquidity problems and fraudulent activity. The bank was closely linked to Venezuela's last major anti-government TV station, Globovisión, which in 2013 sold out to businessmen with ties to the government.[16] Economic mismanagement and manipulation sparked hyperinflation and a massive economic contraction in Venezuela by the late 2010s. For a bank to merely stay afloat began to require either bleeding money or playing fast and loose with official regulatory requirements. This situation rendered them vulnerable to state takeovers.

---

[16] On Globovisión's sale, see Chris Kraul and Mery Mogollon, "Venezuela's last major opposition TV station is sold," *Los Angeles Times*, May 14, 2013.

In early 2018, under considerable threat from the opposition figure Juan Guaidó and selected insider defections, Maduro cast a net of investigations into banks accusing them of acting as "mafias" that were weakening the currency, stoking inflation, and causing shortages of basic goods. It even intervened in the operations of Banesco, Venezuela's largest private bank whose owner Juan Carlos Escotet had long had cordial relations with the regime. The government arrested a suite of Banesco's executives and held them in detainment for two weeks. Its intervention into Banesco's operations lasted nearly a year. In short, the little that had remained of property rights for politically connected bankers began to evaporate as Maduro's ruling coalition shrunk to an ever smaller coterie of military and civilian figures.

Pathways to Markets, Property Rights, and Development

The discussions of subsoil property rights in Mexico and the United States and property rights in the banking sector in Venezuela suggest that there are various pathways to creating or defining markets by shaping property rights. Table 9.3 situates these cases over time within the framework of Table 9.2. The nature of these markets and the property rights that prevail in them in turn drive development outcomes through their effects on competition, investment incentives, access to credit, transaction costs, and other related factors.

Robust markets with strong property rights can arise under either democracy or foreign pressure. The evolution of subsoil mineral rights in the United States from the mid-nineteenth century and subsoil oil rights in Mexico in the late 1800s to early 1900s illustrate these paths. Other examples include stronger property rights in the banking sectors of countries such as Vietnam and Malaysia in the wake of international bailouts and pressure during the 1997 Asian Financial Crisis; in mining in Indonesia since its transition to democracy in 1998; and in agriculture and manufacturing in countries such as Hungary, Poland, and Romania that transitioned to democracy after the fall of the Berlin Wall. Of course, within the broad contours of these markets in which entrants enjoy relatively well-defined and secure property rights, governments still regulate and market players can jockey for power and influence through lobbying or leveraging market power to crush competitors. But the basic rules of the game are clear and arbitrary violations of property rights do not go unchecked.

Markets do not require strong and widespread property rights to flourish for a time. Selective property rights provided to some firms but not others can yield spectacular episodes of growth. Illustrative examples include Venezuela's banking sector in the mid-2000s, the authoritarian developmental states of post–WWII South Korea and Taiwan, Myanmar under military rule in the 1990s and 2000s, or contemporary China or Egypt. The sustained growth of markets in these cases often requires heavy state support to make the promise of hefty profits worth the risks of falling out of favor with the incumbent government.

TABLE 9.3 *The evolution of property rights in various markets in Mexico, the United States, and Venezuela*

	Sectoral balance in coalition	Sectoral balance out of coalition
Dictatorship	Selective property rights in sector to connected actors/firms ("crony capitalism") *Venezuela banking mid-2000s*	Weak property rights across sector *Mexico oil mid-1800s* *Mexico oil 1930s–1990s* *Venezuela banking 2010s*
Democracy	Strong property rights in sector *US mining mid-1800s to present* *Venezuela banking 1960s–1980s*	Sector broadly organized: strong property rights in sector *US mining mid-1800s to present* Sector divided: selective or weak property rights in sector *Venezuela banking mid-1990s*
Foreign pressure for stronger property rights	Strong property rights in sector	Strong property rights in sector *Mexico oil 1880s–1930s* *Venezuela banking late 1990s*

Even then, these markets face inherent limitations. At some point, state support may shift, the market may hit a growth ceiling, or crony capitalism may begin to creak under the weight of corruption. Venezuela's banking sector in the 2010s is a case in point. To continue down a more sustainable development path requires a change. That change could come either from outside pressure or from a shift toward democracy that provides market participants the ability to organize to extend and protect their property rights as a sector.

The counterpoint to markets in which property rights are either well-defined and broadly held or selectively provided to only some actors that operate in the market are markets in which property rights are poorly defined or weakly enforced across the board. Many markets hobble along for years without ever granting participants secure property rights. This can be good politics for the typically authoritarian incumbent government that presides over this arrangement. But it stunts markets and limits their development potential. Mexico's oil industry after the 1938 nationalization of oil is a case in point.

State-owned oil served as a convenient piggy bank to stoke industrialization and enjoyed major government investment over decades. But it eventually became legendary as an exemplar of inefficiency and corruption. Other examples of rampant weak property rights include large swathes of Central Asian economies in countries such as Turkmenistan or Tajikistan and Middle Eastern and North African economies in countries such as Iran, Sudan, and Algeria.

It is no surprise that many of the world's most notorious authoritarian regimes – such as Cuba and North Korea – fail to provide property rights in most markets and pay the economic price for it with underdevelopment. Of course, it is also noteworthy that political regimes in these countries have been long lasting. Withholding property rights from economic agents can generate powerful coercive leverage over society that can be channeled toward maintaining political incumbency. Sluggish development is a price that many authoritarian regimes are willing to pay.

APPENDIX A

Regression Tables for Chapter 4

TABLE A.1 *Regressions for Figure 4.2 (rows 1–8): Political regimes and competing existing explanations for the property rights gap in Latin America, 1920–2010*

	Partial				Full			
	Yearly titling gap		Cumulative titling gap		Yearly titling gap		Cumulative titling gap	
Dependent variable:	Model 1	Model 2	Model 3	Model 4	Model 5	Model 6	Model 7	Model 8
Democracy	-0.477*	-1.007**	-0.556**	-0.826***	-0.371	-0.929**	-0.493**	-0.759**
	(0.243)	(0.426)	(0.237)	(0.292)	(0.233)	(0.459)	(0.232)	(0.315)
State capacity	0.221	0.569	0.288	0.432	-0.106	0.296	-0.023	0.122
	(0.350)	(0.553)	(0.315)	(0.401)	(0.302)	(0.531)	(0.305)	(0.380)
Rural pressure	0.564	-0.884	-0.575	-0.753	0.557	-1.670**	-0.537	-1.133**
	(0.592)	(1.243)	(0.586)	(0.768)	(0.599)	(0.765)	(0.613)	(0.564)
Percent urban	0.032	0.061	0.136***	0.062**	0.040*	0.095**	0.143***	0.082***
	(0.025)	(0.051)	(0.025)	(0.028)	(0.022)	(0.042)	(0.022)	(0.020)
Left ideology	1.042***	1.339**	1.467***	1.951***	0.953**	0.942	1.481***	1.725***
	(0.365)	(0.637)	(0.352)	(0.453)	(0.370)	(0.612)	(0.360)	(0.450)
Revolution	-0.173	-0.442	-0.310	-0.523	-0.031	-0.491	-0.199	-0.569*
	(0.310)	(0.389)	(0.276)	(0.318)	(0.328)	(0.373)	(0.289)	(0.295)
Age of land cadaster	-0.041*	-0.008	0.070***	0.114**	-0.034	0.036	0.069***	0.147***
	(0.025)	(0.052)	(0.017)	(0.051)	(0.025)	(0.061)	(0.017)	(0.055)
Years of prior land conflict	-0.047	-0.025	-0.090*	-0.067	-0.032	-0.028	-0.082	-0.084*
	(0.055)	(0.043)	(0.054)	(0.042)	(0.054)	(0.044)	(0.055)	(0.047)

Years of democracy	0.132**	0.028	0.029	-0.001	0.103*		0.011	
	(0.057)	(0.060)	(0.056)	(0.052)	(0.059)		(0.057)	
Prior land redistribution	-0.002	-0.069*	0.977***	0.945***	0.002	-0.074***	0.981***	0.946***
	(0.024)	(0.038)	(0.023)	(0.026)	(0.024)	(0.027)	(0.022)	(0.019)
Prior land titling	-0.043**	-0.046	-1.030***	-1.026***	-0.066***	-0.062***	-1.035***	-1.030***
	(0.021)	(0.029)	(0.028)	(0.030)	(0.022)	(0.021)	(0.029)	(0.028)
Prior titling (full PR)					-0.066***	-0.062***	-1.035***	-1.030***
					(0.022)	(0.021)	(0.029)	(0.028)
Drop years of no redistribution/ titling	NO	YES	NO	YES	NO	YES	NO	YES
Time trends	YES	YES	YES	YES	YES	YES	YES	YES
Fixed effects	Country	Country	Country	Country	Country	Country	Country	Country
Observations	1150	758	1333	1016	1163	760	1333	1017

* p<0.10, ** p<0.05, *** p<0.01 (two-tailed). All models are estimated via OLS models using Driscoll-Kraay standard errors with a Newey West correction for serial correlation, indicated in parentheses. Country fixed effects are controlled for via a within transformation. Constants and time trends are not shown. Models 2 and 6 drop observations where there is no land redistribution or land titling. Models 4 and 8 drop observations where there has been no previous land redistribution or land titling activity since 1920.

TABLE A.2 *Regressions for Figure 4.2 (rows 9–12): Political regimes and competing existing explanations for the property rights gap in Latin America, 1920–2010*

Dependent variable:	Land redistribution	Land titling	Yearly titling gap	
Property rights measure:		Partial	Partial	Full
	Tobit		2SLS-FE	
	Model 1	Model 2	Model 3	Model 4
Democracy	–1.130*	1.992**	–3.031**	–2.539**
	(0.625)	(0.994)	(1.352)	(1.164)
State capacity	0.483	–0.700	0.222	–0.109
	(0.536)	(0.828)	(0.326)	(0.260)
Rural pressure	1.635	0.682	0.126	0.180
	(1.117)	(0.453)	(0.507)	(0.436)
Percent urban	0.017	0.084**	0.058*	0.064**
	(0.044)	(0.037)	(0.031)	(0.028)
Left ideology	1.882**	0.207	1.591***	1.408***
	(0.767)	(0.507)	(0.515)	(0.483)
Revolution	0.357	0.666	–0.275	–0.110
	(0.387)	(0.662)	(0.275)	(0.285)
Age of land cadaster	0.002	–0.027**	–0.019	–0.018
	(0.007)	(0.013)	(0.034)	(0.034)
Years of prior land conflict	0.124**	0.073	0.004	0.008
	(0.062)	(0.058)	(0.039)	(0.037)
Years of democracy	0.081*	0.021		
	(0.049)	(0.023)		
Prior land redistribution	0.008	0.007	–0.020	–0.011
	(0.005)	(0.009)	(0.020)	(0.018)
Prior land titling		0.061***	–0.046**	–0.074***
		(0.018)	(0.018)	(0.019)
First-stage instrument			0.048***	0.050***
(Sum polity score in region)			(0.011)	(0.011)
First-stage instrument			–0.109***	–0.110***
(Previous transitions to dictatorship)			(0.029)	(0.029)
Drop years of no redistribution/titling	—	—	NO	NO
Time trends	YES	YES	YES	YES
Fixed effects	Region	Region	Country	Country
First-stage F-statistic			14.48	16.11
Hansen-J statistic (Chi-square p-value)			0.49 (0.48)	2.46 (0.12)
Observations	1225	1182	1150	1163

*p<0.10, **p<0.05, ***p<0.01 (two-tailed). Standard, errors clustered by country in parentheses for tobit models. Country-fixed effects are controlled for via a within transformation. Constants and time trends are not shown.

TABLE A.3 *Regressions for Figure 4.3: Political regimes and the property rights gap when accounting for alternative explanations*

Dependent variable:	Yearly titling gap				
	Model 1	Model 2	Model 3	Model 4	Model 5
Democracy		-0.553**	-0.672*	-0.592**	-0.516**
		(0.271)	(0.345)	(0.273)	(0.245)
Democracy (binary)	-1.214***				
	(0.377)				
Foreign aid		-0.017			
		(0.062)			
Military regime			0.229		
			(0.406)		
Personalist regime			-0.746		
			(0.738)		
Single party regime			-2.093		
			(2.175)		
Parties programmatic				0.239	
				(0.465)	
Party weakness					0.056
					(0.044)
State capacity	0.I49	0.189	0.210	0.186	0.133
	(0.330)	(0.407)	(0.336)	(0.406)	(0.388)
Rural pressure	0.781	0.251	0.146	0.504	0.688
	(0.601)	(0.604)	(0.625)	(0.569)	(0.657)
Percent urban	0.039	0.034	0.030	0.030	0.028
	(0.027)	(0.027)	(0.027)	(0.026)	(0.024)
Left ideology	1.237***	1.075**	1.308**	1.024***	1.083***
	(0.403)	(0.419)	(0.512)	(0.371)	(0.362)
Revolution	-0.238	-0.042	-0.078	-0.196	-0.248
	(0.308)	(0.362)	(0.338)	(0.310)	(0.328)
Age of land cadaster	-0.041	-0.034	-0.079**	-0.039	-0.038
	(0.025)	(0.051)	(0.036)	(0.024)	(0.026)
Years of prior land conflict	-0.018	-0.033	-0.030	-0.042	-0.063
	(0.055)	(0.052)	(0.055)	(0.057)	(0.065)
Years of democracy	0.141**	0.111*	0.132**	0.134**	0.125**
	(0.057)	(0.057)	(0.059)	(0.058)	(0.054)
Prior land redistribution	-0.004	-0.004	-0.005	-0.002	-0.001
	(0.024)	(0.026)	(0.024)	(0.024)	(0.025)
Prior land titling	-0.036*	-0.047**	-0.051**	-0.046**	-0.046**
	(0.021)	(0.022)	(0.025)	(0.023)	(0.021)

(*continued*)

TABLE A.3 (*continued*)

Dependent variable:	Yearly titling gap				
	Model 1	Model 2	Model 3	Model 4	Model 5
Controls for prior redistribution/titling	YES	YES	YES	YES	YES
Time trends	YES	YES	YES	YES	YES
Fixed effects	Country	Country	Country	Country	Country
Observations	1150	1037	1067	1138	1138

*p<0.10, **p<0.05, ***p< 0.01 (two-tailed). All models are estimated via OLS models using Driscoll-Kraay standard errors with a Newey West correction for serial correlation, indicated in parentheses. Country fixed effects are controlled for via a within transformation. Constants and time trends are not shown.

TABLE A.4 *Regressions for Figure 4.4: Opening and maintaining property rights gaps: The effects of political regimes and ruling coalitions*

Sample:	Land redistribution	All regimes			
Dependent variable:		Yearly gap	Cumulative gap	Yearly gap	Cumulative gap
			Partial		Full
Property rights measure:	Tobit		OLS-FE		
	Model 1	Model 2	Model 3	Model 4	Model 5
Democracy	1.257	0.501	0.667*	0.939**	1.059***
	(0.832)	(0.464)	(0.357)	(0.398)	(0.312)
Landowners excluded	3.262***	1.582***	2.012***	2.011***	2.474***
	(1.164)	(0.515)	(0.484)	(0.413)	(0.393)
Democracy*Landowners excluded	−3.508***	−1.493**	−2.052***	−2.023***	−2.579***
	(1.042)	(0.592)	(0.525)	(0.572)	(0.522)
State capacity	0.598	0.392	0.408	0.105	0.141
	(0.445)	(0.359)	(0.326)	(0.293)	(0.287)
Rural pressure	1.645	0.653	−0.427	0.691	−0.317
	(1.194)	(0.576)	(0.525)	(0.593)	(0.563)
Percent urban	0.018	0.023	0.099***	0.025	0.097***
	(0.033)	(0.025)	(0.022)	(0.022)	(0.019)
Left ideology	1.279**	0.770**	1.152***	0.662*	1.125***
	(0.539)	(0.367)	(0.328)	(0.370)	(0.332)
Revolution	0.471	−0.100	−0.227	0.064	−0.093
	(0.363)	(0.312)	(0.275)	(0.323)	(0.281)

(*continued*)

TABLE A.4 (*continued*)

	Land redistribution	Yearly gap	Cumulative gap	Yearly gap	Cumulative gap
Sample:	All regimes				
Dependent variable:					
Property rights measure:	Tobit	Partial		Full	
			OLS-FE		
	Model 1	Model 2	Model 3	Model 4	Model 5
Age of land cadaster	−0.006	−0.039	0.057***	−0.033	0.056***
	(0.011)	(0.024)	(0.017)	(0.025)	(0.016)
Years of prior land conflict	0.107*	−0.035	−0.076	−0.013	−0.062
	(0.059)	(0.056)	(0.053)	(0.053)	(0.053)
Years of democracy	0.106*	0.132**	0.040	0.106*	0.026
	(0.060)	(0.058)	(0.057)	(0.059)	(0.058)
Prior land redistribution	0.009	−0.005	0.979***	−0.000	0.983***
	(0.006)	(0.025)	(0.023)	(0.024)	(0.023)
Prior land titling		−0.037*	−1.020***	−0.055**	−1.020***
		(0.020)	(0.026)	(0.022)	(0.028)
Time trends	YES	YES	YES	YES	YES
Fixed effects	Region	Country	Country	Country	Country
Observations	1225	1150	1316	1163	1316

* p<0.10, ** p<0.05, *** p<0.01 (two-tailed). OLS models use Driscoll-Kraay standard errors with a Newey West correction for serial correlation, indicated in parentheses. Country fixed effects are controlled for via a within transformation. Standard errors clustered by country in parentheses for tobit models. Constants and time trends are not shown.

TABLE A.5 *Regressions for Figure 4.6: Closing property rights gaps: The effects of political regimes, ruling coalitions, and external pressure*

Sample:	All regimes	Democracy	Dictatorship	Democracy	Dictatorship
	Model 1	Model 2	Model 3	Model 4	Model 5
Democracy	2.127*				
	(1.187)				
Landowners excluded	0.613				
	(0.868)				
Democracy*Landowners excluded	−0.139				
	(1.345)				
Peasants included		5.260**	1.109		
		(2.033)	(6.620)		
Upper chamber fractionalization		−1.048	−2.978		
		(1.990)	(3.806)		
Upper chamber fractionalization*		−8.812***	9.362		
Peasants in coalition		(2.948)	(8.076)		
Structural adjustment				−0.157	7.814***
				(0.194)	(2.810)
ODA				−0.034	−4.307*
				(0.285)	(2.239)
ODA*structural adjustment				0.313***	2.920**
				(0.096)	(1.134)
State capacity		0.317	4.186	0.179	−11.684***
		(0.365)	(3.157)	(0.386)	(2.428)
Rural pressure		2.464***	−14.487	0.653	1.565
		(0.861)	(9.958)	(0.544)	(3.174)
	−0.681				
	(0.782)				
	0.730				
	(0.480)				

(continued)

TABLE A.5 (continued)

	All regimes	Democracy	Dictatorship	Democracy	Dictatorship
Sample:	Model 1	Model 2	Model 3	Model 4	Model 5
Percent urban	0.083**	0.055	−1.226	0.006	−2.481***
	(0.036)	(0.052)	(0.935)	(0.036)	(0.463)
Left ideology	−0.021	−0.322	3.960	−0.688*	−36.696**
	(0.636)	(0.672)	(3.145)	(0.355)	(17.646)
Revolution	0.662	−0.883***	0.324***	0.187	0.800
	(0.645)	(0.310)	(0.112)	(0.509)	(0.615)
Age of land cadaster	−0.029**	0.010	−0.339	0.007*	−0.821***
	(0.014)	(0.009)	(0.209)	(0.004)	(0.196)
Years of prior land conflict	0.078	0.203*	1.033	−0.013	0.163
	(0.060)	(0.105)	(1.189)	(0.021)	(0.209)
Years of democracy	0.021	0.088*	−0.364	−0.003	−1.410***
	(0.025)	(0.047)	(0.469)	(0.013)	(0.244)
Prior land redistribution	0.006	−0.005	0.178	−0.005	0.663***
	(0.009)	(0.013)	(0.138)	(0.018)	(0.103)
Prior land titling	0.063***	−0.043	−0.469*	0.108***	−0.006
	(0.018)	(0.060)	(0.238)	(0.041)	(0.311)
Time trends	YES	YES	YES	YES	YES
Fixed effects	Region	Region	Region	Region	Region
Observations	1182	264	149	275	74

* $p < 0.10$, ** $p < 0.05$, *** $p < 0.01$ (two-tailed). All models use a tobit specification. The dependent variable in all models is Land Titling. All models use a partial property rights measure. Standard errors clustered by country in parentheses. Constants and time trends are not shown. Democracy cutoff for Models 2–5 is a Polity Score of 0.6 or higher; 0.5 and lower are classified as dictatorships.

TABLE A.6 *Regressions for Figure 4.9: Additional observable implications of the theory*

Dependent variable:	Agricultural prices Model 1	Industrial property rights violation Model 2
Democracy	−0.071***	0.524
	(0.024)	(0.779)
Landowners excluded	−0.129***	
	(0.025)	
Democracy*Landowners excluded	0.113***	
	(0.038)	
Yearly titling gap		0.058
		(0.057)
State capacity	−0.024	0.514
	(0.020)	(0.607)
Rural pressure	0.027	1.767
	(0.051)	(2.573)
Percent urban	−0.007***	0.053
	(0.002)	(0.068)
Left ideology	0.025	0.184
	(0.036)	(0.708)
Revolution	−0.018	0.390*
	(0.011)	(0.228)
Age of land cadaster	0.013*	
	(0.007)	
Years of prior land conflict	−0.008***	
	(0.003)	
Years of democracy	0.005	
	(0.004)	
Controls for prior redistribution/ titling	YES	NO
Time trends	YES	YES
Country fixed effects	YES	YES

* $p < 0.10$, ** $p < 0.05$, *** $p < 0.01$ (two-tailed). Model 1 is estimated via OLS using Driscoll-Kraay standard errors with a Newey West correction for serial correlation, indicated in parentheses. Model 2 is estimated using a conditional logit model with standard errors clustered by country in parentheses. Country fixed effects are controlled for via a within transformation throughout. Constants and time trends are not shown.

APPENDIX B

Regression Tables for Chapter 5

TABLE B.I *Regressions for Figure 5.1: Social and economic consequences of the property rights gap*

Dependent variable:	Economically active population in agriculture	Agricultural productivity per worker	Urban policy bias	Income inequality	Income per capita
	Model 1	Model 2	Model 3	Model 4	Model 5
Cumulative titling gap	0.018** (0.007)	−0.008*** (0.001)	−0.0003** (0.0001)	0.030*** (0.006)	−7.719*** (1.182)
Log (GDP per capita)	−8.538*** (0.910)	0.276* (0.147)	−0.012 (0.017)	1.479 (2.310)	
State capacity	1.574** (0.681)	0.370*** (0.117)	−0.000 (0.006)	0.137 (0.507)	299.686*** (80.611)
Percent urban	−0.346*** (0.042)	−0.016** (0.006)	−0.002*** (0.000)	0.069* (0.035)	31.025*** (7.485)
Left ideology	−2.228*** (0.579)	0.170 (0.713)	−0.082*** (0.007)	−0.991* (0.543)	294.241** (123.123)
Time trends	YES	YES	YES	YES	YES
Country fixed effects	YES	YES	YES	YES	YES
Observations	999	1430	1334	378	1493

*p<0.10, **p<0.05, ***p<0.01 (two-tailed). All models are estimated via OLS models using Driscoll-Kraay standard errors with a Newey West correction for serial correlation, indicated in parentheses. The cumulative titling gap is lagged one period. Country-fixed effects are controlled for via a within transformation. Constants and time trends are not shown.

TABLE B.2 *Regressions for Figure 5.2: Political consequences of the property rights gap*

Dependent variable:	Rural political power	Vote buying
	Model 1	Model 2
Cumulative titling gap	–0.002	0.003
	(0.001)	(0.001)
Log (GDP per capita)	–0.599	0.222
	(0.112)	(0.167)
State capacity	0.114***	0.186***
	(0.038)	(0.045)
Percent urban	–0.008***	–0.007
	(0.002)	(0.005)
Left ideology	0.103*	0.146***
	(0.060)	(0.050)
Time trends	YES	YES
Country fixed effects	YES	YES
Observations	1334	1358

*p<0.10, **p<0.05, ***p<0.01 (two-tailed). All models are estimated via OLS using Driscoll-Kraay standard errors with a Newey West correction for serial correlation, indicated in parentheses. The cumulative titling gap is lagged one period. Country fixed effects are controlled for via a within transformation. Constants and time trends are not shown.

APPENDIX C

Regression Tables for Chapter 7

TABLE C.1 *Regressions for Figure 7.3: Development characteristics prior to a property rights gap*

	Estimated difference	p-value	Bandwidth	Treated obs.	Control obs.
Economically active population in agriculture	−0.036	0.66	40.19	156	186
Literacy rate	−0.062	0.33	54.91	213	232
Poverty (*chozas*)	−0.002	0.72	50.33	174	192
Poverty (dirt floors)	−0.069	0.21	51.39	178	192
Inequality (hacienda power)	0.018	0.37	57.61	224	243

*p<0.10, **p<0.05, ***p<0.01 (two-tailed). Running variable is distance from agrarian reform zonal core boundary. Columns 3–5 report the main optimal band width around the cutoff, the number of treated observations within the bandwidth, and the number of control observations within the bandwidth.

TABLE C.2 *Regressions for Figure 7.4: Covariate balance across Agrarian Reform Zone core boundary*

	Estimated difference	p-value	Bandwidth	Treated obs.	Control obs.
Population	1.343	0.41	57.95	224	245
Road density	0.514	0.98	44.72	178	196
State personnel	0.023	0.89	90.08	300	336
Elevation	−0.526	0.34	51.22	206	223
Slope	−2.221**	0.04	40.72	164	186
District area	0.481	0.51	35.97	147	163
Cultivable land	−0.800	0.33	36.81	148	167
Private land area	1.531	0.21	84.73	291	320
Indigenous population	0.186	0.60	65.38	238	264
Mita zone	−0.388	0.13	102.65	322	364
Prior social movements	0.504	0.13	32.08	125	150

*p<0.10, **p<0.05, ***p<0.01 (two-tailed). Running variable is distance from agrarian reform zonal core boundary. Columns 3–5 report the main optimal band width around the cutoff, the number of treated observations within the bandwidth, and the number of control observations within the bandwidth.

TABLE C.3 *Regressions for Figure 7.5: Effect of land reform on outcomes on eve of property rights reform*

Dependent variable:	Plots with title	Economically active pop. in agriculture	Agricultural productivity	Literacy rate (Urban bias)	Inequality	Poverty
Treatment effect estimate	−1.922** (0.034)	0.720** (0.030)	−1.342* (0.089)	−0.829** (0.022)	1.749** (0.029)	1.064* (0.056)
First-stage estimate	0.074* (0.072)	0.092** (0.037)	0.114*** (0.000)	0.113*** (0.004)	0.090** (0.043)	0.097** (0.024)
Bandwidth	74.78	38.50	28.90	32.68	39.15	36.62
Treated observations	264	157	112	126	159	148
Control observations	295	177	136	152	181	166
Geographic controls	Yes	Yes	Yes	Yes	Yes	Yes
Includes covariates	Yes	Yes	Yes	Yes	Yes	Yes

*p<0.10, **p<0.05, ***p<0.01 (two-tailed). Running variable is distance from agrarian reform zonal core boundary. Robust p-values in parentheses. Each model reports the main optimal bandwidth around the cutoff, the number of treated observations within the bandwidth, and the number of control observations within the bandwidth. Geographic controls include a second-order polynomial in district latitude and longitude, the latitude and longitude coordinates of the nearest point along the zonal border cutoff, and boundary segment fixed effects.

TABLE C.4 *Regressions for Figure 7.6: Placebo tests*

	10 km. outside	5 km. outside	True boundary	5 km. inside	10 km. inside	15 km. inside	Land reform treatment: Uncultivable land	Agrarian Zone 2 periphery/periphery boundary
Treatment effect estimate	−0.014 (0.849)	0.118 (0.782)	−1.922** (0.034)	−0.557 (0.194)	−0.565 (0.349)	−4.001 (0.791)	50.624 (0.946)	−0.230 (0.736)
First-stage estimate	−0.068 (0.146)	−0.034 (0.274)	0.074* (0.072)	0.167*** (0.000)	0.116*** (0.003)	−0.006 (0.519)	−0.002 (0.303)	−0.042 (0.465)
Bandwidth	49.86	44.19	74.78	37.74	49.29	43.34	36.42	30.68
Treated observations	207	170	264	155	184	166	143	30
Control observations	203	203	295	165	221	190	166	34

*p<0.10, **p<0.05, ***p<0.01 (two-tailed). Running variable is distance from agrarian reform zonal core boundary in columns 3 and 7 and distance to the placebo boundary indicated for columns 1–2 and 4–6. In last column, running variable is distance from Agrarian Zone 2 periphery/periphery boundary between Cajamarca and Amazonas/La Libertad. Robust p-values in parentheses. All models include the full set of geographic controls and covariates. Each model reports the main optimal bandwidth around the cutoff, the number of treated observations within the bandwidth, and the number of control observations within the bandwidth. The last column uses the zonal periphery/periphery as the cutoff.

TABLE C.5 *Regressions for Figure 7.7: Effects of early property rights gap on outcomes after property rights gap largely closed*

	Plots with title	Plots with registered title	Economically active population in agriculture	Agricultural productivity	Literacy rate (Urban bias)	Inequality	Poverty	Poverty gap index	Nighttime luminosity
Treatment effect estimate	0.371 (0.496)	0.715 (0.183)	1.398** (0.044)	2.170 (0.366)	-0.490** (0.023)	0.253 (0.118)	0.480 (0.365)	0.519** (0.045)	-0.977* (0.078)
First-stage estimate	0.110*** (0.005)	0.090** (0.042)	0.096** (0.028)	0.093** (0.027)	0.112*** (0.005)	0.116*** (0.002)	0.101** (0.014)	0.096** (0.028)	0.112*** (0.006)
Bandwidth	33.22	39.99	36.93	37.20	33.01	31.53	35.12	36.92	33.35
Treated observations	128	159	149	143	129	124	144	149	132
Control observations	154	184	167	166	154	147	163	167	153

*p<0.10, ** p<0.05, ***p<0.01 (two-tailed). Running variable is distance from agrarian reform zonal core boundary. Robust p-values in parentheses. All models include covariates and the full set of geographic controls. Each model reports the main optimal bandwidth around the cutoff, the number of treated observations within the bandwidth, and the number of control observations within the bandwidth.

TABLE C.6 *Regressions for Figure 7.8: Return to landholding inequality by the time the property rights gap is closed*

Dependent variable:	Land inequality	Agricultural land inequality	Agricultural land inequality excluding communities
Treatment effect estimate	0.651 (0.634)	0.249 (0.918)	–0.014 (0.675)
First-stage estimate	0.087** (0.049)	0.090** (0.037)	0.094** (0.027)
Bandwidth	42.53	39.65	37.72
Treated observations	167	159	149
Control observations	193	182	169

*p<0.10, **p<0.05, ***p<0.01 (two-tailed). Running variable is distance from agrarian reform zonal core boundary. Robust p-values in parentheses. All models include covariates and the full set of geographic controls. Each model reports the main optimal bandwidth around the cutoff, the number of treated observations within the bandwidth, and the number of control observations within the bandwidth. Column 3 excludes indigenous communities from the agricultural landholding Gini.

TABLE C.7 *Regressions for alternative explanations in Chapter 7*

Alternative explanation: Dependent variable:	Selective sorting Immigration, 1987–1992	Conflict intensity Conflict events, 1980–2000
Treatment effect estimate	–25.37 (0.194)	–11.376* (0.063)
First-stage estimate	0.076* (0.097)	0.076* (0.087)
Bandwidth	47.43	46.92
Treated observations	192	192
Control observations	207	206

*p<0.10, **p<0.05, ***p<0.01 (two-tailed). Running variable is distance from agrarian reform zonal core boundary. Robust p-values in parentheses. All models include covariates and the full set of geographic controls. Each model reports the main optimal bandwidth around the cutoff, the number of treated observations within the bandwidth, and the number of control observations within the bandwidth.

References

Abiad, Abdul, Enrica Detragiache, and Thierry Tressel. 2010. "A new database of financial reforms." *IMF Staff Papers* 57(2): 281–302.

Acemoglu, Daron, Simon Johnson, and James Robinson. 2001. "The colonial origins of comparative development: An empirical investigation." *American Economic Review* 91(5): 1369–1401.

Acemoglu, Daron, Simon Johnson, and James Robinson. 2002. "Reversal of fortune: Geography and institutions in the making of the modern world income distribution." *Quarterly Journal of Economics* 117(4): 1231–1294.

Acemoglu, Daron and James Robinson. 2006. *Economic Origins of Dictatorship and Democracy*. Cambridge: Cambridge University Press.

Acosta Peña, Brasil Alberto. 2008. "Cambios en la tenencia de la tierra y la productividad del maíz en México." *Revista Mexicana de Economía Agrícola y de los Recursos Naturales* 1(1): 57–68.

Albertus, Michael. 2013. "Vote buying with multiple distributive goods." *Comparative Political Studies* 46(9): 1082–1111.

Albertus, Michael. 2015a. *Autocracy and Redistribution: The Politics of Land Reform*. New York: Cambridge University Press.

Albertus, Michael. 2015b. "The role of subnational politicians in distributive politics: Political bias in Venezuela's land reform under Chávez." *Comparative Political Studies* 48(13): 1667–1710.

Albertus, Michael. 2015c. "Explaining patterns of redistribution under autocracy: The case of Peru's revolution from above." *Latin American Research Review* 50(2): 107–134.

Albertus, Michael. 2017. "Landowners and democracy: The social origins of democracy reconsidered." *World Politics* 69(2): 233–276.

Albertus, Michael. 2019. "The effect of commodity price shocks on public lands distribution: Evidence from Colombia." *World Development* 113: 294–308.

Albertus, Michael. 2020. "Land reform and civil conflict: Theory and evidence from Peru." *American Journal of Political Science* 64(2): 256–274.

Albertus, Michael, Beatriz Magaloni, Barry Weingast, and Alberto Diaz-Cayeros. 2016. "Authoritarian survival and poverty traps: Land reform in Mexico." *World Development* 77: 154–170.

Albertus, Michael and Oliver Kaplan. 2013. "Land reform as a counterinsurgency policy: Evidence from Colombia." *Journal of Conflict Resolution* 57(2): 198–231.

Albertus, Michael, Thomas Brambor, and Ricardo Ceneviva. 2018. "Land inequality and rural unrest: Theory and evidence from Brazil." *Journal of Conflict Resolution* 62(3): 557–596.

Albertus, Michael and Victor Menaldo. 2018. *Authoritarianism and the Elite Origins of Democracy*. New York: Cambridge University Press.

Alesina, Alberto and Dani Rodrik. 1994. "Distributive politics and economic growth." *Quarterly Journal of Economics* 109: 465–490.

Alexander, Robert. 2007. *History of Organized Labor in Peru and Ecuador*. Westport, Conn: Greenwood Publishing Group.

Alston, Lee, Gary Libecap, and Robert Schneider. 1996. "The determinants and impact of property rights: Land titles on the Brazilian frontier." *The Journal of Law, Economics, and Organization* 12(1): 25–61.

Alston, Lee, Gary Libecap, and Bernardo Mueller. 1999. *Titles, Conflict, and Land Use*. Ann Arbor: University of Michigan Press.

Alvarez, José. 2004. *Cuba's Agricultural Sector*. Gainesville: University Press of Florida.

Anderson, Leslie. 1990. "Alternative action in Costa Rica: Peasants as positive participants." *Journal of Latin American Studies* 22 (1–2): 89–113.

Anderson, Kym and E. Valenzuela. 2008. *Global Estimates of Distortions to Agricultural Incentives, 1955 to 2007*. Washington, DC: World Bank, Dataset available at www.worldbank.org/agdistortions.

Ansell, Ben and David Samuels. 2014. *Inequality and Democracy*. New York: Cambridge University Press.

Arce, Moisés. 2014. *Resource Extraction and Protest in Peru*. Pittsburgh: University of Pittsburgh Press.

Arriola, Carlos. 1976. "Los grupos empresariales frente al Estado (1973–1975)." *Foro internacional* 16(4): 449–495.

Ashton, Basil, Kenneth Hill, Alan Piazza, and Robin Zeitz. 1984. "Famine in China, 1958–61." *Population and Development Review* 10(4): 613–645.

Astorga, Enrique. 1985. *Mercado de trabajo rural en México*. Mexico, DF: Ediciones Era.

Auerbach, Adam, Adrienne LeBas, Aliso Post, and Rebecca Weitz-Shapiro. 2018. "State, society, and informality in cities of the Global South." *Studies in Comparative International Development* 53(3): 261–280.

Baer, Werner. 1972. "Import substitution and industrialization in Latin America: Experiences and interpretations." *Latin American Research Review* 7(1): 95–122.

Bai, Chong-En, Jiangyong Lu, and Zhigang Tao. 2006. "Property rights protection and access to bank loans: Evidence from private enterprises in China." *Economics of transition* 14(4): 611–628.

Baland, Jean Marie and James Robinson. 2008. "Land and power: Theory and evidence from Chile." *American Economic Review* 98(5): 1737–65.

Bandeira, Pablo, José María Sumpsi, and Cesar Falconi. 2010. "Evaluating land administration systems: A comparative method with an application to Peru and Honduras." *Land Use Policy* 27(2): 351–363.

Barbier, Edward. 2010. *Scarcity and Frontiers*. New York: Cambridge University Press.

Barnett, A. Doak. 1953. "China's road to collectivization." *Journal of Farm Economics* 35(2): 188–202.

Barraclough, Solon, ed. 1973. *Agrarian Structure in Latin America*. Lexington: D.C. Heath.

Barreto, António. 1987. *Anatomia de uma Revolução: A reforma agrária em Portugal 1974–1976*. Mem Martins: Publicações Europa-América.

Bartra, Roger. 1993. *Agrarian Structure and Political Power in Mexico*. Baltimore: Johns Hopkins University Press.

Barzel, Yoram. 1997. *Economic Analysis of Property Rights*. New York: Cambridge University Press.

Baten, Joerg and Dácil Juif. 2014. "A story of large landowners and math skills: Inequality and human capital formation in long-run development, 1820–2000." *Journal of Comparative Economics* 42(2): 375–401.

Bates, Robert. 1981. *Markets and States in Tropical Africa*. Berkeley: University of California Press.

Bates, Robert. 1989. *Beyond the Miracle of the Market: The Political Economy of Agrarian Development in Kenya*. New York: Cambridge University Press.

Becker, Lawrence. 1977. *Property Rights: Philosophic Foundations*. New York: Routledge.

Becker, Jasper. 1998. *Hungry Ghosts: Mao's Secret Famine*. New York: Henry Holt.

Berg, Ronald. 1992. "Peasant responses to Shining Path in Andahuaylas." In David Scott Palmer, ed., *The Shining Path of Peru*, pp. 83–104. New York: St. Martin's Press.

Bermeo, Nancy. 1986. *The Revolution within the Revolution: Workers' Control in Rural Portugal*. Princeton: Princeton University Press.

Berry, Albert, and William Cline. 1979. *Agrarian Structure and Productivity in Developing Countries*. Baltimore: Johns Hopkins University Press.

Besley, Timothy and Robin Burgess. 2000. "Land reform, poverty reduction, and growth: Evidence from India." *Quarterly Journal of Economics* 115 (2): 389–430.

Besley, Timothy and Torsten Persson. 2009. "The origins of state capacity: Property rights, taxation, and politics." *American Economic Review* 99(4): 1218–44.

Bhattacharya, Prasad and Mehmet Ulubasoglu. 2010. "How do legal systems affect land distribution? A long-run disaggregated analysis." Working paper.

Bhattacharya, Prasad, Devashish Mitra, and Mehmet Ulubaşoğlu. 2019. "The political economy of land reform enactments: New cross-national evidence (1900–2010)." *Journal of Development Economics* 139: 50–68.

Binswanger-Mkhize, Hans, Camille Bourguignon, and Rogier van den Brink, eds. 2009. *Agricultural Land Redistribution: Toward Greater Consensus*. Washington, D.C.: The World Bank.

Bird, Richard Miller and Naomi Enid Slack, eds. 2004. *International Handbook of Land and Property Taxation*. Northampton, Mass: Edward Elgar Publishing.

Boix, Carles. 2003. *Democracy and Redistribution*. Cambridge: Cambridge University Press.

Boix, Carles, Michael Miller, and Sebastian Rosato. 2013. "A complete data set of political regimes, 1800–2007." *Comparative Political Studies* 46(12): 1523–1554.

Boone, Catherine. 2014. *Property and Political Order: Land Rights and the Structure of Politics in Africa*. New York: Cambridge University Press.

Boone, Catherine. 2018. "Shifting visions of property under competing political regimes: Changing uses of Côte d'Ivoire's 1998 Land Law." *Journal of Modern African Studies* 56(2): 189–216.

Boone, Catherine, Alex Dyzenhaus, Ambreena Manji, Catherine Gateri, Seth Ouma, James Kabugu Owino, Achiba Gargule, and Jacqueline Klopp. 2019a. "Land law reform in Kenya: Devolution, veto players, and the limits of an institutional fix." *African Affairs* 118(471): 215–237.

Boone, Catherine, Arsene Brice Bado, Aristide Mah Dion, and Zibo Irigo. 2019b. "Regional dynamics and complexities of land certification in Côte d'Ivoire." *London School of Economics*. 9/27/2019. Available at: https://blogs.lse.ac.uk /africaatlse/2019/09/27/regional-dynamics-and-complexities-of-land-certification-in-cote-divoire/.

Booth, John. 2007. "Political parties in Costa Rica: Democratic stability and party system change in a Latin American context." In Webb, Paul, and Stephen White, eds., *Party Politics in New Democracies*, pp. 305–344. Oxford: Oxford University Press.

Borras Jr, Saturnino and Jennifer Franco. 2012. "Global land grabbing and trajectories of agrarian change: A preliminary analysis." *Journal of Agrarian Change* 12(1): 34–59.

Boserup, Ester. 1965. *The conditions of agricultural growth: The economics of agrarian change under population pressure*. New Brunswick, NJ: Routledge.

Bottazzi, Patrick and Stephan Rist. 2012. "Changing land rights means changing society: The sociopolitical effects of agrarian reforms under the government of Evo Morales." *Journal of Agrarian Change* 12(4): 528–551.

Bowles, Samuel. 1971. "Cuban education and the revolutionary ideology." *Harvard Educational Review* 41 (November): 472–500.

Brasselle, Anne-Sophie, Frederic Gaspart, and Jean-Philippe Platteau. 2002. "Land tenure security and investment incentives: Puzzling evidence from Burkina Faso." *Journal of Development Economics* 67(2): 373–418.

Bromley, Daniel. 1989. *Economic Interests and Institutions: The Conceptual Foundations of Public Policy*. New York: Basil Blackwell.

Bromley, Daniel, Margaret Mckean, Jere Gilles, Ronald Oakerson, and Fordcoed Runge. 1992. *Making the Commons Work: Theory, Practice, and Policy*. San Francisco: Institute for Contemporary Studies Press.

Bruno, Regina Angela Landim. 2003. "Nova República: A violència patronal rural como prática de classe." *Sociologias* 10 (July/December): 284–310.

Bucheli, Marcelo. 2008. "Multinational corporations, totalitarian regimes and economic nationalism: United Fruit Company in Central America, 1899–1975." *Business History* 50(4): 433–454.

Bunker, Stephen. 1988. *Underdeveloping the Amazon: Extraction, Unequal Exchange, and the Failure of the Modern State*. Chicago: University of Chicago Press.

Caballero, José María. 1981. "From Belaúnde to Belaúnde: Peru's Military Experiment in Third-Roadism." Cambridge: Centre of Latin American Studies, Cambridge University. Working Paper no. 36.

Cabral, Manuel Villaverde. 1978. "Agrarian structures and recent rural movements in Portugal." *The Journal of Peasant Studies* 5(4): 411–445.

Calonico, Sebastian, Matias Cattaneo, and Rocío Titiunik. 2014. "Robust nonparametric confidence intervals for regression-discontinuity designs." *Econometrica* 82(6): 2295–2326.

Cant, Anna. 2012. "'Land for those who work It': A visual analysis of Agrarian reform posters in Velasco's Peru." *Journal of Latin American Studies* 44(1): 1–37.

Cantuarias, Fernando and Miguel Delgado. 2004. "Peru's urban land titling program." Paper presented at conference entitled "Scaling up poverty reduction: A global learning process and Conference." Shanghai, May 25–27. 2004.

Cardoso, António Lopes. 1977. *Luta Pela Reforma Agraria*. Lisbon: Livros Horizonte.

Carter, David and Curtis Signorino. 2010. "Back to the future: Modeling time dependence in binary data." *Political Analysis* 18(3): 271–292.

Carter, Michael and Elena Alvarez. 1989. "Changing paths: The decollectivization of Agrarian reform agriculture in coastal Peru." In William Thiesenhusen, ed., *Searching for Agrarian Reform in Latin America*, pp. 156–87. Boston: Unwin Hyman.

Casanova, Pablo Gonzalez. 1965. "Internal colonialism and national development." *Studies in Comparative International Development* 1(4): 27–37.

Casanova, Pablo González. 1985. *Historia Politica de los Campesinos Latinoamericanos, Vol. 2*. Instituto de Investigaciones Sociales de la U.N.A.M.

Cattaneo, Matias, Nicolas Idrobo, and Rocío Titiunik. 2018. *A Practical Introduction to Regression Discontinuity Designs*. New York: Cambridge University Press.

CEPAL. 1986. Antecentes Estadísticas de la Distribución del Ingreso, Costa Rica, 1958–1982. United Nations: Santiago.

Chen, Xi and William Nordhaus. 2011. "Using luminosity data as a proxy for economic statistics." *Proceedings of the National Academy of Sciences* 108(21): 8589–8594.

Chilcote, Ronald. 2012. *The Portuguese Revolution: State and Class in the Transition to Democracy*. Lanham, MD: Rowman & Littlefield.

Cinnirella, Francesco and Erik Hornung. 2016. "Landownership concentration and the expansion of education." *Journal of Development Economics* 121: 135–152.

Cho, Chae-hong. 1964. *Post-1945 land reforms and their consequences in South Korea*. PhD dissertation, Indiana University.

Cleaves, Peter and Martin Scurrah. 1980. *Agriculture, Bureaucracy, and Military Government in Peru*. Ithaca: Cornell University Press.

Coatsworth, John. 2008. "Inequality, institutions and economic growth in Latin America." *Journal of Latin American Studies* 40(3): 545–569.

Cockburn, Julio Calderón. 1987. "Luchas por la tierra, contradicciones sociales y sistema político: El caso de las zonas ejidales y comunales en la ciudad de México (1980–1984)." *Estudios demográficos y urbanos* 2(2): 301–324.

Colburn, Forrest. 1993. "Exceptions to urban bias in Latin America: Cuba and Costa Rica." *Journal of Development Studies* 29(4): 60.

Collier, David. 1976. *Squatters and Oligarchs: Authoritarian Rule and Policy Change in Peru*. Baltimore: Johns Hopkins University Press.

Comisión de la Verdad y Reconciliación (CVR). 2004. *Informe Final*. Lima, Peru. www .cverdad.org.pe/ifinal/.

Commons, John. 1968. *Legal Foundations of Capitalism*. Madison: University of Wisconsin Press.

Consejo Nacional de Reforma Agraria (CNRA). 1987. *Reorientación de la Reforma Agraria*. La Paz: CNRA.

Coppedge, Michael. 2000. "Venezuelan parties and the representation of elite interests." In Kevin Middlebrook, ed., *Conservative Parties, the Right, and Democracy in Latin America*, pp. 110–36. Baltimore: The Johns Hopkins University Press.

Corrales, Javier and Michael Penfold-Becerra. 2011. *Dragon in the Tropics: Hugo Chávez and the Political Economy of Revolution in Venezuela*. Washington, DC: Brookings Institution Press.

Corvalán, Javier. 2006. "Educación para la población rural en siete países de América Latina. Síntesis y análisis global de resultados por países." *Revista colombiana de educación* 51: 40–79.

Crabtree, John. 2002. "The impact of neo-liberal economics on Peruvian peasant agriculture in the 1990s." *The Journal of Peasant Studies* 29(3–4): 131–161.

Cui, Ernan, Ran Tao, Travis Warner, and Dali Yang. 2015. "How do land takings affect political trust in rural China?" *Political Studies* 63: 91–109.

D'Arcy, Michelle and Marina Nistotskaya. 2017. "State first, then democracy: Using cadastral records to explain governmental performance in public goods provision." *Governance* 30(2): 193–209.

Davis, Diane. 1994. *Urban Leviathan: Mexico City in the Twentieth Century*. Philadelphia: Temple University Press.

de Almeida, Maria Antónia Pires. 2016. "The agrarian reform under the Portuguese revolution, 1974–76: Its roots and reversal." *Studies in People's History* 3(2): 185–196.

de Almeida, Maria Antónia Pires. 2007. "Memory and trauma of the Portuguese agrarian reform: A case study." *Portuguese Journal of Social Science* 6(2): 63–76.

de Barros, Afonso. 1979. *A Reforma Agrária em Portugal: Das Ocupações de terras à formação das novas unidades de produção*. Instituto Gulbenkian de Ciência.

de Barros, Afonso. 1980. "Portuguese agrarian reform and economic and social development." *Sociologia ruralis* 20(1–2): 82–96.

de Celis, Emma Rubin. 1977. *Las CAPS de Piura y sus contradicciones*. Piura: CIPCA.

de Ita, Ana. 2006. "Land concentration in Mexico after PROCEDE." In Peter Rosset, Raj Patel, Michael Courville, eds., *Promised Land: Competing Visions of Agrarian Reform*, pp. 148–164. Oakland, CA: Food First Books.

De Janvry, Alain. 1981. *The Agrarian Question and Reformism in Latin America*. Baltimore: Johns Hopkins University Press.

De Janvry, Alain, Marco Gonzalez-Navarro, and Elisabeth Sadoulet. 2014. "Are land reforms granting complete property rights politically risky? Electoral outcomes of Mexico's certification program." *Journal of Development Economics* 110: 216–225.

de Janvry, Alain, Kyle Emerick, Marco Gonzalez-Navarro, and Elisabeth Sadoulet. 2015. "Delinking land rights from land use: Certification and migration in Mexico." *American Economic Review* 105(10): 3125–3149.

De Soto, Hernando. 2000. *The Mystery of Capital*. New York: Basic Books.

Deere, Carmen. 1992. "Markets, markets everywhere? Understanding the Cuban anomoly." *World Development* 20: 825–839.

Deininger, Klaus. 2003. *Land Policies for Growth and Poverty Reduction*. Washington DC: World Bank.

Deininger, Klaus, et al. 2004. *Land Policy Research Report*. Washington, DC: World Bank.

Deininger, Klaus, Daniel Ayalew Ali, and Takashi Yamano. 2008. "Legal knowledge and economic development: The case of land rights in Uganda." *Land Economics* 84(4): 593–619.

Deininger, Klaus, and Fabrizio Bresciani. 2001. *Mexico's Second Agrarian Reform: Implementation and Impact*. Washington, D.C.: World Bank.

Deininger, Klaus and Fabrizio Bresciani. 2009. *Mexico's "Second Agrarian Reform": Implementation and Impact*. Washington, DC: World Bank.

Deininger, Klaus, Songqing Jin, Shouying Liu, and Fang Xia. 2019. "Property rights reform to support China's rural–urban integration: household-level evidence from the Chengdu experiment." *Australian Journal of Agricultural and Resource Economics* 59: 1–25.

Delahaye, Olivier. 2003. *La Privatización de la Tierra Agrícola en Venezuela, desde Cristóbal Colón: La Titulación (1492–2001).* Caracas: Fondo Editorial Tropykos.

Dell, Melissa. 2010. "The persistent effects of Peru's mining mita." *Econometrica* 78(6): 1863–1903.

Demsetz, Harold. 1967. "Toward a theory of property rights." *American Economic Review* 57(2): 347–359.

Dincecco, Mark. 2017. *State Capacity and Economic Development: Present and Past.* New York: Cambridge University Press.

Do, Quy-Toan and Lakshmi Iyer. 2008. "Land titling and rural transition in Vietnam." *Economic Development and Cultural Change* 56(3): 531–579.

Domínguez, Jorge. 1978. *Cuba: Order and Revolution.* Cambridge, Mass.: Harvard University Press.

Domínguez Rascón, Alonso. 2003. *La política de reforma agraria en Chihuahua, 1920–1924.* México: Instituto Nacional de Antropología e Historia, Plaza y Valdés.

Doner, Richard, Bryan Ritchie, and Dan Slater. 2005. "Systemic vulnerability and the origins of developmental states: Northeast and Southeast Asia in comparative perspective." *International Organization* 59(2): 327–361.

Dong, Yingying, Ying-Ying Lee, and Michael Gou. 2018. "Regression discontinuity designs with a continuous treatment." Unpublished ms., UC Irvine. https://papers.ssrn.com/sol3/papers.cfm?abstract_id=3167541.

Drain, Michel. 1982. *Occupations de Terres et Expropriations dans les Campagnes Portugaises.* Paris: Editions du Centre National de la Recherche Scientifique.

Dugas, John. 2000. "The Conservative Party and the crisis of political legitimacy in Colombia." In Kevin Middlebrook, ed. *Conservative Parties, the Right, and Democracy in Latin America.* pp. 80–109. Baltimore, MD: The Johns Hopkins University Press.

Echevarría, Julio Anibal. 1978. *A Development Programming Model for the Peruvian Agricultural Sector.* PhD Dissertation, Iowa State University.

Eckstein, Salomón. 1968. *El Marco Macroeconómico del Problema Agrario Mexicano.* Mexico: Centro de Investigaciones Agrarias.

Eckstein, Susan. 1982. "The impact of revolution on social welfare in Latin America." *Theory and Society* 11(1): 43–94.

Edelman, Marc. 1992. *The Logic of the Latifundio: The Large Estates of Northwestern Costa Rica since the Late Nineteenth Century.* Stanford, CA: Stanford University Press.

Edelman, Marc. 1999. *Peasants against Globalization: Rural Social Movements in Costa Rica.* Stanford, CA: Stanford University Press.

Edelman, Marc. 2008. "Transnational organizing in agrarian Central America: Histories, challenges, prospects." *Journal of Agrarian Change* 8 (2/3): 229–57.

El-Ghonemy, Mohamad Riad. 1992. *The Political Economy of Rural Poverty: The Case for Land Reform.* London: Routledge.

Elbers, Chris, Jean Lanjouw, and Peter Lanjouw. 2003. "Micro-level estimation of poverty and inequality." *Econometrica* 71(1),355–364.

Ellickson, Robert. 1993. "Property in Land." *Yale Law Journal* 102(6): 1315–1400.

Ellis, Frank. 1983. *Las transnacionales del banano en Centroamérica*. San José, Costa Rica: FLACSO.

Ellis, Frank. 1992. *Agricultural Policies in Developing Countries*. New York: Cambridge University Press.

Ellner, Steve. 2020. "Class strategies in Chavista Venezuela: Pragmatic and populist policies in a broader context." In Steve Ellner, ed., *Latin America's Pink Tide: Breakthroughs and Shortcomings*, pp. 163–192. Lanham, MD: Rowman & Littlefield.

Encinas, Alejandro and Fernando Rascón. 1983. *Reporte y cronología del movimiento campesino e indígena*. Vol. 5. México: Universidad Autónoma de Chapingo.

Engerman, Stanley and Kenneth Sokoloff. 2002. "Factor endowments, inequality, and paths of development among new world economics." *Economia* 3(1): 41–88.

Esquivel, Gerardo. 2011. "The dynamics of income inequality in Mexico since NAFTA." *Economía* 12(1): 155–188.

Esteva, Gustavo. 1980. *La batalla en el México rural*. México: Siglo XXI.

FAO, IFAD, UNCTAD and the World Bank Group. 2010. "Principles for responsible agricultural investment that respects rights, livelihoods and resources." Discussion Note, 25 January 2010.

Fausto, Jordán. 2004. "Reforma Agraria en el Ecuador." In John Vargas Vega, ed., *Proceso agrario en Bolivia y América Latina*, pp. 285–320. La Paz: Plural editores.

Feder, Gershon and David Feeny. 1991."Land tenure and property rights: Theory and implications for development policy." *World Bank Economic Review* 5(1): 135–153.

Feeny, David. 1988. "The development of property rights in land: A comparative study." In Robert Bates, ed., *Toward a Political Economy of Development*, pp. 272–299. Berkeley, CA: University of California Press.

Feeny, David, Fikret Berkes, Bonnie McCay, and James Acheson. 1990. "The tragedy of the commons: Twenty-two years later." *Human Ecology* 18(1): 1–19.

Felix, David. 1977. "Income inequality in Mexico." Current History (pre-1986) 72 (000425): 111–116.

Fergusson, Leopoldo. 2013. "The political economy of rural property rights and the persistence of the dual economy." *Journal of Development Economics* 103: 167–181.

Fernandes, Blasco Hugo. 1973. *Portugal atraves de alguns numeros*. Lisbon: Prelo Press.

Fernández, Angel and Alberto González, eds. 1990. *La reforma agraria peruana: 20 años después*. Chiclayo, Perú: Centro de Estudios Sociales Solidaridad.

Fernández y Fernández, Ramón. 1964. *Notas sobre la reforma agraria mexicana*. Serie Monografías No. 2, Centro de Economía Agrícola, Escuela Nacional de Agricultura. Mexico, D.F.

Ferreira, Hugo Gil and Michael Marshall. 1986. *Portugal's Revolution: Ten Years On*. New York: Cambridge University Press.

Fields, Gary. 1988. "Employment and economic growth in Costa Rica." *World Development* 16(12): 1493–1509.

Findley, Roger. 1972. "Ten years of land reform in Colombia." *Wisconsin Law Review* 3: 880–923.

Firmin-Sellers, Kathryn and Patrick Sellers. 1999. "Expected failures and unexpected successes of land titling in Africa." *World Development* 27(7): 1115–1128.

Food and Agriculture Organization (FAO). 1981. *1970 World Census of Agriculture: Analysis and International Comparison of the Results*. Rome: Food and Agriculture Organization.

Food and Agriculture Organization (FAO). 2000. *Irrigation in Latin American and the Caribbean in Figures*. Rome: Food and Agriculture Organization.

Food and Agriculture Organization (FAO). 2000b. "Peru." In *Agriculture, Trade, and Food Security*. Vol. 2: Country Case Studies. Geneva: Commodities and Trade Division (FAO).

Forster, Nancy. 1981. "Cuban agricultural productivity: A comparison of state and private farm sectors." *Cuban Studies* 11(2): 105.

Fort, Ricardo. 2008. "Assessing the impact of rural titling in Peru: The case of the PETT program." Paper presented at World Bank Conference on New Challenges for Land Policy and Administration, 14–15 February, 2008, Washington D.C.

Frank, André Gunder. 1969. *Capitalism and Underdevelopment in Latin America*. New York: Monthly Review Press.

Frymer, Paul. 2014. "'A rush and a push and the land is ours': Territorial expansion, land policy, and US state formation." *Perspectives on Politics* 12(1): 119–144.

Fu, Teng Margaret. 2005. "Unequal primary education opportunities in rural and urban China." *China Perspectives* 60: 1–9.

Galiani, Sebastian and Ernesto Schargrodsky. 2010. "Property rights for the poor: Effects of land titling." *Journal of Public Economics* 94(9–10): 700–729.

Gall, Norman. 1971. "Peru: The master is dead." *Dissent* 18: 281–320.

Galor, Oded, Omer Moav, and Dietrich Vollrath. 2009. "Inequality in landownership, the emergence of human-capital promoting institutions, and the great divergence." *Review of Economic Studies* 76: 143–79.

García, Antonio. 1970. "Perú: Una reforma agraria radical." *Revista de Comercio Exterior* 5: 390–93.

Garrido, José, ed. 1988. *Historia de la Reforma Agraria en Chile*. Santiago: Editorial Universitaria.

Geddes, Barbara. 2003. *Paradigms and Sand Castles*. Ann Arbor: University of Michigan Press.

Geddes, Barbara, Joseph Wright, and Erica Frantz. 2014. "Autocratic breakdown and regime transitions: A new data set." *Perspectives on Politics* 12(2): 313–331.

Ghai, Dharam, Cristóbal Kay, and Peter Peek. 1988. *Labour and Development in Rural Cuba*. New York: St. Martin's Press.

Gil, Margarita F. 1999. *Security of Land Ownership in the Dominican Republic: A Legal and Historical Analysis*. PhD Dissertation. University of Wisconsin, Madison.

Gilbert, Dennis. 2017. *The Oligarchy and the Old Regime in Latin America, 1880–1970*. Lanham: Rowman & Littlefield.

Gill, Anthony. 1998. *Rendering unto Caesar: The Catholic Church and the State in Latin America*. Chicago: University of Chicago Press.

Giugale, Marcelo, John Newman, and Vicente Fretes-Cibils. 2007. *An Opportunity for a Different Peru: Prosperous, Equitable, and Governable*. Washington D.C: World Bank.

Glavin, Guro, Kristian Stokke, and Henrik Wiig. 2013. "The impact of women's mobilisation: Civil society organisations and the implementation of land titling in Peru." *Forum for Development Studies* 40(1): 129–152.

Gleditsch, Kristian Skrede and Michael Ward. 2006. "Diffusion and the international context of democratization." *International Organization* 60(4): 911–933.

Göbel, Christian and Lynette Ong. 2012. "Social unrest in China." *Europe China Research and Academic Network.* Available at SSRN: https://ssrn.com /abstract=2173073

Goldstein, Markus and Christopher Udry. 2008. "The profits of power: Land rights and agricultural investment in Ghana." *Journal of Political Economy* 116(6): 981–1022.

Goodman, David and Michael Redclift. 1982. *From Peasant to Proletarian: Capitalist Development and Agrarian Transitions.* New York: St. Martin's Press.

Gooneratne, Wilbert and M. Samad. 1979. "Experiences of group production in Sri Lanka." In John Wong, ed., *Group Farming in Asia: Experiences and Potentials.* Singapore: Singapore University Press.

Gordillo, Gustavo, Alain de Janvry, and Elisabeth Sadoulet. 1998. "Between political control and efficiency gains: The evolution of agrarian property rights in Mexico." *Cepal Review* 66: 151–169.

Graham, Lawrence and Douglas Wheeler, eds. 1983. *In Search of Modern Portugal: The Revolution & Its Consequences.* Madison: University of Wisconsin Press.

Greenhalgh, Susan. 2008. *Just One Child: Science and Policy in Deng's China.* Berkeley, CA: University of California Press.

Griffin, Charles. 1949. "Economic and social aspects of the era of Spanish-American independence." *The Hispanic American Historical Review* 29(2): 170–187.

Grindle, Merilee. 1986. *State and Countryside: Development Policy and Agrarian Politics in Latin America.* Baltimore, MD: Johns Hopkins University Press.

Haber, Stephen. 2002. *Crony Capitalism and Economic Growth in Latin America: Theory and Evidence.* Stanford, CA: Hoover Press.

Haber, Stephen, Razo, Armando, and Maurer, Noel. 2003. *The Politics of Property Rights: Political Instability, Credible Commitments, and Economic Growth in Mexico, 1876–1929.* New York: Cambridge University Press.

Haggard, Stephan. 1990. *Pathways from the Periphery: The Politics of Growth in the Newly Industrializing Countries.* Ithaca, NY: Cornell University Press.

Haggard, Stephan and Robert Kaufman. 1995. *The Political Economy of Democratic Transitions.* Princeton, NJ: Princeton University Press.

Haggard, Stephan and Robert Kaufman. 2008. *Development, Democracy, and Welfare States: Latin America, East Asia, and Eastern Europe.* Princeton, NJ: Princeton University Press.

Hall, Linda. 1995. *Oil, Banks, and Politics: The United States and Postrevolutionary Mexico, 1917–1924.* Austin, TX: University of Texas Press.

Hao, Lingxin, Alfred Hu and Jamie Lo. 2014. "Two aspects of the rural–urban divide and educational stratification in China: A trajectory analysis." *Comparative Education Review* 58(3): 509–536.

Handelman, Howard. 1980. "Ecuadorian agrarian reform: The politics of limited change." Reports, American Universities Field Staff No. 49.

Haney, Jr., Emil and Wava Haney. 1987. "Transformation of the agrarian structure in Ecuador with specific reference to the province of Chimborazo." *Land Tenure Center Research Paper* 86: 1–130.

Hansing, Katrin. 2017. "Race and inequality in the New Cuba: Reasons, dynamics, and manifestations." *Social Research* 84(2): 331–349.

Henisz, Witold. 2002. "The institutional environment for infrastructure investment." *Industrial and Corporate Change* 11(2): 355–389.

Henry, James. 2003. *The Blood Bankers: Tales from the Global Underground Economy*. New York: Basic Books.

Hetherington, Kregg. 2009. "Privatizing the private in rural Paraguay: Precarious lots and the materiality of rights." *American Ethnologist* 36(2): 224–241.

Hirschman, Albert. 1968. "The political economy of import-substituting industrialization in Latin America." *Quarterly Journal of Economics* 82(1): 1–32.

Hirschman, Albert. 1973. *Journeys Toward Progress: Studies of Economic Policy-making in Latin America*. New York: WW Norton.

Ho, Peter. 2001. "Who owns China's land? Policies, property rights and deliberate institutional ambiguity." *China Quarterly* 166: 394–421.

Ho, Peter. 2005. *Institutions in Transition: Land Ownership, Property Rights, and Social Conflict in China*. Oxford: Oxford University Press.

Holland, Alisha. 2017. *Forbearance as Redistribution: The Politics of Informal Welfare in Latin America*. New York: Cambridge University Press.

Honig, Lauren. 2017. "Selecting the state or choosing the chief? The political determinants of smallholder land titling." *World Development* 100: 94–107.

Hou, Yue. 2019. *The Private Sector in Public Office: Selective Property Rights in China*. New York: Cambridge University Press.

Huang, Yiping. 1998. *Agricultural Reform in China: Getting Institutions Right*. Cambridge University Press.

Huber, Evelyne and Frank Safford, eds. 1995. *Agrarian Structure Political Power: Landlord and Peasant In The Making Of Latin America*. Pittsburgh: University of Pittsburgh Press.

Huber, Evelyne, John Stephens, Thomas Mustillo, and Jennifer Pribble. 2012. *Latin America and the Caribbean Political Dataset, 1945–2008*. Chapel Hill: University of North Carolina.

Hunefeldt, Christine. 2014. *A Brief History of Peru*. New York: Lexington Associates.

Hunefeldt, Christine. 1997. "The rural landscape and changing political awareness: Enterprises, agrarian producers and peasant communities, 1969–1994." In Maxwell Cameron and Philip Mauceri. eds., *The Peruvian Labyrinth: Polity, Society, Economy*, pp. 107–133. University Park: The Pennsylvania State University Press.

Huntington, Samuel. 1968. *Political Order in Changing Societies*. New Haven: Yale University Press.

Hurst, Willard. 1964. *Law and Economic Growth: The Legal History of the Lumber Industry in Wisconsin, 1836–1915*. Cambridge: Harvard University Press.

Ibarra Mendivil, Julio. 1989. *Propiedad Agraria y Sistema Político en Mexico*. Mexico: M.A. Porrúa.

International Fund for Agricultural Development (IFAD). 2001. "Assets and the rural poor." In *Rural Poverty Report 2001: The Challenge of Ending Rural Poverty*. Oxford: Oxford University Press.

Imbens, Guido and Thomas Lemieux. 2008. "Regression discontinuity designs: A guide to practice." *Journal of Econometrics* 142: 615–635.

Janowitz, Morris. 1977. *Military Institutions and Coercion in the Developing Nations*. Chicago: University of Chicago Press.

Johnson, Chalmers. 1962. *Peasant Nationalism and Communist Power*. Stanford, CA: Stanford University Press.

Kaimowitz, David. 1989. "The role of decentralization in the recent Nicaraguan agrarian reform." In William Thiesenhusen, ed. *Searching for Agrarian Reform in Latin America*, pp. 384–407. Boston: Unwin Hyman.

Kain, Roger and Elizabeth Baigent. 1992. *The Cadastral Map in the Service of the State: A History of Property Mapping*. Chicago, IL: University of Chicago Press.

Kammann, Peter. 1982. *Movimientos campesinos en el Peru: 1900–1968*. Lima: Universidad Mayor de San Marcos.

Kapstein, Ethan. 2017. *Seeds of Stability: Land Reform and US Foreign Policy*. New York: Cambridge University Press.

Kay, Cristobal. 1974. "Comparative development of the European manorial system and the Latin American hacienda system." *Journal of Peasant Studies* 2(1): 69–98.

Kay, Cristóbal. 1985. "Achievements and contradictions of the Peruvian agrarian reform." *Journal of Development Studies* 18(2):141–70.

Kay, Cristóbal. 1998. "Latin America's agrarian reform: Lights and shadows." *Land Reform* 2: 8–31.

Kearney, Michael. 1996. *Reconceptualizing the Peasantry: Anthropology in Global Perspective*. New York: Routledge.

Keele, Luke and Rocío Titiunik. 2015. "Geographic boundaries as regression discontinuities." *Political Analysis* 23: 127–155.

Keswell, Malcolm and Michael Carter. 2014. "Poverty and land redistribution." *Journal of Development Economics* 110: 250–261.

King, Russell. 1978. "Shifting progress in Portugal's land reform." *Geography: Journal of the Geographical Association* 63(2): 118–119.

Klaus, Kathleen. 2020. *Political Violence in Kenya: Land, Elections, and Claim-Making*. New York: Cambridge University Press.

Kohli, Atul. 2004. *State-Directed Development: Political Power and Industrialization in the Global Periphery*. New York: Cambridge University Press.

Kontogiorgi, Elisabeth. 2006. *Population Exchange in Greek Macedonia: The Rural Settlement of Refugees 1922–1930*. Oxford: Oxford University Press.

Kopas, Jacob. 2020. *Legitimizing the State or a Grievance? Property Rights and Political Engagement*. PhD Dissertation, Columbia University.

Kourí, Emilio. 2015. "La invención del ejido." *Nexos* 37(445): 54–61, January 2015.

Kraus, Richard. 1981. *Class Conflict in Chinese Socialism*. New York: Columbia University Press.

Kruijt, Dirk. 1994. *Revolution by Decree: Peru 1968-1975*. Amsterdam: Thela Publishers.

Kung, James Kai-Sing and Shuo Chen. 2011. "The tragedy of the nomenklatura: Career incentives and political radicalism during China's Great Leap famine." *American Political Science Review* 105(1): 27–45.

Labarca, José Tomás. 2016. "Cooperativas Y Estado Subsidiario En El Chile Posdictadura, 1990–2015." *Revista Idelcoop* 218: 135–53.

Ladejinsky, Wolf. 1977. *The Collected Papers of Wolf Ladejinsky*. New York: Oxford University Press.

Lamartine Yates, Paul. 1981. *Mexico's Agricultural Dilemma*. Tucson, AZ: University of Arizona Press.

Landesa. 2012. "Findings from Landesa's survey of rural China published" [online]. Landesa. Available from: www.landesa.org/news/6th-china-survey

Lapp, Nancy. 2004. *Landing Votes*. New York: Palgrave Macmillan.

Larreguy, Horacio, John Marshall, and Laura Trucco. 2018. "Breaking clientelism or rewarding incumbents? Evidence from an urban titling program in Mexico." Working paper, Harvard University.

Larson, Bruce and Daniel Bromley. 1990. "Property rights, externalities, and resource degradation: Locating the tragedy." *Journal of Development Economics* 33(2): 235–262.

Lastarria-Cornhiel, Susana. 1989. "Agrarian reforms of the 1960s and 1970s in Peru." In William Thiesenhusen, ed., *Searching for Agrarian Reform in Latin America*, pp. 156–87. Boston: Unwin Hyman.

LeGrand, Catherine. 1986. *Frontier Expansion and Peasant Protest in Colombia, 1850–1936*. Albuquerque: University of New Mexico Press.

Lehmann, David. 1986. "Two paths of agrarian capitalism, or a critique of Chayanovian Marxism." *Comparative Studies in Society and History* 28(4): 601–27.

Lenin, Vladimir. 1964 [1899]. *The Development of Capitalism in Russia*. Moscow: Progress Publishers.

Levi, Margaret. 1989. *Of Rule and Revenue*. Berkeley: University of California Press.

Lewis, Paul. 1980. *Paraguay under Stroessner*. Chapel Hill: University of North Carolina Press.

Li, Huaiyin. 2018. "Institutions and work incentives in collective farming in Maoist China." *Journal of Agrarian Change* 18(1): 67–86.

Li, Wei, and Dennis Tao Yang. 2005. "The Great Leap Forward: Anatomy of a central planning disaster." *Journal of Political Economy* 113(4): 840–877.

Li, Xiubin. 2011. "Farmland grabs by urban sprawl and their impacts on peasants' livelihood in China: An overview." Paper presented at the Global Land Grabbing, Institute of Development Studies, University of Sussex.

Libecap, Gary. 1978. "Economic variables and the development of the law: The case of western mineral rights." *The Journal of Economic History* 38(2): 338–362.

Libecap, Gary. 1993. *Contracting for Property Rights*. New York: Cambridge University Press.

Libecap, Gary and James Smith. 2002. "The economic evolution of petroleum property rights in the United States." *Journal of Legal Studies* 31(S2): S589-S608.

Lin, Justin Yifu. 1990. "Collectivization and China's agricultural crisis in 1959–1961." *Journal of Political Economy* 98(6): 1228–1252.

Lipton, Michael. 1977. *Why Poor People Stay Poor: A Study of Urban Bias in World Development*. London: Temple Smith.

Lipton, Michael. 2009. *Land Reform in Developing Countries*. New York: Routledge.

Locher, Uli. 2000. "Are the rural poor better off than the urban poor?" *Labour, Capital and Society* 33: 108–35.

Lowenthal, Abraham. 1974. "Armies and Politics in Latin America." *World Politics* 27 (1): 107–30.

Lucena, Manuel. 1977. "A revolução portuguesa: Do desmantelamento da organização corporativa ao duvidoso fim do corporativismo." *Análise Social* 13(51): 541–592.

Machado, Absalón. 1994. *Transformaciones en la Estructura Agraria*. Bogotá: TM Editores.

Machado, Absalón. 2009. *Ensayos para la historia de la política de tierras en Colombia*. Bogotá: Universidad Nacional de Colombia.

Machovec, Frank. 1995. *Perfect Competition and the Transformation of Economics*. London: Routledge.

MacEwan, Arthur. 1981. *Revolution and Economic Development in Cuba*. New York: St. Martin's Press.

Mailer, Phil. 1977. *Portugal: The Impossible Revolution*. London: Solidarity Press.

Mainwaring, Scott and Aníbal Pérez-Liñan. 2014. *Democracies and Dictatorships in Latin America: Emergence, Survival, and Fall*. New York: Cambridge University Press.

Magaloni, Beatriz. 2006. *Voting for Autocracy*. New York: Cambridge University Press.

Mangonnet, Jorge. 2020. Maps of Illegibility: "The politics of land (mis)registration in Brazil." Working paper, Columbia University.

Mann, Michael. 1984. "The autonomous power of the state: Its origins, mechanisms and results." *European Journal of Sociology* 25(2): 185–213.

Mares, Isabela. 2015. *From Open Secrets to Secret Voting: Democratic Electoral Reforms and Voter Autonomy*. New York: Cambridge University Press.

Mares, Isabela and Didac Queralt. 2015. "The non-democratic origins of income taxation." *Comparative Political Studies* 48(14): 1974–2009.

Marsh, Robin and David Runsten. 1996. "Del traspatio a la exportación: potencial para la produccion campesina de frutas y hortalizas en Mexico." In Sara María Lara Flores and Michelle Chauvet, eds., *La sociedad rural mexicana frente al nuevo milenio, Volumen 1*, pp. 167–212. Mexico: Inst. Nacional de Antropología e Historia.

Marx, Karl. 1967 [1867]. *Capital*. Vols I-III. New York: International Publishers.

Mason, David. 1986. "Land reform and the breakdown of clientelist politics in El Salvador." *Comparative Political Studies* 18(4): 487–516.

Mason, David. 1998. "'Take two acres and call me in the morning': Is land reform a prescription for peasant unrest?" *Journal of Politics* 60(1): 199–230.

Masterson, Daniel. 1991. *Militarism and Politics in Latin America*. NY: Greenwood Press.

Matos Mar, José and José Manuel Mejía. 1980. *La reforma agraria en el Perú*. Lima: Instituto de Estudios Peruanos.

Mattheis, Ross and Itzchak Tzachi Raz. 2019. "There's no such thing as free land: The Homestead Act and economic development." Working paper. Available at: https://scholar.harvard.edu/iraz/publications/homestead-act-and-development-american-west

Mattingly, Daniel. 2016. "Elite capture: How decentralization and informal institutions weaken property rights in China." *World Politics* 68(3): 383–412.

Mayer, Enrique. 2009. *Ugly Stories from the Peruvian Agrarian Reform*. Durham: Duke University Press.

McClintock, Cynthia. 1981. *Peasant Cooperatives and Political Change in Peru*. Princeton: Princeton University Press.

McClintock, Cynthia. 1983. "Velasco, officers, and citizens: The politics of stealth." In Cynthia McClintock and Abraham Lowenthal, eds., *The Peruvian Experiment Reconsidered*, pp. 275-308. Princeton: Princeton University Press.

McClintock, Cynthia. 1984. "Why peasants rebel: The case of Peru's Sendero Luminoso." *World Politics* 37(1): 48–84.

McElhinny, Vincent. 2006. *Inequality And Empowerment: The Political Foundations Of Post-War Decentralization And Development In El Salvador, 1992–2000*. PhD Dissertation, University of Pittsburgh.

McNamee, Lachlan. 2018. "Mass resettlement and political violence: Evidence from Rwanda." *World Politics* 70(4): 595–644.

Mellor, John Williams. 1986. "Agriculture on the road to industrialization." In John Lewis and Valeriana Kallab, eds., *Development Strategies Reconsidered*, pp. 67–89. New Brunswick: Transaction Books.

Meltzer, Allan and Scott Richard. 1981. "A rational theory of the size of government." *Journal of Political Economy* 89: 914–927.

Meyer, Carrie. 1989. "Agrarian reform in the Dominican Republic: An associative solution to the collective/individual dilemma." *World Development* 17(8): 1255–1267.

Meyer, Lorenzo. 1972. *Mexico and the United States in the Oil Controversy, 1917–1942*. Austin, TX: University of Texas Press.

Migdal, Joel. 1988. *Strong Societies and Weak States*. Princeton: Princeton University Press.

Migot-Adholla, Shem, Peter Hazell, Benoit Blarel, and Frank Place. 1991. "Indigenous land rights systems in sub-Saharan Africa: A constraint on productivity?." *The World Bank Economic Review* 5(1): 155–175.

Ministerio de Agricultura. 1971a. *Modalidad de Adjudicación del Proyecto Integral de Asentamiento Rural Valle Santa*. Lima: Ministerio de Agricultura.

Ministerio de Agricultura. 1971b. *Seminario Nacional de Reform Agraria para Directores de Zonas Agrarias del Ministerio de Agricultura*. Lima: Ministerio de Agricultura.

Montgomery, John, ed. 1984. *International Dimensions of Land Reform*. Boulder, CO: Westview Press.

Moore, Barrington. 1966. *Social Origins of Dictatorship and Democracy*. Boston: Beacon Press.

Moreno, Julio. 1994. *Los gremios rurales: Rol de las organizaciones rurales en la década de los noventa*. Lima: Fundación Friedrich Ebert.

Morett, Jesús Carlos. 1992. *Alternativas de modernización del ejido*. México: Instituto de Proposiciones Estratégicas.

Morgan, Lynn. 1990. "International politics and primary health care in Costa Rica." *Social Science & Medicine* 30(2): 211–219.

Morley, Samuel. 1995. "Structural adjustment and the determinants of poverty in Latin America," in N. Lustig., ed., *Coping with Austerity: Poverty and Inequality in Latin America*, pp. 42–70. Washington, DC: The Brookings Institution.

Municipio de Cayambe. 1970. *Cayambe: En la mitad del mundo*. Editorial Santo Domingo: Quito, Ecuador.

Muñoz, Jorge. 2017. "VGGT: The global guidelines to secure land rights for all." *World Bank Blogs*, October 5, 2017. Available at: https://blogs.worldbank.org/voices/vggt-global-guidelines-ensure-secure-land-rights-for-all

Muñoz-Mora, Juan Carlos, Santiago Tobón, and Jesse Willem d'Anjou. 2018. "The role of land property rights in the war on illicit crops: Evidence from Colombia." *World Development* 103: 268–283.

Munzer, Stephen. 1990. *A Theory of Property*. New York: Cambridge University Press.

National Land Commission. 1937. *Summary Report of the Land Survey in China*. Nanjing: National Land Commission.

Netting, Robert. 1976. "What alpine peasants have in common: Observations on communal tenure in a Swiss village." *Human Ecology* 4: 135–146.

Netting, Robert. 1981. *Balancing on an Alp*. Cambridge: Cambridge University Press.

Nordlinger, Eric. 1977. *Soldiers in Politics*. Englewood Cliffs, NJ: Prentice Hall.

North, Douglass. 1981. *Structure and Change in Economic History*. New York: Norton.

North, Douglass. 1990. *Institutions, Institutional Change and Economic Performance*. New York: Cambridge University Press.

North, Douglass and Robert Paul Thomas. 1973. *The Rise of the Western World: A New Economic History*. New York: Cambridge University Press.

Nun, José. 1976. "The middle-class military coup revisited." In Abraham Lowenthal, ed., *Armies and Politics in Latin America*, pp. 49–86. New York: Holmes & Meier Publishers.

Oficina Nacional de Estadísticas (ONE). 2018. *Anuario Estadístico de Cuba 2017*. Havana, Cuba: Oficina Nacional de Estadísticas.

Oi, Jean. 1999. *Rural China Takes Off*. Berkeley: University of California Press.

Oi, Jean and Andrew Walder, eds. 1999. *Property Rights and Economic Reform in China* Stanford: Stanford University Press.

Olson, Mancur. 1993. "Dictatorship, democracy, and development." *American Political Science Review* 87: 567–76.

Onoma, Ato Kwamena. 2009. *The Politics of Property Rights Institutions in Africa*. New York: Cambridge University Press.

Ostrom, Elinor. 1990. *Governing the Commons*. Cambridge: Cambridge University Press.

Ostrom, Elinor, Larry Schroeder, and Susan Wynne. 1993a. "Analyzing the performance of alternative institutional arrangements for sustaining rural infrastructure in developing countries." *Journal of Public Administration Research and Theory* 3(1): 11–45.

Ostrom, Elinor, Larry Schroeder, and Susan Wynne. 1993b. *Institutional Incentives and Sustainable Development: Infrastructure Policies in Perspective*. Boulder, CO: Westview Press.

Ostrom, Elinor. 2003. "How types of goods and property rights jointly affect collective action." *Journal of Theoretical Politics* 15(3): 239–270.

Otero, Gerardo. 1989. "Agrarian reform in Mexico: Capitalism and the state." In William Thiesenhusen, ed., *Searching for Agrarian Reform in Latin America*, pp. 276–304. Boston: Unwin Hyman.

Paige, Jeffery. 1975. *Agrarian Revolution*. New York: The Free Press.

Palacios, Marco. 2006. *Between Legitimacy and Violence: A History of Colombia, 1875–2002*. Durham, NC: Duke University Press.

Palma, Isela Ponce, José Nahed Toral, Manuel Roberto Parra Vázquez, Norge Fonseca Fuentes, and Francisco Guevara Hernández. 2015. "Historical changes in the process of agricultural development in Cuba." *Journal of Cleaner Production* 96 (June): 77–84.

Palmer, David Scott. 1986. "Rebellion in rural Peru: The origins and evolution of Sendero Luminoso." *Comparative Politics* 18(2): 127–146.

Paré, Luisa. 1977. *El proletariado agrícola en México*. Mexico City: Siglo XXI.

Pasara, Luis. 2015. "El proceso de Velasco y la organización campesina." *Apuntes: Revista de Ciencias Sociales* 8: 59–80.

Payne, Leigh. 1992. *Brazilian Business and the Democratic Transition: New Attitudes and Influence*. Notre Dame: University of Notre Dame.

Perkins, Dwight and Shahid Yusuf. 1984. *Rural Development in China*. Baltimore: Johns Hopkins University Press.

Peña Huertas, Rocío del Pilar, María Mónica Parada Hernández, and Santiago Zuleta Ríos. 2014. "La regulación agraria en Colombia o el eterno déjà vu hacia la concentración y el despojo: Un análisis de las normas jurídicas colombianas sobre el agro (1991–2010)." *Revista Estudios Socio-Jurídicos* 16(1): 123–167.

Peterson, Glen. 1997. *The Power of Words: Literacy and revolution in South China, 1949–95*. Vancouver: University of British Columbia Press.

Picado, Wilson and Margarita Silva. 2002. *De la colonización al desarrollo rural*. San José: Instituto de Desarrollo Agrario.

Polanyi, Karl. 1944. *The Great Transformation: The Political and Economic Origins of Our Time*. Boston: Beacon Press.

Pop-Eleches, Grigore. 2008. *From Economic Crisis to Reform: IMF Programs in Latin America and Eastern Europe*. Princeton: Princeton University Press.

Powelson, John and Richard Stock. 1990. *The Peasant Betrayed: Agriculture and Land Reform in the Third World*. Washington, D.C.: Cato Institute.

Price, Ronald. 1975. *Education in Communist China*. London: Routledge and Kegan Paul.

Prosterman, Roy and Jeffrey Riedinger. 1987. *Land Reform and Democratic Development*. Baltimore: Johns Hopkins University Press.

Pryor, Frederic. 1992. *The Red and the Green: The Rise and Fall of Collectivized Agriculture in Marxist Regimes*. Princeton: Princeton University Press.

Przeworski, Adam. 1991. *Democracy and the Market: Political and Economic Reforms in Eastern Europe and Latin America*. Cambridge University Press.

Przeworski, Adam, Michael Alvarez, Jose Antonio Cheibub, and Fernando Limongi. 2000. *Democracy and Development: Political Institutions and Well-Being in the World, 1950–1990*. New York: Cambridge University Press.

Quijano, Anibal. 2000. "Coloniality of power and Eurocentrism in Latin America." *International Sociology* 15(2): 215–232.

Radin, Margaret Jane. 1987. "Market-inalienability." *Harvard Law Review* 100(8): 1849–1937.

Rajan, Raghuram and Rodney Ramcharan. 2011. "Land and credit: A study of the political economy of banking in the United States in the early 20th century." *Journal of Finance* 66(6): 1895–1931.

Rajan, Raghuram and Luigi Zingales. 2003. "The great reversals: The politics of financial development in the twentieth century." *Journal of Financial Economics* 69(1): 5–50.

Raven, George. 1988. "The development of the Portuguese agrarian reform." *Journal of Rural Studies* 4(1): 35–43.

Redclift, M. R. 1978. *Agrarian Reform and Peasant Organization on the Ecuadorian Coast*. London: Athlone Press.

Restrepo, Juan Camilo and M.A. Bernal. 2014. *La cuestión agraria: Tierra y Posconflicto en Colombia*. Bogotá: Penguin, Random House.

Rithmire, Meg. 2015. *Land Bargains and Chinese Capitalism: The Politics of Property Rights under Reform*. New York: Cambridge University Press.

Rithmire, Meg. 2017. "Land institutions and Chinese political economy: Institutional complementarities and macroeconomic management." *Politics & Society* 45(1): 123–153.

Rodriguez, Jose. 1987. "Agricultural policy and development in Cuba." *World Development* 15 (1): 23–39.

Rodriguez, Adrian and Stephen Smith. 1994. "A comparison of determinants of urban, rural and farm poverty in Costa Rica." *World Development* 22(3): 381–397.

Rodrik, Dani. 1995. "Getting interventions right: How South Korea and Taiwan grew rich." *Economic Policy* 10(20): 53–107.

Roney, Jennifer. 2000. *Webs of Resistance in a Newly Privatized Polish Firm: Workers React to Organizational Transformation*. New York: Garland Publishing.

Rose-Ackerman, Susan. 1985. "Inalienability and the theory of property rights." *Columbia Law Review* 85(5): 931–969.

Rottenberg, Simon (ed.). 1993. A World Bank comparative study. *Costa Rica and Uruguay – The Political Economy of Poverty, Equity, and Growth*. New York, NY: Oxford University Press.

Rozman, Gilbert and Thomas Bernstein. 1981. *The Modernization of China*. New York: Free Press.

Rueschemeyer, Dietrich, Evelyn Stephens, and John Stephens. 1992. *Capitalist Development and Democracy*. Chicago: University of Chicago Press.

Rutledge, Ian. 1977. "Land reform and the Portuguese revolution." *Journal of Peasant Studies* 5(1): 79–98.

Saffon, Maria Paula. 2015. *Dispossessions as a Cause of Redistributive Land Claims in 20th Century Latin America*. PhD Dissertation, Columbia University.

Sánchez, Gonzalo. 1991. *Guerra y política en la sociedad colombiana*. Bogotá: El Áncora Editores.

Sanderson, Susan Walsh. 1984. *Land Reform in Mexico: 1910–1980*. Orlando, FL: Academic Press.

Sanderson, Steven. 1986. *The Transformation of Mexican Agriculture: International Structure and the Politics of Rural Change*. Princeton: Princeton University Press.

Schlesinger, Arthur. 1965. *A Thousand Days: John F. Kennedy in the White House*. New York: Houghton Mifflin.

Scott, James. 1998. *Seeing Like a State: How Certain Schemes to Improve the Human Condition Have Failed*. New Haven: Yale University Press.

Selden, Mark. 1979. *The People's Republic of China: A Documentary History of Revolutionary Change*. New York: Monthly Review Press.

Seligmann, Linda. 1995. *Between Reform and Revolution: Political Struggles in the Peruvian Andes, 1969–1991*. Stanford: Stanford University Press.

Seligson, Mitchell. 1979. "The impact of agrarian reform: A study of Costa Rica." *The Journal of Developing Areas* 13(2): 161–74.

Seligson, Mitchell. 1980. *Peasants of Costa Rica and the Development of Agrarian Capitalism*. Madison: University of Wisconsin Press.

Seligson, Mitchell. 1984. "Implementing land reform: The case of Costa Rica." *Managing International Development* 1 (2): 29–46.

Servicio de Investigación y Promoción Agraria (SIPA). 1967. *Organización, Funciones, Programación y Metas, Reparticiones y Dependencias*. Lima: Ministerio de Agricultura.

Shouying, Liu. 2019. "The structure and changes of China's land system." *China Agricultural Economic Review* 11(3): 471–488.

Siclari, Paula. 2006. "Recolección y selección de información sobre programas de regularización del suelo e informalidad en Chile." CEPAL, United Nations Documentos de Proyectos, No. 110.

Sikor, Thomas. 2006. "Politics of rural land registration in post-socialist societies: Contested titling in villages of Northwest Vietnam." *Land Use Policy* 23(4): 617–628.

Silva, Ligia and Maria Osório. 1996. *Terras Devolutas e Latifúndio*. Campinas, Brazil: Centro de Memoria Unicamp.

Silva Herzog, Jesus. 1959. *El Agrarismo Mexicano y La Reforma Agraria*. México: Fondo de Cultura Económica.

Simmons, Beth. 2009. *Mobilizing for Human Rights: International Law in Domestic Politics*. New York: Cambridge University Press.

Simpson, Eyler. 1937. *The Ejido: Mexico's Way Out*. Chapel Hill: University of North Carolina Press.

Slater, Dan, Benjamin Smith, and Gautam Nair. 2014. "Economic origins of democratic breakdown? The redistributive model and the postcolonial state." *Perspectives on Politics* 12(2): 353–374.

Smith, Peter. 1979. *Labyrinths of Power: Political Recruitment in Twentieth-Century Mexico*. Princeton: Princeton University Press.

Soifer, Hillel. 2013. "State power and the economic origins of democracy." *Studies in Comparative International Development* 48(1): 1–22.

Soifer, Hillel David. 2015. *State Building in Latin America*. New York: Cambridge University Press.

Songwe, Vera and Klaus Deininger. 2009. "Foreign investment in agricultural production: Opportunities and challenges." *Land Policy and Administration* 45: 1–4.

Staiger, Douglas and James Stock. 1997. "Instrumental variables regression with weak instruments." *Econometrica* 65(3): 557–586.

Stanfield, J. David. 1989. "Agrarian reform in the Dominican Republic." In William Thiesenhusen, ed., *Searching for Agrarian Reform in Latin America*, pp. 305–37. Boston: Unwin Hyman.

Stark, David. 1996. "Recombinant property in East European capitalism." *American Journal of Sociology* 101(4): 993–1027.

Stavenhagen, Rodolfo. 1966. "Social aspects of agrarian structure in Mexico." *Social Research* 33(3): 463–485.

Stokes, Susan. 1997. "Democratic accountability and policy change: Economic policy in Fujimori's Peru." *Comparative Politics* 29(2): 209–226.

Stokes, Susan. 2001. *Mandates and Democracy: Neoliberalism by Surprise in Latin America*. Cambridge University Press.

Stokes, Susan. 2002. *Mandates and Democracy: Neoliberalism by Surprise in Latin America*. New York: Cambridge University Press.

Stokes, Susan, Thad Dunning, Marcelo Nazareno, and Valeria Brusco. 2013. *Brokers, Voters, and Clientelism: The Puzzle of Distributive Politics*. New York: Cambridge University Press.

Strasma, John. 1989. "Unfinished business: Consolidating land reform in El Salvador." In William Thiesenhusen, ed., *Searching for Agrarian Reform in Latin America*, pp. 408–428. Boston: Unwin Hyman.

Sun, Wenyu. 1936. *Yu E Wan Gan si sheng tu di fen lei zhi yan jiu*. Nanjing: Jinling da xue nong ye jing ji xi.

Sun, Shengmin, Rigoberto Lopez, and Xiaoou Liu. 2017. "Property rights, labor mobility and collectivization: The impact of institutional changes on China's agriculture in 1950–1978." *International Review of Economics & Finance* 52: 345–351.

Swinnen, Johan. 1999. "The political economy of land reform choices in Central and Eastern Europe." *Economics of Transition* 7(3): 637–664.

Tang, Chi-yu. 1924. *An Economic Study of Chinese Agriculture*. Ithaca: Cornell University Press.

Tarrow, Sidney. 1994. *Power in Movement: Social Movements, Collective Action and Politics*. New York: Cambridge University Press.

Tawney, Richard Henry. 1932. *Land and Labour in China*. London: George Allen and Unwin Limited.

Taylor, J. Edward, Jorge Mora, Richard Adams, and Alejandro Lopez-Feldman. 2008. "Remittances, inequality and poverty: Evidence from rural Mexico." In Josh DeWind and Jennifer Holdaway, eds., *Migration and Development Within and Across Borders*, pp. 101–130. New York: Social Science Research Council.

Thelen, Kathleen and Wolfgang Streeck. 2005. "Introduction: Institutional change in advanced political economies." In Wolfgang Streeck and Kathleen Thelen, eds., *Beyond Continuity: Institutional Change in Advanced Political Economies*, pp. 1–39. New York: Oxford University Press.

Thiesenhusen, William, ed. 1989. *Searching for Agrarian Reform in Latin America*. Boston: Unwin Hyman.

Thiesenhusen, William. 1995. *Broken Promises: Agrarian Reform and the Latin American Campesino*. Boulder: Westview Press.

Thomas, Hugh. 1971. *Cuba: The Pursuit of Freedom*. New York: Harper & Row.

Tobler, Hans Werner. 1990. "Los campesinos y la formación del Estado revolucionario, 1910–1940." In Friedrich Katz, ed., *Revuelta, rebelión, y revolución*. México, D.F.: Ediciones Era.

Trocki, Carl. 2006. *Singapore: Wealth, Power, and the Culture of Control*. New York: Routledge.

Tsebelis, George. 2002. *Veto Players*. Princeton: Princeton University Press.

Unger, Jonathan. 1985. "The decollectivization of the Chinese countryside: A survey of twenty-eight villages." *Pacific Affairs* 58(4): 585–606.

Urioste, Miguel. 2006. "The agrarian revolution of Evo Morales." *Cuarto Intermedio* 80.

Van de Walle, Nicolas. 2001. *African Economies and the Politics of Permanent Crisis, 1979–1999*. Cambridge University Press.

Vanhanen, Tatu. 2009. *Index of Power Resources*. Tampere: Finnish Social Science Data Archive.

Viladeslau, Tomás Palau. 2003. "'Políticas' agrarias en el Paraguay: Instrumentos de la discriminación." *NovaPolis* 2: 4–23.

Villagómez Ornelas, Paloma. 2019. *Rural Poverty in Mexico: Prevalence and Challenges*. Mexico City: National Council for the Evaluation of Social Development Policy.

Villaveces, Juanita and Sánchez Fabio. 2015. "Tendencias históricas y regionales de la adjudicación de baldíos en Colombia." *Universidad del Rosario*, Serie No. 179. Available at: http://repository.urosario.edu.co/bitstream/handle/10336/10933/12538.pdf

Walder, Andrew. 1986. *Communist Neo-Traditionalism: Work and Authority in Chinese Industry*. Berkeley, CA: University of California Press.

Walder, Andrew and Songhua Hu. 2009. "Revolution, reform, and status inheritance: Urban China, 1949–1996." *American Journal of Sociology* 114(5): 1395–1427.

Wallace, Jeremy. 2014. *Cities and Stability: Urbanization, Redistribution, and Regime Survival in China*. Oxford: Oxford University Press.

Walker, Kenneth. 1966. "A tenth aniversary appraisal: Collectivisation in retrospect: The 'socialist high tide' of Autumn 1955–Spring 1956." *The China Quarterly* 26: 1–43.

Wang, Hui, Pengyu Zhu, Xiao Chen, and Sarah Swider. 2017. "Land expropriation in urbanizing China: An examination of negotiations and compensation." *Urban Geography* 38(3): 401–419.

Wang, Yuhua. 2015. *Tying the Autocrat's Hands: The Rise of the Rule of Law in China.* New York: Cambridge University Press.

Ward, Peter. 1999. *Colonias and Public Policy in Texas and Mexico: Urbanization by Stealth.* Austin, TX: University of Texas Press.

Warman, Arturo. 1979. *Los campesinos: Hijos predilectos del régimen.* México: Editorial Nuestro Tiempo.

Weyland, Kurt. 1996. *Democracy Without Equity: Failures of Reform in Brazil.* Pittsburgh: University of Pittsburgh Press.

Wiarda, Howard and Michael Kryzanek. 1983. "The Dominican Republic." *Latin America and Caribbean Contemporary Record* 1: 544–554(1981–1982).

Wolford, Wendy, Saturnino Borras Jr., Ruth Hall, Ian Scoones, and Ben White. 2013. "Governing global land deals: The role of the state in the rush for land." *Development and Change* 44(2): 189–210.

Wong, John. 1973. *Land Reform in the People's Republic of China: Institutional Transformation in Agriculture.* New York: Praeger.

World Bank. 1978. *Land Reform in Latin America: Bolivia, Chile, Mexico, Peru, and Venezuela.* Staff Working Paper No. 275. Washington, D.C.

World Bank. 1992. "Staff Appraisal Report: Chile Small Farmer Services Project."

World Bank. 2013. *Global Monitoring Report.* Washington, D.C.: World Bank Group.

Yang, Dali. 1996. *Calamity and Reform in China: State, Rural Society, and Institutional Change Since the Great Leap Famine.* Stanford: Stanford University Press.

Yashar, Deborah. 2005. *Contesting Citizenship in Latin America: The Rise of Indigenous Movements and the Postliberal Challenge.* New York: Cambridge University Press.

Yang, Dennis Tao. 2008. "China's agricultural crisis and famine of 1959–1961: A survey and comparison to Soviet famines." *Comparative Economic Studies* 50 (1): 1–29.

Yoo, Dongwoo and Richard Steckel. 2016. "Property rights and economic development: The legacy of Japanese colonial institutions." *Journal of Institutional Economics* 12 (3): 623–650.

Yúnez-Naude, Antonio and Fernando Barceinas. 2006. "The reshaping of agricultural policy in Mexico." In Laura Randall, ed., *Changing Structure of Mexico: Political, Social, and Economic Prospects*, pp. 213–235. Armonk, NY: M.E. Sharpe.

Zamosc, Léon. 1986. *The Agrarian Question and the Peasant Movement in Colombia.* Cambridge: Cambridge University Press.

Zhang, Yongquan and Quanjun Zhao. 1985. *Zhongguo tu di gai ge shi.* Wuhan: Wuhan da xue chu ban she : Xin hua shu dian Hubei fa xing suo fa xing.

Zhao, Yaohui. 1999. "Leaving the countryside: Rural-to-urban migration decisions in China." *American Economic Review* 89(2): 281–286.

Ziblatt, Daniel. 2008. "Does landholding inequality block democratization?" *World Politics* 60(4),610–641.

Ziblatt, Daniel. 2009. "Shaping democratic practice and the causes of electoral fraud: The case of nineteenth-century Germany." *American Political Science Review* 103 (1): 1–21.

Zimbalist, Andrew and Susan Eckstein. 1987. "Patterns of Cuban development: The first twenty-five years." *World Development* 15(1): 5–22.

Ziegler, Melanie, and Walt Vanderbush. 2015. "Necessity is the mother of invention: Cuba's quest for food security in the twenty-first century." In H. Louise Davis, Karyn Pilgrim, and Madhu Sinha, eds., *The Ecopolitics of Consumption: The Food Trade*, pp. 139–157. Lanham, MD: Rowman & Littlefield.

Index